MW00629530

The Prophets

according to

The Scriptures
of
The Reformation

The Writings of

The Prophets

according to

The Scriptures
of
The Reformation

The Writings of

The Prophets

according to

The Scriptures
of
The Reformation

(Isaiah, Jeremiah, Lamentations, Ezekiel, Daniel, Hosea, Joel, Amos, Obadiah, Jonah, Micah, Nahum, Habakkuk, Zephaniah, Haggai, Zehariah, and Malachi)

"the word of our God shall stand for ever" (Isaiah 40:8).

© 1999 Russell Martin Stendal.
May be quoted in other works. May be used freely in all non-profit, non commercial Bible distribution endeavors provided the content is not altered. For all commercial reproduction express written permission from the publisher is required.

Published by:

Ransom Press International
10160 Main Drive
Bonita Springs, Florida 34135
e-mail: gstendal@aol.com

Printed in Colombia, April, 1999

Table of Contents

Therefore become ye converted, and ye shall make a difference between the just and the wicked, between him that serveth God and him that did not serve him.

For, behold, the day cometh, that shall burn as an oven; and all the proud, yea, and all that do wickedly, shall be stubble: and the day that cometh shall burn them up, said the LORD of the hosts, that it shall leave them neither root nor branch.

But unto you that fear my name shall the Sun of righteousness be born, and in his wings *he shall bring* saving health; and ye shall go forth, and jump like calves of the herd.

And ye shall tread down the wicked; for they shall be ashes under the soles of your feet in the day that I make, said the LORD of the hosts.

(Malachi 3:18-4:3).

To the Reader:

Have you ever come across footnotes in the Old Testament saying, "Hebrew Obscure", or "Hebrew Uncertain"? This is not due to any lack of content or clarity in the original text, but rather to the fact that most modern Hebrew scholars simply do not know the precise meaning of many of the original idioms with any degree of certainty. For hundreds of years, Hebrew was studied as a "dead" language (a language that was not spoken in every day life). The difference between studying a "living" versus a "dead" language could be compared to the difference between the study of fossils or museum exhibits of long extinct animals, versus the study of living examples of the same species.

A number of years ago, I was given a copy of an old Spanish Bible translated in the heat and fervor of the Reformation (which was brutally put down in Spain by the Inquisition) during a time when it was common practice to burn Bibles along with their owners. I immediately began to notice a depth and clarity to this translation that brought forth a clear witness of the Spirit of God as to the meanings of many seemingly unfathomable passages (mainly in the Psalms, Proverbs and Prophets) that had intrigued me for years. I began to investigate the unique circumstances of this Spanish translation by Casiodoro de Reina published in 1569.

Casiodoro de Reina was born in 1520. He learned Hebrew in Spain as a young man, apparently from Jews who still spoke Hebrew as a "living" language. The Jews had been officially expulsed from Spain in 1492, but it is estimated that only one fourth of them left at that time (some of those who remained did their best to blend in with the Christians). Eventually, the Spanish Inquisition made it impossible for any Jewish people to survive in Spain speaking their own language. Almost every Hebrew scholar since Casiodoro de Reina has had to learn Hebrew as a "dead" language, which was no longer spoken, until the modern day ongoing resurrection of the Hebrew language in Israel.

Casiodoro began a translation of the Old Testament from Hebrew to Spanish and was forced to flee from Spain in 1551. Several Jewish translations of the Old Testament were published in Spanish about this time (such as the Biblia de Ferrara of 1553) to which Casiodoro had access. He also built on a translation of the Psalms that was published by his friend Juan Pérez de Pineda in 1557. He went to Geneva and was there until the government of Geneva under John Calvin burned Miguel Servet at the stake over differences on points of doctrine. Casiodoro had some strong words about this. He said that Geneva had become a "new Rome" and left for England. The Queen of England (Elizabeth I) allowed Casiodoro to preach to Spanish speakers in the Church of St.

Mary Axe and gave him a monthly income. Casiodoro continued his Bible translation until the Inquisition found out about it and sent agents from Spain, who brought false charges against him and undermined his support from the Queen.

Casiodoro fled to Germany just in time to witness a war between Lutherans and Catholics. He had some words with the Lutherans regarding this and went on into the Low Countries. There he was given a place to preach in a Congregational Church, where he spent quite a bit of time in conflict with the Consistory (the minutes of those meetings still exist). Casiodoro seemed to always maintain an open mind to truth and refused to blindly go along with any given school of doctrine or thought believing that everyone must be responsible before God for their own conscience. After more than twenty years of working on his translation while fleeing with his wife and children, one jump ahead of the Inquisition which was always sending agents to attempt to kill or hinder him, his Bible was finally printed. The Inquisition set up a ring of *retenes* or checkpoints all along the borders and for many years carefully searched every person and/or cargo that entered Spain, making an all out effort to not let even one single Bible into the country. They searched for Bibles with the same intensity that our modern countries search passengers for weapons and drugs! Casiodoro was last heard of at age 70 still one jump ahead of the Inquisition, and it is not known for sure whether they got him in the end or not.

Casiodoro de Reina, although younger, was contemporary with William Tyndale. I have noticed many similarities between the translations of both men (William Tyndale in English and Casiodoro de Reina in Spanish). Studying these two Bibles (they basically agree, yet each brings out unique facets of truth from a slightly different perspective) has been the equivalent of getting the truth of the Scriptures of the Reformation in stereo. The power and clarity of their translations has a much sharper edge than the work that was done in either language even a generation later when the intense heat of the Reformation had died down, and Bible translation had to be officially approved by ecclesiastic and/or secular governments.

It is recognized that the Authorized Version (by King James) in English is basically a revision of Tyndale's work (in many key passages the wording of the AV is ninety percent or more Tyndale's) with the exception of the last half of Old Testament (from Ezra to Malachi). This portion of Tyndale's work is believed to have been lost at sea in a shipwreck (only the book of Jonah survived). Unfortunately, William Tyndale was burned at the stake before he could redo the books that were lost. This disaster has, in my opinion, placed these books of our English AV Bibles on a foundation less than equal in terms of clarity and consistency of translation with the rest of the AV which draws so extensively from the work of Tyndale.

When we edited a recent edition of the Spanish Bible (*Las Sagradas Escrituras, Version Antigua*, published March of 1998) based on the original text of Casiodoro de Reina, I checked much of it against the work of William Tyndale and against the Authorized Version. This strengthened the Spanish Bible in many areas and also tended to confirm the opinion that I gave in the preceding paragraph. Then I decided to diligently compare and align the work of Casiodoro de Reina with the books of the Authorized Version that did not receive the heritage of William Tyndale. The first fruits of this endeavor was a rendition of Psalms, Proverbs, Ecclesiastes and Song of Solomon published in July of 1998 under the Title: *God's Poetry*.

Over the years there have been many revisions of the Authorized Version, some of these under the guise of modernizing the language have watered down the message and introduced errors proceeding from deviant manuscripts, from doctrines of men, and from over simplification of the English language. The same is true regarding the Spanish Bible. Instead of revising "forward" towards modernism and employing modern scholarship, textual criticism, and the like; it has been our intention to revise "back" and return as close as possible to the roots of the pure message and pure language. I believe we are at a place where brilliant scholarship and linguistics alone cannot discern between all the possible variations of meaning, or among what are all being presented as ancient and worthy manuscripts in the original languages. We must have the witness of the Holy Spirit. I have chosen to go with the Hebrew scholarship of Reformers such as William Tyndale and Casiodoro de Reina whose translations of the *Textus Receptus* shined the light of the truth into the spiritual darkness of their day and changed the church and the world for the better, rather than to rely on the modern scholarship which has a penchant for removing the fear of the LORD from among the people of God in this Laodicean hour.

Let us allow the Spirit of Truth to have the last word regarding this matter. We must always bear in mind that even if we were to all learn Hebrew to perfection and could obtain a flawless manuscript of the original text, there would still be a humanly insurmountable language barrier between us and the Truth that can only be bridged by the Spirit of God.

Russell M. Stendal
Editor

For with thee is the fountain of life: in thy light shall we see light. (Psalm:36:9).

Translator's Notes

Amen.   So be it.

Chasten.   Primary meaning: To refine or to purify.
Comes from the root: Chaste.

Earth = Land.   Same word in original. Spiritually this has
to do with the People of God.

Eternal. Primary meaning: Denotes a change in quality, (like
a change of state). Secondary meaning: Unlimited time as a
consequence of coming into another realm (God's realm).

Fools. Those who are governed by carnal thoughts or desires.
This is **folly** in God's eyes.

Halelu.   Praise ye.

Jubilee.   Primary meaning: Freedom, liberty. Secondary
meaning: The joy of being set free.

Life = Soul.   Same word in original. Translated one or the
other according to context.

Right Hand.   Authority (power and strength).

Selah.   Stop and think about it. Meditate on this.

Shadow.   Includes the connotation of covering and protection.

Shophar. Special ram's horn trumpet blown on the Day of Atonement to announce the year of Jubilee and on other special occasions.

Spirit = Wind = Breath. Same word in original. Translated according to context.

Unicorn. Means one horn. In the old Spanish this is the Rhinoceros.

<u>Use of Italics:</u> Words added by the translator either for proper English or for clarification.

<u>Use of pronouns:</u>

Thee, Thou, Thy. Always singular. Note: Serious doctrinal error can result from the consequences of changing **Thee**, **Thou**, or **Thy** to **You** or **Your.** This can cause scriptural promises or directives addressed to the individual to be mistakenly applied to a corporate group. Modern English is ambiguous in this regard and lacks the precision necessary to accurately render the true meaning of the original.

Ye. Always plural. Always denotes a corporate or plural situation. Note: Serious doctrinal error can result from the consequences of changing **ye** to **you** and then indiscriminately applying scriptural promises or directives that apply corporately to the People of God to a given individual. Modern English has lost this important distinction.

You, Your. Third person plural in old English.

The Book of the Prophecies of

Isaiah

Chapter 1

1 The vision of Isaiah the son of Amoz, which he saw concerning Judah and Jerusalem in *the* days of Uzziah, Jotham, Ahaz, *and* Hezekiah, kings of Judah.
2 Hear, O heavens, and give ear, O earth: for the LORD speaketh, I have nourished and brought up children, and they have rebelled against me.
3 The ox knoweth his owner, and the ass his master's crib: *but* Israel doth not know, my people do not have understanding.
4 O sinful nation, people laden with iniquity, generation of evildoers, corrupt sons! They have forsaken the LORD, they have provoked the Holy One of Israel unto anger; they have turned back.
5 Why should I chastise ye any more? ye will revolt more and more: every head is sick, and every heart faint.
6 From the sole of the foot even unto the head *there is* no soundness in him; *but* wounds, and bruises, and putrefying sores: they have not been closed, neither bound up, neither mollified with ointment.
7 Your country *is* desolate, your cities *are* burned with fire: your land, strangers devour it in your presence, and *it is* desolate, as overthrown by strangers.
8 And the daughter of Zion is left as a cottage in a vineyard, as a lodge in a garden of cucumbers, as a besieged city.
9 Except the LORD of the hosts had left unto us a very small remnant, we should have been as Sodom, *and* we should have been like unto Gomorrah.

10 Hear the word of the LORD, ye princes of Sodom; give ear unto the law of our God, ye people of Gomorrah.
11 To what purpose *is* the multitude of your sacrifices unto me? shall the LORD say. I am full of the burnt offerings of rams, and the fat of fed beasts; and I de-

light not in the blood of bullocks, or of lambs, or of he goats.

12 When ye come to appear before me, who hath required this at your hand, to tread my courts?

13 Bring no more vain oblations; the incense is an abomination unto me; the new moons and sabbaths, the calling of assemblies, I cannot stand them; iniquity and the solemn meeting.

14 Your new moons and your appointed feasts my soul hateth: they are a trouble unto me; I am weary to bear *them*.

15 And when ye spread forth your hands, I will hide my eyes from you: yea, when ye make many prayers, I will not hear: your hands are full of blood.

16 Wash you, make you clean; put away the evil of your doings from before my eyes; cease to do evil;

17 learn to do good; seek judgment, restore unto the oppressed, hear the fatherless in right *judgment*, protect the widow.

18 Then come, shall the LORD say, and we shall be even: if your sins were as scarlet, they shall be made as white as snow; if they were red like crimson, they shall become as wool.

19 If ye be willing and hearken, ye shall eat the good of the land:

20 But if ye refuse and rebel, ye shall be devoured with the sword: for the mouth of the LORD hath spoken *it*.

21 How is the faithful city become an harlot! it was full of judgment; righteousness lodged in it; but now murderers.

22 Thy silver is become dross, thy wine mixed with water:

23 Thy princes *are* rebellious, and companions of thieves: every one loveth gifts, and followeth after rewards: they do not hear the fatherless in judgment, neither doth the cause of the widow come unto them.

24 Therefore saith the Lord, the LORD of the hosts, the mighty One of Israel, Ah, I will ease me of my adversaries, and avenge me of my enemies:

25 And I will turn my hand upon thee, and purely purge away thy dross, and take away all thy tin:

26 And I will restore thy judges as at the first, and thy counsellors as at the beginning: afterward thou shalt be called, The city of righteousness, the faithful city.

27 Zion shall be redeemed with judgment, and her converts with righteousness.

28 And the destruction of the transgressors and of the sinners *shall be* together, and they that forsook the LORD shall be consumed.

29 For ye shall be ashamed of the oaks which ye have desired, and ye shall be confounded for the groves that ye have chosen.

30 For ye shall be as an oak whose leaf falleth, and as a garden that hath no water.

31 And the strong *idol* shall be as tow, and the maker of it as a spark, and they shall both burn together, and none *shall be able to* quench *them*.

Chapter 2

1 The word that Isaiah the son of Amoz saw concerning Judah and Jerusalem.

2 And it shall come to pass in the last of the days [*or* times], *that* the mountain of the LORD'S house shall be confirmed as *the* head of the mountains, and shall be exalted above the hills; and all the Gentiles shall flow unto it.

3 And many peoples shall go and say, Come ye, and let us go up to the mountain of the LORD, to the house of the God of Jacob; and he will teach us of his ways, and we will walk in his paths: for out of Zion shall go forth the law, and the word of the LORD from Jerusalem.

4 And he shall judge among the Gentiles, and shall rebuke many peoples: and they shall beat their swords into plowshares, and their spears into pruninghooks: nation shall not lift up sword against nation, neither shall they learn war any more.

5 O house of Jacob, come ye, and let us walk in the light of the LORD.

6 Therefore thou hast forsaken thy people the house of Jacob, because they be replenished from the east, and *are* soothsayers like the Philistines, and they please themselves in the children of strangers.

7 Their land is full of silver and gold, neither *is there any* end of their treasures; their land is also full of horses, neither *is there any* end of their chariots:

8 Their land also is full of idols; they worship the work of their own hands, that which their own fingers have made:

9 And the mean man boweth down, and the great man humbleth himself: therefore thou shalt not forgive them.

10 Enter into the rock, and hide thee in the dust, from the terrible presence of the LORD, and from the glory of his majesty.

11 The lofty looks of man shall be humbled, and the haughtiness of men shall be bowed down, and the LORD alone shall be exalted in that day.

12 For the day of the LORD of the hosts *shall be* upon every *one that is* proud and lofty, and upon every *one that is* lifted up; and he shall be brought low:

13 And upon all the cedars of Lebanon, *that are* high and lifted up, and upon all the oaks of Bashan,

14 And upon all the high mountains, and upon all the hills *that are* lifted up,

15 And upon every high tower, and upon every fenced wall,

16 And upon all the ships of Tarshish, and upon all pleasant pictures.

17 And the loftiness of man shall be bowed down, and the haughtiness of men shall be made low: and the LORD alone shall be exalted in that day.

18 And the idols he shall utterly abolish.

19 And they shall go into the holes of the rocks, and into the caves of the earth, because of the terrible presence of the LORD, and because of the glory of his majesty, when he shall arise to smite the earth.

20 In that day man shall cast his idols of silver, and his idols of gold, (which they made *each one* for himself to worship), into the caves of the moles and of the bats;

21 to go into the clefts of the rocks, and into the caverns of the cliffs, from before the fearful presence of the LORD, and from the glory of his majesty, when he shall arise to smite the earth.

22 Cease ye from man, whose breath *is* in his nostrils: for wherein is he to be accounted of?

Chapter 3

1 For, behold, the Lord, the LORD of the hosts, doth take away from Jerusalem and from Judah the stay and the staff, the whole stay of bread, and the whole stay of water,

2 *The* mighty man, and *the* man of war, *the* judge, and *the* prophet, the fortune-teller, and *the* ancient,

3 the captain of fifty, and *the* honourable man, and *the* counsellor, and *the* cunning artificer, and *the* eloquent wise man.

4 And I will give children *to be* their princes, and young *fools* shall rule over them.

5 And the people shall do violence, every one against another, and every one against his neighbour: the child shall rise up against the ancient, and the base against the honourable.

6 When a man shall take hold of his brother of the house of his father, *saying,* Thou hast clothing, be thou our ruler, and *let* this ruin *be* under thy hand:

7 In that day shall he swear, saying, I will not be an healer; for in my house *is* neither bread nor clothing: make me not a ruler of the people.

8 For Jerusalem is ruined, and Judah is fallen: because their tongue and their doings *have been* against the LORD, to irritate the eyes of his majesty.

9 The appearance of their countenance doth witness against them; and they declare their sin as Sodom, they hide *it* not. Woe unto their soul! for they have rewarded evil unto themselves.

10 Say ye to the righteous, that *it shall be* well *with him*: for they shall eat of the fruit of their doings.

11 Woe unto the wicked! *it shall be* ill *with him*: for according to the work of his hands it shall be done unto him.

12 The oppressors of my people *are* many, and women rule over him. O my people, they which lead thee cause *thee* to err, and twist the way of thy paths.

13 The LORD standeth up to litigate, and is *present* to judge the peoples.

14 The LORD will come with judgment against the elders of his people, and against the his princes: for ye have eaten up the vineyard; the spoil of the poor *is* in your houses.

15 What mean ye *that* ye beat my people to pieces, and grind the faces of the poor? saith the Lord GOD of the hosts.

16 Moreover the LORD saith, Because the daughters of Zion are haughty, and walk with stretched forth necks and wanton eyes, walking and swaggering *as* they go, and making a tinkling with their feet:

17 Therefore the Lord will make bare the crown of the head of the daughters of Zion, and the LORD will uncover that which they are ashamed of.

18 In that day the Lord will take away the adornment of *their* shoes, and *their* hair nets, and *their* crystals,

19 The chains, and the jewels, and the bracelets,

20 The bonnets, and the ornaments of the legs, and the headbands, and the powders, and the earrings,

21 The rings, and nose jewels,

22 The changeable suits of apparel, and the mantles, and the veils, and the crisping pins,

23 The *looking* glasses, and the fine linen, and the hoods, and the hairdos.

24 And it shall come to pass, *that* instead of sweet perfumes there shall be stink; and instead of a girdle a rent; and instead of well set hair baldness; and instead of a stomacher a girding of sackcloth; *and* burning instead of beauty.

25 Thy men shall fall by the sword, and thy mighty in the war.

26 Thy gates shall lament and mourn; and she *being* desolate shall sit upon the ground.

Chapter 4

1 And in that day seven women shall take hold of one man, saying, We will eat our own bread, and wear our own apparel: only let us be called by thy name, to take away our reproach.

2 In that day shall the branch of the LORD be for beauty and glory, and the fruit of the earth for greatness and honour to them that are freed of Israel.

3 And it shall come to pass, *that he that is* left in Zion, and *he that* remaineth in Jerusalem, shall be called holy, *even* every one that is written among the living in Jerusalem:

4 When the Lord shall have washed away the filth of the daughters of Zion, and shall have purged the blood of Jerusalem from the midst thereof by the spirit of judgment, and by the spirit of burning.

5 And the LORD will create upon every dwelling place of mount Zion, and upon the places of her assemblies, a cloud and darkness by day, and the shining of a flaming fire by night: because over all glory *there shall be a* covering.

6 And there shall be a covert for a shadow in the daytime from the heat, and for a place of refuge, and for a shelter from storm and from rain.

Chapter 5

1 Now will I sing to my wellbeloved a song of my beloved touching his vineyard. My wellbeloved had a vineyard in a very fruitful hill:

2 And he had fenced it, and gathered out the stones thereof, and planted it with the choicest vine, and built a tower in the midst of it, and also made a winepress therein: and he looked that it should bring forth grapes, and it brought forth wild grapes.

3 And now, O inhabitants of Jerusalem, and men of Judah, judge, I pray you, betwixt me and my vineyard.

4 What could have been done more to my vineyard, that I have not done in it? wherefore, when I looked that it should bring forth grapes, brought it forth wild grapes?

5 And now go to; I will tell you what I will do to my vineyard: I will take away the hedge thereof, and it shall be eaten up; *and* break down the wall thereof, and it shall be trodden down:

6 And I will lay it waste: it shall not be pruned, nor digged; but there shall come up briers and thorns: I will even command the clouds that they rain no rain upon it.

7 For the vineyard of the LORD of the hosts *is* the house of Israel, and every man of Judah his pleasant plant: and he looked for judgment, but behold oppression; for righteousness, but behold a cry.

8 Woe unto them that join house to house, *that* lay field to field, until they have done away with the borders! Will ye dwell alone in the midst of the earth?

9 In mine ears *said* the LORD of the hosts, Of a truth many houses shall be desolate, *even* great and fair, without inhabitant.

10 Yea, ten acres of vineyard shall yield one bath, and the seed of an homer shall yield an ephah.

11 Woe unto them that rise up early in the morning, *that* they may continue their drunkenness; that continue until night, *until* wine inflame them!

12 And the harp, and the viol, the tambourine, and flutes, and wine, are in their feasts: but they regard not the work of the LORD, neither consider the work of his hands.

13 Therefore my people are gone into captivity, because *they have* no knowledge: their glory died of hunger, and their multitude dried up of thirst.

14 Therefore hell hath enlarged herself, and opened her mouth without measure: and their glory, and their multitude descended into it, and their pomp, and he that rejoiced in him.

15 And the mean man shall be brought down, and the mighty man shall be humbled, and the eyes of the lofty shall be humbled:

16 But the LORD of the hosts shall be exalted in judgment, and God that is holy shall be sanctified with righteousness.

17 Then shall the lambs be fed after their manner, and strangers shall eat the fat ones that are forsaken.

18 Woe unto them that draw iniquity with cords of vanity, and sin as it were with a cart rope:

19 That say, Let him make speed, *and* hasten his work, that we may see *it*: and let the counsel of the Holy One of Israel draw nigh and come, that we may know *it*!

20 Woe unto them that call evil good, and good evil; that put darkness for light, and light for darkness; that put bitter for sweet, and sweet for bitter!

21 Woe unto *them that are* wise in their own eyes, and prudent in their own sight!

22 Woe unto *them that are* mighty to drink wine, and men of strength to mingle strong drink:

23 Which justify the wicked for reward, and take away the righteousness of the righteous from him!

24 Therefore as the fire devoureth the stubble, and the flame consumeth the chaff, *so* their root shall be as rottenness, and their blossom shall go away as dust: because they have cast away the law of the LORD of the hosts, and despised the word of the Holy One of Israel.

25 Therefore is the anger of the LORD kindled against his people, and he hath stretched forth his hand against them, and hath smitten them: and the mountains did tremble, and their carcasses *were* torn in the midst of the streets. For all this his anger is not turned away, but his hand *is* stretched out still.

26 And he will lift up an ensign to Gentiles that are far, and will hiss unto them *that are* in the end of the earth: and, behold, they shall come with speed swiftly:

27 None shall be weary nor stumble among them; none shall slumber nor sleep; neither shall the girdle of their loins be loosed, nor the latchet of their shoes be broken:

28 Whose arrows *are* sharp, and all their bows bent, their horses' hoofs shall be counted like flint, and the *wheels of their chariots* like a whirlwind:

29 Their roaring *shall be* like a lion, they shall roar like young lions: yea, they shall gnash their teeth, and lay hold of the prey, and shall carry *it* away safe, and none shall deliver *it*.

30 And in that day they shall roar against them like the roaring of the sea: and if *one* look unto the land, behold darkness *and* sorrow, and the light is darkened in the heavens thereof.

Chapter 6

1 In the year that king Uzziah died I saw also the Lord sitting upon a throne, high and lifted up, and his train filled the temple.

2 Above it stood the seraphims: each one had six wings; with two he covered his face, and with two he covered his feet, and with two he did fly.

3 And one cried unto another, and said, Holy, holy, holy, *is* the LORD of the hosts: the whole earth *is* full of his glory.

4 And the posts of the door moved at the voice of him that cried, and the house was filled with smoke.

5 Then said I, Woe *is* me! for I am dead; because I *am* a man of unclean lips, and I dwell in the midst of a people of unclean lips: for mine eyes have seen the King, the LORD of the hosts.

6 Then flew one of the seraphim unto me, having a live coal in his hand, *which* he had taken with the tongs from off the altar:

7 And he laid *it* upon my mouth, and said, Behold, this hath touched thy lips; and it shall take away thy guilt, and thy sin shall be cleansed.

8 After this I heard the voice of the Lord, saying,

Whom shall I send, and who will go for us? Then answered I, Here *am* I; send me.

9 Then he said, Go, and tell this people, Hear ye indeed, but understand not; and see ye indeed, but perceive not.

10 Make the heart of this people fat, and make their ears heavy, and blind their eyes; that they not see with their eyes, nor hear with their ears, nor understand with their heart, nor convert, and *there be* healing for him.

11 And *I* said, Lord, how long? And he answered, Until the cities be wasted without inhabitant, and not a man in the houses, and the land be turned into desert;

12 until the LORD has removed men far away, and there be great solitude in the midst of the land.

13 But yet in it shall remain a tenth, and *it* shall return, and shall be razed: as the teil tree, and as the oak, of which the stump *remains alive* when they are cut down, *likewise in these* his stump shall remain, holy seed.

Chapter 7

1 And it came to pass in the days of Ahaz the son of Jotham, the son of Uzziah, king of Judah, *that* Rezin the king of Syria, and Pekah the son of Remaliah, king of Israel, went up toward Jerusalem to war against it, but could not prevail against it.

2 And it was told the house of David, saying, Syria is confederate with Ephraim. And his heart was moved, and the heart of his people, as the trees of the wood are moved with the wind.

3 Then said the LORD unto Isaiah, Go forth now to meet Ahaz, thou, and Shearjashub thy son, at the end of the conduit of the upper pool in the highway of the fuller's field;

4 And say unto him, Take heed, and be quiet; fear not, neither be fainthearted for the two tails of these smoking firebrands, for the fierce anger of Rezin with Syria, and of the son of Remaliah.

5 Because Syria, Ephraim, and the son of Remaliah, have taken evil counsel against thee, saying,

6 Let us go up against Judah, and vex it, and let us divide it between us, and set a king in the midst of it, *even* the son of Tabeal:

7 Thus saith the Lord GOD, It shall not stand, neither shall it come to pass.

8 For the head of Syria shall be Damascus, and the head of Damascus, Rezin; and within threescore and five years shall Ephraim be broken, *and it shall never again be a* people.

9 In the mean time the head of Ephraim *shall be* Samaria, and the head of Samaria, Remaliah's son. If ye will not believe, surely ye shall not be established.

10 Moreover the LORD spoke again unto Ahaz, saying,

11 Ask thee a sign of the LORD thy God; ask it either in the depth, or in the height above.

12 But Ahaz said, I will not ask, neither will I tempt the LORD.

13 *Then* said *Isaiah*, Hear ye now, O house of David; *Is it* a small thing for you to weary men, but will ye weary my God also?

14 Therefore the Lord himself shall give you a sign; Behold, the virgin shall conceive, and bear a son, and shall call his name Immanuel.

15 Butter and honey shall he eat, that he may know to refuse the evil, and choose the good.

16 For before the child shall know to refuse the evil, and choose the good, the land that thou abhorrest shall be forsaken of both her kings.

17 The LORD shall bring upon thee, and upon thy people, and upon thy father's house, days that have not come since the day that Ephraim departed from Judah; *even* unto the king of Assyria.

18 And it shall come to pass in that day, *that* the LORD shall hiss for the fly that *is* in the uttermost part of the rivers of Egypt, and for the bee that *is* in the land of Assyria.

19 And they shall come, and shall rest all of them in the desolate valleys, and in the holes of the rocks, and upon all thorns, and upon all bushes.

20 In the same day shall the Lord raze with a razor that is hired, *namely*, by them beyond the river, by the king of Assyria, the head, and the hair of the feet: and it shall also consume the beard.

21 And it shall come to pass in that day, *that* a man

shall nourish a young cow, and two sheep;

22 and it shall come to pass, for the abundance of milk *that* they shall give he shall eat butter: for butter and honey shall every one eat that is left in the land.

23 And it shall come to pass in that day, that *in* the place where there were a thousand vines that were worth a thousand *shekels* of silver, it shall *even* be for the briers and for the thorns.

24 With arrows and with bows shall *men* come thither; because all the land shall become briers and thorns.

25 But unto all the hills that were digged with the hoe, there shall not come thither the fear of briers and thorns: but they shall be for pasture of oxen, and for the treading of the lesser cattle.

Chapter 8

1 Moreover the LORD said unto me, Take thee a great roll, and write in it with a man's pen concerning Mahershalalhashbaz [Hurry to the spoil, make haste to the prey].

2 And I took unto me faithful witnesses to record, Uriah the priest, and Zechariah the son of Jeberechiah.

3 And I went unto the prophetess; and she conceived, and bare a son. Then said the LORD to me, Call his name Mahershalalhashbaz.

4 For before the child shall have knowledge to cry, My father, and my mother, the riches of Damascus and the spoil of Samaria shall be taken away before the king of Assyria.

5 The LORD spoke also unto me again, saying,

6 Forasmuch as this people refused the waters of Shiloah that go softly, and rejoiced in Rezin and Remaliah's son;

7 Now therefore, behold, the Lord bringeth up upon them the waters of the river, strong and many, *even* the king of Assyria, and all his power: and he shall come up over all his channels, and go over all his banks:

8 And he shall pass through Judah; he shall overflow and go over, he shall reach *even* to the neck; and the stretching out of his wings shall fill the breadth of thy land, O Immanuel.

9 Associate yourselves, O ye people, and ye shall be .

broken in pieces; and give ear, all ye of far countries: prepare yourselves, and ye shall be broken in pieces; gird yourselves, and ye shall be broken in pieces.

10 Take counsel together, and it shall come to nought; speak the word, and it shall not stand: for God *is* with us.

11 For the LORD spoke thus to me with a strong hand, and instructed me that I should not walk in the way of this people, saying,

12 Say ye not, A confederacy, to all *them to* whom this people shall say, A confederacy; neither fear ye their fear, nor be afraid.

13 Sanctify the LORD of the hosts himself; and *let* him *be* your fear, and *let* him *be* your dread.

14 Then he shall be for a sanctuary; but for a stone of stumbling and for a rock of offence to both the houses of Israel, for a snare and for a net to the inhabitants of Jerusalem.

15 And many among them shall stumble, and fall, and be broken, and be snared, and be taken.

16 Bind up the testimony, seal the law among my disciples.

17 And I will wait for the LORD, that hideth his face from the house of Jacob, and I will look for him.

18 Behold, I and the children whom the LORD hath given me *are* for signs and for wonders in Israel from the LORD of the hosts, which dwelleth in mount Zion.

19 And when they shall say unto you, Seek unto them that have familiar spirits, and unto wizards that peep, and that mutter: shall the people not seek unto their God? *Shall we appeal* for the living unto the dead?

20 To the law and to the testimony! If they speak not according to this word, *it is* because *there is* no light in them.

21 Then they shall pass through *this land*, fatigued and hungry: and it shall come to pass, that when they shall be hungry, they shall fret themselves, and curse their king and their God. And raising their face high,

22 they shall look upon the earth; and behold tribulation and gross darkness, darkness and anguish; and they shall be submerged in gross darkness.

Chapter 9

1 Nevertheless *this* darkness *shall* not *be* the same as the affliction that came upon her when they did lightly touch the land of Zebulun and the land of Naphtali; nor afterward when they did more grievously afflict *her by* the way of the sea, beyond Jordan, in Galilee of the Gentiles.

2 The people that walked in darkness have seen a great light: they that dwell in the land of the shadow of death, upon them hath the light shined.

3 As thou hast multiplied the nation, thou hast not increased the joy. They shall rejoice before thee as they rejoice in the harvest, *and* as *men* rejoice when they divide the spoil.

4 For thou hast broken his heavy yoke, and the staff of his shoulder, the rod of his oppressor, as in the day of Midian.

5 For every battle of he who fights *is* with shaking *of the earth*, and the rolling of garments in blood; but *this* shall be with burning *and* consuming of fire.

6 For unto us a child is born, unto us a son is given: and the government is *placed* upon his shoulder: and his name shall be called The Wonderful *One*, The Counsellor, The God, The Mighty *One*, The Eternal Father, The Prince of Peace.

7 The multitude of *his* dominion, and the peace, shall have no end upon the throne of David, and upon his Kingdom, ordering it, and confirming it in judgment and in righteousness from henceforth even for ever. The zeal of the LORD of the hosts will perform this.

8 The Lord sent a word into Jacob, and it hath lighted upon Israel.

9 And all the people shall know, *even* Ephraim and the inhabitant of Samaria, that say in pride and arrogance of heart,

10 The bricks are fallen down, but we will build with hewn stones: the wild fig trees are cut down, but we will put cedars in their place.

11 Therefore the LORD shall set up the adversaries of Rezin against him, and join his enemies together;

12 the Syrians before, and the Philistines behind; and they shall devour Israel with open mouth. For all this his anger is not turned away, but his hand *is* stretched out still.

13 But the people did not turn unto him that smote them, neither did they seek the LORD of the hosts.

14 Therefore the LORD will cut off from Israel head and tail, branch and rush, in one day.

15 The ancient and venerable to look upon is the head; the prophet that teacheth lies, he is *the* tail.

16 For the governors of this people are deceivers; and those who are governed by them *are* lost.

17 Therefore the Lord shall have no joy in their young men, neither shall he have mercy on their fatherless and widows: for every one *is* an hypocrite and an evildoer, and every mouth speaketh folly. For all this his anger is not turned away, but his hand *is* stretched out still.

18 For wickedness burneth as the fire: it shall devour the briers and thorns, and shall kindle in the thickets of the forest, and they shall mount up *like* the lifting up of smoke.

19 Through the wrath of the LORD of the hosts is the land darkened, and the people shall be as the fuel of the fire: no man shall spare his brother.

20 And he shall snatch on the right hand, and be hungry; and he shall eat on the left hand, and they shall not be satisfied: they shall eat every man the flesh of his own arm:

21 Manasseh, Ephraim; and Ephraim, Manasseh: *and* they together *shall be* against Judah. For all this his anger is not turned away, but his hand *is* stretched out still.

Chapter 10

1 Woe unto them that establish unrighteous laws, and that wilfully prescribe tyranny;

2 to turn aside the poor from *right* judgment, and to take away the right from the afflicted of my people, that widows may be their prey, and *that* they may rob the fatherless!

3 And what will ye do in the day of visitation, and in the desolation *which* shall come from far? to whom will ye flee for help? and where will ye leave your glory?

4 They shall bow down among the prisoners, and they shall fall among the slain. For all this his anger is not turned away, but his hand *is* stretched out still.

5 O Assyrian, rod and staff of my anger, in thy hand have I placed my indignation.
6 I will send him against an hypocritical nation, and upon *the* people of my wrath will I send him, to take spoil, and to take prey, and to ready them that they might be tread down like the mire of the streets.

7 Howbeit he shall not think like this, not even in his heart shall he imagine this way *of doing things*; but his thought shall be to destroy and cut off nations not a few.
8 For he shall say, *Are* not my princes altogether kings?
9 *Is* not Calno as Carchemish? *is* not Hamath as Arpad? *is* not Samaria as Damascus?
10 As my hand hath found the kingdoms of the idols, and whose graven images did excel them of Jerusalem and of Samaria;
11 Shall I not, as I have done unto Samaria and her idols, so do to Jerusalem and her idols?
12 Wherefore it shall come to pass, *that* when the Lord hath performed his whole work upon mount Zion and on Jerusalem, I will come upon the fruit of the pride of the heart of the king of Assyria, and upon the glory of his high looks.
13 For he said, By the strength of my hand I have done *it*, and by my wisdom; for I have been prudent: and I have removed the boundaries of the peoples, and have robbed their treasures, and I have cast down as valiant *ones* those who were seated:
14 And my hand hath found as a nest the riches of the peoples: and as one gathereth eggs *that are* left, have I taken control over all the earth; and there was none that moved the wing, or opened the mouth, or peeped.

15 Shall the axe boast itself against him that heweth therewith? *or* shall the saw magnify itself against him that moveth it? as if the rod should rise up against them that lift it up, *or* as if the staff should lift *itself* up. Is it not wood?
16 Therefore shall the Lord, the LORD of the hosts, send among his fat ones leanness; and under his glory he shall kindle a burning like the burning of a fire.
17 And the light of Israel shall be for a fire, and his

Holy One for a flame: and it shall burn and devour his thorns and his briers in one day;

18 And shall consume the glory of his forest, and of his fruitful field, from the soul unto the flesh: and they shall come to be as *a* standard-bearer in defeat.

19 And the trees that shall remain in his forest shall be in number such that a child may count them.

20 And it shall come to pass in that day, *that* those who shall be left of Israel, and those who shall be left of the house of Jacob, shall no more again stay upon him that smote them; but shall stay upon the LORD, the Holy One of Israel, in truth.

21 The remnant shall become converted, *even* the remnant of Jacob, unto the mighty God.

22 For though thy people Israel be as the sand of the sea, *yet* the remnant of them shall become converted: when the consumption comes to an end righteousness shall overflow.

23 For the Lord GOD of the hosts shall make a consumption and an end in the midst of all the land.

24 Therefore thus saith the Lord GOD of the hosts, O my people, dweller of Zion, be not afraid of the Assyrian: he shall smite thee with a rod, and shall lift up his stick against thee, by the way of Egypt;

25 yet from now until a very little while, and the indignation and my anger shall cease, to make an end of them.

26 And the LORD of the hosts shall raise up a scourge against him as the slaughter of Midian at the rock of Oreb: and shall raise up his rod upon the sea, by the way of Egypt.

27 And it shall come to pass in that day, that his burden shall be taken away from off thy shoulder, and his yoke from off thy neck, and the yoke shall be consumed in the presence of the anointing.

28 He is came to Aiath, he is passed unto Migron; in Michmash he shall number his army:

29 They are gone over the fords: they have taken up their lodging at Geba; Ramah is afraid; Gibeah of Saul is fled.

30 Lift up thy voice, O daughter of Gallim: Laish

cause poor Anathoth to hear thee.

31 Madmenah is in up-heaval; the inhabitants of Gebim shall gather them-selves together.

32 Even yet *shall come* a day when he shall rest at Nob: he shall raise his hand unto the mountain of the daughter of Zion, unto the hill of Jerusalem.

33 Behold, the Lord, the LORD of the hosts, shall lop the bough with force: and the high ones of stature *shall be* hewn down, and the haughty shall be humbled.

34 And he shall cut down the thickness of the forest with iron, and Lebanon shall fall by force.

Chapter 11

1 And there shall come forth a rod out of the stem of Jesse, and a Branch shall grow out of his roots:

2 And the Spirit of the LORD shall rest upon him, the Spirit of wisdom and under-standing, the Spirit of coun-sel and might, the Spirit of knowledge and of the fear of the LORD;

3 and shall make him of quick olfactory in the fear of the LORD: and he shall not judge according to the sight of his eyes, neither reprove according to the hearing of his ears:

4 But with righteousness shall he judge the poor, and reprove with equity for the meek of the earth: and he shall smite the earth with the rod of his mouth, and with the spirit of his lips shall he slay the wicked.

5 And righteousness shall be the girdle of his loins, and faith the girdle of his kidneys.

6 The wolf shall dwell with the lamb, and the leopard shall lie down with the kid; and the calf and the young lion and the fatling to-gether; and *a* child shall shepherd them.

7 The cow and the bear shall feed; their young ones shall lie down together: and the lion shall eat straw like the ox.

8 And the sucking child shall play on the hole of the asp, and the weaned child shall put his hand on the cockatrice' den.

9 They shall not hurt nor destroy in all my holy mountain: for the earth shall be full of the knowl-edge of the LORD, as the waters cover the sea.

10 And it shall be in that day, that the Root of Jesse, which shall be *lifted up* as an ensign to the Gentiles; shall be sought by the Gentiles: and his *Kingdom* of peace shall be glorious.

11 And it shall come to pass in that day, *that* the Lord shall return to set his hand again, to possess the remnant of his people which were left from Assyria, and from Egypt, and from Pathros, and from Cush, and from Elam, and from Shinar, and from Hamath, and from the islands of the sea.

12 And he shall set up an ensign for the Gentiles, and shall assemble the outcasts of Israel, and gather together the dispersed of Judah from the four corners of the earth.

13 The envy also of Ephraim shall depart, and the adversaries of Judah shall be cut off: Ephraim shall not envy Judah, and Judah shall not vex Ephraim.

14 But they shall fly upon the shoulders of the Philistines toward the west; they shall spoil them of the east together: they shall lay their hand upon Edom and Moab; and the children of Ammon shall obey them.

15 And the LORD shall utterly dry up the tongue of the Egyptian sea; and shall raise his hand in the strength of his spirit upon the river, and shall smite it into seven streams, and make *men* go over dryshod.

16 And there shall be an highway for the remnant of his people, which shall be left, from Assyria; like as it was for Israel in the day that he came up out of the land of Egypt.

Chapter 12

1 And in that day thou shalt say, O LORD, I will sing unto thee: though thou wast angry with me, thine anger is turned away, and thou hast comforted me.

2 Behold, O God my saving health; I will trust, and not be afraid: for JAH, the LORD, *is* my strength and *my* song; he also is become saving health unto me.

3 Therefore with joy shall ye draw water out of the wells of saving health.

4 And in that day shall ye say, Sing unto the LORD, call upon his name, declare his doings among the peoples, remember how his name is exalted.

5 Sing psalms unto the LORD; for he hath done excellent things: *let* this *be* known in all the earth.

6 Rejoice and sing, thou inhabitant of Zion: for great *is* the Holy One of Israel in the midst of thee.

Chapter 13

1 The burden of Babylon, which Isaiah the son of Amoz did see.

2 Lift ye up *a* banner upon *the* high mountain, exalt the voice unto them, raise the hand, that they may enter in by gates of princes.

3 I have commanded my sanctified ones, I have also called my mighty ones for my anger, that they *might* rejoice with my glory.

4 The noise of a multitude in the mountains, like as of a great people; a tumultuous noise of kingdoms, of Gentiles gathered together: the LORD of the hosts orders the host of the battle.

5 They come from a far land, from the end of the heavens, *even* the LORD, and the instruments of his indignation, to destroy the whole earth.

6 Howl ye; for the day of the LORD *is* at hand; it shall come as destruction from the Almighty.

7 Therefore shall all hands be faint, and every man's heart shall melt:

8 And they shall be filled with terror: anguish and pain shall take hold of them; they shall be in pain as a woman that travaileth: they shall be amazed one at another; their faces *shall be as* flames.

9 Behold, the day of the LORD cometh, cruel and with wrath and fierce anger, to lay the earth desolate: and he shall destroy the sinners thereof out of it.

10 And I will visit evil upon the world, and iniquity upon the wicked; and I will cause the arrogancy of the proud to cease, and will lay low the haughtiness of the strong.

12 I will make the *noble* man more precious than fine gold; and man more than the gold of Ophir.

13 Because I will shake the heavens, and the earth shall be moved out of her place, in the indignation of the LORD of the hosts, and in the day of his fierce anger.

14 Every one that is found shall be thrust through; and every one that is joined *unto them* shall fall by the sword.

16 Their children also shall be dashed to pieces before their eyes; their houses shall be spoiled, and their wives ravished.

17 Behold, I will stir up the Medes against them, which

shall not look for silver; nor covet gold.

18 They shall shoot at the young boys with bows; and they shall have no pity on the fruit of the womb; their eye shall not spare *the* sons.

19 And Babylon, the glory of kingdoms, the beauty of the Chaldees' excellency, shall be as when God overthrew Sodom and Gomorrah.

20 It shall never again be inhabited, neither shall it be dwelt in from generation to generation: neither shall the Arabian pitch tent there; neither shall the shepherds make their fold there.

21 But wild beasts of the desert shall lie there; and their houses shall be full of doleful creatures; and owls shall dwell there, and satyrs shall dance there.

22 And the wild beasts of the islands shall cry in their palaces, and dragons in *their* pleasant palaces: and her time *is* near to come, and her days shall not be prolonged.

Chapter 14

1 For the LORD will have mercy on Jacob, and will yet choose Israel, and cause them to rest in their own land: and the strangers shall be joined with them, and they shall cleave to the house of Jacob.

2 And the peoples shall take them, and bring them to their place: and the house of Israel shall possess them in the land of the LORD for servants and handmaids: and they shall take them captives, whose captives they were; and they shall rule over their oppressors.

3 And it shall come to pass in the day that the LORD shall give thee rest from thy sorrow, and from thy fear, and from the hard bondage wherein thou wast made to serve,

4 that thou shalt take up this proverb against the king of Babylon, and say, How hath the oppressor ceased! the city that coveteth gold hath ceased!

5 The LORD hath broken the staff of the wicked, *and* the sceptre of the rulers;

6 who smote the peoples in wrath with a continual stroke, he that ruled the Gentiles in anger, and who defended not the persecuted.

7 The whole earth is at rest, *and* is quiet: they sing praises.

8 Yea, the fir trees rejoice at thee, *and* the cedars of

Lebanon, *saying*, Since thou art laid down, no feller is come up against us.

9 Hell from beneath is aghast at thee: it stirreth up the dead to meet *thee* at thy coming; it hath raised up from their thrones all the princes of the earth, all the kings of the Gentiles.

10 All they shall shout and say unto thee, Art thou also become sick as we? art thou become like unto us?

11 Thy pride is brought down to the grave, *and* the noise of thy viols: the worm is spread under thee, and the worms cover thee.

12 How art thou fallen from heaven, O Lucifer, son of the morning! *how* art thou cut down to the ground, which didst claim the Gentiles as an inheritance!

13 Thou who said in thine heart, I will ascend into heaven, upon high next to the stars of God I will exalt my throne: and I will sit upon the mount of the testimony, and in the sides of the north:

14 I will ascend above the heights of the clouds; I will be like the most High.

15 Yet thou art cast down in the grave, to the sides of the pit.

16 They that see thee shall narrowly look upon thee, and consider thee, *saying,* Is this the man that made the earth to tremble, that did shake the kingdoms;

17 *That* made the world as a wilderness, and destroyed the cities thereof; *that* opened not the prison to his prisoners?

18 All the kings of the Gentiles, *even* all of them, lie in glory, every one in his own house.

19 But thou art cast out of thy grave like an abominable branch, *and as* the raiment of those that are slain, thrust through with a sword, that went down to the bottom of the pit; as a carcass trodden under feet.

20 Thou shalt not be numbered with them in burial, because thou hast destroyed thy land, *and* slain thy people: the seed of evildoers shall not be forever.

21 Prepare slaughter for his children for the iniquity of their fathers; that they do not rise, nor possess the land, nor fill the face of the world with cities.

22 For I will rise up upon them, saith the LORD of hosts, and cut off from Babylon the name, and remnant, and son, and nephew, saith the LORD.

23 I will also make it a possession for the bittern, and pools of water: and I will sweep it with brooms of destruction, saith the LORD of the hosts.

24 The LORD of the hosts hath sworn, saying, Surely as I have thought, so shall it come to pass; and as I have purposed, *so* shall it stand:

25 That I will break the Assyrian in my land, and upon my mountains tread him under foot: then shall his yoke depart from off them, and his burden depart from off their shoulders.

26 This *is* the counsel that is purposed upon the whole earth: and this *is* the hand that is stretched out upon all the Gentiles.

27 For the LORD of the hosts hath purposed, and who shall disannul *it*? and his hand *is* stretched out, and who shall turn it back?

28 In the year that king Ahaz died was this burden.

29 And the firstborn of the poor shall be fed, and the needy shall lie down in safety: and I will cause thy root to die of famine, and he shall slay thy remnant.

31 Howl, O gate; cry, O city; thou, whole Palestine, *art* dissolved: for there shall come from the north a smoke, and not one *shall be* left in thy assemblies.

32 What shall *one* then answer the messengers of the Gentiles? That the LORD hath founded Zion, and in her the afflicted of his people shall have confidence.

Chapter 15

1 The burden of Moab. Certainly in the night Ar of Moab was laid waste, *and* brought to silence; certainly in the night Kir of Moab was laid waste, *and* brought to silence.

2 He is gone up to Bajith, and to Dibon, the altars, to weep: Moab shall howl over Nebo, and over Medeba: every head among her shall become bald, *and* every beard shall be cut off.

3 In their streets they shall gird themselves with sackcloth: on the tops of their houses, and in their streets, every one shall howl, weeping as they come down.

4 And Heshbon shall cry, and Elealeh: their voice shall be heard *even* unto JAHaz: therefore the armed soldiers of Moab shall cry out; each one of them shall cry out for his soul.

5 My heart shall cry out for Moab; his fugitives shall go up with weeping by the hill of Luhith unto Zoar, an heifer of three years; for in the way of Horonaim they shall raise up a cry of destruction.

6 For the waters of Nimrim have run out: for the grass *of the courtyard* is withered away, the herb faileth, there is no green thing.

7 Therefore that which *each one* has laid up, and their riches, shall they carry away to the brook of the willows.

8 For the cry is gone round about the borders of Moab; the howling thereof unto Eglaim, and the clamour thereof unto Beerelim.

9 For the waters of Dimon shall be full of blood: for I will bring more upon Dimon, lions upon him that escapeth of Moab, and upon the remnant of the land.

Chapter 16

1 Send ye the lamb to the ruler of the land, from the rock of the wilderness unto the mount of the daughter of Zion.

2 For it shall be, *that*, as a wandering bird cast out of the nest, *so* the daughters of Moab shall be at the fords of Arnon.

3 Take counsel, execute judgment; make thy shadow as the night in the midst of the noonday; hide the outcasts; betray not him that escapeth.

4 Let my outcasts dwell with thee, Moab; be thou a covert to them from the presence of the destroyer: for the extortioner shall come to an end, the destroyer shall cease, the oppressor shall be consumed out of the land.

5 And in mercy shall the throne be established: and he shall sit upon it in truth in the tabernacle of David, judging, and seeking judgment, and hastening righteousness.

6 We have heard of the pride of Moab; *he is* very proud: *even* of his haughtiness, and his pride, and his wrath: *but* his lies *shall* not *be* so.

7 Therefore shall Moab howl for Moab, every one shall howl: for the foundations of Kirhareseth shall ye mourn; surely *they are* stricken.

8 For the vines of Heshbon were cut off, *and* the vines of Sibmah: the lords of the Gentiles have trodden down the offshoots thereof, which had come *even* unto Jazer, and extended *through* the wilderness; they had gone over the sea.

9 Therefore I will bewail with the weeping Jazer of the vine of Sibmah: I will cause thee to drink my tears, O Heshbon, and Elealeh: for the song shall cease upon thy summer fruits and thy harvest.

10 And gladness is taken away, and joy out of the fertile field; and in the vineyards there shall be no singing, neither shall there be rejoicing: the treaders shall tread out no wine in *their* presses; I have made *their vintage* song to cease.

11 Wherefore my bowels shall sound like an harp for Moab, and my inward parts for Kirharesh.

12 And it shall come to pass, when it is seen that Moab is weary upon the high places, that he shall come to his sanctuary to pray; but he shall be unable to.

13 This *is* the word that the LORD hath spoken concerning Moab since that time.

14 But now the LORD hath spoken, saying, Within three years, as an hireling *counteth the* years, the glory of Moab shall be cast down, with all *her* great multitude; and the remnant *shall be* few, small *and* feeble.

Chapter 17

1 The burden of Damascus. Behold, Damascus is taken away from *being* a city, and it shall be a ruinous heap.

2 The cities of Aroer *are* forsaken: they shall be for flocks, which shall lie down, and none shall make *them* afraid.

3 The succour of Ephraim shall cease, and the kingdom from Damascus, and the remnant of Syria: they shall be as the glory of the children of Israel, saith the LORD of the hosts.

4 And in that day it shall come to pass, *that* the glory of Jacob shall be made thin, and the fatness of his flesh shall wax lean.

5 And it shall be as when the harvestman gathereth the sheaves, and reapeth the grain with his arm; and it shall be as he that gathereth grain in the valley of Rephaim.

6 Yet gleaning shall be left in it, as when the olive tree is shaken, two *or* three berries *are left* in the top of the uppermost bough, four *or* five in the outmost fruitful branches thereof, saith the LORD God of Israel.

7 At that day shall man look to his Maker, and his

eyes shall see the Holy One of Israel.

8 And he shall not look to the altars, the work of his hands, neither shall he look upon *that* which his fingers have made, either the groves, or the images of the sun.

9 In that day the cities of his strength shall be as the gleanings which remain on the shoots and on the branches, which were left of the children of Israel: and there shall be desolation.

10 Because thou hast forgotten the God of thy saving health, and hast not been mindful of the Rock of thy strength, therefore shalt thou plant pleasant plants, and shalt set it with strange slips:

11 In the day that shalt thou shalt plant them, thou shalt make them to grow, and shalt make thy seed to flourish early: *but* in the day of gathering, the harvest shall flee, and *shall be* desperate sorrow.

12 Woe to the multitude of many peoples, *which* shall make a noise like the noise of the sea; and the rushing of nations, *that* make an uprising like the rushing of mighty waters!

13 The peoples shall make noise like the rushing of great waters: but *God* shall reprehend them, and they shall flee far off, and shall be chased as the chaff of the mountains before the wind, and like the tumbleweed before the whirlwind.

14 And behold at eveningtide trouble; *and* before the morning she *is* not. This *is* the portion of them that tread on us, and the lot of them that spoil us.

Chapter 18

1 Woe to the land which maketh shade with *her* wings, which *is* beyond the rivers of Ethiopia:

2 He who sendeth ambassadors by the sea, even in vessels of bulrushes upon the waters, *saying*, Go, ye swift messengers, to the people scattered and peeled, to the people full of fears from their beginning, and hitherto; *a* people tired of waiting and trodden down, whose land the rivers have spoiled!

3 All ye inhabitants of the world, and neighbours of the land, when he lifteth up an ensign on the mountains, ye shall see it; and when he bloweth a trumpet, ye shall hear it.

4 For so the LORD said unto me, I will take my rest, and I will look forth from my dwelling place; like a clear sun after the rain, *and* like a cloud filled with dew in the heat of the harvest.

5 For before the harvest, when the fruit is perfect, and after the flower is past, the fruit is mature, then he shall both cut off the sprigs with pruning hooks, and take away *and* cut down the branches.

6 They shall be left together unto the fowls of the mountains, and to the beasts of the earth: and the fowls shall summer upon them, and all the beasts of the earth shall winter upon them.

7 In that time shall *the* present be brought unto the LORD of the hosts, the people scattered and peeled, the people full of fears from their beginning and hitherto; *a* people tired of waiting and trodden under foot, whose land the rivers have spoiled, to the place of the name of the LORD of the hosts, to the mount Zion.

Chapter 19

1 The burden of Egypt. Behold, the LORD rideth upon a swift cloud, and shall come into Egypt: and the idols of Egypt shall be moved at his presence, and the heart of Egypt shall melt in the midst of it.

2 And I will set the Egyptians against the Egyptians: and they shall fight every one against his brother, and every one against his neighbour; city against city, *and* kingdom against kingdom.

3 And the spirit of Egypt shall fail in the midst thereof; and I will destroy the counsel thereof: and they shall seek to the idols, and to the charmers, and to them that have familiar spirits, and to the wizards.

4 And the Egyptians will I give over into the hand of a cruel lord; and a violent king shall rule over them, saith the Lord, the LORD of the hosts.

5 And the waters shall fail from the sea, and the river shall be wasted and dried up.

6 And they shall turn the rivers far away; *and* the brooks of defence shall be emptied and dried up: the reeds and flags shall wither.

7 The vegetables by the river, by the mouth of the river, and every thing sown beside the river, shall dry up, wither away, and be no *more*.

8 The fishermen also shall mourn, and all they that cast fishhooks into the river shall lament, and they that spread nets upon the waters shall languish.

9 Moreover they that work in fine flax, and they that weave networks, shall be confounded.

10 Because all their nets shall be broken; all that make ponds to *raise* fish *shall be* discontented.

11 Surely the princes of Zoan *are* fools, the counsel of the prudent counsellors of Pharaoh is become carnal: how say ye unto Pharaoh, I *am* the son of the wise, the son of the ancient kings?

12 Where *are* they? where *are* thy wise *men*? and let them tell thee now, or let them cause thee to know what the LORD of the hosts hath purposed upon Egypt.

13 The princes of Zoan are become fools, the princes of Noph are deceived; they have also seduced Egypt, *even they that are* the stay of the tribes thereof.

14 The LORD hath mingled a perverse spirit in the midst thereof: and they have caused Egypt to err in every work thereof, as a drunken *man* staggereth in his vomit.

15 Neither shall it be of *any* value unto Egypt, any work which the head or tail, branch or rush, may do.

16 In that day shall Egypt be like unto women: and it shall be afraid and fear in the presence of the tall hand of the LORD of the hosts, which he shall raise up over them.

17 And the land of Judah shall be a terror unto Egypt, every one that maketh mention thereof shall be afraid in himself, because of the counsel of the LORD of the hosts, which he hath determined against it.

18 In that day shall five cities in the land of Egypt speak the language of Canaan, and swear to the LORD of the hosts; one shall be called, The city of destruction.

19 In that day shall there be an altar to the LORD in the midst of the land of Egypt, and a pyramid titled: To the LORD, at the border thereof.

20 And it shall be for a sign and for a witness unto the LORD of the hosts in the land of Egypt: for they shall cry unto the LORD because of the oppressors, and he shall send them a Saviour, and a Prince, and he shall deliver them.

21 And the LORD shall be known to Egypt, and the Egyptians shall know the LORD in that day, and shall do sacrifice and oblation; yea, they shall vow vows unto the LORD, and perform them.

22 And the LORD shall smite Egypt: he shall smite and heal *it*: because they shall become converted unto the LORD, and he shall grant them clemency, and shall heal them.

23 In that day shall there be a highway out of Egypt to Assyria, and the Assyrian shall come into Egypt, and the Egyptian into Assyria, and the Egyptians shall serve the LORD with the Assyrians.

24 In that day shall Israel be the third with Egypt and with Assyria, *even* a blessing in the midst of the earth.

25 For the LORD of the hosts shall bless them, saying, Blessed *be* Egypt my people, and Assyria the work of my hands, and Israel my inheritance.

Chapter 20

1 In the year that Tartan came unto Ashdod, (when Sargon the king of Assyria sent him,) and fought against Ashdod, and took it;

2 At the same time spoke the LORD by Isaiah the son of Amoz, saying, Go and loose the sackcloth from off thy loins, and put off thy shoe from thy foot. And he did so, walking naked and barefoot.

3 And the LORD said, Like as my servant Isaiah hath walked naked and barefoot three years *for* a sign and wonder upon Egypt and upon Ethiopia;

4 So shall the king of Assyria lead away the Egyptians prisoners, and the Ethiopians captives, young and old, naked and barefoot, even with *their* buttocks uncovered, to the shame of Egypt.

5 And they shall be afraid and ashamed of Ethiopia their hope, and of Egypt their glory.

6 And the inhabitant of this isle shall say in that day, Behold, such *was* our hope, which we did cling to for help that we might be free from the presence of the king of Assyria. How shall we escape?

Chapter 21

1 The burden of the desert of the sea. As the whirlwinds which pass through the wilderness in the land of the south; *so* come they from the terrible land.

2 A grievous vision is shown unto me. For *one* who is treacherous, another who dealeth treacherously, and for *one* destroyer, *another* destroyer. Rise up, Elam: besiege, Media; all the sighing thereof have I made to cease.

3 Therefore are my loins filled with pain: pangs have taken hold upon me, as the pangs of a woman that travaileth: I was bowed down at the hearing *of it*; I was dismayed at the seeing *of it.*

4 My heart panted, the horror affrighted me: the night of my pleasure hath he turned into fear unto me.

5 Prepare the table, watch in the watchtower, eat, drink: arise, ye princes, *and* anoint the shield.

6 For thus hath the Lord said unto me, Go, set a watchman who shall declare what he seeth.

7 And he saw a chariot *with* a couple of horsemen, a chariot of asses, *and* a chariot of camels; then he looked with more diligence:

8 And he cried, A lion upon the watchman. My lord, I stand continually *all* the day, and all night long upon my watchtower.

9 And, behold, this chariot of men cometh, *with* a couple of horsemen. Afterwards he spoke and said, Babylon is fallen, is fallen; and all the graven images of her gods he hath broken unto the ground.

10 O my harvest, and the people of my threshing floor: that which I have heard of the LORD of the hosts, the God of Israel, have I declared unto you.

11 The burden of Dumah. He calleth to me out of Seir, Watchman, what of this night? Watchman, what of this night?

12 The watchman said, The morning cometh, and then the night: if ye will enquire, enquire ye: return, and come.

13 The burden upon Arabia. In the forest shall ye pass the night in Arabia, O ye walkers of Dedanim.

14 Go ye out to meet them bringing water for the thirsty O inhabitants of the land of Tema; succour those who are fleeing with your bread.

15 For they flee from the presence of the sword, from the presence of the drawn sword, from the presence of the bent bow, from the presence of the grievousness of the battle.

16 For thus hath the Lord said unto me, Within a year, according to the years of an hireling, and all the glory of Kedar shall be undone:

17 And the residue of the number of valiant archers, sons of Kedar, shall be diminished: for the LORD God of Israel hath spoken *it*.

Chapter 22

1 The burden of the valley of the vision. What aileth thee now, that thou art completely gone up to the housetops?

2 Thou that art full of stirs, a tumultuous city, a joyous city: thy dead *are* not slain with the sword, nor slain in battle.

3 All thy princes together fled from the bow, they were bound: all that were found in thee were bound together, *the others* fled far away.

4 Therefore said I, Leave me; I will weep bitterly, labour not to comfort me of the destruction of the daughter of my people.

5 For a day of trouble, and of treading down, and of wearing down by the Lord GOD of the hosts *is sent* in the valley of the vision, to break down the wall, and *give a* cry unto the mountain.

6 Also Elam bare the quiver in chariot of men, and of horsemen, and Kir uncovered the shield.

7 And it came to pass, *that* thy choicest valleys were full of chariots, and the soldiers set themselves in array at the gate.

8 And he discovered the covering of Judah, and thou didst look in that day to the house of weapons of the forest.

9 Ye have seen also the breaches of the city of David, that they are multiplied: and ye gathered together the waters of the lower pool.

10 And ye have numbered the houses of Jerusalem, and ye have broken down houses to fortify the wall.

11 Ye made also a moat between the two walls with the water of the old pool: but ye have not looked unto the maker thereof, neither had respect unto him that fashioned it long ago.

12 Therefore the Lord GOD of the hosts did call in this day unto weeping, and to mourning, and to baldness, and to girding with sackcloth:

13 And behold joy and gladness, slaying oxen, and killing sheep, eating flesh, and drinking wine *while they say*: let us eat and drink; for to morrow we shall die.

14 This was revealed in my ears by the LORD of the hosts, That surely this iniquity shall not be purged from you until ye die, saith the Lord GOD of the hosts.

15 Thus saith the Lord GOD of the hosts, Go, get thee unto this treasurer, *even* unto Shebna, which *is* over the house, *and say*,

16 What hast thou here? or whom hast thou here, that thou hast hewed thee out a sepulchre here, *as* he that heweth him out a sepulchre on a high place, or that graveth an habitation for himself in a rock?

17 Behold, the LORD will carry thee away in a hard captivity, and will surely cover thy face.

18 He will surely violently turn and toss thee *like* a ball into a large country: there shalt thou die, and there the chariots of thy glory *shall come to an end*, the shame of the House of thy Lord.

19 And I will drive thee from thy place, and from thy state shall he pull thee down.

20 And it shall come to pass in that day, that I will call my servant Eliakim the son of Hilkiah:

21 And I will clothe him with thy robe, and strengthen him with thy girdle, and I will commit thy government into his hand: and he shall be a father to the inhabitants of Jerusalem, and to the house of Judah.

22 And the key of the house of David will I lay upon his shoulder; so he shall open, and none shall shut; and he shall shut, and none shall open.

23 And I will fasten him *as* a nail in a sure place; and he shall be for a glorious throne to his father's house.

24 And they shall hang upon him all the glory of his father's house, the sons and the grandsons, all the vessels of small quantity, from the cups to drink *from*, even unto all the instruments of music.

25 In that day, saith the LORD of the hosts, shall the nail that is fastened in the sure place be removed, and be cut down, and fall; and the burden that *was* upon it shall be cut off: for the LORD hath spoken *it*.

Chapter 23

1 The burden of Tyre. Howl, ye ships of Tarshish; for it is laid waste, so that there is no house, no entering in: from the land of Chittim it is revealed to them.

2 Be still, ye inhabitants of the isle; *thou* mart of Zidon, that *by* passing over the sea thou wert replenished.

3 Her provision *was* from the plantings *that grow* with the many waters of the Nile, of the harvest of the river. She was also the mart of the Gentiles.

4 Be thou ashamed, O Zidon: for the sea hath spoken, *even* the strength of the sea, saying, I have never travailed, nor brought forth children, neither did I nourish up young men, *nor* bring up virgins.

5 When the report cometh unto Egypt, they shall be sorely pained at the news from Tyre.

6 Pass ye over to Tarshish; howl, ye inhabitants of the isle.

7 *Is* this your joyous *city*, whose antiquity *is* of ancient days? her own feet shall carry her afar off to sojourn.

8 Who hath decreed this against Tyre, the crowning *city*, whose merchants were princes, whose traders *were* the honourable of the earth?

9 The LORD of the hosts hath purposed it, to stain the pride of all glory, *and* to bring down all *those* who are exalted in the earth.

10 Pass by as a river from thy land, O daughter of Tarshish: for *thou shalt have* no more strength.

11 He stretched out his hand over the sea, he shook the kingdoms: the LORD commanded upon Canaan that her strength should be weakened.

12 And he said, Thou shalt no more rejoice, O thou oppressed virgin, daughter of Zidon: arise, pass over to Chittim, and even there thou shalt have no rest.

13 Behold the land of the Chaldeans; this people was not, *until* the Assyrian founded it for them that dwell in the wilderness: they set up the towers thereof, they raised up the palaces thereof; *and* he brought it to ruin.

14 Howl, ye ships of Tarshish: for your strength is laid waste.

15 And it shall come to pass in that day, that Tyre shall be forgotten seventy years, according to the days of one king: after the end of seventy years shall Tyre sing as an harlot.

16 Take an harp, go about the city, thou harlot that hast been forgotten; make sweet melody, sing the song again, that thou mayest be remembered.

17 And it shall come to pass after the end of seventy years, that the LORD will visit Tyre, and she shall turn to her hire, and shall commit fornication again with all the kingdoms of the world upon the face of the earth.

18 But her profit and her hire shall be consecrated unto the LORD: it shall not be treasured nor laid up; for her profit shall be for them that dwell before the LORD, to eat until they are filled, and to dress honourably.

Chapter 24

1 Behold, the LORD maketh the earth empty, and maketh it naked, and turneth it upside down, and scattereth abroad the inhabitants thereof.

2 And it shall be, as with the people, so with the priest; as with the servant, so with his master; as with the maid, so with her mistress; as with the buyer, so with the seller; as with the lender, so with the borrower; as with the taker of usury, so with the giver of usury to him.

3 The land shall be utterly emptied, and utterly spoiled: for the LORD hath spoken this word.

4 The earth has destroyed itself and fallen, the world has become sick and fallen, the haughty peoples of the earth are become sick.

5 The earth also is become bankrupt under the inhabitants thereof; because they have transgressed the laws, falsified the order, broken the everlasting covenant.

6 Therefore hath the curse consumed the earth, and they that dwell therein are desolate: therefore the inhabitants of the earth are consumed, and few men left.

7 The new wine is lost, the vine is sick, all those who were merryhearted do sigh.

8 The mirth of tambourines ceaseth, the noise of them that rejoice endeth, the joy of the harp ceaseth.

9 They shall not drink wine with a song; the drink shall be bitter to them that would drink it.

10 The city of confusion is broken down: every house is shut up, that no man may come in.

11 *There is* a crying for wine in the streets; all joy is darkened, the mirth of the land is gone.

12 In the city is left desolation, and the gate is smitten with destruction.

13 For thus it shall be in the midst of the land among the peoples, as the shaking of an olive tree, as the gleanings when the vintage is done.

14 These shall lift up their voice, they shall sing joyfully in the majesty of the LORD, they shall lift up their voice from the sea.

15 Therefore glorify ye the LORD in the valleys, Let the LORD God of Israel be called upon by name in the isles of the sea.

16 From the uttermost part of the earth have we heard psalms, *Glory* to the righteous *one*. But I said, My leanness, my leanness, woe unto me!

The treacherous dealers have dealt treacherously; yea, the treacherous dealers have dealt very treacherously.

17 Fear, and the pit, and the snare, *are* upon thee, O inhabitant of the earth.

18 And it shall come to pass, *that* he who shall flee from the noise of the fear shall fall into the pit; and he that shall come up out of the midst of the pit shall be taken in the snare: because from on high windows have been opened, and the foundations of the earth shall shake.

19 The earth shall be utterly broken down, the earth is clean dissolved, the earth is moved exceedingly.

20 The earth shall reel to and fro like a drunkard, and shall be removed like a cottage; and the transgression thereof shall be heavy upon it; and it shall fall, and never rise again.

21 And it shall come to pass in that day, *that* the LORD shall visit *punishment* upon the host of the high ones *that are* on high, and upon the kings of the earth upon the earth.

22 And they shall be gathered together, *as* prisoners are gathered in the pit, and shall be shut up in the prison, and after many days shall they be visited.

23 Then the moon shall be confounded, and the sun ashamed, when the LORD of the hosts shall reign in mount Zion, and in Jerusalem, and in the presence of his ancients he shall be glorious.

Chapter 25

1 O LORD, thou *art* my God; I will exalt thee, I will praise thy name; for thou hast done wonders, the counsels of old, the truth unchanging.

2 That thou hast turned the city into an heap; the defenced city into *a* ruin: the palace of strangers to not be *a* city; it shall never be rebuilt.

3 Therefore shall the strong people glorify thee, the city of the strong Gentiles shall fear thee.

4 For thou hast been strength to the poor, strength to the needy in his distress, refuge from the storm, shadow from the heat, for the force of the violent *is* as a storm *against* the wall.

5 As the heat in a dry place, thou shalt bring down the pride of the strangers; *even as* with heat *that burns* beneath *a* cloud, thou shalt cause the offshoot of the stout ones to whither.

6 And in this mountain shall the LORD of the hosts make unto all people a feast of fat things, a feast of purified wines, of fat things full of marrow, of purified liquids.

7 And he will undo in this mountain the mask of the covering with which all the peoples are covered, and the covering that is extended over all the Gentiles.

8 He will destroy death forever; and the Lord GOD shall wipe away every tear from off all faces; and the rebuke of his people shall he take away from off all the earth: for the LORD hath determined *it*.

9 And it shall be said in that day, Behold, this *is* our God, who we have waited for, and he has saved us: this *is* the LORD, who we have waited for, we will be glad and rejoice in his saving health.

10 For in this mountain shall the hand of the LORD rest, and Moab shall be trodden down under him, even as straw is trodden down for the dunghill.

11 And he shall extend his hand in the midst of him, as he that swimmeth spreadeth forth *his hand* to swim: and he shall bring down his pride with the members of his hands;

12 and lay siege to the fortress of thy high walls; he shall humble it and bring it down to the ground, *even* to the dust.

Chapter 26

1 In that day they shall sing this song in the land of Judah; We have a strong city; *God* has appointed saving health *for* walls and bulwarks.

2 Open ye the gates, that the righteous nation which keepeth the truth may enter in.

3 Thou wilt keep *him* in perfect peace, *whose* mind *is* stayed *on thee*: because he trusteth in thee.

4 Trust ye in the LORD for ever: for in JAH, the LORD *is* the strength of the ages:

5 For he hath brought down them that dwelt on high; he hath humbled the lofty city; he humbled her, *even* to the ground; he brought her down *even* to the dust.

6 The foot shall tread her down, *even the* feet of the poor, *and the* steps of the needy.

7 The way of the just *is* uprightness: thou, most upright, dost weigh the path of the just.

8 Yea, in the way of thy judgments, O LORD, we wait for thee; the desire of *our* soul *is* to thy name, and to the remembrance of thee.

9 With my soul I desire thee in the night; yea, even as long as the spirit is within me I will seek thee early: for as long as thy judgments *are* in the earth, the inhabitants of the world learn righteousness.

10 Let favour be showed to the wicked, *yet* will he not learn righteousness: in the land of uprightness will he deal unjustly, and will not behold the majesty of the LORD.

11 LORD, *when* thy hand is withdrawn, they will not see: *but* they shall see in the end, and be ashamed with the zeal of the people. And fire shall consume thine enemies.

12 LORD, thou wilt ordain peace for us: for thou also hast wrought in us all our works.

13 O LORD our God, *other* lords have had dominion over us without thee: *but* in thee only will we remember thy name.

14 *They are* dead, they shall not live; *they are* deceased, they shall not rise: because thou hast visited and destroyed them, and made all their memory to perish.

15 Thou hast added the Gentiles, O LORD, thou hast

added the Gentiles: thou hast made thyself glorious: thou hast extended thyself *unto* all the ends of the earth.

16 LORD, in the tribulation they have sought thee, they poured out prayer *when* thy chastening *was* upon them.

17 Like as a woman with child, *that* draweth near the time of her delivery, is in pain, *and* crieth out in her pangs; so have we been in thy sight, O LORD.

18 We have conceived, we have had birth pangs, we have as it were brought forth wind; we have not wrought any health in the earth; neither have the inhabitants of the world fallen.

19 Thy dead shall live, and *together with* my body they shall arise. Awake and sing, ye that dwell in dust: for thy dew *is as* the covering of light, and the earth shall cast out the dead.

20 Come, my people, enter thou into thy chambers, and shut thy doors about thee: hide thyself as it were for a little moment, until the indignation be overpast.

21 For, behold, the LORD cometh out of his place to visit the iniquity of the in-habitant of the earth against himself: the earth also shall disclose her blood, and shall no more cover her slain.

Chapter 27

1 In that day the LORD with his sore and great and strong sword shall visit *punishment* upon leviathan the fleeing serpent, and upon leviathan that serpent of double vision; and he shall slay the dragon that *is* in the sea.

2 In that day sing ye unto the vineyard of the red wine.

3 I the LORD do keep it; I will water it every moment: lest *the enemy* visit it, I will keep it night and day.

4 Fury *is* not in me: who would set the briers *and* thorns against me in battle? I would tread them down, I would burn them to-gether.

5 Or *who* shall take hold of my strength? Make peace with me, yea, make peace with me.

6 *Days* shall come when Jacob shall take root: Israel shall blossom and bud, and the face of the world shall be filled with fruit.

7 Has he been smitten, as he who smote him? *or* has

he been slain as those who slew him?

8 In measure, she shall be chastised in her stalks: he stayeth his rough wind in the day of the east wind.

9 Therefore, in this manner shall the iniquity of Jacob be purged; and this *shall be* all the fruit, the removal of his sin; when shall return all the stones of the altar, as chalkstones that are beaten in sunder, that they may not raise up the groves, or the images of the sun.

10 Otherwise the defenced city *shall be* made desolate, *and* the habitation shall be forsaken, and left like a wilderness: there shall the calf feed, and there shall he lie down, and consume the branches thereof.

11 When the boughs thereof are withered, they shall be broken off: women shall come *and* set them on fire: for this *is* not a people of understanding: therefore he that made them will not have mercy on them, and he that formed them will show them no favour.

12 And it shall come to pass in that day, *that* the LORD shall smite from the channel of the river *Eufrates* unto the stream of Egypt, and ye shall be gathered one by one, O ye children of Israel.

13 And it shall come to pass in that day, *that* the great trumpet shall be blown, and they shall come which were ready to perish in the land of Assyria, and the outcasts in the land of Egypt, and shall worship the LORD in the holy mount at Jerusalem.

Chapter 28

1 Woe to the crown of pride, to the drunkards of Ephraim, and to the fading flower of the beauty of their glory, which *is* upon the head of the fertile valley of them that are overcome with wine!

2 Behold, the Lord hath a mighty and strong one, *which* as a tempest of hail *and* a destroying storm, as a flood of mighty waters overflowing, shall cast down to the earth with the hand.

3 The crown of pride, the drunkards of Ephraim, shall be trodden under feet:

4 And the fading flower of the beauty of their glory, which *is* upon the head of the fertile valley, shall be as the early fig, which *cometh* first *before the other fruits* of the summer; which *when* he that looketh upon it seeth it, *as soon as he* hath it in his hand he eateth it up.

5 In that day shall the LORD of the hosts be for a crown of glory, and for a diadem of beauty, unto the residue of his people,

6 And for a spirit of judgment to him that sitteth upon *the throne of* judgment, and for strength to them that turn the battle to the gate.

7 But they also have erred through wine, and through strong drink are out of the way; the priest and the prophet have erred through strong drink, they are swallowed up of wine, they are out of the way through strong drink; they err in vision, they stumble *in* judgment.

8 For all tables are full of vomit *and* filthiness, *so that there is* no place *clean*.

9 Whom shall he teach knowledge? and whom shall he make to understand doctrine? *them that are* weaned from the milk, *and* drawn from the breasts.

10 For precept *must be* upon precept, precept upon precept; line upon line, line upon line; here a little, *and* there a little:

11 For with stammering lips and another tongue will he speak to this people.

12 To whom he said, This *is* the rest *wherewith* ye may cause the weary to rest; and this *is* the refreshing: yet they would not hear.

13 But the word of the LORD shall be unto them precept upon precept, precept upon precept; line upon line, line upon line; here a little, *and* there a little; that they might go, and fall backward, and be broken, and snared, and taken.

14 Therefore hear the word of the LORD, ye scornful men, that have taken rule over this people which *is* in Jerusalem.

15 Because ye have said, We have made a covenant with death, and with the grave are we at agreement; when the overflowing scourge shall pass through, it shall not come unto us: for we have made lies our refuge, and under falsehood have we hid ourselves:

16 Therefore thus saith the Lord GOD, Behold, I lay in Zion for a foundation a stone, a tried stone, a precious corner *stone*, a sure foundation: he that believeth shall not make haste.

17 Judgment also will I lay to the line, and righteousness to the plummet: and the hail shall sweep away the refuge of lies, and the waters shall overflow the hiding place.

18 And your covenant with death shall be disannulled, and your agreement with the grave shall not stand; when the overflowing scourge shall pass through, then ye shall be trodden down by it.

19 From the time that it goeth forth it shall take you: for it shall come suddenly, by day and by night: and it shall be *that* the terror only causes *one to* understand the report.

20 For the bed is shorter than that *a man* can stretch himself *on it*: and the covering narrower than that he can wrap himself *in it*.

21 For the LORD shall rise up as *in* mount Perazim, he shall be wroth as *in* the valley of Gibeon, that he may do his work, his strange work; and bring to pass his act, his strange act.

22 Now therefore be ye not mockers, lest your bands be made strong: for I have heard from the Lord GOD of the hosts that consumption and destruction *are* deter-mined upon the whole earth.

23 Give ye ear, and hear my voice; hearken, and hear my speech.

24 Doth the plowman plow all day to sow? doth he open and break the clods of his ground?

25 When he hath levelled the face thereof, doth he not cast abroad the fitches, and scatter the cummin, and cast in the principal wheat and the appointed barley and the rye in their place?

26 For his God doth teach him to know how to judge, *and* doth instruct him.

27 For the fitches are not threshed with a threshing instrument, neither is a cart wheel turned about upon the cummin; but the fitches are beaten out with a staff, and the cummin with a rod.

28 Grain is thrashed *to make bread*; but he will not ever be threshing it, nor shall he grind *it* with the wheel of his cart, nor crush it with the teeth *of his thrashing instrument*.

29 This also cometh forth from the LORD of the hosts, to make *his* counsel wonderful, and to increase wisdom.

Chapter 29

1 Woe to Ariel, to Ariel, the city *where* David dwelt! add ye one year to another; the lambs shall cease.

2 Yet I will distress Ariel, and there shall be heaviness and sorrow: and it shall be unto me as Ariel.

3 And I will camp against thee round about, and will lay siege against thee with a mount, and I will raise forts against thee.

4 And thou shalt be brought down, *and* shalt speak out of the ground, and thy speech shall be low out of the dust, and thy voice shall be, as of one that hath a familiar spirit, out of the ground, and thy speech shall whisper out of the dust.

5 Moreover the multitude of thy enemies *that shall come from afar* shall be like small dust, and the multitude of the strong ones *shall be* as chaff that passeth away: ye a, it shall be at an instant suddenly.

6 Thou shalt be visited of the LORD of the hosts with thunders, with earthquakes, and with great noise, with whirlwind and tempest, and the flame of devouring fire.

7 And the multitude of all the Gentiles that shall fight against Ariel, even all that shall fight against her and their siege weapons, and those that shall distress her, shall be as a dream of a night vision.

8 It shall even be as he who dreameth that he is hungry, and in his dream, he eateth; but when he awaketh, his soul *is* empty: and *as* he who dreameth that he is thirsty, and, in his dream, he drinketh; but he awaketh, and, behold, *he is* faint, and his soul *is still* thirsty: so shall the multitude of all the Gentiles be, that shall fight against mount Zion.

9 Become ye dumb, and make others dumb; become ye blind, and blind others: they are drunken, but not with wine; they stagger, but not with strong drink.

10 For the LORD hath extended upon you the spirit of deep sleep, and hath closed your eyes: the prophets and your rulers, the seers hath he covered with sleep.

11 And every vision is unto you as the words of a book that is sealed, which if it were delivered to one that knoweth how to read, saying, Read this, I pray thee: he shall say, I cannot; for it *is* sealed:

12 And if the book were delivered to him that knoweth not how to read, saying, Read this, I pray thee: he shall say, I know not how to read.

13 Wherefore the Lord said, Forasmuch as this people sacrifice unto me, and with their lips do honour me, but have removed their heart far from me, and their worship with which they honour me was taught by the commandment of men:

14 Therefore, behold, I will again do a marvellous *work among* this people with *a* fearful miracle: for the wisdom of their wise *men* shall perish, and the prudence of their prudent *men* shall fade away.

15 Woe unto them that hide themselves from the LORD, covering the counsel; and their works are in the dark, and they say, Who seeth us? and who knoweth us?

16 Surely your subversion shall be as the potter's clay: for shall the work say of him that made it, He made me not? or shall the vessel say of him that made it, He did not understand?

17 *Is* it not yet a very little while, and Lebanon shall be turned into Carmel [*a fruitful field*], and shall not Carmel be esteemed as a forest?

18 And in that day shall the deaf hear the words of the book, and the eyes of the blind shall see in the midst of darkness, and of gross darkness.

19 Then the humble shall grow in joy in the LORD, and the poor among men shall rejoice in the Holy One of Israel.

20 For the violent one shall be done away with, and the scorner shall be consumed, and all those that rose early unto iniquity shall be cut off:

21 Those that made men to sin in word; those that layed a snare for him that reproved in the gate, and turned that which is just into vanity.

22 Therefore thus saith the LORD, who redeemed Abraham, unto the house of Jacob, Jacob shall not now be ashamed, neither shall his face now wax pale;

23 for he shall see his children, the work of my hands, in the midst of him, they shall sanctify my name, and shall sanctify the Holy One of Jacob, and shall fear the God of Israel;

24 and those that erred in spirit shall learn understanding, and they that murmured shall learn doctrine.

Chapter 30

1 Woe to the sons that leave, saith the LORD, to make counsel, but not of me; to cover themselves with a covering, and not by my spirit, adding sin unto sin!

2 They leave to descend into Egypt, and have not *asked for a word from* my mouth; to strengthen themselves in the strength of Pharaoh, and to place their hope in the shadow of Egypt.

3 But the strength of Pharaoh shall become your shame, and the hope in the shadow of Egypt *your* confusion.

4 When his princes shall be in Zoan, and his ambassadors have come to Hanes.

5 All shall be ashamed of the people *that* shall not profit them, nor be an help, nor bring them increase, but a shame, and also a reproach.

6 The burden of the beasts of the south: into the land of trouble and anguish, from whence *come* the young and old lion, the viper and fiery flying serpent, they will carry their riches upon the shoulders of young asses, and their treasures upon the bunches of camels, to a people *that* shall not profit *them*.

7 For the Egyptians shall help in vain, and to no purpose: therefore have I cried concerning this, that your strength *should be* to sit still.

8 Now go, write this *vision* before them on a tablet, and note it in a book, that it may remain unto the last day, for ever, unto all ages.

9 That this *is* a rebellious people, lying sons, children *that* did not desire to hear the law of the LORD:

10 Which say to those that see, See not; and to the prophets, Prophesy not unto us right things, speak unto us smooth things, prophesy deceits:

11 Get you out of the way, turn aside out of the path, cause the Holy One of Israel to leave our presence.

12 Wherefore thus' saith the Holy One of Israel, Because ye despise this word, and trust in violence and iniquity, and build upon this:

13 Therefore this sin shall be to you as an open *wall* ready to fall, and as a breach in a high defence, whose breaking cometh suddenly at an instant.

14 And your destruction, shall be as the breaking of *a* potters' vessel, that without mercy is broken to pieces: so that there shall not be found in the bursting of it even a shard to take fire from the hearth, or to take water from *the* well.

15 For the Lord GOD, the Holy One of Israel hath said; In returning and rest shall ye be saved; in quietness and in confidence shall be your strength: and ye would not.

16 But ye said, No; for we will flee upon horses; therefore shall ye flee: and, We will ride upon the swift; therefore shall they that pursue you be even more swift.

17 One thousand *shall flee* at the rebuke of one; at the rebuke of five shall ye *all* flee: until ye be left as a beacon upon the top of a mountain, and as an ensign on an hill.

18 And therefore will the LORD wait *for you*, that he may have mercy on you, and therefore will he be exalted having mercy upon you: for the LORD *is* a God of judgment: blessed *are* all they that wait for him.

19 For the people shall dwell in Zion, in Jerusalem: thou shalt weep no more: he who hath mercy shall show mercy unto thee; at the voice of thy cry; when he shall hear it, he will answer thee.

20 But the Lord shall give you the bread of adversity, and the water of affliction; thy rain shall never more be taken away, but thine eyes shall see thy rain:

21 Then thine ears shall hear a word behind thee, saying, This *is* the way, walk ye in it, that ye not turn to the right hand, and that ye not turn to the left hand.

22 Ye shall defile also the covering of thy graven images of silver, and the protection of thy molten images of gold: thou shalt cast them away as a menstruous cloth; thou shalt say unto it, Get thee hence.

23 Then shall he give the rain unto thy planting, when thou shalt sow the ground; and bread of the fruit of the earth, and it shall be fat and fertile: in that day shall thy cattle feed in large pastures.

24 Thine oxen and thine asses that work the ground shall eat clean grain, which hath been winnowed with the shovel and with the fan.

25 And there shall be upon every high mountain, and upon every high hill, rivers *and* streams of waters in the day of the great slaughter, when the towers shall fall.

26 Moreover the light of the moon shall be as the light of the sun, and the light of the sun shall be sevenfold, as the light of seven days, in the day that the LORD bindeth up the breach of his people, and healeth the stroke of their wound.

27 Behold, the name of the LORD cometh from afar, his face is blazing, and difficult to gaze upon: his lips are full of indignation, and his tongue as a devouring fire:
28 And his Spirit, as an overflowing stream, shall break even unto the neck, to sift the Gentiles with the sieve of vanity: and *to put a* bridle in the jaws of the people, causing *them* to err.
29 Ye shall have a song, as in *the* night *in which* the Passover is kept; and gladness of heart, as when one goeth with a flute to come into the mountain of the LORD, to the mighty One of Israel.

30 And the LORD shall cause the power of his voice to be heard, and shall cause the lighting down of his arm to be seen, with the indignation of *his* countenance, and *with* the flame of a devouring fire, *with* scattering, and tempest, and hailstones.
31 For through the voice of the LORD shall the Assyrian be beaten down, *which* smote with a rod.
32 And *in* every *evil* place there shall be a staff, that the LORD shall cause to lay upon him with tambourines and harps: and with *the* strength of heaven he will fight against her.
33 For Tophet *is* ordained of yesterday for the king *of Babylon*, it is also prepared; he hath deepened *and* enlarged the pile of her fire and much wood; the breath of the LORD, like a stream of brimstone, doth kindle it.

Chapter 31

1 Woe to them that go down to Egypt for help; and trust in horses, and place their hope in chariots, because *they are* many; and in horsemen, because they are valiant; but they did not look unto the Holy One of Israel, neither did they seek the LORD!

2 Yet he also *is* wise to guide evil, and will not cause his words to lie: but will arise against the house of the evildoers, and against the help of them that work iniquity.

3 Now the Egyptian is a man, and not God; and his horses flesh, and not spirit, so that as the LORD shall stretch out his hand, both he that helpeth shall fall, and he that is helped shall fall down, and they all shall fail together.

4 For thus hath the LORD spoken unto me, Like as the lion and the young lion roaring on his prey, even if a multitude of shepherds cometh forth against him, *he* will not be afraid of their voices, nor abase himself for the noise of them: so shall the LORD of the hosts come down to fight for mount Zion, and for his hill.

5 As birds flying, so will the LORD of the hosts defend Jerusalem; defending, delivering, passing over, and saving *it*.

6 Turn ye unto him against whom *ye* have deeply revolted, O sons of Israel.

7 For in that day every man shall cast away his idols of silver, and his idols of gold, which your own sinful hands have made unto you.

8 Then shall the Assyrian fall by the sword, not of a mighty man; and the sword, not of a mean man, shall devour him: but he shall flee from the presence of the sword, and his young men shall faint.

9 And he shall pass over to his strong hold for fear, and his princes shall be afraid of the ensign, saith the LORD, unto whom *there is* fire in Zion, and unto whom *there is a* furnace in Jerusalem.

Chapter 32

1 Behold, *one* king shall reign in righteousness, and princes shall preside unto judgment.

2 And that Man shall be as an hiding place from the wind, and a covert from the tempest; as rivers of water in a dry *place*, as the shadow of a great rock in a hot land.

3 And the eyes of them that see shall not be dim, and the ears of them that hear shall hearken.

4 The heart also of the rash shall understand knowledge, and the tongue of the stammerers shall be ready to speak plainly.

5 The vile person shall be no more called liberal, nor

the greedy said *to be* bountiful.

6 For the vile person will speak villainy, and his heart will invent iniquity, to work unrighteousness, and to speak scornfully against the LORD, leaving the soul of the hungry empty, and taking away the drink of the thirsty.

7 Certainly the greedy *use* evil measures: he deviseth wicked devices to ensnare the simple with lying words, and to speak in judgment *against* the poor.

8 But the liberal deviseth liberal things; and by liberal things shall he rise.

9 Rise up, ye women that are at ease; hear my voice, ye careless daughters; give ear unto my speech.

10 Many days and years shall ye be troubled, ye careless women: for the vintage shall fail, and the harvest shall not come in.

11 Tremble, ye women that are at ease; be troubled, ye careless ones: strip you, and make you bare, and gird *sackcloth* upon *your* loins.

12 Upon their breasts they shall lament for the pleasant fields, for the fruitful vine.

13 Upon the land of my people shall come up thorns *and* briers; yea, upon all the houses of joy *in* the joyous city:

14 Because the palaces shall be forsaken; the noise of the city shall be cease; the forts and towers shall be for dens for ever, a joy of wild asses, a pasture of flocks;

15 until the spirit be poured upon us from on high, and the wilderness be turned into a fruitful field, and the fruitful field be counted for a forest.

16 Then judgment shall dwell in the wilderness, and righteousness shall remain in the fruitful field.

17 And the work of righteousness shall be peace; and the effect of righteousness rest and security for ever.

18 And my people shall dwell in an habitation of peace, and in secure dwellings, and in the refreshing of rest.

19 And the hail, when it shall come down, *shall be* in the forest; and the city shall be completely laid low.

20 Blessed *are* ye that sow upon all *the* waters, ye that plow with the ox and with the ass.

Chapter 33

1 Woe to thee that spoilest, and thou *wast* not spoiled; and thou dealest treacherously, and they dealt not treacherously with thee! when thou shalt cease to spoil, thou shalt be spoiled; *and* when thou shalt make an end to deal treacherously, they shall deal treacherously with thee.

2 O LORD, have mercy on us; we wait for thee: *thou* wert the strength of thy people in the beginning, be also our saving health in the time of tribulation.

3 At the noise of the tumult the peoples fled; at the lifting up of thyself the Gentiles were scattered.

4 And your spoil shall be gathered *like* the gathering of the caterpillar: as the running to and fro of locusts shall he run upon them.

5 The LORD shall be exalted; he who dwelleth on the heights: *for* he hath filled Zion with judgment and righteousness.

6 And in thy times wisdom and knowledge, and the strength of salvation shall reign: the fear of the LORD *shall be* his treasure.

7 Behold, their ambassadors shall cry without: the messengers of peace shall weep bitterly.

8 The highways shall be broken down, the travellers shall cease: he hath broken the covenant, he hath despised the cities, he regardeth not man.

9 The earth mourneth *and* languisheth: Lebanon is ashamed *and* hewn down: Sharon is like a wilderness; and Bashan and Carmel were shaken.

10 Now will I rise up, saith the LORD; now will I be exalted; now will I be lifted up.

11 Ye shall conceive chaff, ye shall bring forth stubble: your breath, *as* fire, shall devour you.

12 And the peoples shall be *as* the burnings of lime: *as* thorns cut up shall they be burned in the fire.

13 Hear, ye *that are* far off, what I have done; and, ye *that are* near, acknowledge my might.

14 The sinners in Zion are afraid; fearfulness hath surprised the hypocrites. Who among us shall dwell with the devouring fire? who among us shall dwell with eternal flames?

15 He that walketh in righteousness, he that speaketh uprightly; he that despiseth the gain of violence, he that shaketh his hands from receiving bribes; he that stoppeth his ears, to not hear of blood; he who shutteth his eyes, to not see evil;

16 he shall dwell upon the high places: fortresses of rocks shall be his place of refuge: bread shall be given him; his waters *shall be* sure.

17 Thine eyes shall see the king in his beauty: they shall behold the land that is very far off.

18 Thine heart shall imagine the terror. Where *is* the scribe? where *is* the receiver *of tribute*? where *is* he that counted the towers?

19 Thou shalt not see that fierce people, a people of a dark speech than thou canst perceive; of a stammering tongue, *that thou canst* not understand.

20 Thou shalt see Zion, the city of our solemnities: thine eyes shall see Jerusalem a quiet habitation, a tabernacle *that* shall not be taken down; not one of the stakes thereof shall ever be removed, neither shall any of the cords thereof be broken.

21 For the LORD shall surely be strong unto us there, a place of broad rivers *and* wide streams; wherein shall go no galley with oars, neither shall *any* great ship pass thereby.

22 For the LORD *shall be* our judge, the LORD *shall be* our lawgiver, the LORD shall be our king; he himself will save us.

23 Thy tacklings are loosed; they could not well strengthen their mast, they could not spread the sail: then is the prey of a great spoil to be divided; *even* the lame shall take prey.

24 And the inhabitant shall not say, I am sick: the people that dwell therein *shall be* absolved from sin.

Chapter 34

1 Come near, ye Gentiles, to hear; and hearken, ye peoples: let the earth hear, and all that is therein; the world, and all things that come forth of it.

2 For the indignation of the LORD *is* upon all the Gentiles, and *his* fury upon the entire army of them: he shall destroy them, and deliver them to the slaughter.

3 Their slain shall be cast out, and their stink shall come up out of their carcasses, and the mountains shall be melted with their blood.

4 And all the host of heavens shall be dissolved, and

the heavens shall be rolled together as a scroll: and all their host shall fall down, as the leaf falleth off from the vine, and as the *leaf* falleth from the fig tree.

5 For in the heavens my sword shall become drunk: behold, it shall come down upon Idumea [*or Edom*], and upon the people of my anathema.

6 The sword of the LORD is filled with blood, it is made fat with fatness, *and* with the blood of lambs and goats, with the fat of the kidneys of rams: for the LORD hath a sacrifice in Bozrah, and a great slaughter in the land of Idumea.

7 And the unicorns shall fall with them, and the bulls with the calves; and their land shall become drunk with blood, and their dust shall be greased with fatness.

8 For *it shall be* the day of the LORD'S vengeance, *and* the year of recompenses for the controversy of Zion.

9 And the streams thereof shall be turned into pitch, and the dust thereof into sulphur, and the land thereof shall become burning pitch.

10 It shall not be quenched night nor day; the smoke thereof shall go up for ever: from generation to generation it shall lie waste; none shall pass through it for ever and ever.

11 But the cormorant and the bittern shall possess it; the owl also and the raven shall dwell in it: and he shall stretch out upon it the line of confusion, and the level of desolation.

12 They shall call the princes thereof, princes without a kingdom; and all her great ones shall be nothing.

13 And thorns shall come up in her palaces, nettles and brambles in the fortresses thereof: and it shall be an habitation of dragons, *and* a court for young owls.

14 The wild beasts of the desert shall also meet with the wild beasts of the island, and the satyr shall cry to his fellow; the screech owl shall have his seat there, and find for himself a place of rest.

15 There shall the great owl make his nest, and conserve *his eggs*, and hatch his young, and gather them under his wings: there shall the vultures also be gathered, every one with his mate.

16 Seek ye out *that which is written in* the book of the LORD, and read: if one of these is lacking, none is missing with his mate: for his mouth hath commanded it, and his same Spirit it hath gathered them.

17 And he hath cast the lot for them, and his hand hath divided it unto them by line: therefore they shall have it as an inheritance for ever, from generation to generation shall they dwell therein.

Chapter 35

1 The wilderness and the solitary place shall be glad; the desert shall rejoice, and blossom as the lily.

2 It shall blossom abundantly, and shall also praise and sing with jubilee: the honour of Lebanon shall be given unto it, the beauty of Carmel and Sharon. They shall see the glory of the LORD, *and* the beauty of our God.

3 Comfort ye the tired hands, and strengthen the knees that tremble.

4 Say to them *that are* of a fearful heart, Be comforted, fear not: behold, your God cometh with vengeance, with recompense; God himself will come and save you.

5 Then the eyes of the blind shall be opened, and the ears of the deaf shall be unstopped.

6 Then the lame *one* shall leap as *an* hart, and the tongue of the dumb shall praise: for waters shall be dug in the wilderness, and streams in the desert.

7 The parched ground shall become a pool, and the thirsty land springs of water: in the habitation of dragons, where each lay, *shall be* grass with reeds and rushes.

8 And an highway shall be there, and a way, and it shall be called The Way of Holiness; the unclean shall not pass over it; and for those in it there *shall be* someone to go with them, in such a manner that the foolish shall not err *therein.*

9 No lion shall be there, nor *any* ravenous beast shall go up thereon, it shall not be found there; so that the redeemed can walk *there*:

10 And the ransomed of the LORD shall return, and come to Zion with songs; and everlasting joy *shall be* upon their heads: they shall retain joy and gladness, and sorrow and sighing shall flee away.

Chapter 36

1 Now it came to pass in the fourteenth year of king Hezekiah, *that* Sennacherib king of Assyria came up against all the defenced cities of Judah, and took them.

2 And the king of Assyria sent Rabshakeh from Lachish to Jerusalem unto king Hezekiah with a great army. And he camped by the conduit of the upper pool in the highway of the fuller's field.

3 Then came forth unto him Eliakim, Hilkiah's son, which was over the house, and Shebna the scribe, and Joah, Asaph's son, the recorder.

4 And Rabshakeh said unto them, Say ye now to Hezekiah, Thus saith the great king, the king of Assyria, What confidence *is* this wherein thou trustest?

5 I say, *sayest thou*, (but *they are but* vain words) *I have* counsel and strength for war: now on whom dost thou trust, that thou rebellest against me?

6 Behold, thou trustest in the staff of this broken reed, on Egypt; whereon if a man lean, it will go into his hand, and pierce it: so *is* Pharaoh king of Egypt to all that trust in him.

7 But if thou say to me, We trust in the LORD our God: *is it* not he, whose high places and whose altars Hezekiah hath taken away, and said to Judah and to Jerusalem, Ye shall worship before this altar?

8 Now therefore give pledges, I pray thee, to my master the king of Assyria, and I will give thee two thousand horses, if thou be able on thy part to set riders upon them.

9 How, therefore, wilt thou turn away the face of one captain of the least of my master's servants, even if thou art trusting in Egypt for chariots and for horsemen?

10 And peradventure am I now come up without the LORD against this land to destroy it? the LORD said unto me, Go up against this land, and destroy it.

11 Then said Eliakim and Shebna and Joah unto Rabshakeh, Speak, I pray thee, unto thy servants in the Syrian language; for we understand *it*: and speak not to us in the Jewish language, in the ears of the people that *are* on the wall.

12 But Rabshakeh said, Hath my master sent me to thy master and to thee to speak these words? *hath he* not *sent me* to the men that sit upon the wall, that they may eat their own dung, and drink their own piss with you?

13 Then Rabshakeh stood, and cried with a loud voice in the Jewish language, and said, Hear ye the words of the great king, the king of Assyria.

14 Thus saith the king, Let not Hezekiah deceive you: for he shall not be able to deliver you.

15 Neither let Hezekiah make you trust in the LORD, saying, The LORD will surely deliver us: this city shall not be delivered into the hand of the king of Assyria.

16 Hearken not to Hezekiah: for thus saith the king of Assyria, Make peace with me, and come out to me: and eat ye every one of his vine, and every one of his fig tree, and drink ye every one the waters of his own cistern;

17 until I come and take you away to a land like your own land, a land of grain and wine, a land of bread and vineyards.

18 *Beware* lest Hezekiah persuade you, saying, The LORD will deliver us. Hath any of the gods of the Gentiles delivered his land out of the hand of the king of Assyria?

19 Where *is* the god of Hamath and Arphad? Where *is* the god of Sepharvaim? Have they delivered Samaria out of my hand?

20 What god is there among all the gods of these lands, that have delivered their land out of my hand, that the LORD should deliver Jerusalem out of my hand?

21 But they held their peace, and answered him not a word: for the king's commandment was, saying, Answer him not.

22 *Then* came Eliakim, the son of Hilkiah, that *was* over the household, and Shebna the scribe, and Joah, the son of Asaph, the recorder, to Hezekiah with *their* clothes rent, and told him the words of Rabshakeh.

Chapter 37

1 And it came to pass, when king Hezekiah heard *it*, that he rent his clothes, and covered himself with sackcloth, and went into the house of the LORD.

2 And he sent Eliakim, who *was* over the household, and Shebna the scribe, and the elders of the priests covered with sackcloth, unto Isaiah the prophet the son of Amoz.

3 And they said unto him, Thus saith Hezekiah, This day *is* a day of trouble, and of rebuke, and of blasphemy: for the sons are come to the breaking *of the water*, and *there is* no strength in her who is to bring *them* forth.

4 It may be the LORD thy God will hear the words of Rabshakeh, whom the king of Assyria his master hath sent to blaspheme the living God, and to reprove with the words which the LORD thy God hath heard: wherefore lift up *thy* prayer for the remnant that is still left.

5 So the servants of king Hezekiah came to Isaiah.

6 And Isaiah said unto them, Thus shall ye say unto your master, Thus saith the LORD, Be not afraid of the words that thou hast heard, wherewith the servants of the king of Assyria have blasphemed me.

7 Behold, that I am sending *a* spirit in him, and he shall hear *a* rumour, and return to his own land; and I will cause him to fall by the sword in his own land.

8 So Rabshakeh returned, and found the king of Assyria warring against Libnah: for he had heard that he was departed from Lachish.

9 And he heard say concerning Tirhakah king of Ethiopia, He is come forth to make war with thee. And when he heard *it*, he sent messengers to Hezekiah, saying,

10 Thus shall ye speak to Hezekiah king of Judah, saying, Let not thy God, in whom thou trustest, deceive thee, saying, Jerusalem shall not be given into the hand of the king of Assyria.

11 Behold, thou hast heard what the kings of Assyria have done to all lands by destroying them utterly; and shalt thou be delivered?

12 Have the gods of the Gentiles delivered them which my fathers have destroyed, *as* Gozan, and Haran, and Rezeph, and the sons of Eden which *were* in Telassar?

13 Where *is* the king of Hamath, and the king of Arphad, and the king of the city of Sepharvaim, Hena, and Ivah?

14 And Hezekiah took the letters from the hand of the messengers, and read them: and Hezekiah went up unto the house of the LORD, and spread them before the LORD.

15 And Hezekiah prayed unto the LORD, saying,

16 O LORD of the hosts, God of Israel, that dwellest *between* the cherubim, thou *art* the God, *even* thou alone, of all the kingdoms of the earth: thou hast made the heavens and earth.

17 Incline thine ear, O LORD, and hear; open thine eyes, O LORD, and see: and hear all the words of Sennacherib, which hath sent *his messengers* to blaspheme the living God.

18 Of a truth, LORD, the kings of Assyria have laid waste all the nations, and their countries,

19 and have cast their gods into the fire: for they *were* no gods, but the work of men's hands, wood and stone: therefore they have destroyed them.

20 Now therefore, O LORD our God, save us from his hand, that all the kingdoms of the earth may know that thou *art* the LORD, *even* thou only.

21 Then Isaiah the son of Amoz sent unto Hezekiah, saying, Thus saith the LORD God of Israel, Whereas thou hast prayed to me against Sennacherib king of Assyria:

22 This *is* the word which the LORD hath spoken concerning him, Hath he despised thee? Hath he laughed the to scorn O virgin daughter of Zion? Hath he shaken his head behind thy back O daughter of Jerusalem?

23 Whom hast thou reproached and blasphemed? and against whom hast thou exalted *thy* voice, and lifted up thine eyes on high? *even* against the Holy One of Israel.

24 By the hand of thy servants hast thou reproached the Lord, and hast said, By the multitude of my chariots shall I come up to the height of the mountains, to the sides of Lebanon; and I will cut down the tall cedars thereof, *and* the choice fir trees thereof: and I will enter into the height of his border, *and* the forest of his Carmel.

25 I have digged, and drunk water; and with the sole of my feet have I shall up all the rivers of sustenance.

26 Hast thou not heard long ago, *how* I have done it; *and* of ancient times, that I have formed it? now have I brought it to pass, that thou shouldest be to lay waste defenced cities *into* ruinous heaps.

27 And their inhabitants, of little strength, dismayed and confounded: shall be *as* the grass of the field, and *as* the green shrub, *as* the grass on the housetops, that before it cometh to maturity it is dried up.

28 I have understood thy state, thy going out, and thy coming in, and thy rage against me.

29 Because thy rage against me, and thy tumult, is come up into my ears, therefore will I put my hook in thy nose, and my bridle in thy lips, and I will turn thee back by the way by which thou camest.

30 And this *shall be* a sign unto thee, Ye shall eat *this* year such as groweth of itself; and the second year that which springeth of the same: and in the third year ye shall sow, and shall reap, and shall plant vineyards, and shall eat the fruit thereof.

31 And the remnant that is escaped of the house of Judah shall again take root downward, and bear fruit upward:

32 For out of Jerusalem shall go forth a remnant, and from mount Zion shall come an escape: the zeal of the LORD of the hosts shall do this.

33 Therefore thus saith the LORD concerning the king of Assyria, He shall not come into this city, nor shoot an arrow there, nor come before it with shields, nor cast a bank against it.

34 By the way that he came, by the same shall he return, and shall not come into this city, saith the LORD.

35 For I will defend this city to save it for my own sake, and for my servant David's sake.

36 Then the angel of the LORD went forth, and smote in the camp of the Assyrians a hundred and fourscore and five thousand: and when they arose early in the morning, behold, they *were* all dead corpses.

37 So Sennacherib king of Assyria departed, and went and returned, and dwelt at Nineveh.

38 And it came to pass, as he was worshipping in the house of Nisroch his god, that Adrammelech and Sharezer his sons smote him with the sword; and they escaped into the land of Armenia: and Esarhaddon his son reigned in his stead.

Chapter 38

1 In those days was Hezekiah sick unto death. And Isaiah the prophet the son of Amoz came unto him, and said unto him, Thus saith the LORD, Set thine house in order: for thou shalt die, and not live.

2 Then Hezekiah turned his face toward the wall, and prayed unto the LORD,

3 And said, Remember now, O LORD, I beseech thee, how I have walked before thee in truth and with a perfect heart, and have done *that which is* good in thy sight. And Hezekiah wept sore.

4 Then came the word of the LORD to Isaiah, saying,

5 Go, and say to Hezekiah, Thus saith the LORD, the God of David thy father, I have heard thy prayer, I have seen thy tears: behold, I will add unto thy days fifteen years.

6 And I will deliver thee and this city out of the hand of the king of Assyria: and I will defend this city.

7 And this *shall be* a sign unto thee from the LORD, that the LORD will do this thing that he hath spoken;

8 Behold, I will bring again the shadow of the degrees, which is gone down in the sun dial of Ahaz, ten degrees backward. So the sun returned ten degrees, by which degrees it was gone down.

9 The writing of Hezekiah king of Judah, when he had been sick, and was recovered of his sickness:

10 I said in the cutting off of my days, I shall go to the gates of the grave: I am deprived of the residue of my years.

11 I said, I shall not see JAH, *even* JAH, in the land of the living: I shall behold man no more with the inhabitants of the world.

12 My dwelling place has been moved, and is removed from me as a shepherd's tent: he hath cut off my life like a weaver: he hath cut me off with sickness: from day *even* to night wilt thou shalt consume me.

13 I reckoned that I had until morning. As a lion, he broke all my bones: from the morning *even* unto the night thou shalt make an end of me.

14 Like a crane *or* a swallow, so did I complain: I did mourn as a dove: I raised my eyes upward: O LORD, I am suffering violence; comfort me.

15 What shall I say? he hath both spoken unto me, and himself hath done *it*: I shall walk softly all my years in the bitterness of my soul.

16 O Lord, even unto all those that shall live, *in these fifteen years I shall proclaim* the life of my spirit in them; and how thou caused me to sleep, and *afterwards* hast given me life

17 Behold, for peace I had great bitterness: but it has pleased thee to *deliver* my life from the pit of corruption: for thou hast cast all my sins behind thy back.

18 For the grave shall not confess thee, nor shall death praise thee; nor shall they that go down into the pit wait for thy truth.

19 He who liveth, he who liveth, even he shall confess thee, as I *do* this day: the father to the children shall make known thy truth.

20 The LORD *is ready* to save me: therefore we will sing our psalms in the house of he LORD all the days of our life.

21 Isaiah then said, Let them take a lump of figs, and lay *it* for a plaster upon the boil, and he shall be healed.

22 And Hezekiah had said, What *is* the sign that I shall go up to the house of the LORD?

Chapter 39

1 At that time Merodach-baladan, the son of Baladan, king of Babylon, sent letters and presents to Hezekiah: for he had heard that he had been sick, and was recovered.

2 And Hezekiah rejoiced with them, and showed them the house of his precious things, the silver, and the gold, and the spices, and the precious ointments, and all the house of his weapons, and all that was found in his treasures: there was nothing in his house, nor in all his dominion, that Hezekiah showed them not.

3 Then came Isaiah the prophet unto king Hezekiah, and said unto him, What said these men? and from whence came they unto thee? And Hezekiah said, They are come from a far country unto me, *even* from Babylon.

4 Then said he, What have they seen in thine house? And Hezekiah answered, All that *is* in my house have they seen: there is nothing among my treasures that I have not showed them.

5 Then said Isaiah to Hezekiah, Hear *the* word of the LORD of the hosts:

6 Behold, the days come, that all that *is* in thine house, and *that* which thy fathers have laid up in store until this day, shall be carried to Babylon: nothing shall be left, saith the LORD.

7 And of thy sons that shall issue from thee, which thou shalt beget, shall they take away; and they shall be eunuchs in the palace of the king of Babylon.

8 Then said Hezekiah to Isaiah, Good *is* the word of the LORD which thou hast spoken. He said moreover, At least there shall be peace and truth in my days.

Chapter 40

1 Comfort ye, comfort ye my people, saith your God.

2 Speak ye according to the heart of Jerusalem, and cry unto her, that her time is now fulfilled, that her iniquity is pardoned: for she hath received of the LORD'S hand double for all her sins.

3 The voice *of him* that crieth in the wilderness, Prepare ye the way of the LORD, make straight in the desert a highway for our God.

4 Every valley shall be exalted, and every mountain and hill shall be made low: and the crooked shall be made straight, and the rough places made plain:

5 And the glory of the LORD shall be manifested, and all flesh shall see *it* together: for the mouth of the LORD hath spoken *it*.

6 *The* voice that said, Cry. And *I* said, What shall I cry? All flesh *is* grass, and all the goodliness thereof *is* as the flower of the field:

7 The grass withereth, the flower fadeth: because the spirit of the LORD bloweth upon it: surely the people *is* grass.

8 The grass withereth, the flower fadeth: but the word of our God shall stand for ever.

9 O Zion, that bringest good tidings, get thee up into the high mountain; lift up thy voice with strength O bearer of good tidings of Jerusalem; lift *it* up, be not afraid; say unto the cities of Judah, Behold your God!

10 Behold, the Lord GOD will come with strong *hand*, and his arm shall rule for him: behold, his reward *is* with him, and his work before him.

11 He shall feed his flock like a shepherd: he shall gather the lambs with his arm, and carry *them* in his bosom, *and* shall gently lead those that are with young.

12 Who hath measured the waters in the hollow of his hand, and prepared the heavens with his palm, and with three fingers measured the dust of the earth; and weighed the mountains in a balance, and the hills with weights?

13 Who hath directed the Spirit of the LORD, or *being* his counsellor hath taught him?

14 With whom took he counsel, and *who* instructed him? who taught him in the path of judgment, and taught him knowledge, and showed to him the way of understanding?

15 Behold, the nations *are* as a drop of a bucket, and are counted as the small dust of the balance: behold, he causeth the isles to disappear as dust.

16 And all Lebanon *is* not sufficient for the fire, nor all the beasts thereof sufficient for the sacrifice.

17 All the Gentiles *are* as nothing before him; and they are counted to him as vanity and *as* less than nothing.

18 To whom then will ye liken God? or what likeness will ye compare unto him?

19 The workman prepareth the graven image, and the goldsmith spreadeth it over with gold, and *casteth* silver chains.

20 He that *is* so impoverished that he hath no oblation chooseth a tree *that* will not rot; he seeketh unto him a cunning workman to prepare a graven image, *that* shall not be moved.

21 Have ye not known? have ye not heard? hath it not been told you from the beginning? have ye not been taught since the land was founded?

22 He is seated upon the circle of the earth, and the inhabitants thereof *are* as grasshoppers; he stretcheth out the heavens as *a* curtain, and spreadeth them out as *a* tent to dwell in:

23 He bringeth the powerful to nothing; he maketh the judges of the earth as if they had never been.

24 As if they had never been planted; as if they had never been sown: as if their stock had never taken root in the earth; even blowing upon them, and they wither, and the whirlwind taketh them away as stubble.

25 To whom then will ye liken me, or what shall ye compare me to? saith the Holy One.

26 Lift up your eyes on high, and behold who hath created these *things*, he bringeth out his host by number: he calleth them all by their names; none shall be lacking by the greatness of his might, and by the strength of *his* power.

27 Why sayest thou, *O* Jacob, and speakest *thou*, O Israel, My way is hid from the LORD, and my judgment is passed over from my God?

28 Hast thou not known? hast thou not heard, *that* the God of the age is the LORD, the Creator of the ends of the earth? He fainteth not, neither is weary; and there is no one that can attain to his understanding.

29 He giveth power to the faint; and to *them that have* no might he increaseth strength.

30 The young men faint and are weary, the children stumble and fall;

31 but they that wait for the LORD shall have new strength; they shall mount up with wings as eagles; they shall run, and not be weary; *and* they shall walk, and not faint.

Chapter 41

1 Listen unto me, O islands; and let the peoples strengthen themselves: let them come near; then let them speak: let us come near together to judgment.

2 Who raised up righteousness from the east, called him that he might follow him, gave the Gentiles before him, and made *him* rule over kings? he gave *them* as the dust to his sword, *and* as driven stubble to his bow.

3 He pursued them, *and* passed in peace by the way *that* his feet had never entered.

4 Who hath wrought and done *it*? Who calleth the generations from the beginning? I the LORD, the first, and I, myself am with those who are last.

5 The isles saw *it*, and feared; the ends of the earth were afraid; they congregated, and came.

6 They helped every one his neighbour; and *every one* said to his brother, Be of good courage.

7 So the carpenter encouraged the goldsmith, *and* he that smootheth *with* the hammer him that smote the anvil, saying, It *is* well joined: and he strengthened it with nails, *that* it should not be moved.

8 But thou, Israel, my servant, Jacob whom I have chosen, *art* the seed of Abraham my friend.

9 For I have taken thee from the ends of the earth, and called thee from the boundaries thereof, and said unto thee, Thou *shalt be* my servant; I have chosen thee, and not cast thee away.

10 Fear thou not; for I *am* with thee: be not dismayed; for I *am* thy God, who strengtheneth thee; I will help thee always; I will always uphold thee with the right hand of my righteousness.

11 Behold, all they that were incensed against thee shall be ashamed and confounded: they shall be as nothing; and they that strive with thee shall perish.

12 Thou shalt seek them, and shalt not find them, *even* them that contended with thee: they that war against thee shall be as nothing, and as a thing of nought.

13 For I *am* the LORD thy God that holdeth thy right hand, and sayeth unto thee, Fear not; I will help thee.

14 Fear not, thou worm Jacob, ye dead of Israel; I will help thee, saith the LORD, and thy Redeemer, the Holy One of Israel.

15 Behold, I have placed thee as a threshing instrument, as a new *sharp* threshing instrument having teeth: thou shalt thresh the mountains, and beat *them* small, and shalt make the hills as chaff.

16 Thou shalt fan them, and the wind shall carry them away, and the whirlwind shall scatter them: but thou shalt rejoice in the LORD, thou shalt glory in the Holy One of Israel.

17 The poor and needy seek the waters that are not; their tongue faileth for thirst; I the LORD will hear them, *I* the God of Israel will not forsake them.

18 I will open rivers in high places, and fountains in the midst of the plains: I will turn the wilderness into pools of water, and the dry land into springs of water.

19 I will bring forth in the wilderness cedars, thorns, myrtles, and olive trees; I will set in the desert the fir tree, *and* the pine, and the box tree together:

20 That they may see, and know, and take warning, and understand together, that the hand of the LORD doeth this, and the Holy One of Israel hath created it.

21 Explain your cause, saith the LORD; bring forth your foundations, saith the King of Jacob.

22 Let them bring forth, and declare unto us what shall happen: tell us what hath happened from the beginning, and we shall consider it in our hearts; and we shall know what his end shall be, and cause us to understand that which is to come.

23 Give us news of that which is to come hereafter, that we may know that ye *are* gods: or at least do good, or do evil, that we may have something to tell, and together we shall marvel.

24 Behold, ye *are* of nothing, and your works of vanity: an abomination *is he that* chooseth you.

25 I have raised up *one* from the north, and he came: from the rising of the sun he called in my name: and came unto princes as clay, and as the potter treadeth clay.

26 Who hath declared from the beginning, that we shall know? and beforetime, that we shall say, *He is* righteous? yea, *there is* none that declareth this, yea, *there is* none that teacheth, yea, *there is* none that heareth your words.

27 I *am* the first that hath taught these things unto Zion, and unto Jerusalem I brought the news.

28 For I beheld, and *there was* no one; and *I asked* regarding these things, and *there was* no counsellor; I asked them, and they answered not a word.

29 Behold, they *are* all vanity; their works *are* nothing: their molten images *are* wind and confusion.

Chapter 42

1 Behold my servant, whom I uphold; my elect, *in whom* my soul delighteth; I have put my Spirit upon him: he shall give judgment unto the Gentiles.

2 He shall not cry, nor lift up, nor cause his voice to be heard in the streets.

3 A bruised reed shall he not break, and the smoking flax shall he not quench: he shall bring forth judgment unto truth.

4 He shall not tire nor faint, until he hath set judgment in the earth: and the isles shall wait for his law.

5 Thus saith God the LORD, the Creator of the heavens, and he that stretcheth them out; he that spreadeth forth the earth, and that which cometh out of it; he that giveth breath unto the people upon it, and spirit to them that walk therein:

6 I the LORD have called thee in righteousness, and will hold thee by thine hand; I will keep thee, and place thee as *my* covenant unto the people, as light unto *the* Gentiles;

7 that thou might open *the* eyes of *the* blind, that thou might bring out the prisoners from the prison, *and* them that sit in darkness out of the prison house.

8 I *am* the LORD. This *is* my name: and my glory will I not give to another, neither my praise to graven images.

9 Behold, the former things are come to pass, and new things do I declare: before they spring forth I tell you of them.

10 Sing unto the LORD a new song, *and* his praise from the end of the earth, ye that go down to the sea, and all that is therein; the isles, and the inhabitants thereof.

11 Let the wilderness and the cities thereof lift up *their* voice*, the villages *that* Kedar doth inhabit: let the inhabitants of the rock sing, let them *shout with* jubilee from the top of the mountains.

12 Let them give glory unto the LORD, and declare his praise in the islands.

13 The LORD shall go forth as a giant, he shall stir up jealousy like a man of war: he shall cry, yea, roar; he shall prevail against his enemies.

14 I have long time held my peace; I have been still, *and* refrained myself: *now* will I cry like a travailing woman; I will destroy and devour at once.

15 I will make waste mountains and hills, and dry up all their herbs; and I will make the rivers islands, and I will dry up the pools.

16 And I will bring the blind by a way *that* they knew not; I will cause them to walk in paths *that* they have not known: I will make darkness light before them, and crooked things straight. These things will I do unto them, and not forsake them.

17 They shall be turned back, they shall be greatly ashamed, that trust in graven images, that say to the molten images, Ye *are* our gods.

18 Hear, ye deaf; and look, ye blind, that ye may see.

19 Who *is* blind, but my servant? or deaf, as my messenger *that* I sent? Who *is* blind as *he that is* perfect, and blind as the servant of the LORD,

20 who seeth many things and warneth not; who openeth his ears and heareth not.

21 The LORD, jealous for his righteousness, will magnify the law, and enlarge *it*.

22 Therefore this people *is* robbed and spoiled; all of them shall be snared in holes, and hid in prison houses: they shall be for a prey, and none delivereth; for a spoil, and none saith, Restore.

23 Who among you will give ear to this? *who* will warn and consider regarding the time to come?

24 Who gave Jacob for a spoil, and Israel to the robbers? did not the LORD? Because we sinned against him and they did not desire to walk in his ways, neither did they hearken unto his law.

25 Therefore he hath poured upon him the fury of his anger, and the strength of battle: he put fire round about him, yet he was careless; and it set him on fire, yet he laid *it* not to heart.

Chapter 43

1 But now thus saith the LORD that created thee, O Jacob, and he that formed thee, O Israel, Fear not: for I have redeemed thee, I have named thee; Thou *art* mine.

2 When thou passest through the waters, I *will be* with thee; and through the rivers, they shall not overflow thee: when thou walkest through the same fire, thou shalt not be burned; neither shall the flame kindle upon thee.

3 For I *am* the LORD thy God, the Holy One of Israel, thy Keeper: I gave Egypt *for* thy ransom, Ethiopia and Seba for thee.

4 Because thou wast precious in my sight, thou wast worthy of honour, and I have loved thee.

5 Fear not: for I *am* with thee: I will bring thy generation from the east, and gather thee from the west;

6 I will say to the north *wind*, Give up; and to the south, Keep not back: bring my sons from far, and my daughters from the ends of the earth;

7 *Even* every one that is called by my name: for I have created them for my glory, I have formed them; yea, I have made them.

8 Bring forth the people that is blind that have eyes, and the deaf that have ears.

9 Let all the Gentiles be gathered together as one, and let the peoples be joined: who among them can declare this, and show us former things? let them bring forth their witnesses, that they may be justified: or let them hear, and say, *It is* truth.

10 Ye *are* my witnesses, saith the LORD, and my servant whom I have chosen: that ye may know and believe me, and understand that I *am* he: before me there was no God formed, neither shall there be after me.

11 I, *even* I, *am* the LORD; and beside me *there is* no saviour.

12 I have declared, and have saved, and I have showed, when *there was* no strange *god* among you: therefore ye *are* my witnesses, saith the LORD, that I *am* God.

13 Yea, before the day *was* I existed; and *there is* none that can deliver out of my hand: *if* I work, who shall hinder it?

14 Thus saith the LORD, your redeemer, the Holy One of Israel; For your sake I have sent to Babylon, and caused fugitives to descend unto all of them, and clamour of Chaldeans in the ships.

15 I *am* the LORD, your Holy One, the creator of Israel, your King.

16 Thus saith the LORD, which maketh a way in the sea, and a path in the mighty waters;

17 *when* he bringeth forth the chariot and horse, the army and the power; they shall fall together, and never rise: they are extinct, they are quenched as wick.

18 Remember ye not the former things, neither consider the things of old.

19 Behold, I will do a new thing; it shall come to light quickly; shall ye not know it? I will again make a way in the wilderness, *and* rivers in the desert.

20 The beast of the field shall honour me, the dragons and the owls: because I give waters in the wilderness, *and* rivers in the desert, to give drink to my people, my chosen.

21 This people have I formed for myself; they shall show forth my praise.

22 But thou hast not called upon me, O Jacob; but thou hast been weary of me, O Israel.

23 Thou hast not brought me the animals of thy burnt offerings; neither hast thou honoured me with thy sacrifices. I have not caused thee to serve with an offering, nor wearied thee with incense.

24 Thou hast bought me no sweet cane with money, neither hast thou filled me with the fat of thy sacrifices: but thou hast made me to serve with thy sins, thou hast wearied me with thine iniquities.

25 I, *even* I, *am* he that uprooteth thy rebellions for mine own sake, and will not remember thy sins.

26 Cause me to remember: let us enter into judgment together: declare thou, that it may be put to thy account.

27 Thy first father hath sinned, and thy teachers have transgressed against me.

28 Therefore I have profaned the princes of the sanctuary, and have set up Jacob as anathema, and Israel as a reproach.

Chapter 44

1 Yet now hear, O Jacob my servant; and Israel, whom I have chosen:

2 Thus saith the LORD that made thee, and formed thee from the womb, *which* will help thee; Fear not, O Jacob, my servant; and thou, Jesurun, *the upright one* whom I have chosen.

3 For I will pour water upon him that is thirsty, and floods upon the dry ground: I will pour my spirit upon thy seed, and my blessing upon thine offspring:

4 And they shall spring up *as* among the grass, as willows by the water courses.

5 One shall say, I *am* the LORD'S; and another shall call *himself* by the name of Jacob; and another shall subscribe *with* his hand unto the LORD, and surname *himself* by the name of Israel.

6 Thus saith the LORD the King of Israel, and his redeemer the LORD of the hosts; I *am* the first, and I *am* the last; and beside me *there is* no God.

7 And who shall call as I *do*, and declare this *in advance*, and set it in order for me, since I made the people of the world? Let them declare unto them the things that are nigh and the things that shall come.

8 Fear ye not, neither be afraid: have not I caused thee to hear from of old, and declared unto thee beforehand *that which was to come*? Then ye *are* my witnesses that there is no God but me, yea, *there is* no Strong One that I do not know.

9 They that make a graven image *are* all of them vanity; and that which is most precious to them is useful for nothing; and they *are* their own witnesses, that they see not, nor understand; therefore they shall be ashamed.

10 Who hath formed God? And who cast a graven image *that* is profitable for nothing?

11 Behold, all his fellows shall be ashamed: for the workmen, they *are* of men: Even if all of them be gathered together and stand, they shall fear, and shall be ashamed together.

12 The smith *shall take* the tongs, he shall work among the coals; he shall give it form with the hammers, and bring forth in it the arm of his strength: though *he be* hungry, and his strength faileth: he shall not drink water, even if he faint.

13 The carpenter stretcheth out *his* rule; he measureth it with a line; he fitteth it with planes, he marketh it out with the compass; he maketh it after the form of a *noble* man, in the likeness of *the* beauty *of a* man; that it may remain in the house.

14 He shall hew down cedars, and take the cypress and the oak, and he shall strengthen himself with the trees of the forest: he shall plant a fir tree, which shall be nourished with the rain.

15 The man shall then use of it for firewood: for he will take thereof, and warm himself; he will kindle *it*, and bake bread; he will also make a god, and worship *it*; he will fabricate an idol, and shall kneel down before it.

16 He shall burn part thereof in the fire; with *another* part thereof he shall eat flesh; he shall roast meat, and shall satisfy himself. Afterwards he shall warm *himself*, and say, Aha, I have warmed myself, I have seen fire:

17 The residue thereof he turneth into god, into his graven image: he humbleth himself before it, and worshippeth *it*, and prayeth unto it, and saith, Deliver me; for thou *art* my god.

18 They did not know nor understand: for *he* hath anointed their eyes, that they see not; *and* their hearts, that they understand not.

19 He doth not return to his right mind, he doth not have knowledge nor understanding to say, I have burned part of it in the fire; yea, also I have baked bread upon the coals thereof; I have roasted flesh, and eaten *it*: and shall I make the residue thereof an abomination? do I have to humble myself before the trunk of a tree?

20 The ashes feedeth *him*: his deceived heart inclineth him, that he not deliver his soul, and say, *Is* not the lie at my right hand?

21 Remember these things, O Jacob and Israel; that thou *art* my servant: I have formed thee; thou *art* my servant: O Israel, do not forget me.

22 I have undone, as a cloud, thy rebellions, and thy sins, as a mist: return unto me; for I have redeemed thee.

23 Sing praises, O *ye* heavens; for the LORD hath done *it*: shout with jubilee, *ye* lower parts of the earth: break forth into praise, *ye* mountains, O forest, and every tree therein: for the LORD hath redeemed Jacob, and in Israel he shall be glorified.

24 Thus saith the LORD, thy redeemer, and he that formed thee from the womb, I *am* the LORD that maketh all *things*; that stretcheth forth the heavens alone; that spreadeth abroad the earth by myself;

25 that undoeth the signs of the fortune tellers, and maketh the diviners mad; that turneth the wise *men* backward, and maketh their wisdom fade away;

26 that awaketh the word of his servant, and fulfilleth the counsel of his messengers; that saith to Jerusalem, Thou shalt be inhabited; and to the cities of Judah, Ye shall be rebuilt, and I will raise up thy ruins;

27 that saith to the deep, Be dry, and I will dry up thy rivers;

28 that calleth Cyrus, my shepherd, and all that I desire, he shall fulfil, by saying to Jerusalem, Thou shalt be built; and to the temple, Thy foundation shall be laid.

Chapter 45

1 Thus saith the LORD to his Messiah, to Cyrus, who I have taken by his right hand, to subdue Gentiles before him, and to loose the loins of kings. To open before him the *two-leaved* gates; and the gates shall not be shut:

2 I will go before thee, and make the crooked places straight: I will break in pieces the gates of brass, and cut in sunder the bars of iron:

3 And I will give thee the hidden treasures, and the well guarded secrets, that thou mayest know that I *am* the LORD, the God of Israel, which give *thee* thy name.

4 For Jacob my servant's sake, and Israel my elect, I have even called thee by thy name: I have surnamed thee, though thou hast not known me.

5 I *am* the LORD, and *there is* none else, *there is* no God beside me: I shall gird thee, though thou hast not known me:

6 That it may be know from the rising of the sun, and from whence it goeth down, that *there is* none beside me. I *am* the LORD, and *there is* none else.

7 I form the light, and create darkness: I make peace, and create evil: I *am* the LORD that doeth all this.

8 Release, ye heavens, from above, and the clouds shall pour down righteousness: let the earth open *up*, and let salvation and righteousness bear their fruit; let them produce *fruit* together; I the LORD have created it.

9 Woe unto him that striveth with his Maker! *Let* the potsherd *strive* with the potsherds of the earth. Shall the clay say to him that fashioneth it, What makest thou; thy work *hath* no form?

10 Woe unto him that saith unto *his* father, Why begettest thou? or to the woman, Why hast thou brought forth?

11 Thus saith the LORD, the Holy One of Israel, and his Maker, Ask me of things to come; inquire of me concerning my sons, and concerning the work of my hands.

12 I have made the earth, and created man upon it: I, *even* my hands, have stretched out the heavens, and all their host have I commanded.

13 I have awakened him in righteousness, and I will make straight all his ways: he shall build my city, and he shall loose my captives, not for price nor for gifts, saith the LORD of the hosts.

14 Thus saith the LORD, The labour of Egypt, and merchandise of Ethiopia and of the Sabeans, men of stature, shall come over unto thee, and they shall be thine: they shall come after thee; in chains they shall come over, and they shall fall down unto thee, they shall make supplication unto thee, *saying*, Surely God *is* in thee; and *there is* none else, *there is* none *other* beside God.

15 Verily thou *art* God, that thou *might* hide thyself; God of Israel, who saves.

16 They shall be ashamed, and also confounded, all of them: all the makers of idols shall go forth ashamed.

17 Israel is saved in the LORD, eternal saving health: ye shall never be ashamed nor confounded through all ages.

18 For thus hath the LORD said that createth the heavens; God himself that formeth the earth, he who made it, and established it. He created it not in vain; he created it to be inhabited: I *am* the LORD; and *there is* none else.

19 I have not spoken in secret, in *a* place of land of darkness. Not without substance did I say unto the seed of Jacob, Seek ye me; I *am* the LORD who speaketh righteousness, who declareth things that are right.

20 Assemble yourselves and come; draw near together, all ye *that are* escaped of the Gentiles. They have no knowledge that set up the wood of their graven image, and pray unto the god *that* does not save.

21 Tell ye, and bring *them* near; yea, let them take counsel together: who caused this to be heard from the beginning, and hath declared it from that time, except I, the LORD? and *there is* no God beside me; a just God and a Saviour; *there is* none beside me.

22 Look unto me, and be ye saved, all the ends of the earth: for I *am* God, and *there is* none else.

23 I have sworn by myself, the word is gone out of my mouth *in* righteousness, and shall not return, That unto me every knee shall bow, every tongue shall swear.

24 And unto me he shall say, Surely in the LORD *is* the righteousness and the strength; until he shall come; and all that are incensed against him shall be ashamed.

25 In the LORD shall all the generation of Israel be justified, and shall glory.

Chapter 46

1 Bel bowed down, Nebo is fallen, their images were placed *upon* animals, and upon beasts *of burden*: that will carry you laden with yourselves, burden of weariness.

2 They stoop, they are fallen together; they could not escape from the burden, and their soul had to go into captivity.

3 Hearken unto me, O house of Jacob, and all the remnant of the house of Israel, which are borne *by me* from the belly, which are carried from the womb:

4 And *even* to *your* old age I *am* he; and *even* to grey hairs will I carry *you*: I have made, and I will bear; even I will carry, and will deliver *you*.

5 To whom will ye liken me, and make *me* equal, and compare me, that we may be like?

6 They lavish gold out of the bag, and weigh silver in the balance, *and* hire a goldsmith; and he maketh it a god: they fall down, yea, they worship.

7 They bear him upon the shoulder, they carry him, and set him in his place. There he is; he doth not move from his place; they cry unto him, and neither doth he answer, nor save from the tribulation.

8 Remember this, and be ashamed: bring *it* again to mind, O ye transgressors.

9 Remember the former things of old: for I *am* God, and *there is* none else; I *am* God, and *there is* none like me,

10 declaring the end from the beginning, and from ancient times *the things* that are not *yet* done, saying, My counsel shall stand, and I will do all my pleasure:

11 Calling a ravenous bird from the east, the man that executeth my counsel from a far country: yea, I have spoken *it*, I will also bring it to pass; I have purposed *it*, I will also do it.

12 Hearken unto me, ye hard of heart, that *are* far from righteousness:

13 I cause my righteousness to come nigh; it shall not go away, and my saving health shall not be stayed: and I will place saving health in Zion; and my glory in Israel.

Chapter 47

1 Come down, and sit in the dust, O virgin daughter of Babylon, sit on the ground: without a throne, O daughter of the Chaldeans: for thou shalt no more be called tender and delicate.

2 Take the millstones, and grind meal: uncover thy locks, remove the shoes from thy feet, uncover the thigh, pass over the rivers.

3 Thy nakedness shall be uncovered, yea, thy shame shall be seen: I will take vengeance, and I will not help *any* man.

4 *As for* our redeemer, the LORD of the hosts *is* his name, the Holy One of Israel.

5 Sit, be silent, and get thee into darkness, O daughter of the Chaldeans: for thou shalt no more be called, The lady of kingdoms.

6 I was wroth with my people, I have profaned my inheritance, and given them into thine hand: thou didst show them no mercy; upon the ancient hast thou very heavily laid thy yoke.

7 And thou saidst, I shall be a lady for ever. Until now thou hast not layed these *things* to heart, neither didst thou remember thy latter end.

8 Therefore hear now this, *thou* delicate one, that sittest in confidence, that sayest in thine heart, I *am*, and none else beside me; I shall not sit *as* a widow, neither shall I be fatherless.

9 But these two *things* shall come to thee in a moment in one day, the loss of thy fathers, and widowhood: they shall come upon thee in their perfection for the multitude of thy sorceries, *and* for the great abundance of thine enchantments.

10 For thou hast trusted in thy wickedness: thou hast said, None seeth me. Thy wisdom and thine *own* knowledge, it hath deceived thee; for thou hast said in thine heart, I *am*, and none else beside me.

11 Therefore shall evil come upon thee; thou shalt not know from whence it riseth: and mischief shall fall upon thee; thou shalt not be able to put it off: and destruction shall come upon thee suddenly, *which* thou shalt not know.

12 Stand now with thine enchantments, and with the multitude of thy sorceries, wherein thou hast laboured from thy youth; if so be thou shalt be able to better thyself, if so be thou mayest prevail.

13 Thou art wearied in the multitude of thy counsels. Let now those that contemplate the heavens, those that speculate regarding the stars, those that teach the courses of the moon, stand up, and defend thee from *these things* that shall come upon thee.

14 Behold, they shall be as stubble; the fire shall burn them; they shall not deliver their lives from the hand of the flame: *there shall* not *be* a coal left to warm at, *nor* light to sit before it.

15 Thus shall they be unto thee with whom thou hast laboured, *even* thy merchants, from thy youth: they shall wander every one to his own way; there *shall be* none to save thee.

Chapter 48

1 Hear ye this, O house of Jacob, which call yourselves by the name of Israel, those that are come forth out of the waters of Judah, those which swear by the name of the LORD, and make mention of the God of Israel, *but* not in truth, nor in righteousness.

2 For they call themselves of the holy city, and stay themselves upon the God of Israel; The LORD of the hosts *is* his name.

3 That which happened, I have already declared many days ago; and it went forth out of my mouth, and I published it; I did *it* suddenly, and it came to pass.

4 Because I know that thou *art* obstinate, and thy neck *is* an iron sinew, and thy brow brass;

5 I have already declared it many days ago; before it came to pass I showed *it* thee: lest thou shouldest say, My idol hath done it, my graven image, and my molten image, hath commanded these things.

6 Thou hast heard it, thou hast seen it all; and will not ye declare *it*? I have showed thee new things from this time, even hidden things, and thou didst not know them.

7 They are created now, and not in days past; nor before this day hast thou heardest them; lest thou shouldest say, Behold, I knew them.

8 Certainly thou hast never heard this; certainly thou hast never known this; certainly thine ear was never before opened: for I knew that being unfaithful thou wouldest disobey, therefore

I called thee a rebel from the womb.

9 For my name's sake will I defer my anger, and for my praise will I wait patiently for thee, that I cut thee not off.

10 Behold, I have refined thee, and not as silver; I have chosen thee in the furnace of affliction.

11 For mine own sake, *even* for mine own sake, will I do *it*: for how should *my name* be profaned? and I will not give my glory unto another.

12 Hearken unto me, O Jacob and Israel, my called; I *am* he; I *am* the first, I also *am* the last.

13 Certainly my hand founded the earth, and my right hand measured the heavens with the palm: as I named them, they appeared together.

14 All ye, assemble yourselves, and hear; who is there among them that declareth these *things*? The LORD hath loved him: the one who will execute his will on Babylon, and his arm *upon* the Chaldeans.

15 I, *even* I, have spoken; yea, I have called him: I have brought him, and his way shall be prospered.

16 Come ye near unto me, hear ye this; I have not spoken in secret from the beginning; from the time that it was done, I was there: and now the LORD God hath sent me, and his Spirit.

17 Thus hath the LORD, thy Redeemer, the Holy One of Israel said; I *am* the LORD thy God which teacheth thee to profit, which causeth thee to walk by the way *in which* thou walkest.

18 O that thou wouldest look unto my commandments! then would thy peace be as a river, and thy righteousness as the waves of the sea:

19 Thy seed would be as the sand, and the offspring of thy bowels like the gravel thereof; his name would never be cut off nor destroyed from before me.

20 Come out of Babylon, flee ye from among the Chaldeans. Give news of this with a voice of joy; publish this, take this *news* to the end of the earth; say ye, The LORD hath redeemed his servant Jacob.

21 And they thirsted not *when* he led them through the deserts: he caused water to flow out of the rock for them: he clave the rock, and the waters gushed out.

22 *There is* no peace for the wicked, said the LORD.

Chapter 49

1 Listen, O isles, unto me; and hearken, ye peoples, from far; The LORD hath called me from the womb; from the bowels of my mother hath he remembered my name.

2 And he hath made my mouth like a sharp sword; with the shadow of his hand hath he covered me, and made me a clean arrow; in his quiver hath he kept me.

3 And he said unto me, Thou *art* my servant, O Israel, in thee I will glory.

4 But I said, I have laboured in vain, I have spent my strength for nought, and in vain: *yet* surely my judgment *is* before the LORD, and my recompense with my God.

5 And now, saith the LORD, he that formed me from the womb *to be* his servant, so that Jacob might be converted unto him. But *if* Israel will not be gathered, even so, yet shall I be esteemed in the eyes of the LORD, and my God shall be my strength.

6 And he said, It is a light thing that thou shouldest be my servant to wake up the tribes of Jacob, and to restore the desolations of Israel: I have also given thee for a light to the Gentiles, that thou mayest be my saving health unto the end of the earth.

7 Thus hath the LORD said, the Redeemer of Israel, his Holy One, to him whom man despiseth, to him whom the Gentiles abhorreth, to the servant of the tyrants, Kings shall see and be raised up *as* princes, and shall worship because of the LORD, for faithful *is* the Holy One of Israel, who hath chosen thee.

8 Thus hath the LORD said, In an acceptable time have I heard thee, and in the day of saving health have I helped thee: and I will preserve thee, and give thee for a covenant of people, that thou might awaken the earth, that thou might inherit *the* desolate heritages;

9 That thou mayest say to the prisoners, Go forth; and unto them that *are* in darkness, Show yourselves. Upon the ways shall they be fed, and upon all the high places *shall be* their pastures.

10 They shall never hunger nor thirst; neither shall the heat nor sun smite them: for he that hath mercy on them shall lead them, even by the springs of water shall he feed them.

11 And I will turn all my mountains *into* a way, and my highways shall be exalted.

12 Behold, these shall come from far: and, behold, these from the north and from the west; and these from the land of Sinim.

13 Sing, O heavens; and be joyful, O earth; and break forth into singing, O mountains: for the LORD hath comforted his people, and will have mercy upon his afflicted.

14 But Zion said, The LORD hath forsaken me, and my Lord hath forgotten me.

15 Can a woman forget her sucking child, that she should not have compassion on the son of her womb? yea, they may forget, yet will I not forget thee.

16 Behold, I have graven thee upon the palms of *my* hands; thy walls *are* continually before me.

17 Thy builders shall come in haste; thy destroyers and they that made thee waste shall go forth of thee.

18 Lift up thine eyes round about, and behold: all these gather themselves together, *and* come to thee. *As* I live, saith the LORD, thou shalt surely clothe thee with them all, as with a garment of honour, and shalt be girded by them as a bride.

19 For thy waste and thy desolate places, and the land of thy destruction, shall even now be too narrow by reason of the inhabitants, and they that swallowed thee up shall be separated far away.

20 Even thy children which were fatherless, shall say in thine ears, The place *is* too strait for me: give place to me that I may dwell.

21 Then shalt thou say in thine heart, Who hath begotten me these, seeing I had lost my children, and *was* desolate, a stranger, removed from my land? and who hath brought up these? Behold, I was left alone; these, where *had* they *been*?

22 Thus hath the Lord GOD said, Behold, I will lift up my hand to the Gentiles, and raise up my standard to the peoples: and they shall bring thy sons in *their* arms, and thy daughters shall be carried upon *their* shoulders.

23 And kings shall be thy nursing fathers, and their queens thy nursing mothers: they shall bow down to thee with *their* face toward the earth, and lick up the dust of thy feet; and thou shalt know that I *am* the LORD: for they that wait for me shall not be ashamed.

24 Shall the prey be taken from the mighty, or the lawful captive delivered?

25 But thus saith the LORD, Even the captives of the mighty shall be taken away, and the prey of the terrible shall be delivered: for I will contend with him that contendeth with thee, and I will save thy children.

26 And I will feed them that oppress thee with their own flesh; and they shall be drunken with their own blood, as with sweet wine: and all flesh shall know that I the LORD *am* thy Saviour and thy Redeemer, the mighty One of Jacob.

Chapter 50

1 Thus saith the LORD, Where *is* the bill of your mother's divorcement, whom I have put away? or which of my creditors *is it* to whom I have sold you? Behold, for your iniquities are ye sold, and for your rebellions was your mother put away,

2 for I came, and no one showed himself; I called, and no one answered. Is my hand shortened at all, that it cannot redeem? or have I no power to deliver? behold, at my rebuke I dry up the sea, I make the rivers a wilderness: their fish stinketh, because *there is* no water, and dieth for thirst.

3 I clothe the heavens with blackness, and I make sackcloth their covering.

4 The Lord GOD hath given me the tongue of the wise, that I should know how to speak a word in season to *him that is* weary: he wakeneth up early, early shall he awaken *my* ear, that I might hear, as the wise.

5 The Lord GOD hath opened my ear, and I was not rebellious, neither turned away back.

6 I gave my back to the smiters, and my cheeks to them that plucked off the hair: I hid not my face from shame and spitting.

7 For the Lord GOD will help me; therefore I was not ashamed: therefore have I set my face like a flint, and I know that I shall not be ashamed.

8 *He is* near that justifieth me; who will contend with me? let us stand together: who *is* my adversary? let him come near to me.

9 Behold, the Lord GOD will help me; who *is* he *that* shall condemn me? behold, they all shall wax old as a garment; the moth shall eat them up.

10 Who *is* among you that feareth the LORD? Hearken unto the voice of his servant. He who walked *in* darkness, and had no light; let him trust in the name of the LORD, and stay upon his God.

11 Behold, that all of you kindle fire, and are compassed about with sparks; walk in the light of your fire, and of the sparks *that* ye have kindled. From my hand hath come this; ye shall be buried in sorrow.

Chapter 51

1 Hearken to me, ye that follow after righteousness, ye that seek the LORD: look unto the rock *whence* ye are hewn, and to the hole of the pit *whence* ye are digged.

2 Look unto Abraham your father, and unto Sarah *that* bare you: for I called him alone, and blessed him, and multiplied him.

3 For the LORD shall surely comfort Zion: he will comfort all her waste places; and he will make her wilderness like Eden, and her desert like the garden of the LORD; joy and gladness shall be found therein, thanksgiving, and the voice of singing.

4 Hearken unto me, my people; and give ear unto me, O my nation: for the law shall proceed from me, and I will uncover my judgment for a light of the peoples.

5 My righteousness *is* near; my saving health is gone forth, and my arms shall judge the people; the isles shall wait upon me, and on my arm shall they place their hope.

6 Lift up your eyes to the heavens, and look upon the earth beneath: for the heavens shall vanish away like smoke, and the earth shall wax old like a garment, and they that dwell therein shall perish in like manner: but my saving health shall be for ever, and my righteousness shall never perish.

7 Hearken unto me, ye that know righteousness, the people in whose heart *is* my law; fear ye not the reproach of men, neither be ye afraid of their revilings.

8 For the moth shall eat them up like a garment, and the worm shall eat them like wool: but my righteousness shall be for ever, and my saving health from age to age.

9 Awake, awake, put on strength, O arm of the LORD; awake, as in the ancient days, in ages past. *Art thou not he who cut off the proud *one*, and he who smote the dragon?

10 Art thou not he who dried up the sea, the waters of the great deep; he who turned the depths of the sea into a way, that the redeemed might pass over?

11 Therefore the redeemed of the LORD shall return, and come with singing unto Zion; and everlasting joy *shall be* upon their head: they shall obtain gladness and joy; *and* sorrow and mourning shall flee away.

12 I, *even* I, *am* he that comforteth you. Who *art* thou, that thou shouldest be afraid of man, that is mortal, and of the son of man *which* shall be counted as stubble?

13 And thou hast already forgotten the LORD thy maker, that hath stretched forth the heavens, and laid the foundations of the earth; and hast feared continually every day the fury of the oppressor, when he was ready to destroy. But, where *is* the fury of the oppressor?

14 The prisoner is anxious that he may be loosed, and that he should not die in the pit, nor that his bread should fail.

15 And I *am* the LORD thy God, that divideth the sea, and the waves roar: I am thy God; the LORD of the hosts *is* his name.

16 That hath placed my words in thy mouth, and I have covered thee with the shadow of my hand, that thou mayest plant the heavens, and lay the foundations of the earth, and say unto Zion, Thou *art* my people.

17 Awake, awake, stand up, O Jerusalem, which hast drunk at the hand of the LORD the cup of his fury; thou hast drunken of the dregs of the cup of trembling, *and* wrung *them* out.

18 There is none to guide her among all the sons *whom* she hath brought forth; neither *is there any* that taketh her by the hand of all the sons *that* she hath brought up.

19 These two *things* are come unto thee; who shall be sorry for thee? desolation, and destruction, and the famine, and the sword. Who shall comfort thee?

20 Thy sons have fainted, they lie at the head of all the streets, as a wild bull in a net: they are full of the fury of the LORD, the rebuke of thy God.

21 Therefore hear now this, thou afflicted, and drunken, but not with wine:

22 Thus hath thy Lord said, I AM thy God who pleadeth the cause of his people, Behold, I have taken out of thine hand the cup of trembling, *even* the dregs of the cup of my fury; thou shalt no more drink it again:

23 But I will put it into the hand of them that afflict thee; which have said to thy soul, Bow down, that we may go over: and thou hast laid thy body as the ground, and as the street, to them that went over.

Chapter 52

1 Awake, awake; put on thy strength, O Zion; put on thy beautiful garments, O Jerusalem, the holy city: for henceforth there shall no more come into thee the uncircumcised and the unclean.

2 Shake thyself from the dust; arise, *and* sit down, O Jerusalem: loose thyself from the bands of thy neck, O captive daughter of Zion.

3 For thus saith the LORD, Ye have sold yourselves for nought; and ye shall be redeemed without money.

4 For thus hath the Lord GOD said, My people went down aforetime into Egypt to sojourn there; and the Assyrian captured them without cause.

5 Now therefore, what have I here, saith the LORD, that my people is taken away for nought? And those among my people that take rule over them make them to howl, saith the LORD; and my name continually every day *is* blasphemed.

6 Therefore my people shall know my name for this reason in that day: for even I that speaketh, behold, I shall be present.

7 How beautiful are upon the mountains are the feet of him that bringeth good tidings, that publisheth peace; that bringeth good tidings of good, that publisheth saving health; that saith unto Zion, Thy God reigneth!

8 The voice of thy watchmen! They shall lift up the voice, together they shall *sound the* jubilee: for they shall see eye to eye, how the LORD shall return to bring again Zion.

9 Sing praises, rejoice together, ye waste places of Jerusalem: for the LORD hath comforted his people, he hath redeemed Jerusalem.

10 The LORD hath made bare the arm of his holiness before the eyes of all the Gentiles; and all the ends of the earth shall see the saving health of our God.

11 Depart ye, depart ye, go ye out from thence, touch no unclean *thing*; go ye out of the midst of her; be ye clean, that bear the vessels of the LORD.

12 For ye shall not go out with haste, nor go by flight: for the LORD will go before you; and the God of Israel will gather you together.

13 Behold, my servant shall be prospered, he shall be exalted and extolled, and be very high.

14 As many rejected thee, in such manner was his likeness, and his beauty, disfigured from the sons of men:

15 But he shall sprinkle many Gentiles; the kings shall shut their mouths over him: for *that* which had not been told them shall they see; and *that* which they had not heard shall they understand.

Chapter 53

1 Who shall believe our report? and upon whom shall the arm of the LORD be manifested?

2 With all this he shall grow up before him as a tender sprout, and as a root out of a dry ground. There is no outward appearance in him, nor beauty. We shall see him, yet nothing attractive about him that we should desire him.

3 He is despised and rejected among men; a man of sorrows, and acquainted with weakness: and we hid as it were *our* faces from him; he was despised, and we esteemed him not.

4 Surely he hath borne our sicknesses, and suffered our pain: and we considered him stricken, smitten of God, and cast down.

5 But he *was* wounded for our rebellions, *he was* bruised for our iniquities: the chastisement of our peace *was* upon him; and by his stripes healing was provided for us.

6 All we like sheep have become lost; we have turned every one to his own way; and the LORD transposed in him the iniquity of us all.

7 He was oppressed, and he was afflicted, yet he opened not his mouth: he was brought as a lamb to the slaughter, and as a sheep before her shearers is dumb, so he openeth not his mouth.

8 He was taken from prison and from judgment: and who shall count his generation? for he was cut off out of the land of the living: for the rebellion of my people was he smitten.

9 And he made his grave with the wicked, and his death with the rich; even though he had never done evil, neither *was any* deceit in his mouth.

10 With all this the LORD chose to bruise him; subjecting him to grief.

When he shall have offered his soul for atonement, he shall see *his* seed, he shall prolong *his* days, and the will of the LORD shall be prospered in his hand.

11 He shall see of the travail of his soul, *and* shall be satisfied.

And by his knowledge shall my righteous servant justify many; for he shall bear their iniquities.

12 Therefore will I divide him *a portion* with the great, and he shall divide the spoil unto the strong; because he hath poured out his soul unto death: and he was numbered with the rebellious, having

born the sin of many, and made intercession for the transgressors.

Chapter 54

1 Rejoice, O barren, thou *that* didst not bear; break forth into singing, and cry aloud with jubilee, thou *that* didst not travail with child: for more *shall be* the children of the desolate than the children of the married wife, said the LORD.

2 Enlarge the place of thy tent, and let them stretch forth the curtains of thine habitations: spare not, lengthen thy cords, and strengthen thy stakes;

3 For thou shalt break forth on the right hand and on the left; and thy seed shall inherit the Gentiles, and make the desolate cities to be inhabited.

4 Fear not; for thou shalt not be ashamed: neither be thou confounded; for thou shalt not be put to shame: for thou shalt forget the shame of thy youth, and shalt not remember the reproach of thy widowhood any more.

5 For thy Maker *shall be* thine husband; the LORD of the hosts *is* his name; and thy Redeemer the Holy One of Israel; The God of the whole earth shall he be called.

6 For as a woman forsaken and grieved in spirit hath the LORD called thee, and young woman who is put away, said thy God.

7 For a small moment have I forsaken thee; but with great mercies will I gather thee.

8 In a little wrath I hid my face from thee for a moment; but with eternal mercy will I have compassion on thee, said the LORD thy Redeemer.

9 For this *is as* the waters of Noah unto me: for *as* I have sworn that the waters of Noah should no more go over the earth; so have I sworn that I would not be wroth *again* with thee, nor reprehend thee.

10 For the mountains shall be removed, and the hills shall tremble; but my kindness shall not depart from thee, neither shall the covenant of my peace be changed, said the LORD that hath mercy on thee.

11 O thou afflicted, tossed with tempest, *and* not comforted, behold, I will cement thy stones upon carbuncle, and lay thy foundations upon sapphires.

12 And I will make thy windows of precious stones, and thy gates of carbuncles, and all thy borders of stones of great price.

13 And all thy children *shall be* taught of the LORD; and the peace of thy children shall be multiplied.

14 With righteousness shalt thou be adorned: thou shalt be far from oppression; for thou shalt not fear *it*: and from terror; for it shall not come near thee.

15 If anyone should conspire against thee, it *shall be* without me, *but* not by me: whosoever would conspire against thee shall fall before thee.

16 Behold, I have created the smith that bloweth the coals in the fire, and that bringeth forth the instrument for his work; and I have created the waster to destroy.

17 No weapon that is formed against thee shall prosper; and every tongue *that* shall rise against thee in judgment thou shalt condemn. This *is* the heritage of the servants of the LORD, and their justice from me, said the LORD.

Chapter 55

1 Ho, every one that thirsteth, come ye to the waters, and he that hath no money; come ye, buy, and eat; yea, come, buy wine and milk without money and without price.

2 Wherefore do ye spend money for *that which is* not bread? and your labour for *that which* satisfieth not? hearken diligently unto me, and eat ye *that which is* good, and let your soul delight itself in fatness.

3 Incline your ear, and come unto me: hear, and your soul shall live; and I will make an eternal covenant with you, *even* the sure mercies of David.

4 Behold, I have gave him *for* a witness to the peoples, a captain and teacher to the peoples.

5 Behold, thou shalt call a people *that* thou knowest not, and Gentiles *that* knew not thee shall run unto thee because of the LORD thy God, and for the Holy One of Israel; for he hath honoured thee.

6 Seek ye the LORD while he may be found, call ye upon him while he is near:

7 Let the wicked forsake his way, and the unrighteous man his thoughts: and let him return unto the LORD, and he will have mercy upon him; and to our God, for he will abundantly pardon.

8 For my thoughts *are* not *as* your thoughts, neither *are* your ways *as* my ways, saith the LORD.

9 For *as* the heavens are higher than the earth, so are my ways higher than your ways, and my thoughts more than your thoughts.

10 For as the rain cometh down, and the snow from the heavens, and returneth not thither, but watereth the earth, and maketh it bring forth and bud, that it may give seed to the sower, and bread to the eater:

11 So shall my Word be that goeth forth out of my mouth: it shall not return unto me void, but it shall accomplish that which I please, and it shall be prospered in that for which I sent it.

12 For ye shall go out with joy, and be returned with peace: the mountains and the hills shall break forth before you into singing, and all the trees of the field shall clap *their* hands.

13 Instead of the thorn shall come up the fir tree, and instead of the brier shall come up the myrtle tree: and it shall be to the LORD for a name, for an eternal sign *that* shall not be cut off.

Chapter 56

1 Thus saith the LORD, Keep ye judgment, and do justice: for my saving health *is* near to come, and my righteousness to be manifested.

2 Blessed *is* the man *that* doeth this, and the son of man *that* layeth hold on it; that keepeth the sabbath from polluting it, and keepeth his hand from doing any evil.

3 Neither let the son of the stranger, that hath joined himself to the LORD, speak, saying, The LORD shall utterly separate me from his people: neither let the eunuch say, Behold, I *am* a dry tree.

4 For thus hath the LORD said unto the eunuchs that keep my sabbaths, and choose *the things* that please me, and take hold of my covenant;

5 even unto them will I give in my house and within my walls a place and a name better than of sons and of daughters: I will give them an everlasting name, that shall never be cut off.

6 Also the sons of the stranger, that join themselves to the LORD, to serve him, and that love the name of the LORD, to be his servants, every one that keepeth the sabbath from polluting it, and taketh hold of my covenant;

7 even them will I bring to the mountain of my holiness, and refresh them in the house of my prayer: their burnt offerings and their sacrifices *shall be* accepted upon my altar; for my house shall be called, House of prayer for all peoples.

8 The Lord GOD which gathereth the outcasts of Israel saith, I will still gather upon him his gathered ones.

9 All ye beasts of the field, all ye beasts of the forest; come to devour.

10 His watchmen *are* blind: they are all ignorant, they *are* all dumb dogs, they cannot bark; sleeping, lying down, they love to slumber.

11 And these anxious dogs are insatiable, and even the shepherds did not know enough to understand: they all look to their own ways, every one for his gain, from his quarter.

12 Come ye, *say they*, I will fetch wine, and we will fill ourselves with strong drink; and to morrow shall be as this day, *or* much more excellent.

Chapter 57

1 The righteous perisheth, and no man layeth *it* to heart: and merciful men *are* taken away, none considering that the righteous is taken away from the evil *to come.*

2 He shall enter into peace: they shall rest in their beds, *each one* walking *in* his uprightness.

3 But draw near hither, ye sons of the sorceress, generation of the adulterer and the whore.

4 Against whom do ye sport yourselves? against whom make ye a wide mouth, *and* draw out the tongue? *are* ye not rebellious sons, a lying seed of transgression,

5 enflaming yourselves with idols under every green tree, slaying the children in the valleys under the clefts of the rocks?

6 Among the smooth *stones* of the valley *is* thy portion; they, they *are* thy lot: even to them hast thou poured a drink offering, thou hast offered a grain offering. Should I not avenge these things?

7 Upon the lofty and high mountain hast thou set thy bed: even thither wentest thou up to offer sacrifice.

8 Behind the doors also and the posts hast thou set up thy remembrance: for thou hast discovered *thyself to another* than me, and art gone up; thou hast enlarged thy bed, and made thee *a covenant* with them;

thou lovedst their bed wherever thou sawest *it.*

9 And thou wentest to the king with ointment, and didst multiply thy perfumes, and didst send thy messengers far off, and didst debase *thyself even* unto hell.

10 Thou became wearied in the multitude of thy ways; *yet* saidst thou not, There is no remedy: thou hast found that which thou wast searching for; therefore thou repented not.

11 And of whom hast thou reverenced or feared? Why dost thou lie; that thou hast not remembered me, nor have I come to thy thought? Have not I held my peace even of old, and thou hast never feared me?

12 I will declare thy righteousness, and thy works; for they shall not profit thee.

13 When thou criest, let thy companions deliver thee; but the wind shall carry them all away; vanity shall take *them*: but he that waiteth in me shall have the land by inheritance, and shall possess the mountain of my holiness.

14 And shall say, Clear away, clear away, level the way, take away the stumblingblocks out of the way of my people.

15 For thus hath said the high and lofty One that inhabiteth eternity, whose name *is* The Holy *One*; I dwell in the high place and in holiness; and with him also *that is* of a contrite and humble spirit, to cause the spirit of the humble to live, and to cause the heart of the contrite ones to live.

16 For I will not contend for ever, neither will I be always wroth: for by me is the spirit covered by the body, and I have made the souls.

17 For the iniquity of his covetousness was I wroth, and smote him: I hid *my face*, and was wroth, and he went on rebelliously in the way of his heart.

18 I have seen his ways, and will heal him: I will lead him also, and restore comforts unto him and to his mourners.

19 I create the fruit of the lip s; Peace, peace to *him that is* far off, and to *him that is* near, said the LORD; and healed him.

20 But the wicked *are* like sea in tempest, that cannot rest, whose waters cast up mire and dirt.

21 *There is* no peace, saith my God, for the wicked.

Chapter 58

1 Cry aloud, do not hold back, lift up thy voice like a trumpet, and preach to my people their rebellion, and to the house of Jacob their sin.

2 That they seek me daily, and want to know my ways, as people that do righteousness, and have not forsaken the rights of their God: they ask me of the rights of righteousness, and desire to approach God.

3 Wherefore have we fasted, *say they*, and thou seest not? *wherefore* have we afflicted our soul, and thou takest no knowledge? Behold, in the day of your fast ye find *your own* pleasure, and exact your own estates.

4 Behold, ye fast for strife and debate, and to smite with the fist of wickedness: ye shall not fast as *ye do this* day, to make your voice to be heard on high.

5 Is it such a fast that I have chosen? a day for a man to afflict his soul? *is it* to bow down his head as a bulrush, and to spread sackcloth and ashes *under him*? wilt thou call this a fast, and an acceptable day to the LORD?

6 *Is* not rather the fast that I have chosen, to loose the bands of wickedness, to undo the ties of oppression, to release *into freedom* those who are broken, and that ye break every yoke?

7 *Is it* not to share thy bread with the hungry, and that thou bring the poor that are cast out to thy house? when thou seest the naked, that thou cover him; and that thou hide not thyself from thy brother?

8 Then shall thy light break forth as the morning, and thine health shall spring forth speedily: and thy righteousness shall go before thee; the glory of the LORD shall be thy rereward.

9 Then shalt thou call, and thou shalt hear the LORD; thou shalt cry, and he shall say, Here I *am*. If thou take away from the midst of thee the yoke, the putting forth of the finger, and speaking vanity;

10 and *if* thou pour out thy soul to the hungry, and satisfy the afflicted soul; then shall thy light rise in obscurity, and thy darkness *be* as the noonday:

11 And the LORD shall guide thee continually, and satisfy thy soul in drought, and make fat thy bones: and thou shalt be like a watered garden, and like a spring of water, whose waters fail not.

12 And *they* shall build up out of thee the old waste places: thou shalt raise up the *fallen* foundations of many generations; and thou shalt be called, The repairer of the breach, The restorer of paths to dwell in.

13 If thou turn away thy foot from the sabbath, *from* doing thy will on my holy day; and call the sabbath *the* delightful, holy, glorious *day* of the LORD; and shalt honour him by not doing thine own ways, nor seeking thine own will, nor speaking *thine own* words:

14 Then shalt thou delight thyself in the LORD; and I will cause thee to ride upon the high places of the earth, and cause thee to eat of the heritage of Jacob thy father: for the mouth of the LORD hath spoken *it*.

Chapter 59

1 Behold, the LORD'S hand is not shortened, that it cannot save; neither his ear heavy, that it cannot hear:

2 But your iniquities have separated between you and your God, and your sins have hid *his* face from you, that he will not hear.

3 For your hands are defiled with blood, and your

fingers with iniquity; your lips pronounce lies, your tongue speaketh evil.

4 None calleth for righteousness, nor *any* judgeth by the truth: they trust in vanity, and speak vanities: they conceive trouble, and bring forth iniquity.

5 They hatch cockatrice' eggs, and weave the spider's web: whosoever shall eat of their eggs shall die, and if they should squeeze them, a viper shall come out.

6 Their cloth is unfit to be a garment, neither shall they cover themselves with their works: their works *are* works of iniquity, and the work of iniquity *is* in their hands.

7 Their feet run to evil, and they make haste to shed innocent blood: their thoughts *are* thoughts of iniquity; wasting and destruction are their paths.

8 The way of peace they knew not; nor is there anything straight about their ways: they have wilfully made themselves crooked paths: whosoever goeth therein shall not know peace.

9 Therefore hath judgment withdrawn from us, and righteousness hath never overtaken us: we wait for light, but behold obscurity; for brightness, *but* we walk in darkness.

10 We grope for the wall like the blind, and as if *we had* no eyes we walk by touch: we stumble at noonday as in the night; *we are* in graves as dead *men.*

11 We all roar like bears, and mourn sore like doves: we look for judgment, but *there is* none; for saving heath, *but* it has withdrawn from us.

12 For our rebellions are multiplied before thee, and our sins have testified against us: for our iniquities *are* with us; and we know our sins:

13 To rebel and to lie against the LORD, and to depart away from our God; the speaking of libel and rebellion, to conceive, and to speak from the heart words of falsehood.

14 And that which is right hath departed, and righteousness withdrew afar off: for truth is fallen in the street, and equity could not enter.

15 And the truth was taken captive; and he *that* departed from evil *was* imprisoned: and the LORD saw *it,* and it was displeasing in his eyes, because that which is right was lost.

16 And he saw that *there was* no man, and wondered that *there was* no intercessor: therefore his arm brought salvation unto him; and his righteousness, it sustained him.

17 For he put on righteousness as a breastplate, and an helmet of saving health upon his head; and he put on the garments of vengeance *for* clothing, and was clad with zeal as a cloak,

18 so as to give payment, so as to repay the vengeance of his enemies, and repay his adversaries; to the islands he will repay recompense.

19 So shall they fear the name of the LORD from the west, and his glory from the rising of the sun; for he shall come like a violent river impelled by the breath of the LORD.

20 And the Redeemer shall come to Zion, and unto them that turı from the iniquity in Jacob, said the LORD.

21 And this shall be my covenant with them, said the LORD; My spirit that *is* upon thee, and my words which I have put in thy mouth, shall not depart out of thy mouth, nor out of the mouth of thy seed, nor out of the mouth of thy seed's seed, saith the LORD, from henceforth and for ever.

Chapter 60

1 Arise, shine; for thy light is come, and the glory of the LORD is risen upon thee.

2 For, behold, the darkness shall cover the earth, and gross darkness the peoples: but the LORD shall arise upon thee, and his glory shall be seen upon thee.

3 And the Gentiles shall walk to thy light, and the kings to the brightness of thy birth.

4 Lift up thine eyes round about, and see: all they gather themselves together, they come to thee: thy sons shall come from far, and thy daughters shall be nursed at *thy* side.

5 Then thou shalt see, and thou shall shine, and thine heart shall marvel, and be enlarged; because the abundance of the sea shall be converted unto thee, the strength of the Gentiles shall have come unto thee.

6 The multitude of camels shall cover thee, the dromedaries of Midian and Ephah; all they from Sheba shall come: they shall bring gold and incense; and they shall show forth the praises of the LORD.

7 All the flocks of Kedar shall be gathered together unto thee, rams of Nebaioth shall be served unto thee: they shall offered up with grace upon my altar, and I will glorify the house of my glory.

8 Who *are* these *that* fly as a cloud, and as the doves to their windows?

9 For the isles shall wait for me, and the ships of Tarshish from the first, to bring thy sons from far, their silver and their gold with them, unto the name of the LORD thy God, and to the Holy One of Israel, who hath glorified thee.

10 And the sons of strangers shall build up thy walls, and their kings shall serve thee: for in my wrath I smote thee, but in my good favour shall I have mercy on thee.

11 Therefore thy gates shall be open continually; they shall not be shut day nor night; that the strength of the Gentiles may be brought unto thee, and their kings guided.

12 For the people or the kingdom that will not serve thee shall perish; and shall be utterly wasted.

13 The glory of Lebanon shall come unto thee, the fir tree, the pine tree, and the box together, to beautify the place of my sanctuary; and I will honour the place of my feet.

14 The sons also of them that afflicted thee shall come humbled unto thee; and at the steps of thy feet all they that despised thee shall bow themselves down; and they shall call thee, The city of the LORD, The Zion of the Holy One of Israel.

15 Whereas thou hast been forsaken and hated, so that no man went through *thee*, I will place thee in eternal glory, in joy from generation to generation.

16 Thou shalt also suck the milk of the Gentiles, and shalt suck the breast of the kings: and thou shalt know that I the LORD *am* thy Saviour and thy Redeemer, the mighty One of Jacob.

17 For brass I will bring gold, and for iron I will bring silver, and for wood brass, and for the stones iron: I will also put peace *in the place of* thy government, and righteousness *in the place of* thine oppressors.

18 Violence shall no more be heard in thy land, wasting nor destruction within thy borders; but thou shalt call thy walls Saving Health, and thy gates Praise.

19 The sun shall be no more thy light by day; neither for brightness shall the moon give light unto thee: but the LORD shall be unto thee an everlasting light, and thy God thy glory.

20 Thy sun shall set no more; neither shall thy moon wane: for the LORD shall be thine everlasting light, and the days of thy mourning shall be ended.

21 Thy people also *shall be* all righteous: they shall inherit the land for ever; they shall be shoots of my planting, the work of my hands, that I may be glorified.

22 The small one *shall be* as a thousand; the youngest as a strong nation: I the LORD will hasten it in his time.

Chapter 61

1 The Spirit of the Lord GOD *is* upon me; because the LORD hath anointed me; he hath sent me to preach good tidings unto those who are cast down; to bind up *the wounds* of the brokenhearted, to proclaim liberty to the captives, and the opening of the prison to *them that are* bound;

2 to proclaim the year of the LORD's favour, and *the* day of vengeance of our God; to comfort all that mourn;

3 to order in Zion those that mourn, to give unto them beauty for ashes, the oil of joy for mourning, the garment of praise for the spirit of heaviness; that they might be called trees of righteousness, the planting of the LORD, that he might be glorified.

4 And they shall build the old wastes, they shall raise up the former desolations, and they shall restore the waste cities, the desolations of many generations.

5 And strangers shall stand and feed your flocks, and the sons of the alien *shall be* your plowmen and your vinedressers.

6 But ye shall be named the Priests of the LORD: *men* shall call you the Ministers of our God: ye shall eat the riches of the Gentiles, and with their glory ye shall be lifted up.

7 Instead of your double shame, and your dishonour, they shall praise you in your inheritance: therefore in your land ye shall possess the double, and ye shall have everlasting joy.

8 For I the LORD love *that which is* right, I hate robbery for burnt offering; and I will confirm your work in truth, and I will make an everlasting covenant with them.

9 And their seed shall be known among the Gentiles, and their offspring among the peoples: all that saw them shall acknowledge them, that they *are* the seed *which* the LORD hath blessed.

10 I will greatly rejoice in the LORD, my soul shall be joyful in my God; for he hath clothed me with the garments of saving health, he hath surrounded me with the robe of righteousness, as a bridegroom hath he arrayed me, and as a bride made up of his jewels.

11 For as the earth bringeth forth her shoot, and as the garden causeth her seed to spring forth; so the Lord GOD will cause righteousness and praise to spring forth before all the Gentiles.

Chapter 62

1 For Zion's sake will I not hold my peace, and for Jerusalem's sake I will not rest, until her righteousness go forth as brightness, and the her saving health be lit as a flaming torch.

2 And the Gentiles shall see thy righteousness, and all the kings thy glory: and thou shalt be given *a* new name, which the mouth of the LORD shall name.

3 Thou shalt also be a crown of glory in the hand of the LORD, and a kingdom diadem in the hand of thy God.

4 Thou shalt no more be termed Forsaken; neither shall thy land any more be termed Desolate: but thou shalt be called Hephzibah [*my will in her*], and thy land Beulah [*married*]: for the will of the LORD *shall be* in thee, and thy land shall be married.

5 For *as* a young man marrieth a virgin, *so* shall thy sons marry thee: and *as* the bridegroom rejoiceth with the bride, *so* shall thy God rejoice with thee.

6 I have set watchmen upon thy walls, O Jerusalem, *which* shall never hold their peace day nor night: ye that make mention of the LORD, keep not silence,

7 and give him no rest, until he establish, and until he make Jerusalem a praise in the earth.

8 The LORD hath sworn by his right hand, and by the arm of his strength, Surely I will no more give thy wheat *to be* food for thine enemies; and the sons of the stranger shall not drink thy wine, for the which thou hast laboured:

9 But they that have gathered it shall eat it, and praise the LORD; and they that have brought it together shall drink it in the courts of my holiness.

10 Go through, go through the gates; prepare ye the way of the people; clear up, clear up the highway; gather out the stones; lift up a standard for the people.

11 Behold, the LORD hath caused it to be heard unto the end of the earth, Say ye to the daughter of Zion, Behold, thy Saviour cometh; behold that his reward *is* with him, and his work before him.

12 And they shall call them, The holy people, The redeemed of the LORD: and thou shalt be called, Sought out, A city not forsaken.

Chapter 63

1 Who *is* this that cometh from Edom, with red garments from Bozrah? this *that is* glorious in his apparel, travelling in the greatness of his strength? I that speak in righteousness, mighty to save.

2 Wherefore *art thou* red in thine apparel, and thy garments like him that treadeth in the winefat?

3 I have trodden the winepress alone; and of the peoples *there was* none with me: for I have trodden them with my anger, and have trampled them with my fury; and their blood sprinkled my garments, and stained all my raiment.

4 For the day of vengeance *is* in my heart, and the year of my redeemed is come.

5 And I looked, and *there was* none to help; and I wondered that *there was* none to uphold *me*: therefore my own arm brought salvation unto me; and my fury, it upheld me.

6 And I have trampled down the people with my anger, and made them drunk in my fury, and I brought down their strength to the earth.

7 I will mention the mercies of the LORD, *and* the praises of the LORD, according to all that the LORD hath bestowed on us, and the greatness of his goodness toward the house of Israel, which he hath bestowed on them according to his mercies, and according to the multitude of his lovingkindnesses.

8 For he said, Surely they *are* my people, children *that* do not lie: and he was their Saviour.

9 In all their affliction he was afflicted, and the Angel of his face saved them: with his love and with his clemency he redeemed them; and he bare them, and carried them all the days of the age.

10 But they were rebels, and angered his holy Spirit: therefore he was turned to be their enemy, *and* he himself fought against them.

11 Then he remembered the days of old, of Moses, *and* his people, *saying*, Where *is* he that brought them up out of the sea with the shepherd of his flock? where *is* he that put his Holy Spirit within him?

12 He that led *them* by the right hand of Moses with the arm of his glory, he who divided the water before them, thus making himself an everlasting name?

13 He that led them through the deep, as *an* horse in the wilderness, they never stumbled.

14 The Spirit of the LORD pastored them, as a beast, that goeth down into the valley: so didst thou lead thy people, to make thyself a glorious name.

15 Look down from heaven, and behold from the habitation of thy holiness and of thy glory: where *is* thy zeal and thy strength, the feeling of thy bowels and of thy mercies toward me? are they restrained?

16 Doubtless thou *art* our father, though Abraham be ignorant of us, and Israel acknowledge us not: thou, O LORD, *art* our father, our everlasting Redeemer is thy name.

17 O LORD, why hast thou made us to err from thy ways? Hast thou hardened our heart to thy fear? Return for thy servants, for the tribes of thine inheritance.

18 The people of thy holiness have possessed *the promised land* but a little while: our adversaries have trodden down thy sanctuary.

19 We have been like those whom thou never barest rule over, who were never called by thy name.

Chapter 64

1 Oh that thou wouldest rend the heavens, that thou wouldest come down, that the mountains might flow down at thy presence,

2 As *when* the melting fire burneth, the fire causeth the waters to boil, to make thy name known to thine adversaries, *that* the Gentiles may tremble at thy presence!

3 *As* thou camest down when thou didst terrible things *which* we looked not for, *that* the mountains flowed down at thy presence.

4 Nor have *men* heard, nor perceived by the ear, neither hath the eye seen a God beside thee, that thou might do *it again* for the one who waiteth in him.

5 Thou camest out to meet him that with rejoicing had worked righteousness. In thy ways they remembered thee. Behold, thou art wroth; for we have sinned: thy ways are eternal, and *we* shall be saved.

6 But we were all as an unclean *thing*, and all our righteousnesses as filthy rags; and we all fell as the leaves *of a tree*; and our iniquities, like the wind, have taken us away.

7 And *there* is none that calleth upon thy name, that waketh up himself to take hold *of thee*: therefore thou hast hid thy face from us, and hast allowed us to wither in the power of our iniquities.

8 But now, O LORD, thou *art* our father; we *are* the clay, and thou our potter; such that we all *are* the work of thy hands.

9 Be not wroth very sore, O LORD, neither remember iniquity for ever: behold, see, we beseech thee, we *are* all thy people.

10 Thy holy cities are a wilderness, Zion is a wilderness, Jerusalem a desolation.

11 Our house of our Sanctuary and of our glory, where our fathers praised thee, was burned up with fire: and all our precious things were destroyed.

12 Wilt thou refrain thyself regarding these *things*, O LORD? wilt thou hold thy peace, and afflict us very sore?

Chapter 65

1 I was sought of *them that* asked not *for me*; I was found of *them that* sought me not: I said, Here I am, Here I am, unto a people *that* did not invoke my name.

2 I have spread out my hands all the day unto a rebellious people, which walketh in a way *that was* not good, after their own thoughts;

3 A people that provoketh me to anger continually to my face; that sacrificeth in

gardens, and burneth incense upon altars of brick;
4 which remain *asleep* among the graves, and lodge in the deserts, which eat swine's flesh, and broth of abominable *things is in* their vessels;
5 which say, Stand by thyself, come not near to me; for I am holier than thou. These *are* a smoke in my nose, a fire that burneth all the day.
6 Behold, *it is* written before me: I will not keep silence, but will recompense, even recompense into their bosom,
7 For your iniquities, and the iniquities of your fathers together, saith the LORD, which have burned incense upon the mountains, and blasphemed me upon the hills: therefore will I measure their former work into their bosom.

8 Thus hath the LORD said, As when *one* hath found new wine in a cluster, and saith, Destroy it not; for a blessing *is* in it: so will I do for my servants' sakes, that I may not destroy them all.
9 And I will bring forth a seed out of Jacob, and out of Judah an inheritor of my mountains: and my elect shall possess the land for and inheritance, and my servants shall dwell there.
10 And Sharon shall be for a fold of flocks, and the valley of Achor a place for the herds to lie down in, for my people that have sought me.
11 But ye that forsake the LORD, that forget the mountain of my holiness, that prepare a table unto fortune, and that furnish the drink offering for destiny;
12 I also will destine you to the sword, and ye shall all bow down to the slaughter: because when I called, ye did not respond; I spoke, and ye did not hear; but did evil before my eyes, and did choose that which displeased *me.*

13 Therefore thus hath the Lord GOD said, Behold, my servants shall eat, but ye shall be hungry: behold, my servants shall drink, but ye shall be thirsty: behold, my servants shall rejoice, but ye shall be ashamed:
14 Behold, my servants shall jubilee by the joy of *their* heart, but ye shall cry for sorrow of *your* heart, and shall howl for the destruction of spirit.
15 And ye shall leave your name for a curse unto my chosen: for the Lord GOD

shall slay thee, and call his servants by another name.

16 He who blesseth himself in the earth shall bless himself in the God of truth; and he that sweareth in the earth shall swear by the God of truth; because the former troubles shall be forgotten, and shall be covered from my eyes.

17 For, behold, I create new heavens and a new earth: and the former shall not be remembered, nor come into mind.

18 But ye shall be glad and rejoice from age to age in the things which I shall create: for, behold, I create joy unto Jerusalem, and unto her people joy.

19 And I will be glad with Jerusalem, and rejoice with my people: and the voice of weeping shall be no more heard in her, nor the voice of crying.

20 There shall be no more thence an infant of days, nor an old man that hath not filled his days: for the child shall die an hundred years old; and he who sinneth at one hundred years of age, shall be accursed.

21 And they shall build houses, and inhabit *them*; and they shall plant vine-yards, and eat the fruit of them.

22 They shall not build, and another inhabit; they shall not plant, and another eat: for as the days of the trees shall be the days of my people, and my elect shall perpetuate the work of their hands.

23 They shall not labour in vain, nor give birth with fear; for their *births* are the seed of the blessed of the LORD, and their offspring shall be with them.

24 And it shall come to pass, that before they call, I will answer; and while they are yet speaking, I will hear.

25 The wolf and the lamb shall be fed together, and the lion shall eat straw like the ox: and dust *shall be the* serpent's food. They shall not afflict nor do evil in all my holy mountain, said the LORD.

Chapter 66

1 Thus saith the LORD, The heaven *is* my throne, and the earth *is* my footstool: where *shall remain* this house that ye built unto me? and where *shall remain* this place of my rest?

2 For all these *things* hath my hand made, *by my hand* hath these *things* been, said the LORD: but to this *man* will I look, *even* to *him that is* poor and of a contrite spirit, and trembleth at my word.

3 He that killeth an ox *is as if* he slew a man; he that sacrificeth a lamb, *as if* he cut off a dog's neck; he that offereth an oblation, *as if he offered* swine's blood; he that burneth incense, *as if* he blessed iniquity. Yea, they have chosen their own ways, and their soul delighteth in their abominations.

4 I also will choose their delusions, and will bring their fears upon them; because I called, and no one answered; I spoke, and they did not hear: but they did evil before my eyes, and chose that which displeased *me.*

5 Hear the word of the LORD, ye that tremble at his word; Your brethren that hate you, that deny you for my name's sake, said, Let the LORD be glorified: but he shall appear to your joy, and they shall be ashamed.

6 *A* voice of noise from the city, *a* voice of the temple, *a* voice of the LORD that rendereth recompense to his enemies.

7 Before she travailed, she brought forth; before her pain came, she was delivered of a man child.

8 Who hath heard such a thing? who hath seen such things? Shall the earth bring forth in one day? shall an *entire* nation be born at once? that Zion travailed, and shall bring forth her children together?

9 I, who make births *to happen,* shall I not be with child? saith the LORD: I, who cause conception, shall I be stopped? saith thy God.

10 Rejoice ye with Jerusalem, and be glad with her, all ye that love her: be filled with her with joy, all ye that mourn for her:

11 That ye may suck, and be satisfied with the breasts of her consolations; that ye may milk out, and be delighted with the splendour of her glory.

12 For thus saith the LORD, Behold, I will extend peace to her like a river, and the glory of the Gentiles like a flowing stream: then shall ye suck, ye shall be borne upon *her* sides, and be dandled upon *her* knees.

13 As a manchild whom his mother comforteth, so will I comfort you; and ye shall be comforted in Jerusalem.

14 And ye shall see, your heart shall rejoice, and your

bones shall flourish like an herb: and the hand of the LORD shall be known toward his servants, and *his* indignation toward his enemies.

15 For, behold, the LORD will come with fire, and with his chariots like a whirlwind, to render his anger with fury, and his rebuke with flames of fire.

16 For by fire and by his sword will the LORD judge all flesh: and the slain of the LORD shall be multiplied.

17 They that sanctify themselves, and purify themselves in the gardens, one behind another; those that eat swine's flesh, and abomination, and the mouse, shall be cut off together, saith the LORD.

18 For I *understand* their works and their thoughts.

The time shall come to gather all the Gentiles and tongues; and they shall come, and see my glory.

19 And I will set a sign among them, and I will send those that escape of them unto the Gentiles, *to* Tarshish, Pul, and Lud, that draw the bow, *to* Tubal, and Javan, *to* the isles afar off, that have never heard my name, nor seen my glory; and they shall declare my glory among the Gentiles.

20 And they shall bring all your brethren *for* an offering unto the LORD from among all the Gentiles, upon horses, and in chariots, and in litters, and upon mules, and upon camels, to my holy mountain of Jerusalem, saith the LORD, so that the sons of Israel bring the offering in clean vessels to the house of the LORD.

21 And I will also take of them for priests *and* for Levites, saith the LORD.

22 For as the new heavens and the new earth, which I make, shall remain before me, saith the LORD, so shall your seed and your name remain.

23 And it shall come to pass, *that* from one new moon to another, and from one sabbath to another, shall all flesh come to worship before me, said the LORD.

24 And they shall go forth, and look upon the carcasses of the men that rebelled against me: for their worm shall not die, neither shall their fire be quenched; and they shall be an abhorring unto all flesh.

The Book of the Prophecies of

Jeremiah

Chapter 1

1 The words of Jeremiah the son of Hilkiah, of the priests that *were* in Anathoth in the land of Benjamin:

2 To whom the word of the LORD came in the days of Josiah the son of Amon king of Judah, in the thirteenth year of his reign.

3 It came also in the days of Jehoiakim the son of Josiah king of Judah, unto the end of the eleventh year of Zedekiah the son of Josiah king of Judah, unto the carrying away of Jerusalem captive in the fifth month.

4 Then the word of the LORD came unto me, saying,

5 Before I formed thee in the belly I knew thee; and before thou camest forth out of the womb I sanctified thee, *and* I ordained thee a prophet unto the Gentiles.

6 Then I said, Ah, Lord GOD! behold, I know not how to speak: for I *am* a child.

7 But the LORD said unto me, Say not, I *am* a child: for thou shalt go to all that I shall send thee, and whatsoever I command thee thou shalt speak.

8 Be not afraid of their faces: for I *am* with thee to deliver thee, saith the LORD.

9 Then the LORD put forth his hand, and touched my mouth. And the LORD said unto me, Behold, I have put my words in thy mouth.

10 See, I have placed thee in this day over Gentiles and over kingdoms, to root out, and to destroy, and to throw out, and to cast down, to build, and to plant.

11 Moreover the word of the LORD came unto me, saying, Jeremiah, what seest thou? And I said, I see a rod of an almond tree.

12 Then the LORD said unto me, Thou hast seen well: for I will hasten my word to perform it.

13 And the word of the LORD came unto me the second time, saying, What seest thou? And I said, I see a seething pot; and the face thereof *is* toward the north.

14 Then the LORD said unto me, Out of the north an evil shall break forth upon all the inhabitants of the land.

15 For, behold, I will call all the families of the kingdoms of the north, saith the LORD; and they shall come, and they shall set every one his seat at the entering of the gates of Jerusalem, and near all the walls thereof round about, and near all the cities of Judah.

16 And I will utter my judgments against them touching all their wickedness, who have forsaken me, and have burned incense unto other gods, and worshipped the works of their own hands.

17 Thou therefore gird up thy loins, and thou shalt arise, and speak unto them all that I shall command thee: do not fear them, lest I confound thee before them.

18 For, behold, I have made thee this day as a defenced city, and as an iron pillar, and as wall of brass upon all the earth, against the kings of Judah, against the princes thereof, against the priests thereof, and against the people of the land.

19 And they shall fight against thee; but they shall not prevail against thee; for I *am* with thee, saith the LORD, to deliver thee.

Chapter 2

1 Moreover the word of the LORD came to me, saying,

2 Go and cry in the ears of Jerusalem, saying, Thus saith the LORD; I remember thee, the mercy of thy youth, the love of thine espousals, when thou wentest after me in the wilderness, in a land *that was* not sown.

3 Israel *was* holiness unto the LORD, *and* the firstfruits of his increase: all that devour him shall offend; evil shall come upon them, saith the LORD.

4 Hear ye the word of the LORD, O house of Jacob, and all the families of the house of Israel:

5 Thus hath the LORD said, What iniquity have your fathers found in me, that they are gone far from me, and have walked after vanity, and are become vain?

6 Neither said they, Where *is* the LORD that brought us up out of the land of Egypt, that led us through the wilderness, through a land of deserts and of pits, through a land of drought, and of the shadow of death, through a land that no man passed through, and where no man dwelt?

7 And I brought you into a plentiful country, to eat the fruit thereof and the goodness thereof; but when ye entered, ye defiled my land, and made my heritage an abomination.

8 The priests said not, Where *is* the LORD? and they that handled the law knew me not: the pastors also rebelled against me, and the prophets prophesied by Baal, and walked after *things that* do not profit.

9 Wherefore I will yet enter into judgment with you, saith the LORD, and with your children's children will I plead.

10 For pass over the isles of Chittim, and see; and send unto Kedar, and consider diligently, and see if there be such a thing.

11 Hath a nation changed *their* gods? Even though they are not gods. But my people have changed their glory for *that which* doth not profit.

12 Be astonished, O ye heavens, at this, and be horribly afraid, be ye very desolate, said the LORD.

13 For my people have committed two evils; they have forsaken me the fountain of living waters, to hew them out cisterns, broken cisterns, that can hold no water.

14 *Is* Israel a servant? *is* he a homeborn *slave*? why has he been *given over* as a prey?

15 The young lions roared upon him, *and* yelled, and they made his land waste: his cities are deserted without inhabitant.

16 Also the children of Noph and Tahapanes have broken the crown of thy head.

17 Could this not have come upon you peradventure because thou hast forsaken the LORD thy God, when he led thee by the way?

18 And now what hast thou to do in the way of Egypt? to drink the waters of the Nile? or what hast thou to do in the way of Assyria? to drink the waters of the river *Eufrates*?

19 Thine own wickedness shall chastise thee, and thy backslidings shall reprove thee: know therefore and see how evil and bitter it is, that thou hast forsaken the LORD thy God, and that my fear *is* lacking in thee, saith the Lord GOD of the hosts.

20 For of old time I have broken thy yoke, *and* burst thy bands; and thou saidst, I will not serve [*sin*]. With all this, upon every high hill and under every green tree thou wanderest, playing the harlot.

21 Yet I had planted thee a noble vine, a seed of Truth, all of her: how then art thou turned into the degenerate plant of a strange vine unto me?

22 For though thou wash thee with nitre, and take thee much soap, *yet* thine iniquity is sealed before me, saith the Lord GOD.

23 How canst thou say, I am not polluted, I have not gone after Baalim? see thy way in the valley, know what thou hast done: *thou art* a swift dromedary traversing her ways;

24 a wild ass used to the wilderness, that breatheth according to the desire of her soul; from her lust, who shall stop her? all they that seek her will not weary themselves; in her month they shall find her.

25 Withhold thy foot from being unshod, and thy throat from thirst: but thou saidst, There is no hope: no; for I have loved strangers, and after them will I go.

26 As the thief is ashamed when he is taken, so shall the house of Israel be ashamed; they, their kings, their princes, and their priests, and their prophets,

27 saying to a *piece of* firewood, Thou *art* my father; and to a stone, Thou hast brought me forth: for they have turned *their* back unto me, and not *their* face: but in the time of their trouble they say, Arise, and deliver us.

28 But where *are* thy gods that thou hast made thee? let them arise, if they can save thee in the time of thy trouble: for *according to* the number of thy cities were thy gods, O Judah.

29 Wherefore will ye plead with me? ye all have rebelled against me, saith the LORD.

30 In vain have I smitten your children; they have received no correction: your own sword hath devoured your prophets, like a destroying lion.

31 O generation, see ye the word of the LORD. Have I been a wilderness unto Israel? a land of darkness? wherefore say my people, We are lords; we will come no more unto thee?

32 Shall the virgin, perchance, forget her ornaments, *or* a bride her attire? yet my people have forgotten me days without number.

33 Why trimmest thou thy way to seek love? therefore hast thou also taught the wicked ones thy ways.

34 Even in thy skirts is found the blood of the souls of the poor innocents: thou didst not find any trespass in them, but by all these things.

35 Yet thou sayest, Because I am innocent, surely his anger shall turn from me. Behold, I will enter into judgment with thee, because thou hast said, I did not sin.

36 Why talkest thou so much, changing thy ways? thou also shalt be ashamed of Egypt, as thou wast ashamed of Assyria.

37 Yea, thou shalt also go forth from him with thine hands upon thine head: for the LORD hath rejected thy confidences, and thou shalt not prosper in them.

Chapter 3

1 They say, If a man put away his wife, and she go from him, and become another man's, shall he return unto her again? Is she not a land that is now completely polluted? but thou hast played the harlot with many lovers; yet return again to me, said the LORD.

2 Lift up thine eyes unto the high places, and see where thou hast not been lien with. In the ways hast thou sat for them, as the Arabian in the wilderness; and thou hast polluted the land with thy whoredoms and with thy wickedness.

3 Therefore the rain have been withheld, and there hath been no latter rain; and thou hadst a whore's forehead, thou refusedst to be ashamed.

4 Wilt thou not from this time cry unto me, My father, thou *art* the guide of my youth?

5 Will he reserve *his anger* for ever? will he keep *it* to the end? Behold, thou hast spoken and done evil things as thou couldest.

6 The LORD said unto me in the days of Josiah the king, Hast thou seen *that* which rebellious Israel hath done? she is gone up upon every high mountain and under every green tree, and there hath played the harlot.

7 And I said after she had done all these *things*, Turn thou unto me. But she returned not. And her rebellious sister Judah saw *it*.

8 And I saw, when for all the causes whereby rebellious Israel committed adultery I had put her away, and given her a bill of divorce; yet her rebellious sister Judah feared not, but went and played the harlot also.

9 And it came to pass through *her judging* her whoredom to be a light *thing*, that the land became defiled, and committed adultery with stones and with stocks.

10 And yet for all this her rebellious sister Judah hath never turned unto me with her whole heart, but untruthfully, said the LORD.

11 And the LORD said unto me, The rebellious Israel hath justified her soul in comparison to the treacherous Judah.

12 Go and proclaim these words toward the north *wind*, and say, Return, thou rebellious Israel, said the LORD; *and* I will not cause my anger to fall upon you: for I *am* merciful, said the LORD, *and* I will not keep *anger* for ever.

13 Only acknowledge thine iniquity, that thou hast rebelled against the LORD thy God, and hast scattered thy ways to the strangers under every green tree, and ye have not heard my voice, said the LORD.

14 Turn, O rebellious sons, said the LORD; for I am your Lord: and I will take you one of a city, and two of a family, and I will bring you to Zion:

15 And I will give you pastors according to my heart, which shall feed you with knowledge and understanding.

16 And it shall come to pass, when ye be multiplied and increased in the land, in those days, said the LORD, they shall say no more, The ark of the covenant of the LORD: neither shall it come to mind: neither shall they remember it; neither shall they visit *it*; neither shall *that* be done any more.

17 At that time they shall call Jerusalem the throne of the LORD; and all the Gentiles shall congregate unto it in the name of the LORD in Jerusalem: neither shall they walk any more after the hardness of their evil heart.

18 In those times they shall go out from the house of Judah unto the house of Israel, and they shall come together out of the land of the north *wind* to the land which I caused your fathers to inherit.

19 But I said, How shall I place thee as sons, and give thee the desirable land, the heritage that the hosts of Gentiles desire? and I said, Thou shalt call me, My father; and shalt not turn away from following me.

20 Surely *as* the woman breaketh the faith of her husband, so have ye dealt treacherously with me, O house of Israel, said the LORD.

21 A voice was heard upon the high places, weeping of the supplications of the children of Israel: for they have perverted their way, *and* they have forgotten the LORD their God.

22 Return, ye rebellious sons, *and* I will heal your rebellion. Behold, we come unto thee; for thou *art* the LORD our God.

23 Truly the hills are vanity, the multitude of mountains: truly in the LORD our God *is* the saving health of Israel.

24 For shame hath devoured the labour of our fathers from our youth; their flocks and their herds, their sons and their daughters.

25 We lie down in our shame, and our confusion covereth us: for we have sinned against the LORD our God, we and our fathers, from our youth even unto this day, and have not heard the voice of the LORD our God.

Chapter 4

1 If thou wilt return unto me, O Israel, said the LORD, thou shalt have rest: and if thou wilt put away thine abominations out of my sight, then shalt thou not go *into captivity*.

2 And thou shalt swear, The LORD liveth, in truth, in judgment, and in righteousness; and the Gentiles shall bless themselves in him, and in him shall they glory.

3 For thus hath the LORD said to every man of Judah and of Jerusalem, Break up your fallow ground, and sow not among thorns.

4 Circumcise yourselves to the LORD, and take away the foreskins of your heart, ye men of Judah and inhabitants of Jerusalem: lest my fury come forth like fire, and burn that none can quench *it*, because of the evil of your doings.

5 Declare ye in Judah, and publish in Jerusalem; and say, Blow ye the shophar in the land: cry, gather together, and say, Assemble yourselves, and let us go into the defenced cities.

6 Set up the standard in Zion: come together, do not delay: for I bring evil from the north *wind*, and a great destruction.

7 The lion is come up from his den, and the destroyer of the Gentiles is on his way; he is gone forth from his place to make thy land desolate; *and* thy cities shall be laid waste, without an inhabitant.

8 For this gird you with sackcloth, lament and howl: for the fierce anger of the LORD is not turned back from us.

9 And it shall come to pass at that day, saith the LORD, *that* the heart of the king shall perish, and the heart of the princes; and the priests shall be astonished, and the prophets shall wonder.

10 (Then I said, Ah, Lord GOD! surely thou hast greatly deceived this people and Jerusalem, saying, Ye shall have peace; whereas the sword reacheth unto the soul).

11 At that time shall it be said to this people and to Jerusalem, A dry wind of the high places of the wilderness came toward the daughter of my people, not to fan, nor to cleanse,

12 *Even* a wind much more violent than these shall come unto me: for now also will I speak judgments against them.

13 Behold, he shall come up as a cloud, and his chariots as a whirlwind: his horses are swifter than eagles. Woe unto us, for we are given over to be spoiled!

14 O Jerusalem, wash thine heart from wickedness, that thou mayest be saved. How long shalt thou entertain the thoughts of thy iniquity within thee?

15 For the voice *is heard* from he who bringeth the news from Dan, and from he who causeth to hear the affliction from mount Ephraim.

16 Say ye of the Gentiles; behold, cause it to be heard upon Jerusalem, Watchmen come from a far country, and shall give out their voice upon the cities of Judah.

17 As the watchmen of the heritages, they were upon her round about; because she hath been rebellious against me, saith the LORD. **18** Thy way and thy doings have procured these *things* unto thee; this *is* thy wickedness, because it is bitter, because it reacheth unto thine heart.

19 My bowels, my bowels! I am pained at my very heart; my heart maketh a noise in me; I cannot hold my peace, because thou hast heard, O my soul, the sound of the shophar, the alarm of war.

20 Destruction upon destruction is cried; for the whole land is destroyed: suddenly are my tents destroyed, *and* my curtains in a moment.

21 How long shall I see the standard, *and* hear the voice of the shophar?

22 For my people *are* foolish; the ignorant children with no understanding have not known me; they *are* wise to do evil, but to do good they have no knowledge.

23 I beheld the earth, and, behold, *it was* without form, and void; and the heavens, and they *had* no light.

24 I beheld the mountains, and, behold, they trembled, and all the hills were destroyed.

25 I beheld, and, behold, *there was* no man, and all the birds of the heavens had fled.

26 I beheld, and, behold, the fruitful place [*Carmel*] *was* a wilderness, and all the cities thereof were broken down at the presence of the LORD, *and* by his fierce anger.

27 For thus hath the LORD said, The whole land shall be desolate; yet I will not make a full end.

28 For this shall the earth be made desolate, and the heavens above be darkened: because I spoke, I purposed, and did not repent, neither will I turn back from it.

29 The whole city fled from the thunder of the horsemen and bowmen; they went into the thickets of the forests, and climbed up upon the rocks: every city was forsaken, and not a man dwelleth therein.

30 And thou who art destroyed, what wilt thou do? Though thou clothest thyself with crimson, though thou deckest thee with ornaments of gold, though thou paintest thy eyes with antimony, in vain shalt thou make thyself fair; *thy* lovers will despise thee, they will seek thy life.

31 For I have heard a voice as of a woman in travail, the anguish as of her that bringeth forth her first child, the voice of the daughter of Zion, *that* bewaileth herself, *that* spreadeth her hands, *saying*, Woe *is* me now! for my soul is faint because of the murderers.

Chapter 5

1 Run ye to and fro through the streets of Jerusalem, and see now, and find out, and seek in the broad places thereof, if ye can find a man, if there be *any* that executeth judgment, that seeketh the truth; and *I* will pardon the city.

2 And if they should say, The LORD liveth; surely they swear falsely.

3 O LORD, *are* not thine eyes upon the truth? thou hast stricken them, but they did not feel it; thou hast consumed them, *but* they have refused to receive chastisement: they have made their faces harder than a rock; they have refused to return.

4 Therefore I said, Surely these *are* poor; they have become foolish: for they know not the way of the LORD, *nor* the judgment of their God.

5 I will go unto the great men, and will speak unto them; for they have known the way of the LORD, *and* the judgment of their God: but these have altogether broken the yoke, *and* burst the bonds.

6 Wherefore a lion out of the forest shall slay them, *and* a wolf of the desert shall destroy them, a tiger shall lie in wait over their cities: every one that goeth out thence shall be torn in pieces: because their rebellions have been multiplied, *and* their backslidings are increased.

7 How shall I pardon thee for this? thy sons have forsaken me, and sworn by *them that are* not gods: when I had fed them to the full, they then committed adultery, and assembled themselves by troops in the harlots' houses.

8 They were *as* fed horses in the morning: every one neighed after his neighbour's wife.

9 Shall I not visit for these *things*? said the LORD: and shall not my soul be avenged on such a nation as this?

10 Go ye up upon her walls, and destroy; but make not a full end: take away her battlements; for they *are* not the LORD'S.

11 For the house of Israel and the house of Judah have made a firm decision to rebel against me, saith the LORD.

12 They have denied the LORD, and said, He *is* not; and evil shall not come upon us; neither shall we see sword nor famine;

13 but the prophets shall become like wind, and there is no word in them: thus shall it be done unto them.

14 Wherefore thus hath the LORD God of the hosts said, Because ye have spoken this word, behold, I will make my words in thy mouth fire, and this people wood, and it shall devour them.

15 Behold, I will bring a nation upon you from afar, O house of Israel, saith the LORD: it *is* a mighty nation, it *is* an ancient nation, a nation whose language thou knowest not, neither understandest what they say.

16 Their quiver *is* as an open sepulchre, they *are* all mighty men.

17 And they shall eat up thine harvest, and thy bread, *which* thy sons and thy daughters should eat: they shall eat up thy flocks and thine herds: they shall eat up thy vines and thy fig trees: and thy fenced cities, wherein thou trustedst, they shall bring to nothing with the sword.

18 Nevertheless in those days, saith the LORD, I will not make a full end with you.

19 And it shall come to pass, when ye shall say, Wherefore doeth the LORD our God all these *things* unto us? then shalt thou answer them, Like as ye have forsaken me, and served strange gods in your land, so shall ye serve strangers in a land *that is* not yours.

20 Declare this in the house of Jacob, and publish it in Judah, saying,

21 Hear now this, O foolish people, and without heart; which have eyes, and see not; which have ears, and hear not:

22 Fear ye not me? saith the LORD: will ye not tremble at my presence, which placed the sand *for* the bound of the sea by an eternal order, which cannot be broken? Storms shall raise themselves up, yet they shall not prevail; their waves shall roar, yet they shall not pass over it.

23 But this people hath a false and rebellious heart; they are revolted and gone.

24 Neither say they in their heart, Let us now fear the LORD our God, that giveth rain, both the former and the latter, in his season: he shall keep us *with* the appointed weeks of the harvest.

25 Your iniquities have turned away these *things*, and your sins have withheld good *things* from you.

26 For among my people were found wicked *men*: they layed in wait, as he that setteth snares; they set a trap of perdition to catch men.

27 As a cage full of birds, so *are* their houses full of deceit: therefore they are become great, and waxen rich.

28 They are waxen fat, they shine: yea, they overpass in deeds of wickedness: they judged not the cause, the cause of the fatherless, with all this they made themselves prosperous; and the cause of the poor they did not judge.

29 Shall I not visit for these *things*? saith the LORD: shall not my soul be avenged on such a nation as this?

30 A horrible and ugly thing is committed in the land;

31 The prophets prophesied falsely, and the priests bore rule by their hands; and my people love *to have it* so. What will ye do in the end thereof?

Chapter 6

1 O ye children of Benjamin, gather yourselves to flee out of the midst of Jerusalem, and blow the shophar in Tekoa, and set up as a sign smoke in Bethhaccerem: for evil appeareth out of the north *wind*, and great destruction.

2 I have shall liken the daughter of Zion to a comely and delicate *woman*.

3 The shepherds with their flocks shall come unto her; they shall pitch *their* tents against her round about; they shall feed every one his portion.

4 Prepare ye war against her; arise, and let us go up towards the south. Woe unto us! for the day goeth away, for the shadows of the evening are stretched out.

5 Arise, and let us go up by night, and let us destroy her palaces.

6 For thus hath the LORD of the hosts said, Hew ye down trees, and cast a mount against Jerusalem: this *is* the city that all of her is to be visited; *there is* violence in the midst of her.

7 As the waters never cease to flow from a fountain, so her wickedness never ceaseth to flow: injustice and robbery is heard in her; before me continually *is* sickness and wounds.

8 Chastise Jerusalem, lest peradventure my soul depart from thee; lest per-adventure I make thee desolate, a land not inhabited.

9 Thus hath the LORD of the hosts said, They shall thoroughly glean the remnant of Israel as a vine: turn back thine hand as a grapegatherer into the baskets.

10 To whom shall I speak, and give warning, that they may hear? behold, their ears *are* uncircumcised, and they cannot hearken: behold, the word of the LORD is unto them a reproach; they have no delight in it.

11 Therefore I am full of the fury of the LORD; I have worked hard to hold myself in from pouring it out upon the children in the street, and upon the assembly of young men together: for the husband with the wife shall also be taken, the aged with *him that is* full of days.

12 And their houses shall be turned unto others, *with their* fields and wives together: for I will stretch out my hand upon the inhabitants of the land, saith the LORD.

13 For from the least of them even unto the greatest of them every one *is* given to greed; and from the prophet even unto the priest every one dealeth falsely.

14 They treat also the destruction *of the daughter* of my people lightly, saying, Peace, peace; when *there is* no peace.

15 Were they ashamed when they had committed abomination? nay, they were not at all ashamed, neither could they blush: therefore they shall fall among them that shall fall: at the time *that* I visit them they shall fall, saith the LORD.

16 Thus hath the LORD said, Stand ye in the ways, and see, and ask for the old paths, where *is* the good way, and walk therein, and ye shall find rest for your souls. But they said, We will not walk *therein*.

17 Also I set watchmen over you, *saying*, Hearken to the sound of the shophar. But they said, We will not hearken.

18 Therefore hear, ye Gentiles, and know, O congregation of *Gentiles*.

19 Hear, O earth: behold, I will bring evil upon this people, *even* the fruit of their thoughts, because they have not hearkened unto my words, and they hated my law.

20 To what purpose cometh there to me this incense from Sheba, and the sweet cane from a far country? your burnt offerings *are* not according to my will, nor *are* your sacrifices sweet unto me.

21 Therefore thus saith the LORD, Behold, I will lay stumblingblocks before this people, and the fathers and the sons together shall fall upon them; the neighbour and his friend shall perish.

22 Thus hath the LORD said, Behold, a people cometh from the land of the north *wind*, and a great nation shall be raised from the sides of the earth.

23 They shall lay hold on bow and spear; they *are* cruel, and they shall have no mercy; their voice shall roar like the sea; and they shall ride upon horses, set in array as men for war against thee, O daughter of Zion.

24 We have heard the fame thereof: our hands wax feeble: anguish hath taken hold of us, *and* pain, as of a woman in travail.

25 Go not forth into the field, nor walk by the way; for the sword of the enemy *and* fear *is* on every side.

26 O daughter of my people, gird *thee* with sackcloth, and wallow thyself in ashes: make thee mourning, *as for* an only son, most bitter lamentation: for the destroyer shall suddenly come upon us.

27 I have set thee *for* a tower *and* a fortress among my people; thou shalt know and examine their way.

28 They *are* all rebellious princes, they walk with deception: *they are* brass and iron; they *are* all corrupters.

29 The bellows are burned, the lead is consumed of the fire; the founder melteth in vain: for the wicked are not plucked away.

30 Reprobate silver shall *men* call them, because the LORD hath rejected them.

Chapter 7

1 The word that was sent to Jeremiah from the LORD, saying,

2 Stand in the gate of the LORD'S house, and proclaim there this word, and say, Hear the word of the LORD, all *ye of* Judah, that enter in at these gates to worship the LORD.

3 Thus hath the LORD of the hosts the God of Israel said, Amend your ways and your doings, and I will cause you to dwell in this place.

4 Trust ye not in lying words, saying, The temple of the LORD, The temple of the LORD, The temple of the LORD, *are* these.

5 For if ye thoroughly amend your ways and your doings; if ye thoroughly do right between a man and his neighbour;

6 *if* ye oppress not the stranger, the fatherless, and the widow, and shed not innocent blood in this place, neither walk after other gods to your hurt:

7 Then I will cause you to dwell in this place, in the land that I gave to your fathers, for ever and ever.

8 Behold, ye trust in lying words, that cannot profit.

9 Will ye steal, murder, and commit adultery, and swear falsely, and burn incense unto Baal, and walk after other gods whom ye know not;

10 and come and stand before me in this house, which is called by my name, and say, We are free to do all these abominations?

11 Is this house, which is called by my name, become a den of robbers in your eyes? Behold, even I have seen *it*, said the LORD.

12 But go ye now unto my place which *was* in Shiloh, where I set my name at the first, and see what I did to it for the wickedness of my people Israel.

13 And now, because ye have done all these works, said the LORD, and I spoke well unto you, rising up early and speaking, but ye heard not; and I called you, but ye answered not;

14 Therefore I will do unto *this* house, which is called by my name, wherein ye trust, and unto this place which I gave to you and to your fathers, as I have done to Shiloh.

15 And I will cast you out of my sight, as I have cast out all your brethren, *even* the whole seed of Ephraim.

16 Therefore pray not thou for this people, neither lift up cry nor prayer for them, neither make intercession to me: for I will not hear thee.

17 Seest thou not what they do in the cities of Judah and in the streets of Jerusalem?

18 The children gather wood, and the fathers kindle the fire, and the women knead *their* dough, to make cakes to the queen of heaven, and to pour out drink offerings unto other gods, that they may provoke me to anger.

19 Shall they provoke me to anger? said the LORD: *do they* not *provoke* themselves to the confusion of their own faces?

20 Therefore thus hath the Lord GOD said; Behold, my anger and my fury shall be poured out upon this place, upon man, and upon beast, and upon the trees of the field, and upon the fruit of the ground; and it shall burn, and shall not be quenched.

21 Thus hath the LORD of the hosts, the God of Israel said; Add your burnt offerings upon your sacrifices, and eat flesh.

22 For I spoke not unto your fathers, nor commanded them in the day that I brought them out of the land of Egypt, concerning burnt offerings or sacrifices:

23 But this thing commanded I them, saying, Hear my voice, and I will be your God, and ye shall be my people: and walk ye in all the way that I have commanded you, that it may be well unto you.

24 But they hearkened not, nor inclined their ear, but walked in *their own* counsels in the imagination of their evil heart, and went backward, and not forward,

25 since the day that your fathers came forth out of the land of Egypt unto this day. I have *even* sent unto you all my servants the prophets, daily rising up early and sending *them*;

26 yet they hearkened not unto me, nor inclined their ear, but hardened their neck: they did worse than their fathers.

27 Therefore thou shalt speak all these words unto them; but they will not hearken to thee: thou shalt even call unto them; but they will not answer thee.

28 Therefore thou shalt say unto them, This *is* the nation that did not hear the voice of the LORD their God, nor received chastisement: the faith is lost, and was cut off from their mouth.

29 Cut off thine hair, *O Jerusalem*, and cast *it* away, and take up a lamentation on high places; for the LORD hath cast off and forsaken the nation of his wrath.

30 For the sons of Judah have done evil in my sight, said the LORD: they have set their abominations in the house which is called by my name, to pollute it.

31 And they have built the high places of Tophet, which *is* in the valley of the son of Hinnom, to burn their sons and their daughters in the fire; which I commanded *them* not, neither came it into my heart.

32 Therefore, behold, the days come, saith the LORD, that it shall no more be called Tophet, nor the valley of the son of Hinnom, but the valley of slaughter: for they shall bury in Tophet, for there shall be no *other* place.

33 And the carcasses of this people shall be food for the fowls of the heaven, and for the beasts of the earth; and there shall be no one to chase *them* away.

34 Then will I cause to cease from the cities of Judah, and from the streets of Jerusalem, the voice of mirth, and the voice of gladness, the voice of the bridegroom, and the voice of the bride: for the land shall be desolate.

Chapter 8

1 At that time, said the LORD, they shall bring out the bones of the kings of Judah, and the bones of his princes, and the bones of the priests, and the bones of the prophets, and the bones of the inhabitants of Jerusalem, out of their graves;

2 and they shall spread them before the sun, and the moon, and all the host of heaven, whom they have loved, and whom they have served, and after whom they have walked, and whom they have sought, and whom they have worshipped: they shall not be gathered, nor be buried; they shall be for dung upon the face of the earth.

3 And death shall be chosen rather than life by all the residue of them that remain of this evil generation, in all the places where I have driven those that remain, said the LORD of the hosts.

4 Moreover thou shalt say unto them, Thus hath the LORD said; The one who falleth, doth he never arise? he who turneth away, doth he never return?

5 Why *then* is this people of Jerusalem rebellious with a perpetual rebellion? they hold fast deceit, they refuse to return.

6 I hearkened and heard, *but* they spoke not aright: no man repented him of his wickedness, saying, What have I done? every one turned to his course, as the horse rusheth into the battle.

7 Even the stork in the heaven knoweth her appointed time; and the turtle *dove* and the crane and the swallow observe the time of their coming; but my people did not know the judgment of the LORD.

8 How do ye say, We *are* wise, and the law of the LORD *is* with us? Behold, certainly in vain did he make the pen; the scribes *were* in vain.

9 The wise *men* are ashamed, they are dismayed and taken: behold, they have rejected the word of the LORD; and what wisdom *is* in them?

10 Therefore I will give their wives unto others, *and* their fields to them that shall inherit *them*: for every one from the least even unto the greatest is given to greed, from the prophet even unto the priest every one dealeth falsely.

11 For they have treated the destruction of the daughter of my people lightly, saying, Peace, peace; when *there is* no peace.

12 Were they ashamed when they had committed abomination? nay, they were not at all ashamed, neither could they blush: therefore shall they fall among them that should fall: when I visit them, they shall fall, saith the LORD.

13 I will surely cut them off completely, said the LORD: *there are* no grapes on the vine, nor figs on the fig tree, and the leaf shall fall; and *the things that* I have given them shall pass away from them.

14 Upon what shall we secure ourselves? assemble yourselves, and let us enter into the defenced cities, and let us be silent there: for the LORD our God hath put us to silence, and given us water of gall to drink, because we have sinned against the LORD.

15 We looked for peace, but no good *came; and* for a time of health, and behold trouble!

16 The snorting of his horses was heard from Dan: the whole earth trembled at the sound of the neighing of his strong ones; for they are come, and have devoured the land,

and all that is in it; the city, and those that dwell therein.

17 For, behold, I send serpents, cockatrices, among you, which *will* not *be* charmed, and they shall bite you, said the LORD.

18 Because of my strong sorrow, my heart *is* faint in me.

19 Behold the voice of the cry of the daughter of my people that cometh from a far country: *Is* not the LORD in Zion? *is* not her king in her? Why have they provoked me to anger with their graven images, *and* with vanities of a strange *god*?

20 The harvest is past, the summer is ended, and we are not saved.

21 For the destruction of the daughter of my people am I devastated; I am in darkness; astonishment hath taken hold on me.

22 *Is there* no balm in Gilead; *is there* no physician there? why then was there no medicine for the daughter of my people?

Chapter 9

1 Oh that my head were waters, and my eyes a fountain of tears, that I might weep day and night for the slain of the daughter of my people!

2 Oh that I had in the wilderness a lodging place of wayfaring men; that I might leave my people, and go from them! for they *are* all adulterers, a congregation of rebels.

3 And they bend their tongues *like* their bow *for* lies: but they are not valiant for the truth upon the earth; for they proceed from evil to evil, and they did not recognise me, said the LORD.

4 Take ye heed every one of his neighbour, and trust ye not in any brother: for every brother will utterly supplant, and every neighbour will walk with slanders.

5 And they will deceive every one his neighbour, and will not speak the truth: they have taught their tongue to speak lies, *and* weary themselves to commit iniquity.

6 Thine habitation *is* in the midst of deceit; through deceit they refuse to know me, saith the LORD.

7 Therefore thus hath the LORD of the hosts said, Behold, I will melt them, and try them; for how shall I do for the daughter of my people?

8 Their tongue *is as* a sharp arrow; it speaketh deceit: *one* speaketh peaceably to his neighbour with his mouth, but in heart he layeth in wait.

9 Shall I not visit them for these *things*? saith the LORD: shall not my soul be avenged on such a nation as this?

10 Upon the mountains will I lift up weeping and wailing, and lamentation upon the habitations of the wilderness, because they are burned up, so that none can pass through *them*; neither can *men* hear the voice of the cattle; both the fowl of the heavens and the even the beasts of the earth are fled; they are gone.

11 And I will make Jerusalem heaps, *and* a den of dragons; and I will make the cities of Judah desolate, without an inhabitant.

12 Who *is* the wise man, that may understand this? and *who is he* to whom the mouth of the LORD hath spoken, that he may declare for what cause the land perisheth *and* is burned up like a wilderness, that none passeth through?

13 And the LORD said, Because they have forsaken my law which I set before them, and have not heard my voice, neither walked therein;

14 but have walked after the imagination of their own heart, and after the Baalim, which their fathers taught them:

15 Therefore thus hath the LORD of the hosts the God of Israel said; Behold, I will feed them, *even* this people, with wormwood, and give them water of gall to drink.

16 I will scatter them also among Gentiles whom neither they nor their fathers have known: and I will send a sword after them, until I have consumed them.

17 Thus hath the LORD of the hosts said, Consider ye, and call for the mourning women, that they may come; and send for cunning *women*, that they may come;

18 and let them make haste, and take up a wailing for us, that our eyes may run down with tears, and our eyelids gush out with waters.

19 For a voice of wailing is heard out of Zion, How are we destroyed! we are greatly confounded. Why have we forsaken the land? Why have our dwellings cast *us* out?

20 Yet hear the word of the LORD, O ye women, and let your ear receive the word of his mouth, and teach your daughters wailing, and every one her neighbour lamentation.

21 For death is come up into our windows, *and* is entered into our palaces, to cut off the children from without, *and* the young men from the streets.

22 Speak, Thus hath the LORD said, Even the carcasses of men shall fall as dung upon the open field, and as the handful after the harvestman, and there shall be none to gather *them*.

23 Thus hath the LORD said, Let not the wise *man* glory in his wisdom, neither let the mighty *man* glory in his might, let not the rich *man* glory in his riches:

24 But let him that glorieth glory in this, that he understandeth and knoweth me, that I *am* the LORD who doeth mercy, judgment, and righteousness, in the earth: for in these *things* I delight, said the LORD.

25 Behold, the days come, saith the LORD, that I will visit all *them which are* circumcised with the uncircumcised;

26 Egypt, and Judah, and Edom, and the children of Ammon, and Moab, and all *that are* in the utmost corners, that dwell in the wilderness: for all the Gentiles *are* uncircumcised, and all the house of Israel *are* uncircumcised in the heart.

Chapter 10

1 Hear ye the word which the LORD hath spoken over you, O house of Israel:

2 Thus hath the LORD said, Learn not the way of the Gentiles, and fear not the signs of heaven; even though the Gentiles fear them.

3 For the customs of the peoples *are* vanity: for *one* cutteth a tree out of the forest, the work of the hands of the workman, with the axe.

4 They deck it with silver and with gold; they fasten it with hammer and nails, that it move not.

5 They compare them to the palm tree, and they speak not: they must needs be borne, because they cannot walk. Be not afraid of them; for they cannot do evil, neither do they have power to do good.

6 Forasmuch as *there is* none like unto thee, O LORD; thou *art* great, and thy name *is* great in might.

7 Who would not fear thee, O King of the Gentiles? for to thee doth it appertain:

forasmuch as among all the wise *men* of the Gentiles, and in all their kingdoms, *there is* none like unto thee.

8 But they shall become altogether carnal and foolish: the stock *is* a doctrine of vanities.

9 Silver spread into plates shall be brought from Tarshish, and gold from Uphaz, shall the workman work, and the hands of the founder: they shall dress them in blue and purple: they *are* all the work of cunning *men*.

10 But the LORD God *is* the Truth, he himself *is* Living God, and Everlasting King: at his wrath the earth trembles, and the Gentiles shall not be able to abide his indignation.

11 Thus shall ye say unto them, The gods that have not made the heavens or the earth, *even* they shall perish from the earth, and from under these heavens.

12 He that maketh the earth by his power, he that ordereth the world with his wisdom, and extendeth the heavens with his discretion;

13 at his voice, *there is* given a multitude of waters in the heavens, and he causeth the clouds to ascend from the ends of the earth; he maketh the lightnings with the rain, and bringeth forth the wind out of his treasures.

14 Every man is carnal in *his* knowledge: let every founder be ashamed of his graven image: for his molten image *is* falsehood, and *there is* no spirit in them.

15 They *are* vanity, *and* the work of scorn: in the time of their visitation they shall perish.

16 The portion of Jacob *is* not like them: for he *is* the Former of all *things*; and Israel *is* the rod of his inheritance: The LORD of the hosts *is* his name.

17 Gather up thy wares out of the lands, O inhabitant of the fortress.

18 For thus hath the LORD said, Behold, that this time I will throw out the inhabitants of the land with a sling, and will afflict them, that they may find *it*.

19 Woe is me for my hurt! my wound is grievous: but I said, Truly this *is* my sickness, and I must bear it.

20 My tent is destroyed, and all my cords *are* broken: my children were taken from me, and they *are* lost: *there is* none to stretch forth my tent any more, and to set up my curtains.

21 For the pastors are become carnal, and have not sought the LORD: therefore they did not understand, and all their flocks scattered.

22 Behold, the voice of the rumour is come, and a great commotion out of the land of the north *wind*, to make the cities of Judah desolate, *and* a den of dragons.

23 O LORD, I know that man is not the lord of his *own* way: *it is* not in man that walketh to order his steps.

24 O LORD, chastise me, but with judgment; not with thine anger, lest thou bring me to nothing.

25 Pour out thy fury upon the Gentiles that know thee not, and upon the nations that call not on thy name: for they have eaten up Jacob, and devoured him, and consumed him, and have destroyed his habitation.

Chapter 11

1 The word that came to Jeremiah from the LORD, saying,

2 Hear ye the words of this covenant, and speak unto every man of Judah, and to every inhabitant of Jerusalem;

3 and thou shalt say unto them, Thus hath the LORD God of Israel said; Cursed *be* the man that heareth not the words of this covenant,

4 which I commanded your fathers the day *that* I brought them forth out of the land of Egypt, from the iron furnace, saying unto them, hear my voice, and comply with my words, according to all which I command you: and ye shall be my people, and I will be your God;

5 that I may confirm the oath which I have sworn unto your fathers, that I would give them a land flowing with milk and honey, as *it is* this day. Then answered I, and said, Amen, O LORD.

6 And the LORD said unto me, Proclaim all these words in the cities of Judah, and in the streets of Jerusalem, saying, Hear ye the words of this covenant, and do them.

7 For I earnestly protested unto your fathers in the day *that* I brought them up out of the land of Egypt, *even* unto this day, rising early and protesting, saying, Hear my voice.

8 Yet they did not hear, nor did they incline their ear, but walked every one in the imagination of their evil heart: therefore I will bring upon them all the words of this covenant, which I commanded *them* to do; but they did *them* not.

9 And the LORD said unto me, A conspiracy is found among the men of Judah, and among the inhabitants of Jerusalem.

10 They have returned to the iniquities of their first fathers, which refused to hear my words; and they went after other gods to serve them: the house of Israel and the house of Judah have broken my covenant which I made with their fathers.

11 Therefore thus hath the LORD said, Behold, I will bring evil upon them, which they shall not be able to escape; and though they shall cry unto me, I will not hearken unto them.

12 Then shall the cities of Judah and inhabitants of Jerusalem go, and cry unto the gods unto whom they offer incense, who shall not be able to save them in the time of their trouble.

13 For *according to* the number of thy cities were thy gods, O Judah; and *according to* the number of thy streets, O Jerusalem, have ye set up altars of confusion, *even* altars to burn incense unto Baal.

14 Therefore pray not thou for this people, neither lift up a cry or prayer for them: for I will not hear *them* in the time that they cry unto me in their trouble.

15 What *part* hath my beloved in my house, *seeing* she hath wrought lewdness with many? The holy flesh shall pass from upon thee, for in thy evil thou didst glory.

16 The LORD called thy name, A green olive tree, beautiful in fruit and in appearance. At the voice of a great word he caused fire to be kindled upon it, and they broke her branches.

17 For the LORD of the hosts, that planted thee, hath pronounced evil against thee, for the evil of the house of Israel and of the house of Judah, which they have done against themselves to provoke me to anger in offering incense unto Baal.

18 And the LORD gave me knowledge *of it*, and I experienced *it*: then thou showedst me their doings.

19 But I *was* like a ram *or* an ox *that* is brought to the slaughter; for I did not understand that they had devised devices against me, *saying*, Let us destroy the tree with the fruit thereof, and let us cut him off from the land of the living, that his name may be no more remembered.

20 But, O LORD of the hosts, that judgest righteously, that triest the kidneys and the heart, let me see thy vengeance on them: for unto thee have I uncovered my cause.

21 Therefore, thus hath the LORD said regarding the men of Anathoth, that seek thy life, saying, Prophesy not in the name of the LORD, that thou die not by our hand:

22 Therefore, thus hath the LORD of the hosts said, Behold, I visit: the young men shall die by the sword; their sons and their daughters shall die by famine:

23 And there shall be no remnant of them: for I will bring evil upon the men of Anathoth, *even* the year of their visitation.

Chapter 12

1 Righteous *art* thou, O LORD, even though I dispute with thee: even so, I will speak judgments with thee: Why doth the way of the wicked prosper?   All

they that completely rebel against thee have peace.

2 Thou hast planted them, yea, they have taken root: they grow, yea, they bring forth fruit: thou *art* near in their mouth, and far from their kidneys.

3 But thou, O LORD, knowest me: thou hast seen me, and tried my heart toward thee: pull them out like sheep for the slaughter, and mark them for the day of slaughter.

4 How long shall the land be desolate, and the herbs of all the field wither, for the wickedness of them that dwell therein? the cattle are lacking, and the birds; because they said, He shall not see our latter end.

5 If thou hast run with the footmen, and they have wearied thee, then how canst thou contend with horses? and *if* in the land of peace, *wherein* thou trustedst, *they wearied thee*, then how wilt thou do in the swelling of Jordan?

6 For even thy brethren, and the house of thy father, even they have dealt treacherously with thee; yea, they have raised their voice after thee, *O* congregation: believe them not, when they speak fair words unto thee.

7 I have forsaken my house, I have left my heritage; I have given the dearly beloved of my soul into the hand of her enemies.

8 My heritage was unto me as a lion in the forest; it cried out against me: therefore I have hated it.

9 My heritage *is* unto me *as* a speckled bird, the birds round about *are* against her; come ye, assemble all the beasts of the field, come to devour her.

10 Many pastors have destroyed my vineyard, they have trodden my heritage under foot, they have made my precious heritage a desolate wilderness.

11 They have made it desolate, it cryeth against me, desolate; the whole land was made desolate, because there was no man that would see.

12 The spoilers are come upon all high places through the wilderness: for the sword of the LORD shall devour from the *one* end of the land even to the *other* end of the land: there is no peace for any flesh.

13 They have sown bread, but shall reap thorns: they had the heritage, but they did not profit: and they shall be ashamed because of your fruits, by the *fierce* anger of the LORD.

14 Thus hath the LORD said against all my evil neighbours, that touch the heritage which I have caused my people Israel to inherit; Behold, I will pluck them out of their land, and pluck out the house of Judah from among them.

15 And it shall come to pass, that after I have plucked them out I will return, and have mercy on them, and will cause them to return, everyone to his heritage, and each one to his land.

16 And it shall come to pass, if they will diligently learn the ways of my people, to swear in my name, *saying, The* LORD liveth; as they taught my people to swear by Baal; then shall they be prospered in the midst of my people.

17 But if they will not hear, I will utterly pluck up and destroy that nation, saith the LORD.

Chapter 13

1 Thus hath the LORD said unto me, Go and buy thee a linen girdle, and put it upon thy loins, and thou shalt not put it in water.

2 And I bought the girdle according to the word of the

LORD, and put *it* on my loins.

3 And the word of the LORD came unto me the second time, saying,

4 Take the girdle that thou hast bought, which *is* upon thy loins, and arise, go to the Euphrates, and hide it there in a hole of the rock.

5 So I went, and hid it in the Euphrates, as the LORD commanded me.

6 And it came to pass after many days, that the LORD said unto me, Arise, go to the Euphrates, and take the girdle from thence, which I commanded thee to hide there.

7 Then I went to the Euphrates, and digged, and took the girdle from the place where I had hid it: and, behold, the girdle was rotted, it was good for nothing.

8 Then the word of the LORD came unto me, saying,

9 Thus hath the LORD said, After this manner will I cause the pride of Judah to rot, and the great pride of Jerusalem.

10 This evil people, which refuse to hear my words, which walk in the imagination of their heart, and went after other gods, to serve them, and to worship them, shall even be as this girdle, which is good for nothing.

11 For as the girdle cleaveth to the loins of a man, so have I caused to cleave unto me the whole house of Israel and the whole house of Judah, saith the LORD; that they might be unto me for a people, and for fame, and for a praise, and for honour: but they did not hear.

12 Therefore thou shalt speak unto them this word; Thus hath the LORD God of Israel said, Every bottle shall be filled with wine: and they shall say unto thee, Do we not certainly know that every bottle shall be filled with wine?

13 Then shalt thou say unto them, Thus hath the LORD said, Behold, I fill all the inhabitants of this land with drunkenness, *even* the kings that sit upon David's throne, and the priests, and the prophets, and all the inhabitants of Jerusalem.

14 And I will break them one against another, even the fathers with the sons together, saith the LORD: I will not pity, nor spare, nor have mercy to not destroy them.

15 Hear ye, and give ear; be not proud: for the LORD hath spoken.

16 Give glory to the LORD your God, before he cause darkness, and before your feet stumble in mountains of darkness, and, while ye look for light, he turn it into the shadow of death, *and* make *it* gross darkness.

17 But if ye will not hear this, my soul shall weep in secret because of *your* pride; and weeping bitterly, my eyes shall be undone in tears, because the LORD'S flock was carried away captive.

18 Say unto the king and to the queen, Humble yourselves, sit down *in the dust*: because the crown of your glory has come down off your heads.

19 The cities of the south were shut up, and none could open *them*: Judah was carried away captive, all of it, it was completely carried away captive.

20 Lift up your eyes, and behold them that come from the north *wind*: where *is* the flock *that* was given thee, the cattle of thy beauty?

21 What wilt thou say when he shall visit thee? for thou hast taught them *to be* princes, *and as* head over thee: shall not sorrows take thee, as a woman in travail?

22 When thou shalt say in thine heart, Wherefore come these things upon me? For the greatness of thine iniquity are thy skirts discovered, *and* thy heels made bare.

23 Can the Ethiopian change his skin, or the leopard his spots? Likewise ye also cannot do good, being taught to do evil.

24 Therefore will I scatter them as the stubble that passeth away by the wind of the wilderness.

25 This *shall be* thy lot, the portion of thy measures from me, said the LORD; because thou hast forgotten me, and trusted in falsehood.

26 Therefore did I uncover thy skirts before thy face, and thy shame was manifested.

27 I have seen thine adulteries, and thy neighings, the lewdness of thy whoredom upon the hills; in the same field I saw thine abominations. Woe unto thee, O Jerusalem! wilt thou not be made clean at last? How long then *shall it be*?

Chapter 14

1 The word of the LORD that was given to Jeremiah concerning the famine.

2 Judah mourneth, and the gates thereof languish; they are black unto the ground; and the cry of Jerusalem is gone up.

3 And their nobles have sent their little ones to the waters: they came to the pits, *and* found no water; they returned with their vessels empty; they were ashamed and confounded, and covered their heads.

4 Because the ground is chapped, for there was no rain in the earth, the plowmen were ashamed, they covered their heads.

5 Yea, the hind also calved in the field, and forsook *it*, because there was no grass.

6 And the wild asses did stand in the high places, they snuffed up the wind like dragons; their eyes did fail, because *there was* no grass.

7 O LORD, though our iniquities testify against us, do thou *it* for thy name's sake: for our rebellions have multiplied; we have sinned against thee.

8 O the hope of Israel, the Keeper thereof in time of trouble, why shouldest thou be as a stranger in the land, and as a wayfaring man *that* turneth aside to tarry for a night?

9 Why shouldest thou be as a speachless man, as a mighty man *that* cannot save? yet thou, O LORD, *art* in the midst of us, and we are called by thy name; leave us not.

10 Thus hath the LORD said unto this people, Thus have they loved to move, nor have they refrained their feet, therefore the LORD doth not have them in *his* will; he will now remember their iniquity, and visit their sins.

11 Then said the LORD unto me, Pray not for this people for *their* good.

12 When they fast, I will not hear their cry; and when they offer burnt offering and an oblation, I will not accept them: but I will consume them by sword, and by famine, and by pestilence.

13 Then I said, Ah, Lord GOD! behold, the prophets say unto them, Ye shall not see the sword, neither shall ye have famine; but I will give you true peace in this place.

14 Then the LORD said unto me, The prophets prophesy lies in my name: I sent them not, neither have I commanded them, neither did I speak unto them: they prophesy unto you a false vision, divination, vanity, and the deceit of their heart.

15 Therefore thus hath the LORD said concerning the prophets that prophesy in my name which I sent not, and that say, Sword and famine shall not be in this land; By sword and famine shall those prophets be consumed.

16 And the people to whom they prophesy shall be cast out in the streets of Jerusalem because of the famine and the sword; and they shall have none to bury them, them, their wives, nor their sons, nor their daughters: for I will pour their wickedness upon them.

17 Therefore thou shalt say this word unto them; Let my eyes run down with tears night and day, and let them not cease: for the virgin daughter of my people is broken with a great breach, with a very grievous blow.

18 If I go forth into the field, then behold the slain with the sword! and if I enter into the city, then behold them that are sick with famine! yea, both the prophet and the priest walked around in circles in the land, and they knew *it* not.

19 Hast thou utterly rejected Judah? hath thy soul loathed Zion? why didst thou cause us to be smitten when no healing remaineth for us? we waited for peace, and *there was* no good; and for the time of healing, and behold trouble!

20 We acknowledge, O LORD, our wickedness, *and* the iniquity of our fathers: for we have sinned against thee.

21 Do not cast *us* away, for thy name's sake, do not disgrace the throne of thy glory: remember, break not thy covenant with us.

22 Are there *any* among the vanities of the Gentiles that can cause it to rain? or can the heavens give rain? *art* not thou he, O LORD our God? therefore we will wait upon thee: for thou hast made all these *things*.

Chapter 15

1 Then the LORD said unto me, Though Moses and Samuel stood before me, *yet* my will *would* not *be* toward this people: cast *them* out of my sight, and let them go forth.

2 And it shall come to pass, if they say unto thee, Where shall we go forth? then thou shalt tell them, Thus hath the LORD said; Such as *are* for death, to death; and such as *are* for the sword, to the sword; and such as *are* for the famine, to the famine; and such as *are* for the captivity, to the captivity.

3 And I will visit over them four kinds *of evil,* saith the LORD: the sword to slay, and the dogs to tear, and the fowls of the heaven, and the beasts of the earth, to devour and destroy.

4 And I will give them over to be sifted by all the kingdoms of the earth, because of Manasseh the son of Hezekiah king of Judah, for *that* which he did in Jerusalem.

5 For who shall have pity upon thee, O Jerusalem? or who shall bemoan thee? or who is to come to ask regarding thy peace?

6 Thou hast forsaken me, saith the LORD, thou art gone backward: therefore I stretched out my hand over thee, and cast thee away; I am tired of repenting.

7 And I fanned them with a fan unto the gates of the land; I bereaved *them* of children, I wasted my people; they did not turn from their ways.

8 Their widows are multiplied unto me more than the sand of the sea: I have brought upon them a destroyer at noonday against the young: I have caused *him* to fall upon her suddenly, and terrors upon the city.

9 She that hath borne seven languisheth: her soul is filled with sorrow; her sun is gone down while *it was* yet day: she hath been ashamed and confounded: and the residue of them will I deliver to the sword before their enemies, saith the LORD.

10 Woe is me, my mother, that thou hast borne me a man of strife and a man of contention to the whole earth! I have neither lent on usury, nor men have lent to me on usury; *yet* every one of them doth curse me.

11 The LORD said, Verily it shall be well with thy remnant; verily I will cause the enemy to entreat thee *well* in the time of evil and in the time of affliction.

12 Shall iron break the iron from the place of the north *wind* and the bronze?

13 Thy riches and thy treasures I will give to the spoil without price, and *that* for all thy sins, even in all thy borders.

14 And I will make *thee* to serve thine enemies in a land *which* thou knowest not: for a fire is kindled in my anger, *which* shall burn upon you.

15 O LORD, thou knowest: remember me, and visit me, and revenge me of my enemies; take me not away in the prolongation of thy anger: know that for thy sake I have suffered rebuke.

16 Thy words were found, and I did eat them; and thy word was unto me the joy and rejoicing of my heart: for thy name was called upon me, O LORD God of the hosts.

17 I sat not in the assembly of the mockers, nor did I become puffed up by reason of thy prophecy; I sat alone because thou hast filled me with indignation.

18 Why was my pain perpetual, and my wound incurable, *which* refuseth to be healed? wilt thou be altogether unto me as a liar, *and as* waters *that* fail?

19 Therefore thus hath the LORD said, If thou return, then I will bring thee again, *and* thou shalt stand before me: and if thou take forth the precious from the vile, thou shalt be as my mouth: let them return unto thee; but return not thou unto them.

20 And I will give thee unto this people as a fenced brazen wall: and they shall fight against thee, but they shall not prevail against thee: for I *am* with thee to keep thee and to defend thee, said the LORD.

21 And I will deliver thee out of the hand of the wicked, and I will redeem thee out of the hand of the strong.

Chapter 16

1 And the word of the LORD came unto me, saying,

2 Thou shalt not take thee a wife, neither shalt thou have sons or daughters in this place.

3 For thus hath the LORD said concerning the sons and *concerning* the daughters that would be born in this place, and *concerning* their mothers that would bare them, and *concerning* their fathers that would beget them in this land;

4 They shall die of grievous deaths; they shall not be lamented; neither shall they be buried; *but* they shall be as dung upon the face of the earth: and they shall be consumed by the sword, and by famine; and their carcasses shall be food for the fowls of heaven, and for the beasts of the earth.

5 For thus hath the LORD said, Enter not into the house of mourning, neither go to lament nor comfort them: for I have taken away my peace from this people, said the LORD, *even* loving-kindness and mercies.

6 Both the great and the small shall die in this land: they shall not be buried, neither shall *men* lament for them, nor cut themselves, nor make themselves bald for them:

7 Neither shall they break *the bread* of mourning for them, to comfort them for the dead; neither shall *men* give them the cup of consolation to drink for their father or for their mother.

8 In the same manner thou shalt not go into the house of feasting, to sit with them to eat and to drink.

9 For thus hath the LORD of the hosts, the God of Israel said; Behold, I will cause to cease in this place, before your eyes, and in your days, every voice of mirth, and every voice of gladness, every voice of the bridegroom, and every voice of the bride.

10 And it shall come to pass, when thou shalt show this people all these things, they shall say unto thee, Wherefore hath the LORD pronounced all this great evil against us? or what *is* our iniquity? or what *is* our sin that we have committed against the LORD our God?

11 Then shalt thou say unto them, Because your fathers have forsaken me, saith the LORD, and have walked after other gods, and have served them, and have worshipped them, and have forsaken me, and have not kept my law;

12 and ye have done worse than your fathers; for, behold, ye walk every one after the imagination of his evil heart, not hearkening unto me:

13 Therefore I will cause you to be cast out of this land into a land that ye know not, *neither* ye nor your fathers; and there shall ye serve other gods day and night; for I will not grant you mercy.

14 Therefore, behold, the days come, said the LORD, that it shall no more be said, The LORD liveth, that caused the children of Israel to come up out of the land of Egypt;

15 but, The LORD liveth, that caused the children of Israel to come up out of the land of the north *wind*, and from all the lands where he had driven them: and I will bring them again into their land that I gave unto their fathers.

16 Behold, I send many fishers, saith the LORD, and they shall fish them; and after will I send many hunters, and they shall hunt them from every mountain, and from every hill, and out of the holes of the rocks.

17 For my eyes *are* upon all their ways: which they have not hid from me, neither does their iniquity hide from the presence of my eyes.

18 But first I will recompense their iniquity and their sin double; because they have defiled my land with the carcasses of their abominations, and they have filled my inheritance with abominable things.

19 O LORD, my strength, and my fortress, and my refuge in the time of the affliction; Gentiles shall come unto thee from the ends of the earth, and shall say, Surely our fathers have inherited lies, vanity, and *things* wherein *there is* no profit.

20 Shall a man make gods unto himself? But they *shall* not *be* gods.

21 Therefore, behold, I will cause them to know this time, I will cause them to know my hand and my might; and they shall know that my name *is* The LORD.

Chapter 17

1 The sin of Judah *is* written with a pen of iron, *and* with the point of a diamond: *it is* graven upon the table of their heart, and upon the horns of your altars;

2 that their children might remember their altars and their groves, by the green trees and upon the high hills.

3 My mountain dweller! In the field are thy riches; all thy treasures will I give to the spoil, because of the sin of thy high places throughout all thy borders.

4 And thou, even thyself, shalt discontinue from thine heritage that I gave thee; and I will cause thee to serve thine enemies in the land which thou knowest not: for ye have kindled a fire in my anger, *which* shall burn for ever.

5 Thus hath the LORD said; Cursed *be* the man that trusteth in man, and maketh flesh his arm, and whose heart departeth from the LORD.

6 For he shall be like the heath in the desert, and shall not see when good cometh; but shall inhabit the parched places in the wilderness, *in* a salt land and not inhabited.

7 Blessed *is* the man that is steadfast in the LORD, and whose trust is the LORD.

8 For he shall be as a tree planted by the waters, and *that* spreadeth out her roots by the river, and shall not see when heat cometh, but her leaf shall be green; and shall not be fatigued in the year of drought, neither shall cease from yielding fruit.

9 The heart *is* deceitful above all *things*, and desperately wicked: who shall know it?

10 I the LORD search the heart, *I* try the kidneys, even to give every man according to his ways, *and* according to the fruit of his doings.

11 As the partridge that stealeth that which she did not hatch, *is* he that getteth riches, and not with righteousness; in the midst of his days he shall leave them, and at his end shall be a fool.

12 The throne of glory, height from the beginning, *is* the place of our sanctification.

13 O hope of Israel! LORD, all that forsake thee shall be ashamed; *and* they that depart from me shall be written in the dust; because they have forsaken the LORD, the fountain of living waters.

14 Heal me, O LORD, and I shall be healed; save me, and I shall be saved: for thou *art* my praise.

15 Behold, they say unto me, Where *is* the word of the LORD? let it come now.

16 For I did not take it upon myself to be a pastor following thee: neither have I desired the woeful day; thou knowest: that which came out of my lips hath come forth in thy presence.

17 Be thou not a terror unto me: thou *art* my hope in the day of evil.

18 Let them be confounded that persecute me, but let not me be confounded: let them be dismayed, but let not me be dismayed: bring upon them the day of evil, and destroy them with double destruction.

19 Thus said the LORD unto me; Go and stand in the gate of the children of the people, whereby the kings of Judah come in, and by the which they go out, and in all the gates of Jerusalem;

20 and say unto them, Hear ye the word of the LORD, ye kings of Judah, and all Judah, and all the inhabitants of Jerusalem, that enter in by these gates:

21 Thus hath the LORD said; Take heed for your lives, and bring no burden on the sabbath day, to bring *it* in by the gates of Jerusalem;

22 neither carry forth a burden out of your houses on the sabbath day, neither do ye any work, but sanctify ye the sabbath day, as I commanded your fathers;

23 who did not hear, neither inclined their ear, but made their neck stiff, that they might not hear, nor receive correction.

24 And it shall come to pass, if ye diligently hearken unto me, saith the LORD, to bring in no burden through the gates of this city on the sabbath day, but sanctify the sabbath day, to do no work therein;

25 *then* shall there enter in by the gates of this city, the kings and the princes, who sit upon the throne of David, *riding* in chariots and on horses, they, and their princes, the men of Judah, and the inhabitants of Jerusalem: and this city shall be inhabited for ever.

26 And they shall come from the cities of Judah, and from the places about Jerusalem, and from the land of Benjamin, and from the fields, and from the mountain, and from the south, bringing burnt offerings, and sacrifices, and *grain offerings*, and incense, and bringing *the* sacrifice of praise, unto the house of the LORD.

27 But if ye will not hearken unto me to sanctify the sabbath day, and not to bring burdens nor bring it in through the gates of Jerusalem on the sabbath day; then I will kindle a fire in the gates thereof, and it shall devour the palaces of Jerusalem, and it shall not be quenched.

Chapter 18

1 The word which came to Jeremiah from the LORD, saying,

2 Arise, and go down to the potter's house, and there I will cause thee to hear my words.

3 Then I went down to the potter's house, and, behold, he wrought a work upon *a* wheel.

4 And the vessel that he made of clay was broken in the hand of the potter: so he made it again another vessel, as seemed good to the potter to make *it*.

5 Then the word of the LORD came to me, saying,

6 O house of Israel, cannot I do with you as this potter? saith the LORD. Behold, as the clay *is* in the potter's hand, so *are* ye in my hand, O house of Israel.

7 In an instant I shall speak against Gentiles and against kingdoms, to pluck up, and to pull down, and to destroy.

8 But if these Gentiles shall turn from their evil, I will repent of the evil that I thought to do unto them.

9 And in an instant I shall speak concerning the nation, and concerning the kingdom, to build and to plant *it*;

10 But if it should do evil in my sight, not hearing my voice, then I will repent of the good that I had determined to do unto them.

11 Now therefore go to, speak to every man of Judah, and to the inhabitants of Jerusalem, saying, Thus hath the LORD said; Behold, I ordain evil against you, and devise plans against you: return ye now every one from his evil way, and better your ways and your doings.

12 And they said, This is useless: for we must walk after our own devices, and we must every one do the imagination of his evil heart.

13 Therefore thus hath the LORD said; Ask ye now among the Gentiles, who hath heard such things: the virgin of Israel hath done a very horrible thing.

14 Will anyone leave the snow of the rock of the field that flows from Lebanon? *or* shall they forsake the singular, cold, flowing waters?

15 Because my people have forgotten me, they have burned incense to vanity, and they have caused them to stumble in their ways, in the ancient paths, to walk in paths, *in* a way not trodden;

16 to make their land desolate, and a perpetual hissing; every one that passeth thereby shall be astonished, and wag his head.

17 I will scatter them as with an east wind before the enemy; I will show them the back, and not the face, in the day of their perdition.

18 Then said they, Come, and let us devise devices against Jeremiah; for the

law shall not perish from
the priest, nor counsel from
the wise, nor the word from
the prophet. Come, and let
us smite him with the
tongue, and let us not consider any of his words.
19 Consider me, O LORD,
and hear the voice of them
that contend with me.
20 Shall evil be recompensed for good? for they
have digged a pit for my
soul. Remember that I
stood before thee to speak
good for them, *and* to turn
away thy wrath from them.
21 Therefore deliver up
their children to the famine,
and pour out their *blood* by
the force of the sword; and
let their wives be bereaved
of their children, and *be*
widows; and let their men
be put to death; *let* their
young men *be* slain by the
sword in battle.
22 Let a cry be heard from
their houses, when thou
shalt bring a troop sud-
denly upon them: for they
have digged a pit to take
me, and hid snares for my
feet.
23 Yet, LORD, thou knowest all their counsel against
me to slay *me*: forgive not
their iniquity, neither blot
out their sin from thy sight,
but let them be overthrown
before thee; deal *thus* with
them in the time of thine
anger.

Chapter 19

1 Thus hath the LORD said,
Go and buy a potter's
earthen bottle, and *take* of
the elders of the people, and
of the elders of the priests;
2 and go forth unto the valley of the son of Hinnom,
which *is* by the entry by the
east gate, and proclaim
there the words that I shall
tell thee.
3 Therefore thou shalt say,
Hear ye the word of the
LORD, O kings of Judah,
and inhabitants of Jerusalem; Thus saith the LORD
of the hosts, God of Israel;
Behold, I bring evil upon
this place, the which whosoever heareth, his ears
shall tingle.
4 Because they have forsaken me, and have es-
tranged this place, and
have burned incense in it
unto other gods, whom neither they nor their fathers
have known, nor the kings
of Judah, and have filled
this place with the blood of
innocents;
5 and have built high
places unto Baal, to burn
their sons with fire *for* burnt
offerings unto this same
Baal, which I commanded
not, nor spoke *it*, neither
came *it* into my mind:

6 Therefore, behold, the days come, said the LORD, that this place shall no more be called Tophet, nor The valley of the son of Hinnom, but The valley of the slaughter.

7 And I will make void the counsel of Judah and Jerusalem in this place; and I will cause them to fall by the sword before their enemies, and by the hands of them that seek their souls: and their carcasses will I give to be food for the fowls of the heaven, and for the beasts of the earth.

8 And I will make this city desolate, and an hissing; every one that passeth thereby shall be astonished and hiss because of all the plagues thereof.

9 And I will cause them to eat the flesh of their sons and the flesh of their daughters, and they shall eat every one the flesh of his friend in the siege and straitness, wherewith their enemies, and they that seek their souls, shall straiten them.

10 Then shalt thou break the bottle in the sight of the men that go with thee,

11 and shalt say unto them, Thus hath the LORD of the hosts said; Even so will I break this people and this city, as *one* breaketh a potter's vessel, that cannot be restored again: and they shall bury *them* in Tophet, for there shall be no *other* place to bury.

12 Thus will I do unto this place, saith the LORD, and to the inhabitants thereof, and *even* make this city as Tophet:

13 And the houses of Jerusalem, and the houses of the kings of Judah, shall be as the place of Tophet, defiled, because of all the houses upon whose roofs they have burned incense unto all the host of the heaven, and have poured out drink offerings unto other gods.

14 Then returned Jeremiah from Tophet, where the LORD had sent him to prophesy; and he stood in the court of the LORD'S house; and said to all the people,

15 Thus hath the LORD of the hosts, God of Israel said; Behold, *I* bring upon this city and upon all her towns all the evil that I have spoken against her, because they have hardened their necks, that they might not hear my words.

Chapter 20

1 And Pashur *the* priest, the son of Immer, who presided as prince in the house of the LORD, heard Jeremiah who prophesied these things.

2 Then Pashur smote Jeremiah the prophet, and put him in the stocks that *were* at the gate of Benjamin on the high *place*, which *is* in the house of the LORD.

3 And it came to pass on the morrow, that Pashur brought forth Jeremiah out of the stocks. Then said Jeremiah unto him, The LORD hath not called thy name Pashur [*Prosperity all around*], but Magormissabib [*Fear from every side*].

4 For thus hath the LORD said, Behold, I will make thee a terror to thyself, and to all those that love thee well: and they shall fall by the sword of their enemies, and thine eyes shall behold *it*: and I will give all Judah into the hand of the king of Babylon, and he shall carry them captive into Babylon, and shall smite them with the sword.

5 Moreover I will deliver all the strength of this city, and all the labours thereof, and all the precious things thereof, and all the treasures of the kings of Judah will I give into the hand of their enemies, which shall spoil them, and take them, and carry them to Babylon.

6 And thou, Pashur, and all that dwell in thine house shall go into captivity: and thou shalt come to Babylon, and there thou shalt die, and shalt be buried there, thou, and all those who love thee well, unto whom thou hast prophesied with lies.

7 O LORD, thou hast seduced me, and I was seduced: thou wert stronger than I, and hast overcome me: I am in derision daily, every one mocketh me.

8 For since I spoke *out*, I raised my voice crying, Violence and destruction; because the word of the LORD has been a reproach unto me, and a derision, daily.

9 And I said, I will not make mention of him, nor speak any more in his name. But he was in my heart as a burning fire *and* within my bones; I tried to forbear, and I could not.

10 For I heard the murmuring of many, fear on every side, Report, and we will report it. All my friends watched to see if I would stumble. Peradventure he will deceive himself, they said, and we shall prevail against him, and we shall take our revenge on him.

11 But the LORD *is* with me as a powerful giant: therefore my persecutors shall stumble, and they shall not prevail: they shall be greatly ashamed; for they shall not prosper: they shall have everlasting confusion which shall never be forgotten.

12 O LORD of the hosts, who examineth that which is just, who seest the kidneys and the heart, let me see thy vengeance on them: for unto thee have I opened my cause.

13 Sing unto the LORD, praise ye the LORD: for he hath delivered the soul of the poor from the hand of evildoers.

14 Cursed *be* the day wherein I was born: let not the day wherein my mother bore me be blessed.

15 Cursed *be* the man who brought tidings to my father, saying, A man child is born unto thee; making him very glad.

16 And let that man be as the cities which the LORD overthrew, and repented not: and let him hear the cry in the morning, and the shouting at noontide;

17 because he slew me not in the womb, and my mother would have been

my grave, and her womb perpetual conception.

18 Wherefore came I forth out of the womb? To see labour and sorrow, that my days should be consumed with shame?

Chapter 21

1 The word which came unto Jeremiah from the LORD, when king Zedekiah sent unto him Pashur the son of Melchiah, and Zephaniah *the* priest, the son of Maaseiah, saying,

2 Enquire, I pray thee, of the LORD for us; for Nebuchadrezzar king of Babylon maketh war against us; peradventure the LORD will deal with us according to all his wondrous works, and *he* will go up from upon us.

3 And said Jeremiah unto them, Thus shall ye say to Zedekiah:

4 Thus hath the LORD God of Israel said; Behold, I turn back the weapons of war that *are* in your hands, wherewith ye fight against the king of Babylon, and *against* the Chaldeans, which besiege you without the walls, and I will assemble them into the midst of this city.

5 And I myself will fight against you with an outstretched hand and with a strong arm, even in anger, and in fury, and in great wrath.

6 And I will smite the inhabitants of this city, both man and beast: they shall die of a great pestilence.

7 And afterward, thus hath the LORD said, I will deliver Zedekiah king of Judah, and his servants, and the people, and such as are left in this city from the pestilence, from the sword, and from the famine, into the hand of Nebuchadrezzar king of Babylon, and into the hand of their enemies, and into the hand of those that seek their souls: and *he* shall smite them with the edge of the sword; he shall not forgive them, neither have pity, nor have mercy.

8 And unto this people thou shalt say, Thus hath the LORD said; Behold, I set before you the way of life, and the way of death.

9 He that abideth in this city shall die by the sword, or by the famine, or by the pestilence: but he that goeth out, and falleth to the Chaldeans that besiege you, he shall live, and his soul shall be unto him for a spoil.

10 For I have set my face against this city for evil, and not for good, saith the LORD: it shall be given into the hand of the king of Babylon, and he shall burn it with fire.

11 And to the house of the king of Judah, *say*, Hear ye the word of the LORD;

12 O house of David, thus hath the LORD said; Execute judgment early, and deliver *him that is* oppressed out of the hand of the oppressor, lest my fury go forth like fire, and burn that none can quench *it*, because of the evil of your doings.

13 Behold, I *am* against thee, O inhabitant of the valley of the rock of the plain, saith the LORD; which say, Who shall come up against us? or who shall enter into our habitations?

14 I will visit you according to the fruit of your doings, said the LORD: and I will kindle a fire in your forest, and it shall devour all things round about it.

Chapter 22

1 Thus hath the LORD said; Go down to the house of the king of Judah, and speak there this word,

2 And say, Hear the word of the LORD, O king of Judah, that sittest upon the throne of David, thou, and thy servants, and thy people that enter in by these gates:

3 Thus hath the LORD said; Execute ye judgment and righteousness, and deliver the oppressed out of the hand of the oppressor: and do not deceive, neither steal from the stranger, nor from the fatherless, nor from the widow, neither shed innocent blood in this place.

4 For if ye effectively obey this word, then shall there enter in by the gates of this house the kings seated by David upon his throne, riding in chariots and on horses, he, and his and his servants, and his people.

5 But if ye will not hear these words, I swear by myself, said the LORD, that this house shall become a desolation.

6 For thus hath the LORD said regarding the house of the king of Judah; Thou *art* Gilead unto me, *and* the head of Lebanon: *yet* surely I will make thee a wilderness, *and* cities *which* are not inhabited.

7 And I will appoint destroyers against thee, every one with his weapons: and they shall cut down thy choice cedars, and cast *them* into the fire.

8 And many Gentiles shall pass by this city, and they shall say every man to his neighbour, Wherefore hath the LORD done thus unto this great city?

9 Then they shall answer, Because they have forsaken the covenant of the LORD their God, and worshipped other gods, and served them.

10 Weep ye not for the dead, neither bemoan him: *but* weep sore for him that goeth away: for he shall return no more, nor see his native country.

11 For thus hath the LORD said of Shallum the son of Josiah king of Judah, which reigned instead of Josiah his father, He who went forth out of this place, shall not return thither any more;

12 but he shall die in the place where they have led him captive, and shall see this land no more.

13 Woe unto him that buildeth his house and not in righteousness, and his chambers and not in judgment, using his neighbour's service without wages, and giving him not *the wages of* his work!

14 That saith, I will build me a wide house and large chambers, and cutteth him out windows; and covereth it with cedar, and painteth it with vermilion.

15 Shalt thou reign, because thou closest *thyself*

in cedar? did not thy father eat and drink, and do judgment and justice, *and* then *it was* well with him?

16 He judged the cause of the poor and needy; then *it was* well *with him.* Is this not to know me? said the LORD.

17 But thine eyes and thine heart *are* not but for thy covetousness, and for to shed innocent blood, and for oppression, and for violence, to do *it.*

18 Therefore thus hath the LORD said concerning Jehoiakim the son of Josiah king of Judah; They shall not lament for him, *saying,* Ah my brother! and, Ah sister! they shall not lament for him, *saying,* Ah lord! or, Ah his glory!

19 He shall be buried with the burial of an ass, drawn and cast forth beyond the gates of Jerusalem.

20 Go up to Lebanon, and cry; and lift up thy voice in Bashan, and cry unto all parts: for all thy lovers are destroyed.

21 I spoke unto thee in thy prosperity; *but* thou saidst, I will not hear. This *hath been* thy way from thy youth, that thou hast never heard my voice.

22 The wind shall eat up all thy pastors, and thy lovers shall go into captivity: surely then shalt thou be ashamed and confound thyself because of all thy malice.

23 Thou didst inhabit Lebanon, thou didst make thy nest in the cedars. How shalt thou cry out when pangs come upon thee, the pain as of a woman in travail!

24 *As* I live, saith the LORD, though Coniah the son of Jehoiakim king of Judah were the signet upon my right hand, yet would I pluck thee thence;

25 and I will give thee into the hand of them that seek thy soul, and into the hand *of them* whose face thou fearest, even into the hand of Nebuchadrezzar king of Babylon, and into the hand of the Chaldeans.

26 And I will cast thee out, and thy mother that bore thee, into another country, where ye were not born; and there shall ye die.

27 But to the land whereunto they desire to return, thither shall they not return.

28 *Is* this man Coniah a despised broken idol? *is he* a vessel wherein *is* no pleasure? wherefore are they cast out, he and his generation, and are cast into a land which they know not?

29 O earth, earth, earth, hear the word of the LORD.
30 Thus hath the LORD said, Write *what shall be* of this man deprived of *a* generation, a man unto whom nothing shall prosper in all the days of his life: for no man of his seed who sitteth upon the throne of David and ruleth over Judah shall prosper.

Chapter 23

1 Woe be unto the pastors that waste and scatter the sheep of my pasture! said the LORD.
2 Therefore thus hath the LORD God of Israel said unto the pastors that feed my people; Ye have scattered my flock, and driven them away, and have not visited them: behold, *I* visit upon you the evil of your doings, said the LORD.
3 And I will gather the remnant of my sheep out of all the lands where I have driven them, and will cause them to return to their folds; and they shall be fruitful and increase.
4 And I will set up shepherds over them which shall feed them: and they shall fear no more, nor be dismayed, neither shall they be lacking, said the LORD.
5 Behold, the days come, saith the LORD, that I will raise unto David a righteous Branch, and a King shall reign and prosper, and shall execute judgment and righteousness in the earth.
6 In his days Judah shall be saved, and Israel shall dwell safely: and this *shall be* his name whereby they shall call him, THE LORD OUR RIGHTEOUSNESS.
7 Therefore, behold, the days come, said the LORD, and they shall no more say, The LORD liveth, which brought up the children of Israel out of the land of Egypt;
8 But, The LORD liveth, which brought up and brought the seed of the house of Israel out of the land of the north *wind*, and from all the lands where I had driven them; and they shall dwell in their *own* land.
9 My heart is broken within me because of the prophets; all my bones shake; I was like a drunken man, and like a man whom wine hath overcome, before the LORD, and before of the words of his holiness.
10 For the land is full of adulterers; for because of the oath the land is de-

serted; the booths of the wilderness are dried up, and their course was evil, and their force *was* not right.

11 For both prophet and priest are feigned; even in my house have I found their wickedness, said the LORD.

12 Wherefore their way shall be unto them as slippery *ways* in the darkness: they shall be driven on, and fall therein: for I will bring evil upon them, *even* the year of their visitation, saith the LORD.

13 And I have seen folly in the prophets of Samaria; they prophesied in Baal, and caused my people Israel to err.

14 I have seen also in the prophets of Jerusalem a horrible thing: they committed adultery, and walked by lies: they strengthened also the hands of evildoers, that none is converted from his malice: they are all of them unto me as Sodom, and the inhabitants thereof as Gomorrah.

15 Therefore, thus hath the LORD of the hosts said against those prophets; Behold, I will cause them to eat wormwood, and make them drink the waters of gall: for from the prophets of Jerusalem is hypocrisy gone forth upon all the land.

16 Thus hath the LORD of the hosts said, Hearken not unto the words of the prophets that prophesy unto you: they make you vain: they speak a vision of their own heart, *and* not out of the mouth of the LORD.

17 They say boldly unto those that stir me to anger, The LORD hath said, Ye shall have peace; and they say unto every one that walketh after the imagination of his own heart, No evil shall come upon you.

18 For who hath stood in the secret of the LORD, and hath seen and heard his word? who hath marked his word, and heard *it*?

19 Behold, that the whirlwind of the LORD shall go forth with fury, and the whirlwind which is ready, shall fall *grievously* upon the head of the wicked.

20 The anger of the LORD shall not return, until he hath executed, and until he hath performed the thoughts of his heart: in the last of the days ye shall understand it with understanding.

21 I did not send those prophets, yet they ran: *I* did not speak to them, yet they prophesied.

22 But if they had stood in my secret, they would also have caused my people to hear my words, and they would have caused them to return from their evil way, and from the evil of their doings.

23 *Am* I God of the near *only*, said the LORD, and not God of the far?

24 Can any hide himself in hiding places that I shall not see him? said the LORD. Do not I fill heaven and earth? said the LORD.

25 I have heard what those prophets said, that prophesy lies in my name, saying, I have dreamed, I have dreamed.

26 How long shall *this* be in the heart of the prophets that prophesy lies and that prophesy the deceit of their own heart?

27 Do they not think to cause my people to forget my name by their dreams which they tell every man to his neighbour, so much that their fathers have forgotten my name for Baal?

28 The prophet with whom *the* dream came, let him tell *the* dream; and he with whom my word came, let him speak my true word. What *is* the chaff to the wheat? said the LORD.

29 *Is* not my word like as a fire? saith the LORD; and like a hammer *that* breaketh the rock in pieces?

30 Therefore, behold, I *am* against the prophets, saith the LORD, that steal my words every one from his neighbour.

31 Behold, I *am* against the prophets, saith the LORD, that sweeten their tongues, and say, He said.

32 Behold, I *am* against them that prophesy false dreams, saith the LORD, and did tell them, and caused my people to err by their lies, and by their flattery; yet I sent them not, nor commanded them: and they did not profit this people at all, said the LORD.

33 And when this people, or the prophet, or the priest, shall ask thee, saying, What *is* the burden of the LORD? thou shalt then say unto them, What burden? I will even forsake you, said the LORD.

34 And *as for* the prophet, and the priest, and the people, that shall say, The burden of the LORD, I will visit upon that man and upon his house.

35 Thus shall ye say every one to his neighbour, and every one to his brother,

What hath the LORD answered? and, What hath the LORD spoken?

36 And never again shall it come to *your* memory to say, The burden of the LORD: for every man's word shall be his burden; for ye have perverted the words of the living God, of the LORD of the hosts, our God.

37 Thus shalt thou say to the prophet, What hath the LORD answered thee? and, What hath the LORD spoken?

38 But if ye say, The burden of the LORD; therefore thus hath the LORD said; Because ye say this word, The burden of the LORD, and I have sent unto you, saying, Ye shall not say, The burden of the LORD;

39 therefore, behold, I, even I, will utterly forget you, and I will uproot you from my presence, and the city that I gave you and your fathers:

40 And I will place an everlasting reproach upon you, and eternal shame, which shall never be forgotten.

Chapter 24

1 The LORD showed me, and, behold, two baskets of figs *were* set before the temple of the LORD, after that Nebuchadrezzar king of Babylon had carried away captive Jeconiah the son of Jehoiakim king of Judah, and the princes of Judah, with the carpenters and smiths, from Jerusalem, and had taken them to Babylon.

2 One basket *had* very good figs, *even* like the figs *that are* first ripe: and the other basket *had* very evil figs, which could not be eaten, they were so evil.

3 Then said the LORD unto me, What seest thou, Jeremiah? And I said, Figs; the good figs, very good; and the evil, very evil; so evil that they cannot be eaten.

4 Again the word of the LORD came unto me, saying,

5 Thus hath the LORD God of Israel said; Like these good figs, so will I acknowledge them that are carried away captive of Judah, whom I have sent out of this place into the land of the Chaldeans for *their* good.

6 For I will set my eyes upon them for good, and I will return them to this land: and I will build them, and not pull *them* down; and I will plant them, and not pluck *them* up.

7 And I will give them a heart that they might know me, that I *am* the LORD: and they shall be my people, and I will be their God: for

they shall return unto me
with their whole heart.

8 And as the evil figs, which
cannot be eaten, they are
so evil; surely thus saith the
LORD, So will I give
Zedekiah the king of Judah,
and his princes, and the
residue of Jerusalem, that
remained in this land, and
that dwell in the land of
Egypt:

9 And I give them for a reproach, for evil unto all the
kingdoms of the earth; for
infamy, and for example,
and for a proverb, and for a
curse unto all the places
where I shall drive them.

10 And I will send the
sword, the famine, and the
pestilence, upon them, until they be consumed from
off the land that I gave unto
them and to their fathers.

Chapter 25

1 The word that came to
Jeremiah concerning all the
people of Judah in the
fourth year of Jehoiakim
the son of Josiah king of
Judah, which *is* the first
year of Nebuchadrezzar
king of Babylon;

2 this spoke Jeremiah the
prophet unto all the people
of Judah, and to all the inhabitants of Jerusalem,
saying,

3 From the thirteenth year
of Josiah the son of Amon

king of Judah, even to
this day, which are twenty-
three years, the word of the
LORD hath come unto me,
and I have spoken unto
you, rising early and giving
notice; but ye have not
hearkened.

4 And the LORD hath sent
unto you all his servants
the prophets, rising early
and sending *them*; but ye
have not hearkened, nor
inclined your ear to hear,

5 when they said, Turn ye
again now every one from
his evil way, and from the
evil of your doings, and
dwell in the land that the
LORD hath given unto you
and to your fathers for ever
and ever:

6 And go not after other
gods to serve them, and to
worship them, and provoke
me not to anger with the
works of your hands; and I
will do you no hurt.

7 Yet ye have not hearkened unto me, saith the
LORD; that ye might pro-
voke me to anger with the
works of your hands to your
own hurt.

8 Therefore thus saith the
LORD of the hosts; Because
ye have not heard my
words,

9 behold, I will send and
take all the families of the
north *wind*, saith the LORD,

and Nebuchadrezzar the king of Babylon, my servant, and will bring them against this land, and against the inhabitants thereof, and against all these nations round about, and will utterly destroy them, and make them an astonishment, and an hissing, and perpetual desolations.

10 And I will cause them to lose the voice of mirth, and the voice of gladness, the voice of the bridegroom, and the voice of the bride, the sound of the millstones, and the light of the candle.

11 And this whole land shall be a desolation, *and* an astonishment; and these Gentiles shall serve the king of Babylon seventy years.

12 And it shall come to pass, when seventy years are accomplished, *that* I will visit upon the king of Babylon, and upon that people their *own* evil, said the LORD, and upon the land of the Chaldeans, and will make it perpetual desolations.

13 And I will bring upon that land all my words which I have spoken against it, with all that is written in this book, prophesied by Jeremiah against all the Gentiles.

14 For many Gentiles and great kings shall serve themselves of them also: and I will recompense them according to their deeds, and according to the works of their own hands.

15 For thus hath the LORD God of Israel said unto me; Take the wine cup of this fury from my hand, and cause all the Gentiles, to whom I send thee, to drink of it.

16 And they shall drink, and be moved, and become mad, before the sword that I will send among them.

17 Then took I the cup from the LORD'S hand, and made all the Gentiles to drink, unto whom the LORD had sent me:

18 Unto Jerusalem, and to the cities of Judah, and to the kings thereof, and to the princes thereof, that I might place them into desolation, into astonishment, and into hissing, and into *a* curse, as this day;

19 unto Pharaoh king of Egypt, and to his servants, and to his princes, and to all his people;

20 and to all the mingled people, and to all the kings of the land of Uz, and to all the kings of *the* land of Palestine, and to Ashkelon, and *to* Gaza, and *to* Ekron, and to the remnant of Ashdod;

21 to Edom, and *to* Moab, and to the children of Ammon,

22 and to all the kings of Tyre, and to all the kings of Zidon, and to all the kings of the isles which are of that side of the sea;

23 and to Dedan, and *to* Tema, and *to* Buz, and to all *that are* in the utmost corners;

24 and to all the kings of Arabia, and to all the kings of the *mingled* peoples, the Arabia that dwelleth in the desert;

25 and to all the kings of Zimri, and to all the kings of Elam, and to all the kings of the Medes;

26 and to all the kings of the north *wind*, those of far and those of near, one with another, and to all the kingdoms of the earth, which *are* upon the face of the earth: and the king of Sheshach [*Babylon*] shall drink after them.

27 Therefore thou shalt say unto them, Thus hath the LORD of the hosts, the God of Israel said; Drink ye, and be drunken, and vomit, and fall, and ye shall not rise in the presence of the sword which I send among you.

28 And it shall be, if they refuse to take the cup from thine hand to drink, then shalt thou say unto them, Thus hath the LORD of the hosts said; Ye must certainly drink.

29 For, Behold, I begin to bring evil upon the city which is called by my name, and should ye only be absolved? Ye shall not be absolved: for I bring *the* sword upon all the inhabitants of the earth, said the LORD of the hosts.

30 Therefore, thou shalt prophesy against them all these words, and say unto them, The LORD shall roar from on high, and from the habitation of his holiness he shall utter his voice; in fury he shall roar upon his habitation; he shall sing the song of those that tread *grapes*, against all the inhabitants of the earth.

31 The noise came *even* to the ends of the earth; for it is judgment of the LORD with the Gentiles: he is the Judge of all flesh; he will give them *that are* wicked to the sword, said the LORD.

32 Thus saith the LORD of the hosts, Behold, the evil goeth forth from nation to nation, and a great whirlwind shall be raised up from the coasts of the earth.

33 And the slain of the LORD shall be in that day from *one* end of the earth even unto the *other* end of the earth: they shall not be lamented, neither gathered, nor be buried; they shall be as dung upon the ground.

34 Howl, ye shepherds, and cry; and wallow yourselves *in the ashes*, ye principals of the flock: for the days of your slaughter and of your dispersions are accomplished; and ye shall fall like an enticing vessel.

35 And the shepherds shall have no way to flee, nor *for* the principals of the flock to escape.

36 *The* voice of the cry of the shepherds, and an howling of the principals of the flock, *shall be heard!* For the LORD hath spoiled their pasture.

37 And the quiet pastures shall be cut off by the fierce anger of the LORD.

38 He hath forsaken his habitation, as the *young* lion: for their land is desolate because of the fierceness of the oppressor, and because of his fierce anger.

Chapter 26

1 In the beginning of the reign of Jehoiakim the son of Josiah king of Judah came this word from the LORD, saying,

2 Thus hath the LORD said; Stand in the court of the LORD'S house, and speak unto all the cities of Judah, which come to worship in the LORD'S house, all the words that I commanded thee to speak unto them; diminish not a word:

3 Peradventure they will hearken, and turn every man from his evil way, that I may repent me of the evil, which I purpose to do unto them because of the evil of their doings.

4 And thou shalt say unto them, Thus hath the LORD said; If ye will not hearken to me, to walk in my law, which I have set before you,

5 to hearken to the words of my servants the prophets, whom I send unto you, rising up early and sending *them*, unto whom ye have not hearkened;

6 then will I make this house like Shiloh, and will give this city as *a* curse to all the Gentiles of the earth.

7 And the priests, the prophets and all the people heard Jeremiah speaking these words in the house of the LORD.

8 Now it came to pass, when Jeremiah had made an end of speaking all that the LORD had commanded *him* to speak unto all the people, that the priests and the prophets and all the people took him, saying, Thou shalt surely die.

9 Why hast thou prophesied in the name of the LORD, saying, This house shall be like Shiloh, and this city shall be desolate without an inhabitant? And all the people were gathered against Jeremiah in the house of the LORD.

10 When the princes of Judah heard these things, then they came up from the king's house unto the house of the LORD, and sat down in the entry of the new gate of the LORD'S *house.*

11 Then spoke the priests and the prophets unto all the princes and to all the people, saying, This man *is* worthy to die; for he hath prophesied against this city, as ye have heard with your ears.

12 Then spoke Jeremiah unto all the princes and to all the people, saying, The LORD sent me to prophesy against this house and against this city all the words that ye have heard.

13 Therefore now amend your ways and your doings, and hear the voice of the LORD your God; and the LORD himself will repent of the evil that he hath pronounced against you.

14 As for me, behold, I *am* in your hands: do with me as seemeth good and meet un to you.

15 But know ye for certain, that if ye put me to death, ye shall surely bring innocent blood upon yourselves, and upon this city, and upon the inhabitants thereof: for of a truth the LORD hath sent me unto you to speak all these words in your ears.

16 Then said the princes and all the people unto the priests and to the prophets; This man *is* not worthy to die: for he hath spoken to us in the name of the LORD our God.

17 Then rose up certain of the elders of the land, and spoke to all the congregation of the people, saying,

18 Micah the Morasthite prophesied in the days of Hezekiah king of Judah, and spoke to all the people of Judah, saying, Thus hath the LORD of the hosts said; Zion shall be plowed *like* a field, and Jerusalem shall become heaps, and the temple mount as the high places of a forest.

19 Did Hezekiah king of Judah and all Judah put him at all to death? did he not fear the LORD, and besought the LORD, and the LORD himself repented of the evil which he had pronounced against them? Shall we commit such great evil against our souls?

20 There was also a man that prophesied in the name of the LORD, Urijah the son of Shemaiah of Kirjathjearim, who prophesied against this city and against this land according to all the words of Jeremiah:

21 And Jehoiakim the king heard his words, and all his mighty men, and all the princes, and the king sought to put him to death: but when Urijah understood it, he was afraid, and fled, and went into Egypt.

22 And Jehoiakim the king sent men into Egypt, *namely,* Elnathan the son of Achbor, and *certain* men with him into Egypt;

23 and they fetched forth Urijah out of Egypt, and brought hi . unto Jehoiakim the king; who slew him with the sword, and cast his dead body into the graves of the common people.

24 Nevertheless the hand of Ahikam the son of Shaphan was with Jeremiah, that they should not give him into the hand of the people to put him to death.

Chapter 27

1 In the beginning of the reign of Jehoiakim the son of Josiah king of Judah came this word unto Jeremiah from the LORD, saying,

2 Thus hath the LORD said unto me; Make thee bonds and yokes, and put them upon thy neck;

3 and thou shalt send them to the king of Edom, and to the king of Moab, and to the king of the Ammonites, and to the king of Tyre, and to the king of Zidon, by the hand of the ambassadors which come to Jerusalem unto Zedekiah king of Judah;

4 And thou shalt command them to say unto their masters, Thus hath the LORD of the hosts, the God of Israel said; Thus shall ye say unto your masters;

5 I have made the earth, the man and the beast that *are* upon the face of the earth, by my great power and by my outstretched arm, and have given it unto whom was upright in my eyes.

6 And now have *I* given all these lands into the hand of Nebuchadnezzar the king of Babylon, my servant; and even the beasts of the field have I given him that they might serve him.

7 And all the Gentiles shall serve him, and his son, and his son's son, until the time of his own land shall come also: and many nations and great kings shall serve him.

8 And it shall come to pass, *that* the people and the kingdom which will not serve Nebuchadnezzar the king of Babylon, and that will not put their neck under the yoke of the king of Babylon, that people will I visit, saith the LORD, with the sword, and with the famine, and with the pestilence, until I have finished placing *all of them* under his hand.

9 Therefore hearken not ye to your prophets, nor to your diviners, nor to your dreams, nor to your sorcerers, nor to your enchanters, which speak unto you, saying, Ye shall not serve the king of Babylon:

10 For they prophesy a lie unto you, to remove you far from your land; and that *I* should drive you out, and ye should perish.

11 But the people that submit their neck under the yoke of the king of Babylon, and serve him, those will I let remain still in their own land, said the LORD; and they shall till it, and dwell therein.

12 I spoke also to Zedekiah king of Judah according to all these words, saying, Submit your necks under the yoke of the king of Babylon, and serve him and his people, and live.

13 Why will ye die, thou and thy people, by the sword, by the famine, and by the pestilence, as the LORD hath spoken unto the people that will not serve the king of Babylon?

14 Therefore hearken not unto the words of the prophets that speak unto you, saying, Ye shall not serve the king of Babylon: for they prophesy a lie unto you.

15 For I have not sent them, saith the LORD, yet they prophesy a lie in my name; that I might drive you out, and that ye might perish, ye, and the prophets that prophesy unto you.

16 Also I spoke to the priests and to all this people, saying, Thus hath the LORD said; Hearken not unto the words of your prophets that prophesy unto you, saying, Behold, the vessels of the LORD'S house shall now shortly be brought again from Babylon: for they prophesy a lie unto you.

17 Hearken not unto them; serve the king of Babylon, and live: wherefore should this city be laid waste?

18 But if they *be* prophets, and if the word of the LORD be with them, let them pray now unto the LORD of hosts, that the vessels which are left in the house of the LORD, and *in* the house of the king of Judah, and at Jerusalem, go not to Babylon.

19 For thus hath the LORD of the hosts said concerning the pillars, and concerning the sea, and concerning the bases, and concerning the residue of the vessels that remain in this city,

20 which Nebuchadnezzar king of Babylon took not, when he carried away captive Jeconiah the son of Jehoiakim king of Judah from Jerusalem to Babylon, and all the nobles of Judah and Jerusalem;

21 Yea, thus hath the LORD of the hosts the God of Israel said concerning the vessels that remained in the house of the LORD, and in the house of the king of Judah and in Jerusalem;

22 they shall be carried to Babylon, and there shall they be until the day that I visit them, said the LORD; and afterwards I will bring them up, and restore them to this place.

Chapter 28

1 And it came to pass the same year, in the beginning of the reign of Zedekiah king of Judah, in the fourth year, *and* in the fifth month, *that* Hananiah the son of Azur the prophet, which *was* of Gibeon, spoke unto me in the house of the LORD, in the presence of the priests and of all the people, saying,

2 Thus hath the LORD of the hosts the God of Israel spoken, saying, I have broken the yoke of the king of Babylon.

3 Within two full years will I bring again into this place all the vessels of the LORD'S house, that Nebuchadnezzar king of Babylon took away from this place, and carried them to Babylon:

4 And I will bring again to this place Jeconiah the son of Jehoiakim king of Judah, with all the captives of Judah, that went into Babylon, saith the LORD: for I will break the yoke of the king of Babylon.

5 Then the prophet Jeremiah said unto the prophet

Hananiah in the presence of the priests, and in the presence of all the people that stood in the house of the LORD,

6 therefore the prophet Jeremiah said, Amen: the LORD do so: the LORD confirm thy words with which thou hast prophesied that the vessels of the LORD'S house, and all those that are carried away captive, are to be returned from Babylon unto this place.

7 Nevertheless hear thou now this word that I speak in thine ears, and in the ears of all the people,

8 The prophets that have been before me and before thee of old prophesied both against many countries, and against great kingdoms, of war, and of evil, and of pestilence.

9 The prophet which prophesied of peace, when the word of the prophet should come to pass, *then* shall the prophet be known, that the LORD hath truly sent him.

10 Then Hananiah the prophet took the yoke from off the prophet Jeremiah's neck, and broke it.

11 And Hananiah spoke in the presence of all the people, saying, Thus hath the LORD said; Even so will

I break the yoke of Nebuchadnezzar king of Babylon from the neck of all the Gentiles within the space of two full years. And the prophet Jeremiah went his way.

12 And after Hananiah the prophet had broken the yoke from off the neck of the prophet Jeremiah, the word of the LORD came unto Jeremiah, saying,

13 Go and tell Hananiah, saying, Thus hath the LORD said; Thou hast broken the yokes of wood; but thou shalt make yokes of iron instead.

14 For thus hath the LORD of the hosts the God of Israel said; I have put a yoke of iron upon the neck of all these Gentiles, that they may serve Nebuchadnezzar king of Babylon; and they shall serve him: and I have even given him the beasts of the field.

15 Then said the prophet Jeremiah unto Hananiah the prophet, Hear now, Hananiah; The LORD hath not sent thee; and thou hast made this people to trust in a lie.

16 Therefore thus hath the LORD said; Behold, I will send thee away from upon the face of the earth: this year thou shalt die, because thou hast spoken rebellion against the LORD.

17 So Hananiah the prophet died the same year in the seventh month.

Chapter 29

1 Now these *are* the words of the letter that Jeremiah the prophet sent from Jerusalem unto the residue of the elders which were carried away captives, and to the priests, and to the prophets, and to all the people whom Nebuchadnezzar had carried away captive from Jerusalem to Babylon;

2 (after that Jeconiah the king, and the queen, and the eunuchs, the princes of Judah and Jerusalem, and the carpenters, and the smiths, were departed from Jerusalem;)

3 by the hand of Elasah the son of Shaphan, and Gemariah the son of Hilkiah, (whom Zedekiah king of Judah sent unto Babylon to Nebuchadnezzar king of Babylon) saying,

4 Thus hath the LORD of the hosts the God of Israel said, unto all that are carried away captives, whom I have caused to be carried away from Jerusalem unto Babylon,

5 Build ye houses, and dwell *in them*; and plant gardens, and eat the fruit of them;

6 take ye wives, and beget sons and daughters; give wives unto your sons, and give husbands unto your daughters, that they may bear sons and daughters; that ye may be multiplied there, and not diminished.

7 And seek the peace of the city where I have caused you to be carried away captives, and pray unto the LORD for it: for in the peace thereof shall ye have peace.

8 For thus hath the LORD of the hosts the God of Israel said; Let not your prophets and your diviners that *be* in the midst of you, deceive you, neither hearken to your dreams which ye dream.

9 For they prophesy falsely unto you in my name: I have not sent them, said the LORD.

10 For thus hath the LORD said, That after seventy years be accomplished at Babylon I will visit you, and quicken my good word upon you, to cause you to return to this place.

11 For I know the thoughts that I think concerning you, said the LORD, thoughts of peace, and not of evil, to give you the end that you wait for.

12 Then shall ye call upon me, and ye shall walk *in my ways* and pray unto me, and I will hearken unto you.

13 And ye shall seek me, and find *me*, for ye shall seek me with all your heart.

14 And I will be found of you, said the LORD: and I will turn away your captivity, and I will gather you from all the Gentiles, and from all the places where I have driven you, said the LORD; and I will bring you again into the place whence I caused you to be carried away captive.

15 But ye have said, The LORD hath raised us up prophets in Babylon;

16 *Know* that thus hath the LORD said of the king that sitteth upon the throne of David, and of all the people that dwelleth in this city, *and* of your brethren that are not gone forth with you into captivity;

17 thus hath the LORD of the hosts said; Behold, I will send upon them the sword, the famine, and the pestilence, and will make them like the evil figs, that cannot be eaten, they are so evil.

18 And I will persecute them with the sword, with the famine, and with the pestilence, and will give them over as a reproach to all the kingdoms of the earth, as a curse, and as an astonishment, and an hissing, and an affront, unto all the Gentiles where I have driven them:

19 Because they did not hearken unto my words, said the LORD, which I sent unto them by my servants the prophets, rising up early and sending *them*; but ye did not hear, said the LORD.

20 Hear ye therefore the word of the LORD, all ye of the captivity, whom I have cast out of Jerusalem unto Babylon:

21 Thus hath the LORD of the hosts the God of Israel said *regarding* Ahab the son of Kolaiah, and *regarding* Zedekiah the son of Maaseiah, which prophesy falsely unto you in my name; Behold, *I* deliver them into the hand of Nebuchadrezzar king of Babylon; and he shall slay them before your eyes;

22 and of them shall be taken up a curse by all the captivity of Judah which *are* in Babylon, saying, The LORD make thee like Zedekiah and like Ahab, whom the king of Babylon roasted in the fire;

23 because they have committed villainy in Israel, and have committed adultery with their neighbours' wives, and have spoken a word falsely in my name, which I have not commanded them; even I know, and *am* a witness, saith the LORD.

24 *Thus* shalt thou also speak to Shemaiah the Nehelamite, saying,
25 Thus hath the LORD of the hosts the God of Israel spoken, saying, Because thou hast sent letters in thy name unto all the people that *are* at Jerusalem, and to Zephaniah the priest, the son of Maaseiah, and to all the priests, saying,
26 The LORD hath made thee priest in the stead of Jehoiada the priest, that ye should preside in the house of the LORD over every man *that is* furious and prophesieth, putting him in the prison, and in the stocks.
27 Now therefore why hast thou not reprehended Jeremiah of Anathoth, for prophesying *falsely* unto you?
28 For therefore he sent unto us *in* Babylon, saying, This *captivity is* long: build ye houses, and dwell *in*

them; and plant gardens, and eat the fruit of them.
29 And Zephaniah the priest read this letter in the ears of Jeremiah the prophet.
30 Then came the word of the LORD unto Jeremiah, saying,
31 Send to all them of the captivity, saying, Thus hath the LORD said *concerning* Shemaiah the Nehelamite; Because that Shemaiah hath prophesied unto you, and I sent him not, and he caused you to trust upon *a* lie:
32 Therefore thus hath the LORD said; Behold, I visit upon Shemaiah the Nehelamite, and upon his generation: he shall not have a man to dwell among this people; neither shall he behold that good which I do unto my people, said the LORD; because he hath spoken rebellion against the LORD.

Chapter 30

1 The word that came to Jeremiah from the LORD, saying,
2 Thus hath the LORD God of Israel spoken, saying, Write thee all the words that I have spoken unto thee in a book.
3 For, Behold, the days come, said the LORD, that I

will turn the captivity of my people Israel and Judah, said the LORD: and I will cause them to return to the land that I gave to their fathers, and they shall possess it.

4 And these *are* the words that the LORD spoke concerning Israel and *concerning* Judah.

5 For thus hath the LORD said; We have heard a voice of trembling, of terror, and not of peace.

6 Ask ye now, and see whether the man doth travail with child? for I have seen that every man hath his hands on his loins, as a woman in travail, and all faces have turned pale.

7 Alas! for that day *is* great, so that none *is* like it: it *is* even the time of Jacob's trouble; but he shall be saved out of it.

8 For it shall come to pass in that day, saith the LORD of the hosts, *that* I will break his yoke from off thy neck, and will burst thy bonds, and strangers shall no more place him in servitude,

9 but they shall serve the LORD their God, and David their king, whom I will raise up unto them.

10 Therefore fear thou not, O my servant Jacob, saith the LORD; neither be dismayed, O Israel: for, behold, I am he that saveth thee from afar, and thy seed from the land of their captivity; and Jacob shall turn, and shall rest, and be quiet, and there shall be no one *left* to scatter *him.*

11 For I *shall be* with thee, saith the LORD, to save thee: and I shall make a full end in all Gentiles among whom I scattered thee, yet I will not make a full end of thee: but I will chastise thee with judgment, and will not cut thee off altogether.

12 For thus hath the LORD said, Thy breach *is* incurable, *and* thy sore *is* grievous.

13 *There is* none to judge thy cause unto health; there is no cure, nor *are there* any medicines for thee.

14 All thy lovers have forgotten thee; they seek thee not; for I have wounded thee with the wound of an enemy, with the whip of a cruel one, for the multitude of thine iniquity; *because* thy sins were increased.

15 Why criest thou for thine affliction? thy sorrow *is* incurable for the greatness of thine iniquity: *because* thy sins were increased, I have done these things unto thee.

16 Therefore all they that devour thee shall be devoured; and all those that afflict thee, every one of them, shall go into captivity; and they that trampled upon thee shall be trodden down, and all that prey upon thee will I give for a prey.

17 For I will cause healing to come for thee, and I will heal thee of thy wounds, said the LORD; because they called thee an Outcast, *saying*, This *is* Zion, whom no man seeketh after.

18 Thus hath the LORD said; Behold, I will turn the captivity of Jacob's tents, and have mercy on his dwelling places; and the city shall be builded upon her own hill, and the temple according to her judgment shall stand.

19 And out of them shall proceed thanksgiving and the voice of people that *live* in joy: and I will multiply them, and they shall not be decreased; I will multiply them, and they shall not be cut down.

20 Their sons also shall be as at first, and their congregation shall be confirmed before me, and I will visit all their oppressors.

21 And of him shall be their Rock, and from the midst of him shall their Governor come forth; and I will cause him to come near, and he shall draw near unto me: for who *is* this that softened his heart to approach unto me? said the LORD.

22 And ye shall be my people, and I will be your God.

23 Behold, the whirlwind of the LORD goeth forth with fury, the whirlwind which is preparing itself: it shall remain upon the head of the wicked.

24 The fierce anger of the LORD shall not return, until he have done *it*, and until he have performed the intents of his heart: in the end of the days ye shall understand this.

Chapter 31

1 In that time, said the LORD, *I* will be the God unto all the families of Israel, and they shall be my people.

2 Thus hath the LORD said, The people *which were* left of the sword found grace in the wilderness; as *I* went to cause Israel to find rest.

3 The LORD hath appeared of old unto me, *saying*, Yea, I have loved thee with an eternal love: therefore have I put up with thee with mercy.

4 Again I will build thee, and thou shalt be built, O

virgin of Israel: thou shalt again be adorned with thy tambourines, and shalt go forth in the chorus of dancers.

5 Thou shalt yet plant vines upon the mountains of Samaria: the planters shall plant, and shall eat *them* as common things.

6 For there shall be a day in which the watchmen upon the mount Ephraim shall cry, Arise ye, and let us go up into Zion unto the LORD our God.

7 For thus hath the LORD said; Rejoice in Jacob with joy, and *give shouts of* jubilee at the head of the Gentiles: publish ye, praise ye, and say, O LORD, save thy people, the remnant of Israel.

8 Behold, I turn them from the land of the north *wind,* and gather them from the coasts of the earth; there shall be blind and lame among them, and women with child and those that travaileth with child together: a great company shall return thither.

9 They shall come with weeping, but with mercies will I cause them to return: I will cause them to walk by the rivers of waters in a straight way, wherein they shall not stumble: for I

shall be a father to Israel, and Ephraim *shall be* my firstborn.

10 Hear the word of the LORD, O ye Gentiles, and cause it to be known in the isles afar off, and say, He that scattered Israel will gather him, and keep him, as a shepherd *doth* his flock.

11 For the LORD hath redeemed Jacob, and ransomed him from the hand of *him that was* stronger than he.

12 Therefore they shall come and do praises in the height of Zion, and shall run unto the goodness of the LORD, unto the bread, and unto the wine, and unto the oil, and unto the gain of the flock and of the herd: and their soul shall be as a watered garden; and they shall not sorrow any more at all.

13 Then shall the virgin rejoice in the dance, both young men and old together: for I will turn their mourning into joy, and will comfort them, and make them rejoice from their sorrow.

14 And I will satiate the soul of the priest with fatness, and my people shall be filled with my goodness, said the LORD.

15 Thus hath the LORD said; A voice was heard in Ramah, lamentation, *and* bitter weeping; Rachel weeping for her sons, she refused to be comforted regarding her sons, because they perished.

16 Thus hath the LORD said; Refrain thy voice from weeping, and thine eyes from tears: for thy work shall be rewarded, saith the LORD; and they shall come again from the land of the enemy.

17 There is also hope for thine end, saith the LORD, and the sons shall come again to their own border.

18 I have surely heard Ephraim bemoaning himself *thus*; Thou hast afflicted me, and I was chastised, as an indomitable bullock: turn thou me, and I shall be turned; for thou *art* the LORD my God.

19 Surely after that I was turned, I repented; and after that I was instructed, I smote upon *my* thigh: I was ashamed, yea, even confounded, because I did bear the reproach of my youth.

20 Peradventure is Ephraim a precious son unto me? Peradventure *is he unto me* a delightful child? With all this since I spoke of him, I have remembered him constantly. Therefore my bowels are troubled for him; in tenderness I will surely have mercy upon him, saith the LORD.

21 Establish signs, make thee high markers: consider the highway with great care, *even* the way *which* thou camest: return, O virgin of Israel, return unto these thy cities.

22 How long wilt thou wander, O thou backsliding daughter? for the LORD will bring forth a new thing upon the earth, A woman shall compass the man.

23 Thus hath the LORD of the hosts the God of Israel said; Even yet shall they speak this word in the land of Judah and in the cities thereof, when I shall turn their captivity; The LORD bless thee, O habitation of justice, *and* mountain of holiness.

24 And Judah shall dwell in her, and also in all her cities, husbandmen, and they *that* go forth with flocks.

25 For I have satiated the weary soul, and I have filled every sorrowful soul.

26 Upon this I awaked, and beheld; and my sleep was sweet unto me.

27 Behold, the days come, said the LORD, that I will

sow the house of Israel and the house of Judah with the seed of man, and with the seed of beast.

28 And it shall come to pass, *that* like as I have watched over them, to pluck up, and to break down, and to throw down, and to destroy, and to afflict; so will I watch over them, to build, and to plant, said the LORD.

29 In those days they shall say no more, The fathers have eaten the sour grapes, and the children's teeth are set on edge.

30 But every one shall die for his own iniquity: every man that eateth the sour grapes, his teeth shall be set on edge.

31 Behold, the days come, said the LORD, in which I will make a new covenant with the house of Jacob, and with the house of Judah:

32 Not according to the covenant that I made with their fathers in the day *that* I took them by the hand to bring them out of the land of Egypt; because they invalidated my covenant, and although I was an husband unto them, said the LORD:

33 But this is the covenant that I will make with the house of Israel after those days, said the LORD, I will give my law in their souls, and write it in their hearts; and will be their God, and they shall be my people.

34 And they shall no longer teach every man his neighbour, and every man his brother, saying, Know the LORD: for they shall all know me, from the least of them unto the greatest of them, said the LORD: for I will forgive their iniquity, and I will remember their sin no more.

35 Thus hath the LORD said, who giveth the sun for light by day, *and* the laws of the moon and of the stars for light by night, who divideth the sea and the waves thereof roar; The LORD of the hosts *is* his name:

36 If these laws depart from before me, said the LORD, *then* the seed of Israel also shall cease from being a nation before me for ever.

37 Thus hath the LORD said; If the heavens above can be measured, and the foundations of the earth searched out beneath, I will also cast off all the seed of Israel for all that they have done, said the LORD.

38 Behold, the days come, said the LORD, and the city shall be built unto the LORD from the tower of Hananeel unto the gate of the corner. **39** And the measuring line shall extend before him upon the hill Gareb, and shall compass about to Goath.

40 And the whole valley of the dead bodies, and of the ashes, and all the fields unto the brook of Kidron, unto the corner of the horse gate toward the east, *shall be* holy unto the LORD; it shall not be plucked up, nor thrown down any more for ever.

Chapter 32

1 The word that came to Jeremiah from the LORD in the tenth year of Zedekiah king of Judah, which *was* the eighteenth year of Nebuchadrezzar.

2 For then the king of Babylon's army besieged Jerusalem: and Jeremiah the prophet was shut up in the court of the guard, which *was* in the king of Judah's house.

3 For Zedekiah king of Judah had shut him up, saying, Why dost thou prophesy, and say, Thus hath the LORD said, Behold, I give this city into the hand of the king of Babylon, and he shall take it?

4 And Zedekiah king of Judah shall not escape out of the hand of the Chaldeans, but shall surely be delivered into the hand of the king of Babylon, and shall speak with him mouth to mouth, and his eyes shall behold his eyes;

5 and he shall lead Zedekiah to Babylon, and there shall he be until I visit him, said the LORD: if ye fight with the Chaldeans, ye shall not prosper?

6 And Jeremiah said, The word of the LORD came unto me, saying,

7 Behold, Hanameel the son of Shallum thine uncle cometh unto thee, saying, Buy thee my field that *is* in Anathoth: for the right of redemption *is* thine to buy *it*.

8 So Hanameel my uncle's son came to me in the court of the guard according to the word of the LORD, and said unto me, Buy my field, I pray thee, that *is* in Anathoth, which *is* in the country of Benjamin: for the right of inheritance *is* thine, and the redemption *is* thine; buy *it* for thyself. Then I knew that this *was* the word of the LORD.

9 And I bought the field of Hanameel my uncle's son, that *was* in Anathoth, and weighed him the money, *even* seventeen shekels of silver.

10 And I subscribed the evidence, and sealed *it*, and took witnesses, and weighed *him* the money in the balances.

11 So I took the evidence of the purchase, *both* that which was sealed *according* to the law and custom, and that which was open:

12 And I gave the evidence of the purchase unto Baruch the son of Neriah, the son of Maaseiah, in the sight of Hanameel my uncle's *son*, and in the presence of the witnesses that subscribed the book of the purchase, before all the Jews that were in the court of the guard.

13 And I charged Baruch before them, saying,

14 Thus hath the LORD of the hosts the God of Israel said; Take these evidences, this evidence of the purchase, both which is sealed, and this evidence which is open; and put them in an earthen vessel, that they may continue many days.

15 For thus hath the LORD of the hosts the God of Israel said; Houses and fields and vineyards shall be bought *and sold* again in this land.

16 Now when I had delivered the evidence of the purchase unto Baruch the son of Neriah, I prayed unto the LORD, saying,

17 Ah Lord GOD! behold, thou hast made the heaven and the earth by thy great power and stretched out arm, *and* there is nothing hidden from thee;

18 that thou showest mercy in thousands, and recompensest the iniquity of the fathers into the bosom of their children after them: the Great, the Mighty God, the LORD of the hosts, *is* his name,

19 great in counsel, and magnificent in works: for thine eyes *are* open upon all the ways of the sons of men: to give every one according to his ways, and according to the fruit of his doings;

20 who hast set signs and wonders in the land of Egypt, *even* unto this day, and in Israel, and in the man; and hast made thee a name, as at this day;

21 and hast brought forth thy people Israel out of the land of Egypt with signs, and with wonders, and with a strong hand, and with a stretched out arm, and with great terror;

22 and hast given them this land, which thou didst swear to their fathers to give them, a land flowing with milk and honey;

23 and they came in, and possessed it; but they did not hear thy voice, neither did they walk in thy law; they have done nothing of all that thou commandedst them to do: therefore thou hast caused all this evil to come upon them.

24 Behold the siege engines are come unto the city to take it; and the city is given into the hand of the Chaldeans, that fight against it, because of the sword, and of the famine, and of the pestilence: and what thou hast spoken is come to pass; and, behold, thou seest *it*.

25 And thou hast said unto me, O Lord GOD, Buy thee the field for money, and take witnesses; and the city is given into the hand of the Chaldeans.

26 Then came the word of the LORD unto Jeremiah, saying,

27 Behold, I *am* the LORD, the God of all flesh: peradventure shall any thing be covered unto me?

28 Therefore thus hath the LORD said; Behold, I give this city into the hand of *the* Chaldeans, and into *the* hand of Nebuchadrezzar king of Babylon, and he shall take it:

29 And the Chaldeans, that fight against this city, shall come and set fire on this city, and burn it with the houses, upon whose roofs they have offered incense unto Baal, and poured out drink offerings unto other gods, to provoke me to anger.

30 For the children of Israel and the children of Judah have only done evil before me from their youth: for the children of Israel have only provoked me to anger with the work of their hands, said the LORD.

31 For this city hath been to me *as* a provocation of my anger and of my fury from the day that they built it even unto this day; that I should remove it from before my face,

32 because of all the evil of the children of Israel and of the children of Judah, which they have done to provoke me to anger, they, their kings, their princes, their priests, and their prophets, and the men of Judah, and the inhabitants of Jerusalem.

33 And they have turned unto me the back, and not the face: when I taught them, rising up early and teaching *them*, yet they did not hearken to receive chastisement;

34 but they set their abominations in the house, which is called by my name, to defile it.

35 And they built altars unto Baal, which *are* in the valley of the son of Hinnom, to cause their sons and their daughters to pass through *the fire* unto Molech; which I commanded them not, neither came it into my mind, that they should do this abomination, to cause Judah to sin.

36 And now therefore thus saith the LORD, the God of Israel, unto this city, whereof ye say, It shall be delivered into the hand of the king of Babylon by the sword, and by the famine, and by the pestilence;

37 behold, I will gather them out of all countries, where I have driven them in my anger, and in my fury, and in great wrath; and I will bring them again unto this place, and I will cause them to dwell safely:

38 And they shall be my people, and I will be their God:

39 And I will give them one heart, and one way, that they may fear me for ever, for the good of them, and of their children after them:

40 And I will make an eternal covenant with them, that I will not turn away from doing them good, and I will put my fear in their hearts, that they shall not depart from me.

41 And, I will rejoice with them doing them good, and I will plant them in this land with truth, with my whole heart and with my whole soul.

42 For thus hath the LORD said; Like as I have brought all this great evil upon this people, so will I bring upon them all the good that I speak regarding them.

43 And they shall possess inheritance in this land, whereof ye say, *It is* desolate without man or beast; it is given into the hands of the Chaldeans.

44 Men shall buy fields for money, and subscribe evidences, and seal *them*, and take witnesses in the land of Benjamin, and in the places about Jerusalem, and in the cities of Judah, and in the cities of the mountains, and in the cities of the valley, and in the cities of the south: for I will cause their captivity to turn, saith the LORD.

Chapter 33

1 Moreover the word of the LORD came unto Jeremiah the second time, while he was yet shut up in the court of the guard, saying,

2 Thus hath said the LORD that maketh it, the LORD that formeth it to establish it; the LORD *is* his name;

3 Call unto me, and I will answer thee, and show thee great and difficult things, which thou knowest not.

4 For thus hath the LORD the God of Israel said, concerning the houses of this city, and concerning the houses of the kings of Judah, which are thrown down by the siege engines, and by the sword

5 (because they came to fight with the Chaldeans, to fill them with the dead bodies of men, whom I have slain in my anger and in my fury, and because I hid my face from this city due to all her wickedness):

6 Behold, I will bring her healing and medicine, and I will cure them, and will reveal unto them the abundance of peace and truth.

7 And I will cause the captivity of Judah and the captivity of Israel to turn, and will build them, as at the first.

8 And I will cleanse them from all their iniquity, whereby they have sinned against me; and I will pardon all their sins, whereby they have sinned against me, and with which they rebelled against me.

9 And it shall be unto me a name of joy, of praise and of glory among all the Gentiles of the earth, who shall have heard all the good that I do unto them: and they shall fear and tremble for all the good and for all the peace that I shall do unto them.

10 Thus hath the LORD said; Again there shall be heard in this place, which ye say is desolate without man and without beast, *even* in the cities of Judah, and in the streets of Jerusalem, that are desolate, without man, and without inhabitant, and without beast,

11 the voice of joy, and the voice of gladness, the voice of the bridegroom, and the voice of the bride, the voice of them that shall say, Praise the LORD of the hosts: for the LORD *is* good; for his mercy *endureth* for ever: *and* of them that shall bring the sacrifice of praise into the house of the LORD. For I will cause the captivity of the land to turn, as at the first, said the LORD.

12 Thus hath the LORD of the hosts said; Again in this place, which is desolate without man and without beast, and in all the cities thereof, shall there be booths of shepherds who shall cause *the* flocks to lie down.

13 In the cities of the mountains, in the cities of the vale, and in the cities of the south, and in the land of Benjamin, and in the places about Jerusalem, and in the cities of Judah, shall the flocks pass again under the hands of him that counteth *them*, said the LORD.

14 Behold, the days come, said the LORD, that I will confirm the good Word which I have promised unto the house of Israel and to the house of Judah.

15 In those days, and at that time, I will cause the Branch of righteousness to grow up unto David; and he shall execute judgment and righteousness in the land.

16 In those days shall Judah be saved, and Jerusalem shall dwell safely: and this *is the name* wherewith she shall be called, The LORD our righteousness.

17 For thus hath the LORD said; David shall never lack a man to sit upon the throne of the house of Israel;

18 neither shall the priests the Levites lack a man before me to offer burnt offerings, and to kindle grain offerings, and to do sacrifice continually.

19 And the word of the LORD came unto Jeremiah, saying,

20 Thus hath the LORD said; If ye can break my covenant with the day, and my covenant with the night, such that there should not be day nor night in their season;

21 *then* may also my covenant be broken with David my servant, that he should not have a son to reign upon his throne; and with the Levites and priests, my ministers.

22 As the host of heaven cannot be numbered, neither the sand of the sea measured: so will I multiply the seed of David my servant, and the Levites that minister unto me.

23 Moreover the word of the LORD came to Jeremiah, saying,

24 Considerest thou not what this people have spoken, saying, The two families which the LORD hath chosen, he hath even cast them off? thus they have despised my people, that they should be no more a nation before them.

25 Thus hath the LORD said; If my covenant *remain*

not with the day and the night, *and if* I have not appointed the laws of the heaven and the earth;

26 then will I cast away the seed of Jacob, and David my servant, *so* that I will not take *any* of his seed *to be* rulers over the seed of Abraham, of Isaac, and of Jacob: for I will cause their captivity to turn, and I will have mercy on them.

Chapter 34

1 The word which came unto Jeremiah from the LORD, (when Nebuchadnezzar king of Babylon, and all his army, and all the kingdoms of the earth of his dominion, and all the peoples, fought against Jerusalem, and against all the cities thereof,) saying,

2 Thus hath the LORD God of Israel said; Go and speak to Zedekiah king of Judah, and tell him, Thus hath the LORD said; Behold, I give this city into the hand of the king of Babylon, and he shall burn it with fire:

3 And thou shalt not escape out of his hand, but shalt surely be taken, and delivered into his hand; and thine eyes shall behold the eyes of the king of Babylon, and he shall speak with thee mouth to mouth, and thou shalt go to Babylon.

4 Yet hear the word of the LORD, O Zedekiah king of Judah; Thus hath the LORD said of thee, Thou shalt not die by the sword:

5 *But* thou shalt die in peace: and according to the burnings of thy fathers, the former kings which were before thee, so shall they burn *odours* for thee; and they will lament thee, *saying*, Ah lord! for I have pronounced the word, said the LORD.

6 Then Jeremiah the prophet spoke all these words unto Zedekiah king of Judah in Jerusalem,

7 when the king of Babylon's army fought against Jerusalem, and against all the cities of Judah that were left, against Lachish, and against Azekah: for of the strong cities of Judah these had remained.

8 *This is* the word that came unto Jeremiah from the LORD, after that the king Zedekiah had made a covenant with all the people which *were* at Jerusalem, to proclaim liberty unto them;

9 that every man should let his manservant, and every man his maidservant, *being* an Hebrew or an Hebrewess, go free; that none should use of his brethren, the Jews, as a slave.

10 Now when all the princes, and all the people, which had entered into the covenant, heard that every one should let his manservant, and every one his maidservant, go free, that none should use them any more as servants, then they listened, and let *them* go.

11 But afterward they repented, and caused the servants and the handmaids, whom they had let go free, to return, and brought them into subjection for servants and for handmaids.

12 Therefore the word of the LORD came to Jeremiah from the LORD, saying,

13 Thus saith the LORD God of Israel; I made a covenant with your fathers in the day that I brought them forth out of the land of Egypt, out of the house of slavery, saying,

14 At the end of seven years let ye go every man his Hebrew brother, who hath been sold unto thee; therefore he shall serve thee six years and thou shalt send him forth free from thee: but your fathers hearkened not unto me, neither inclined their ear.

15 And ye were now converted, and had done right in my sight, in proclaiming liberty every man to his neighbour; and ye had made a covenant before me in the house which is called by my name:

16 But ye turned and polluted my name, and caused every man his servant, and every man his handmaid, whom ye had set at liberty at their pleasure, to return, and brought them into subjection, to be unto you for servants and for handmaids.

17 Therefore thus hath the LORD said; Ye have not hearkened unto me, in proclaiming liberty, every one to his brother, and every man to his neighbour: behold, I proclaim a liberty for you, said the LORD, to the sword, to the pestilence, and to the famine; and I will make you to be removed into all the kingdoms of the earth.

18 And I will give the men that have transgressed my covenant, which have not performed the words of the covenant which they had made before me, when they cut the calf in two, and passed between the parts thereof,

19 the princes of Judah, and the princes of Jerusalem, the eunuchs, and the priests, and all the people of the land, which passed between the parts of the calf;

20 I will even give them into the hand of their enemies, and into the hand of them that seek their soul: and their dead bodies shall be for food unto the fowls of the heaven, and to the beasts of the earth.

21 And Zedekiah king of Judah and his princes will I give into the hand of their enemies, and into the hand of them that seek their soul, and into the hand of the king of Babylon's army, which are gone up from you.

22 Behold, I command, said the LORD, and will cause them to return to this city; and they shall fight against her, and take her, and burn her with fire: and I will give the cities of Judah unto desolation until they be without an inhabitant.

Chapter 35

1 The word which came unto Jeremiah from the LORD in the days of Jehoiakim the son of Josiah king of Judah, saying,

2 Go unto the house of the Rechabites, and speak with them, and bring them into the house of the LORD, into one of the chambers, and give them wine to drink.

3 Then I took Jaazaniah the son of Jeremiah, the son of Habaziniah, and his brethren, and all his sons, and the whole house of the Rechabites;

4 and I brought them into the house of the LORD, into the chamber of the sons of Hanan, the son of Igdaliah, a man of God, which *was* by the chamber of the princes, which *was* above the chamber of Maaseiah the son of Shallum, the keeper of the vessels:

5 And I set before the sons of the house of the Rechabites pots full of wine, and cups, and I said unto them, Drink ye wine.

6 But they said, We will drink no wine: for Jonadab the son of Rechab our father commanded us, saying, Ye shall drink no wine, *neither ye*, nor your sons for ever:

7 Neither shall ye build house, nor sow seed, nor plant vineyard, nor have *any*: but all your days ye shall dwell in tents; that ye may live many days in the land where ye *be* strangers.

8 Thus have we obeyed the voice of Jonadab our father,

the son of Rechab, in all that he hath charged us, to drink no wine all our days, we, our wives, our sons, nor our daughters;

9 nor to build houses for us to dwell in: neither have we vineyard, nor field, nor seed:

10 But we have dwelt in tents, and have obeyed, and done according to all that Jonadab our father commanded us.

11 But it came to pass, nevertheless, when Nebuchadrezzar king of Babylon came up into the land, that we said, Come, and let us go to Jerusalem *from* before the army of the Chaldeans, and *from* before of the army of the Syrians: and so we remain in Jerusalem.

12 Then came the word of the LORD unto Jeremiah, saying,

13 Thus hath the LORD of the hosts, the God of Israel said; Go and tell the men of Judah and the inhabitants of Jerusalem, Will ye never receive chastisement hearkening to my words? said the LORD.

14 The word of Jonadab the son of Rechab, that he commanded his sons not to drink wine, was not moved; for unto this day they drink none, but obey their father's commandment: notwithstanding I have spoken unto you, rising early and speaking; but ye hearkened not unto me.

15 I have sent also unto you all my servants the prophets, rising up early and sending *them*, saying, Turn ye now every man from his evil way, and amend your doings, and go not after other gods to serve them, and ye shall live in the land which I have given to you and to your fathers: but ye have not inclined your ear, nor hearkened unto me.

16 Certainly the sons of Jonadab the son of Rechab have not moved the commandment of their father, which he commanded them; but this people hath not hearkened unto me:

17 Therefore thus hath the LORD God of the hosts, the God of Israel said; Behold, I bring upon Judah and upon all the inhabitants of Jerusalem all the evil that I have pronounced against them: because I spoke unto them, but they did not hear; and I called unto them, but they did not answer.

18 And Jeremiah said unto the house of the Rechabites, Thus hath the LORD of the hosts, God of Israel said; Because ye listened to the commandment of Jonadab your father, and kept all his commandments, and have done according unto all that he hath commanded you:

19 Therefore thus hath the LORD of the hosts, God of Israel said; Jonadab the son of Rechab shall not lack a man to stand before me for ever.

Chapter 36

1 And it came to pass in the fourth year of Jehoiakim the son of Josiah king of Judah, *that* this word came unto Jeremiah from the LORD, saying,

2 Take thee a roll of a book, and write therein all the words that I have spoken unto thee against Israel, and against Judah, and against all the Gentiles, from the day I *began* to speak unto thee, from the days of Josiah, unto today.

3 If peradventure the house of Judah will hear all the evil which I purpose to do unto them; that they may turn every one from his evil way; and I will forgive their iniquity and their sin.

4 Then Jeremiah called Baruch the son of Neriah: and Baruch wrote from the mouth of Jeremiah all the words of the LORD, which he had spoken unto him, upon a roll of a book.

5 And Jeremiah commanded Baruch, saying, I *am* shut up; I cannot go into the house of the LORD:

6 Therefore go thou, and read from the roll, which thou hast written from my mouth, the words of the LORD in the ears of the people in the LORD'S house upon the day of fasting: and also in the ears of all Judah that come out of their cities. Thou shalt read them

7 if peradventure their prayer will fall into the presence of the LORD, and they shall turn every one from his evil way: for great *is* the anger and the fury that the LORD hath pronounced against this people.

8 And Baruch the son of Neriah did according to all that Jeremiah the prophet commanded him, reading in the book the words of the LORD in the LORD'S house.

9 And it came to pass in the fifth year of Jehoiakim the son of Josiah king of Judah, in the ninth month, *that* they proclaimed a fast before the LORD to all the people of Jerusalem, and to all the people that came from the cities of Judah unto Jerusalem.

10 Then read Baruch in the book the words of Jeremiah in the house of the LORD, in the chamber of Gemariah the son of Shaphan the scribe, in the higher court, at the entry of the new gate of the LORD'S house, in the ears of all the people.

11 When Michaiah the son of Gemariah, the son of Shaphan, had heard out of the book all the words of the LORD,

12 then he went down into the king's house, into the scribe's chamber: and, behold, all the princes sat there, *even* Elishama the scribe, and Delaiah the son of Shemaiah, and Elnathan the son of Achbor, and Gemariah the son of Shaphan, and Zedekiah the son of Hananiah, and all the princes.

13 Then Michaiah declared unto them all the words that he had heard, when Baruch read the book in the ears of the people.

14 Therefore all the princes sent Jehudi the son of Nethaniah, the son of Shelemiah, the son of Cushi, unto Baruch, saying, Take in thine hand the roll wherein thou hast read in the ears of the people, and come. So Baruch the son of Neriah took the roll in his hand, and came unto them.

15 And they said unto him, Sit down now, and read it in our ears. So Baruch read *it* in their ears.

16 Now it came to pass, when they had heard all the words, each one turned to his companion in fear, and they said unto Baruch, We will surely tell the king of all these words.

17 And they asked Baruch, saying, Tell us now, How didst thou write all these words at his mouth?

18 Then Baruch answered them, He pronounced all these words unto me with his mouth, and I wrote *them* with ink in the book.

19 Then said the princes unto Baruch, Go, hide thee, thou and Jeremiah; and let no man know where ye be.

20 And they went in to the king into the court, but they laid up the roll in the chamber of Elishama the scribe, and told all the words in the ears of the king.

21 So the king sent Jehudi to fetch the roll: and he took it out of Elishama the scribe's chamber. And Jehudi read in it in the ears of the king, and in the ears of all the princes which stood beside the king.

22 Now the king sat in the winterhouse in the ninth month: and *there was a fire* on the hearth burning before him.

23 And it came to pass, *that* when Jehudi had read three or four leaves, he cut it with the penknife, and cast *it* into the fire that *was* on the hearth, until all the roll was consumed in the fire that *was* on the hearth.

24 Yet they were not afraid, nor rent their garments, *neither* the king, nor any of his servants that heard all these words.

25 Nevertheless Elnathan and Delaiah and Gemariah made intercession to the king that he not burn the roll: he would not hear them.

26 But the king commanded Jerahmeel the son of Hammelech, and Seraiah the son of Azriel, and Shelemiah the son of Abdeel, to take Baruch the scribe and Jeremiah the prophet: but the LORD hid them.

27 Then the word of the LORD came to Jeremiah, after the king burned the roll, the words which Baruch had written at the mouth of Jeremiah, saying,

28 Take thee again another roll, and write in it all the former words that were in the first roll, which Jehoiakim the king of Judah hath burned.

29 And thou shalt say to Jehoiakim king of Judah, Thus hath the LORD said; Thou hast burned this roll, saying, Why hast thou written therein, saying, The king of Babylon shall certainly come and destroy this land, and shall cause to cease from thence man and beast?

30 Therefore thus hath the LORD said unto Jehoiakim king of Judah; He shall have none to sit upon the throne of David: and his body shall be cast out in the day to the heat, and in the night to the frost.

31 And I will visit upon him, and upon his seed, and upon his servants, their iniquity; and I will bring upon them, and upon the inhabitants of Jerusalem, and upon the men of Judah, all the evil that I have pronounced against them; but they hearkened not.

32 Then took Jeremiah another roll, and gave it to Baruch the scribe, the son of Neriah; who wrote therein from the mouth of Jeremiah all the words of the book which Jehoiakim king of Judah had burned in the fire: and there were added besides upon them many like words.

Chapter 37

1 And king Zedekiah the son of Josiah reigned instead of Coniah the son of Jehoiakim, whom Nebuchadrezzar king of Babylon made king in the land of Judah.

2 But neither he, nor his servants, nor the people of the land, did hearken unto the words of the LORD, which he spoke by the prophet Jeremiah.

3 And Zedekiah the king sent Jehucal the son of Shelemiah and Zephaniah the son of Maaseiah the priest to the prophet Jeremiah, saying, Pray now unto the LORD our God for us.

4 (Now Jeremiah came in and went out among the people: for they had not put him into prison.

5 And as Pharaoh's army was come forth out of Egypt: and when the Chaldeans that besieged Jerusalem heard tidings of them, they departed from Jerusalem.)

6 Then came the word of the LORD unto the prophet Jeremiah, saying,

7 Thus hath the LORD, the God of Israel said; Thus shall ye say to the king of Judah, that sent you unto me to enquire of me; Behold, Pharaoh's army, which had come forth to help you, has returned to Egypt into their own land.

8 And the Chaldeans shall come again, and fight against this city, and take it, and burn it with fire.

9 Thus hath the LORD said; Deceive not yourselves, saying, The Chaldeans have surely depart from us: for they shall not depart.

10 For though ye had smitten the whole army of the Chaldeans that fight against you, and there remained *but* wounded men among them, *yet* should they rise up every man from his tent, and burn this city with fire.

11 And it came to pass, that when the army of the Chaldeans was broken up from Jerusalem for fear of Pharaoh's army,

12 then Jeremiah went forth out of Jerusalem to go into the land of Benjamin, to separate himself thence in the midst of the people.

13 And when he was in the gate of Benjamin, a captain of the ward *was* there, whose name *was* Irijah, the son of Shelemiah, the son of Hananiah; and he took

Jeremiah the prophet, saying, Thou fallest away to the Chaldeans.

14 Then said Jeremiah, *It is* false; I fall not away to the Chaldeans. But he hearkened not to him: so Irijah took Jeremiah, and brought him to the princes.

15 Wherefore the princes were wroth with Jeremiah, and smote him, and put him in prison in the house of Jonathan the scribe: for they had made that the prison.

16 When Jeremiah was entered into the dungeon, and into the cabins, and Jeremiah had remained there many days;

17 then Zedekiah the king sent, and took him out: and the king asked him secretly in his house, and said, Is there *any* word from the LORD? And Jeremiah said, There is: for, said he, thou shalt be delivered into the hand of the king of Babylon.

18 Moreover Jeremiah said unto king Zedekiah, What have I sinned against thee, or against thy servants, or against this people, that ye have put me in prison?

19 Where *are* now your prophets which prophesied unto you, saying, The king of Babylon shall not come against you, nor against this land?

20 Therefore hear now, I pray thee, O my lord the king: let my supplication, I pray thee, be accepted before thee; that thou cause me not to return to the house of Jonathan the scribe, lest I die there.

21 Then Zedekiah the king commanded that they should commit Jeremiah into the court of the guard, and that they should give him daily a piece of bread out of the bakers' street, until all the bread in the city was spent. Thus Jeremiah remained in the court of the guard.

Chapter 38

1 Then Shephatiah the son of Mattan, and Gedaliah the son of Pashur, and Jucal the son of Shelemiah, and Pashur the son of Malchiah, heard the words that Jeremiah had spoken unto all the people, saying,

2 Thus hath the LORD said, He that remaineth in this city shall die by the sword, by the famine, and by the pestilence: but he that goeth forth to the Chaldeans shall live; for he shall have his life for a prey, and shall live.

3 Thus hath the LORD said, This city shall surely be

given into the hand of the king of Babylon's army, which shall take it.

4 Therefore the princes said unto the king, We beseech thee, let this man be put to death: for thus he weakeneth the hands of the men of war that remain in this city, and the hands of all the people, in speaking such words unto them: for this man seeketh not the peace of this people, but the hurt.

5 Then Zedekiah the king said, Behold, he *is* in your hand: for the king can not do *any* thing against you.

6 Then took they Jeremiah, and cast him into the dungeon of Malchiah the son of Hammelech, that *was* in the court of the guard: and they let down Jeremiah with cords. And in the dungeon *there was* no water, but mire: so Jeremiah sunk in the mire.

7 Now when Ebedmelech the Ethiopian, one of the eunuchs which was in the king's house, heard that they had put Jeremiah in the dungeon; the king then sitting in the gate of Benjamin;

8 Ebedmelech went forth out of the king's house, and spoke to the king, saying,

9 My lord the king, these men have done evil in all that they have done to Jeremiah the prophet, whom they have cast into the dungeon; and he is like to die for hunger in the place where he is: for *there is* no more bread in the city.

10 Then the king commanded Ebedmelech the Ethiopian, saying, Take from hence thirty men with thee, and take up Jeremiah the prophet out of the dungeon, before he dies.

11 So Ebedmelech took the men with him, and went into the house of the king under the treasury, and took thence old cast clouts and old rotten rags, and let them down by cords into the dungeon to Jeremiah.

12 And Ebedmelech the Ethiopian said unto Jeremiah, Put now *these* old cast clouts and rotten rags under thine armholes under the cords. And Jeremiah did so.

13 So they drew up Jeremiah with cords, and took him up out of the dungeon: and Jeremiah remained in the court of the guard.

14 Then Zedekiah the king sent, and took Jeremiah the prophet unto him into the third entry that *is* in the house of the LORD: and the king said unto Jeremiah, I will ask thee a word; hide nothing from me.

15 Then Jeremiah said unto Zedekiah, If I declare *it* unto thee, wilt thou not surely put me to death? and if I give thee counsel, thou wilt not hearken unto me.

16 So Zedekiah the king swore secretly unto Jeremiah, saying, *As* the LORD liveth, that made us this soul, I will not put thee to death, neither will I give thee into the hand of these men that seek thy life.

17 Then said Jeremiah unto Zedekiah, Thus hath the LORD, the God of the hosts, the God of Israel said; If thou wilt assuredly go forth unto the king of Babylon's princes, then thy soul shall live, and this city shall not be burned with fire; and thou shalt live, and thine house:

18 But if thou wilt not go forth to the king of Babylon's princes, then shall this city be given into the hand of the Chaldeans, and they shall burn it with fire, and thou shalt not escape out of their hand.

19 And Zedekiah the king said unto Jeremiah, I am afraid of the Jews that are fallen to the Chaldeans, lest they deliver me into their hand, and they mock me.

20 But Jeremiah said, They shall not deliver *thee*. Hear now the voice of the LORD, which I speak unto thee: so it shall be well unto thee, and thy soul shall live.

21 But if thou refuse to go forth, this *is* the word that the LORD hath showed me:

22 And, behold, all the women that are left in the king of Judah's house *shall be* brought forth to the king of Babylon's princes, and those *women* shall say, Thy friends have deceived thee, and have prevailed against thee: thy feet are sunk in the mire, *and* they are turned away back.

23 So they shall bring out all thy wives and thy children to the Chaldeans: and thou shalt not escape out of their hand, but shalt be taken by the hand of the king of Babylon: and thou shalt cause this city to be burned with fire.

24 Then said Zedekiah unto Jeremiah, Let no man know of these words, and thou shalt not die.

25 But if the princes hear that I have talked with thee, and they come unto thee, and say unto thee, Declare unto us now what thou hast said unto the king, hide it not from us, and we will not put thee to death; also what the king said unto thee:

26 Then thou shalt say unto them, I presented my supplication before the king, that he would not cause me to return to Jonathan's house, to die there.

27 Then came all the princes unto Jeremiah, and asked him: and he told them according to all these words that the king had commanded. So they left off speaking with him; for the matter was not perceived.

28 So Jeremiah abode in the court of the guard until the day that Jerusalem was taken: and he was *there* when Jerusalem was taken.

Chapter 39

1 In the ninth year of Zedekiah king of Judah, in the tenth month, came Nebuchadrezzar king of Babylon and all his army against Jerusalem, and they besieged it.

2 *And* in the eleventh year of Zedekiah, in the fourth month, the ninth *day* of the month, the city was broken up.

3 And all the princes of the king of Babylon came in, and sat in the middle gate, *even* Nergalsharezer, Samgarnebo, Sarsechim, Rabsaris, Nergalsharezer, Rabmag, with all the residue of the princes of the king of Babylon.

4 And it came to pass, *that* when Zedekiah the king of Judah saw them, and all the men of war, then they fled, and went forth out of the city by night, by the way of the king's garden, by the gate betwixt the two walls: and *the king* went out by the way of the desert.

5 But the Chaldeans' army pursued after them, and overtook Zedekiah in the plains of Jericho: and when they had taken him, they brought him up to Nebuchadnezzar king of Babylon to Riblah in the land of Hamath, where he gave judgment upon him.

6 Then the king of Babylon slew the sons of Zedekiah in Riblah before his eyes: also the king of Babylon slew all the nobles of Judah.

7 Moreover he put out Zedekiah's eyes, and bound him with chains, to carry him to Babylon.

8 And the Chaldeans burned the king's house, and the houses of the people, with fire, and broke down the walls of Jerusalem.

9 Then Nebuzaradan the captain of the guard carried away captive into Babylon the remnant of the people that remained in the city, and those that had come over to him, with the rest of the people that remained.

10 But Nebuzaradan the captain of the guard left of the poor of the people, which had nothing, in the land of Judah, and gave them vineyards and fields at the same time.

11 Now Nebuchadrezzar king of Babylon gave charge concerning Jeremiah to Nebuzaradan the captain of the guard, saying,

12 Take him, and look well to him, and do him no harm; but do unto him even as he shall say unto thee.

13 So Nebuzaradan the captain of the guard sent, and Nebushasban, Rabsaris, and Nergalsharezer, Rabmag, and all the king of Babylon's princes·

14 even they sent, and took Jeremiah out of the court of the guard, and committed him unto Gedaliah the son of Ahikam the son of Shaphan, that he should carry him home: so he dwelt among the people.

15 Now the word of the LORD had come unto Jeremiah, while he was shut up in the court of the prison, saying,

16 Go and speak to Ebed-melech the Ethiopian, saying, Thus hath the LORD of the hosts, the God of Israel said; Behold, I will bring my words upon this city for evil, and not for good; and they shall be *accomplished* in that day before thee.

17 But I will deliver thee in that day, said the LORD: and thou shalt not be given into the hand of the men of whom thou *art* afraid.

18 For I will surely deliver thee, and thou shalt not fall by the sword, but thy life shall be for a prey unto thee: because thou hast put thy trust in me, said the LORD.

Chapter 40

1 The word that came to Jeremiah from the LORD, after Nebuzaradan the captain of the guard had let him go from Ramah, when he had taken him being bound in chains among all that were carried away captive of Jerusalem and Judah, which were carried away captive unto Babylon.

2 And the captain of the guard took Jeremiah, and said unto him, The LORD thy God hath pronounced this evil upon this place.

3 Now the LORD hath brought *it*, and done according as he had said: because ye sinned against the LORD, and did not listen to his voice, therefore this thing is come upon you.

4 And now, behold, I loose thee this day from the chains which *were* upon thine hand. If it seem good unto thee to come with me into Babylon, come; and I will look well unto thee: but if it seem ill unto thee to come with me into Babylon, forbear: behold, all the land *is* before thee: where it seemeth good and convenient for thee to go, thither go.

5 Now while he had *not yet replied* that he would go back, *the captain said*, Go back also to Gedaliah the son of Ahikam the son of Shaphan, whom the king of Babylon hath made governor over the cities of Judah, and dwell with him among the people: or go wherever it seemeth convenient unto thee to go. So the captain of the guard gave him victuals and a reward, and sent him forth.

6 Then came Jeremiah unto Gedaliah the son of Ahikam to Mizpah; and dwelt with him among the people that were left in the land.

7 And all the princes of the army which *were* in the field, *even* they and their men, heard that the king of Babylon had made Gedaliah the son of Ahikam governor over the land, and had committed unto him the men, and the women, and the children, and the poor of the land; those that were not carried away captive to Babylon;

8 then they came to Gedaliah to Mizpah, even Ishmael the son of Nethaniah, and Johanan and Jonathan the sons of Kareah, and Seraiah the son of Tanhumeth, and the sons of Ephai the Netophathite, and Jezaniah the son of a Maachathite, they and their men.

9 And Gedaliah the son of Ahikam the son of Shaphan sware unto them and to their men, saying, Fear not to serve the Chaldeans: dwell in the land, and serve the king of Babylon, and it shall be well with you.

10 As for me, behold, I dwell in Mizpah to serve the Chaldeans, which will come unto us: but ye, gather ye the wine, and the bread, and the oil, and put *them* in your vessels, and dwell in your cities that ye have taken.

11 Likewise when all the Jews that *were* in Moab, and among the Ammonites, and in Edom, and that *were* in all the lands, heard how the king of Babylon had left a remnant in Judah, and that he had set over them Gedaliah the son of Ahikam the son of Shaphan;

12 all these Jews returned out of all places where they were driven, and came to the land of Judah, to Gedalias in Mizpah, and gathered wine and much fruit.

13 Moreover Johanan the son of Kareah, and all the princes of the armies that *were* in the fields, came to Gedaliah to Mizpah,

14 and said unto him, Dost thou certainly know that Baalis the king of the Ammonites hath sent Ishmael the son of Nethaniah to slay thee? But Gedaliah the son of Ahikam believed them not.

15 Then Johanan the son of Kareah spoke to Gedaliah in Mizpah secretly, saying, I will go now, and I will slay Ishmael the son of Nethaniah, and no man shall know *it*: wherefore should he slay thee, that all the Jews which are gathered unto thee should be scattered, and the remnant in Judah perish?

16 But Gedaliah the son of Ahikam said unto Johanan the son of Kareah, Thou shalt not do this thing: for thou speakest falsely of Ishmael.

Chapter 41

1 Now it came to pass in the seventh month, *that* Ishmael the son of Nethaniah the son of Elishama, of the royal seed, and *some* princes of the king, and ten men with him, came unto Gedaliah the son of Ahikam in Mizpah; and there they did eat bread together in Mizpah.

2 Then arose Ishmael the son of Nethaniah, and the ten men that were with him, and smote Gedaliah the son of Ahikam the son of Shaphan with the sword, and slew him, whom the king of Babylon had made governor over the land.

3 Ishmael also slew all the Jews that were with him, *even* with Gedaliah, at Mizpah, and the Chaldean soldiers that were found there.

4 And it came to pass the second day after he had

slain Gedaliah, when no one knew of it yet,

5 that there came certain men of Shechem, of Shiloh, and of Samaria, eighty men, having their beards shaven, and their clothes rent, and having cut themselves, with offerings and incense in their hand, to bring *them* to the house of the LORD.

6 And Ishmael the son of Nethaniah went forth from Mizpah to meet them, weeping all along as he went: and it came to pass, as he met them, he said unto them, Come to Gedaliah the son of Ahikam.

7 And it was *so*, when they came into the midst of the city, that Ishmael the son of Nethaniah slew them, *and cast them* into the midst of a pit, he, and the men that *were* with him.

8 But ten men were found among them that said unto Ishmael, Slay us not: for we have treasures in the field, of wheat, and of barley, and of oil, and of honey. So he forbare, and slew them not among their brethren.

9 Now the pit wherein Ishmael had cast all the dead bodies of the men, whom he had slain because of Gedaliah, *was* the same which Asa the king had made for fear of Baasha king of Israel: *and* Ishmael the son of Nethaniah filled it with *them that were* slain.

10 Then Ishmael carried away captive all the residue of the people that *were* in Mizpah, *even* the king's daughters, and all the people that remained in Mizpah, whom Nebuzaradan the captain of the guard had committed to Gedaliah the son of Ahikam: and Ishmael the son of Nethaniah carried them away captive, and departed to go over to the Ammonites.

11 But when Johanan the son of Kareah, and all the princes of the armies that *were* with him, heard of all the evil that Ishmael the son of Nethaniah had done,

12 then they took all the men, and went to fight with Ishmael the son of Nethaniah, and found him by the great waters that *are* in Gibeon.

13 Now it came to pass, *that* when all the people which *were* with Ishmael heard Johanan the son of Kareah, and all the princes of the armies that *were* with him, then they were glad.

14 So all the people that Ishmael had carried away

captive from Mizpah cast about and returned, and went unto Johanan the son of Kareah.

15 But Ishmael the son of Nethaniah escaped from Johanan with eight men, and went to the Ammonites.

16 Then took Johanan the son of Kareah, and all the princes of the armies that *were* with him, all the remnant of the people which had turned from Ishmael the son of Nethaniah, from Mizpah, after he had slain Gedaliah the son of Ahikam; men of war, and the women, and the children, and the eunuchs, whom Johanan had caused to turn from Gibeon:

17 And they departed, and dwelt in the habitation of Chimham, which is by Bethlehem, that they might go and enter into Egypt,

18 because of the Chaldeans: for they were afraid of them, because Ishmael the son of Nethaniah had slain Gedaliah the son of Ahikam, whom the king of Babylon made governor in the land.

Chapter 42

1 Then all the princes of the armies, and Johanan the son of Kareah, and Jezaniah the son of Hoshaiah, and all the people from the least even unto the greatest, came near,

2 And said unto Jeremiah the prophet, Let, we beseech thee, our supplication be accepted before thee, and pray for us unto the LORD thy God, *even* for all this remnant; (for we are left *but* a few of many, as thine eyes do behold us:)

3 That the LORD thy God may show us *the* way wherein we walk, and that which we should do.

4 Then Jeremiah the prophet said unto them, I have heard *you*; behold, I will pray unto the LORD your God according to your words; and it shall come to pass, *that* whatsoever thing the LORD shall answer you, I will declare *it* unto you; I will keep nothing back from you.

5 Then they said to Jeremiah, The LORD be a true and faithful witness between us, if we do not even according to all things for the which the LORD thy God shall send thee to us.

6 Whether *it be* good, or whether *it be* evil, we will hear the voice of the LORD our God, to whom we send thee; that, obeying the voice

205

of the LORD our God, it may be well with us.

7 And it came to pass after ten days, that the word of the LORD came unto Jeremiah.

8 Then called he Johanan the son of Kareah, and all the princes of the armies which *were* with him, and all the people from the least even to the greatest,

9 and said unto them, Thus hath the LORD, the God of Israel said, unto whom ye sent me to present your supplication before him;

10 If ye will still abide in this land, then I will build you, and not pull *you* down, and I will plant you, and not pluck *you* up: for I repent me of the evil that I have done unto you.

11 Be not afraid of the king of Babylon, of whom ye are afraid; be not afraid of him, said the LORD: for I *am* with you to save you, and to deliver you from his hand.

12 And I will show mercies unto you, that he may have mercy upon you, and cause you to dwell in your *own* land.

13 But if ye say, We will not dwell in this land, not listening to the voice of the LORD your God,

14 saying, No; but we will go into the land of Egypt, where we shall see no war, nor hear the sound of the trumpet, nor have hunger of bread; and there will we dwell:

15 And now therefore hear the word of the LORD, ye remnant of Judah; Thus hath the LORD of the hosts, the God of Israel said; If ye altogether set your faces to enter into Egypt, and go to sojourn there;

16 then it shall come to pass, *that* the sword, which ye feared, shall overtake you there in the land of Egypt, and the famine, whereof ye were afraid, shall follow close after you there in Egypt; and there ye shall die.

17 So shall it be with all the men that set their faces to go into Egypt to sojourn there; they shall die by the sword, by the famine, and by the pestilence: and none of them shall remain or escape from the evil that I will bring upon them.

18 For thus hath the LORD of the hosts, the God of Israel said; As my anger and my fury hath been poured forth upon the inhabitants of Jerusalem; so shall my fury be poured forth upon you, when ye shall enter into Egypt: and ye shall be an execration, and an astonishment, and a curse, and a reproach; and ye shall see this place no more.

19 The LORD hath said concerning you, O ye remnant of Judah; Go ye not into Egypt: know certainly that I have admonished you this day.

20 Why did ye cause your souls to err? For ye sent me unto the LORD your God, saying, Pray for us unto the LORD our God; and according unto all that the LORD our God shall say, so declare unto us, and we will do *it*.

21 And *now* I have this day declared *it* to you; but ye have not obeyed the voice of the LORD your God, nor any *thing* for the which he hath sent me unto you.

22 Now therefore know certainly that ye shall die by the sword, by the famine, and by the pestilence, in the place where ye desire to go *and* to sojourn.

Chapter 43

1 And it came to pass, *that* when Jeremiah had made an end of speaking unto all the people all the words of the LORD their God, for which the LORD their God had sent him to them, *even* all these words,

2 Then spoke Azariah the son of Hoshaiah, and Johanan the son of Kareah, and all the proud men, saying unto Jeremiah, Thou speakest falsely: the LORD our God hath not sent thee to say, Go not into Egypt to sojourn there:

3 But Baruch the son of Neriah setteth thee on against us, for to deliver us into the hand of the Chaldeans, that they might put us to death, and carry us away captives into Babylon.

4 So Johanan the son of Kareah, and all the princes of the armies, and all the people, did not hear the voice of the LORD, to dwell in the land of Judah.

5 But Johanan the son of Kareah, and all the princes of the armies, took all the remnant of Judah, that had returned from *among* all the Gentiles, where they had been driven, to dwell in the land of Judah;

6 men, and women, and children, and the king's daughters, and every soul that Nebuzaradan the captain of the guard had left with Gedaliah the son of Ahikam the son of Shaphan, and Jeremiah the prophet, and Baruch the son of Neriah;

7 and they left for the land of Egypt: because they did

not listen to the voice of the LORD: thus came they *even* to Tahpanhes.

8 Then came the word of the LORD unto Jeremiah in Tahpanhes, saying,

9 Take great stones in thine hand, and cover them with clay in a brickkiln, which *is* at the entry of Pharaoh's house in Tahpanhes, in the sight of the men of Judah;

10 and say unto them, Thus hath the LORD of the hosts, the God of Israel said; Behold, I will send and take Nebuchadrezzar the king of Babylon, my servant, and will set his throne upon these stones that I have hid; and he shall spread his royal pavilion over them.

11 And he shall come and smite the land of Egypt, *and deliver* such *as are* for death to death; and such *as are* for captivity to captivity; and such *as are* for the sword to the sword.

12 And I will put fire to the houses of the gods of Egypt; and he shall burn them, and carry them away captives: and he shall array himself with the land of Egypt, as a shepherd putteth on his garment; and he shall go forth from thence in peace.

13 He shall break also the images of Bethshemesh, that *is* in the land of Egypt; and the houses of the gods of the Egyptians shall he burn with fire.

Chapter 44

1 The word that came to Jeremiah concerning all the Jews which dwelt in the land of Egypt, which dwelt at Migdol, and at Tahpanhes, and at Noph, and in the country of Pathros, saying,

2 Thus hath the LORD of the hosts, the God of Israel said; Ye have seen all the evil that I have brought upon Jerusalem, and upon all the cities of Judah; and, behold, this day they *are* a desolation, and no man dwelleth therein,

3 because of their wickedness which they have committed to provoke me to anger, in that they went to burn incense, *and* to serve other gods, whom they knew not, *neither* they, ye, nor your fathers.

4 Howbeit I sent unto you all my servants the prophets, rising early and sending *them*, saying, Oh, do not this abominable thing that I hate.

5 But they hearkened not, nor inclined their ear to turn from their wickedness, to burn no incense unto other gods.

6 Wherefore my fury and my anger was poured forth, and was kindled in the cities of Judah and in the streets of Jerusalem; and they are wasted *and* desolate, as at this day.

7 Therefore now thus hath the LORD, the God of the hosts, the God of Israel said; Why commit ye *this* great evil against your souls, that ye be cut off, man and woman, child and suckling, out of Judah. Why do ye not desire to have a remnant?

8 In that ye provoke me unto wrath with the works of your hands, burning incense unto other gods in the land of Egypt, where ye be gone to dwell. Why do ye cut yourselves off that ye might be a curse and a reproach to all the Gentiles of the earth?

9 Have ye forgotten the wickedness of your fathers, and the wickedness of the kings of Judah, and the wickedness of their wives, and your own wickedness, and the wickedness of your wives, which was committed in the land of Judah, and in the streets of Jerusalem?

10 They are not broken *even* unto this day, neither have they feared, nor walked in my law, nor in my rights, that I set before you and before your fathers.

11 Therefore thus hath the LORD of the hosts, the God of Israel said; Behold, I will set my face against you for evil, and to cut off all Judah.

12 And I will take the remnant of Judah, that have set their faces to go into the land of Egypt to dwell there, and they shall all be consumed, *and* fall in the land of Egypt; they shall *even* be consumed by the sword *and* by the famine: they shall die, from the least even unto the greatest, by the sword and by the famine: and they shall be for an oath, *and* an astonishment, and a curse, and a reproach.

13 For I will visit them that dwell in the land of Egypt, as I visited Jerusalem, with the sword, with famine, and with pestilence:

14 So that none of the remnant of Judah, which are gone into the land of Egypt to dwell there, shall escape or remain alive to return into the land of Judah, to the which they have a desire to return to dwell there: for none shall return but some fugitives.

15 Then all the men which knew that their wives had burned incense unto other gods, and all the women that stood by, a great multitude, even all the people that dwelt in the land of Egypt, in Pathros, answered Jeremiah, saying,

16 *As for* the word that thou hast spoken unto us in the name of the LORD, we will not hearken unto thee.

17 But we will certainly do whatsoever thing goeth forth out of our own mouth, to burn incense unto the queen of heaven, and to pour out drink offerings unto her, as we have done, we, and our fathers, our kings, and our princes, in the cities of Judah, and in the streets of Jerusalem: for *then* had we plenty of victuals, and were well, and saw no evil.

18 But since we left off to burn incense to the queen of heaven, and to pour out drink offerings unto her, we have lacked all *things*, and have been consumed by the sword and by the famine.

19 And when we burned incense to the queen of heaven, and poured out drink offerings unto her, did we make her cakes to worship her, and pour out drink offerings unto her, without our men?

20 Then Jeremiah said unto all the people, to the men, and to the women, and to all the people which had given him *that* answer, saying,

21 The incense that ye burned in the cities of Judah, and in the streets of Jerusalem, ye, and your fathers, your kings, and your princes, and the people of the land, did not the LORD remember them, and came it *not* into his mind?

22 So that the LORD could no longer bear, because of the evil of your doings, *and* because of the abominations which ye have committed; therefore is your land a desolation, and an astonishment, and a curse, without an inhabitant, as at this day.

23 Because ye have burned incense, and because ye have sinned against the LORD, and have not listened to the voice of the LORD, nor walked in his law, nor in his rights, nor in his testimonies; therefore this evil has come upon you, as at this day.

24 Moreover Jeremiah said unto all the people, and to all the women, Hear the word of the LORD, all Judah that *are* in the land of Egypt:

25 Thus hath spoken the LORD of the hosts, the God of Israel, saying; Ye and your wives have both spoken with your mouths, and fulfilled with your hand, saying, We will surely perform our vows that we have vowed, to burn incense to the queen of heaven, and to pour out drink offerings unto her: ye will surely accomplish your vows, and surely perform your vows.

26 Therefore hear ye the word of the LORD, all Judah that dwell in the land of Egypt; Behold, I have sworn by my great name, said the LORD, that my name shall no more be named in the mouth of any man of Judah in all the land of Egypt, saying, The Lord GOD liveth.

27 Behold, I will watch over them for evil, and not for good: and all the men of Judah that *are* in the land of Egypt shall be consumed by the sword and by the famine, until there be an end of them.

28 Yet a small number that escape the sword shall return out of the land of Egypt into the land of Judah; so that all the remnant of Judah, that are gone into the land of Egypt to dwell there, shall know whose words shall stand, mine, or theirs.

29 And this *shall be* a sign unto you, saith the LORD, that I will visit you in this place, that ye may know that my words shall surely stand against you for evil:

30 Thus hath the LORD said; Behold, I will give Pharaohhophra king of Egypt into the hand of his enemies, and into the hand of them that seek his soul; as I gave Zedekiah king of Judah into the hand of Nebuchadrezzar king of Babylon, his enemy, and that sought his soul.

Chapter 45

1 The word that Jeremiah the prophet spoke unto Baruch the son of Neriah, when he had written these words in a book at the mouth of Jeremiah, in the fourth year of Jehoiakim the son of Josiah king of Judah, saying,

2 Thus hath the LORD, the God of Israel said unto thee, O Baruch;

3 Thou didst say, Woe is me now! for the LORD hath added grief to my sorrow; I fainted in my sighing, and I have found no rest.

4 Thus shalt thou say unto him, The LORD said thus;

211

JEREMIAH 46:11

Behold, I destroy those whom I have built up, and those whom I have planted I pluck up, even this whole land.

5 And seekest thou great things for thyself? seek *them* not: for, behold, I bring evil upon all flesh, said the LORD: but thy life will I give unto thee as a spoil *of battle* in all places where thou goest.

Chapter 46

1 The word of the LORD which came to Jeremiah the prophet against the Gentiles;

2 To Egypt: against the army of Pharaohnecho king of Egypt, which was by the river Euphrates in Carchemish, which Nebuchadrezzar king of Babylon smote in the fourth year of Jehoiakim the son of Josiah king of Judah.

3 Order ye the buckler and shield, and draw near to battle.

4 Harness the horses; and get up, ye horsemen, and stand forth with *your* helmets; furbish the spears, *and* put on the brigandines.

5 Wherefore have I seen them dismayed *and* turned away back? and their mighty ones are beaten down, and are fled in haste, and look not back: *for* fear

was round about, said the LORD.

6 Let not the swift flee away, nor the mighty man escape; they stumbled, and fell toward the north by the river Euphrates.

7 Who *is* this *that* cometh up as a flood, whose waters move as rivers?

8 Egypt riseth up like a flood, and *his* waters move like rivers; and he said, I will go up, *and* will cover the earth; I will destroy the city and the inhabitants thereof.

9 Come up, ye horses; and rage, ye chariots; and let the mighty men come forth; the Ethiopians and the Libyans, that handle the shield; and the Lydians, that handle *and* bend the bow.

10 But this day *shall be* unto the Lord GOD of the hosts, a day of vengeance, that he may avenge him of his adversaries: and the sword shall devour, and it shall be satiated and made drunk with their blood: for it *shall be a* slaughter unto the Lord GOD of the hosts in the north country *by* the river Euphrates.

11 Go up into Gilead, and take balm, O virgin, the daughter of Egypt: in vain shalt thou use many medicines; *for* there is no cure for thee.

12 The nations have heard of thy shame, and thy cry hath filled the land: for the mighty man hath stumbled against the mighty, *and* they are fallen both together.

13 The word that the LORD spoke to Jeremiah the prophet, how Nebuchadrezzar king of Babylon should come *and* smite the land of Egypt.

14 Declare ye in Egypt, and publish in Migdol, and publish in Memphis and in Tahpanhes: say ye, Stand fast, and prepare thee; for the sword shall devour round about thee.

15 Why is thy fortress swept away? It could not stand, because the LORD did push it *over.*

16 He multiplied the fallen, yea, one fell upon another: and they said, Arise, and let us go again to our own people, and to the land of our nativity, away from the overcoming sword.

17 They did cry there, Pharaoh king of Egypt *is but* a noise; he allowed the appointed time to pass *by.*

18 As I live, saith the King, whose name *is* the LORD of the hosts, Surely as Tabor *is* among the mountains,

and as Carmel by the sea, *so* shall he come.

19 O thou daughter dwelling in Egypt, furnish thyself to go into captivity: for Memphis shall be a pasture and shall be made desolate without an inhabitant.

20 Egypt *is like* a very fair heifer, *but* destruction cometh; it cometh out of the north.

21 Also her soldiers *are* in the midst of her like fatted bullocks; for they also turned back, *and* all fled away without stopping: because the day of their calamity was come upon them, *and* the time of their visitation.

22 Her voice shall go forth like a serpent; for they shall march with an army, and come against her with axes, as hewers of wood.

23 They shall cut down her forest, saith the LORD, for they cannot be counted; because they are more than the locusts; they *are* innumerable.

24 The daughter of Egypt shall be confounded; she shall be delivered into the hand of the people of the north.

25 The LORD of the hosts, the God of Israel, said; Behold, I will visit the multitude of Alexandria, and

Pharaoh, and Egypt, with their gods, and their kings; even Pharaoh, and *all* them that trust in him:

26 And I will deliver them into the hand of those that seek their soul, and into the hand of Nebuchadrezzar king of Babylon, and into the hand of his servants: and afterward it shall be inhabited, as in the days of old, saith the LORD.

27 But fear not thou, O my servant Jacob, and be not dismayed, O Israel: for, behold, I will save thee from afar off, and thy seed from the land of their captivity; and Jacob shall return, and be in rest and be prospered, and none shall make *him* afraid.

28 Fear thou not, O Jacob my servant, saith the LORD: for I *am* with thee; for I will make a full end of all the Gentiles where I have driven thee: but I will not make a full end of thee, but I will chastise thee with judgment; and I will not completely cut thee off.

Chapter 47

1 The word of the LORD that came to Jeremiah the prophet against the Palestinians, before Pharaoh smote Gaza.

2 Thus hath the LORD said; Behold, waters rise up out of the north, and shall be an overflowing flood, and shall overflow the land, and all that is therein; the cities, and them that dwell therein: then the men shall cry, and all the inhabitants of the land shall howl.

3 At the noise of the stamping of the hoofs of his strong *horses*, at the rushing of his chariots, *and at* the rumbling of his wheels, the fathers shall not look back to *their* children for feebleness of hands;

4 because of the day that cometh to destroy all the Palestinians, *and* to cut off from Tyre, and Zidon, every helper that remaineth: for the LORD will destroy the Palestinians, the remnant of the island of Caphtor.

5 Baldness is come upon Gaza; Ashkelon is cut off *with* the remnant of their valley: how long wilt thou cut thyself?

6 O thou sword of the LORD, how long *will it be* ere thou be quiet? put up thyself into thy scabbard, rest, and be still.

7 How can it be quiet, seeing the LORD hath given it a charge against Ashkelon, and against the sea shore? there hath he appointed it.

Chapter 48

1 Against Moab thus hath the LORD of the hosts, the God of Israel said; Woe unto Nebo! for it is destroyed, it is confounded: Kiriathaim is taken: Misgab is confounded and dismayed.

2 Moab shall no longer be praised: they have devised evil against Heshbon, saying, Come, and let us cut it off from *being* a nation. Also thou shalt be cut down, O Madmen; the sword shall pursue thee.

3 A voice of crying *shall be* from Horonaim, spoiling and great destruction.

4 Moab is destroyed; they have caused the cry of her little ones to be heard.

5 For in the ascending *road* of Luhith he that weepeth shall go up weeping; for in the descending *road* of Horonaim the enemies have heard a cry of destruction.

6 Flee, save your lives, and be like the heath in the wilderness.

7 For because thou hast trusted in thy works; in thy treasures, thou shalt also be taken: and Chemosh shall go forth into captivity *with* his priests and his princes together.

8 And the spoiler shall come upon every city, and no city shall escape: the valley also shall perish, and the plain shall be destroyed, as the LORD hath spoken.

9 Give wings unto Moab, that he may flee and get away: for his cities shall be desolate, without any to dwell therein.

10 Cursed *be* he that doeth the work of the LORD deceitfully, and cursed *be* he that keepeth back his sword from blood.

11 Moab hath been at ease from his youth, and he hath settled on his lees, and hath not been emptied from vessel to vessel, neither hath he gone into captivity: therefore his taste remained in him, and his scent is not changed.

12 Therefore, behold, the days come, said the LORD, that I will send unto him captors, that shall take him captive, and shall empty his vessels, and break his wineskins.

13 And Moab shall be ashamed of Chemosh, as the house of Israel was ashamed of Bethel their confidence.

14 How say ye, We *are* mighty and strong men for the war?

15 Moab is spoiled, and his cities destroyed, and his chosen young men are gone down to the slaughter, said the King, whose name *is* the LORD of the hosts.

16 The calamity of Moab *is* near to come, and his affliction hasteneth fast.

17 All ye that are about him, bemoan him; and all ye that know his name, say, How is the strong staff broken; the beautiful rod!

18 Thou daughter that dost inhabit Dibon, come down from *thy* glory, and sit in thirst; for the spoiler of Moab has come against thee, *and* hath dissipated thy strong holds.

19 O inhabitant of Aroer, stand by the way, and watch; ask her that fleeth, and her that escapeth, *and* say, What has happened?

20 Moab is confounded; for it is broken down: howl and cry; tell ye it in Arnon, that Moab is spoiled,

21 and judgment is come upon the plain country; upon Holon, and upon Jahazah, and upon Mephaath,

22 and upon Dibon, and upon Nebo, and upon Bethdiblathaim,

23 and upon Kiriathaim, and upon Bethgamul, and upon Bethmeon,

24 and upon Kerioth, and upon Bozrah, and upon all the cities of the land of Moab, those that are far and those that are near.

25 The horn of Moab is cut off, and his arm is broken, said the LORD.

26 Make ye him drunken: for he magnified *himself* against the LORD: Moab also shall wallow in his vomit, and he also shall be in derision.

27 For was not Israel a derision unto thee, as if he were found among thieves? for since thou hast spoken of him, thou hast slipped.

28 O ye that dwell in Moab, leave the cities, and dwell in the rock, and be like the dove *that* maketh her nest in the sides of the hole's mouth.

29 We have heard the pride of Moab, (he is exceeding proud) his loftiness, and his arrogancy, and his pride, and the haughtiness of his heart.

30 I know his wrath, saith the LORD; but it shall have no effect; his lies shall not be to his advantage.

31 Therefore will I weep over Moab, and I will cry out for all Moab; *my heart* shall mourn for the men of Kirheres.

32 O vine of Sibmah, I will weep for thee with the weeping of Jazer: thy shoots are gone over the sea, they reach *even* to the sea of Jazer: the spoiler is fallen upon thy summer fruits and upon thy vintage.

33 And joy and gladness shall be taken from the plentiful field, and from the land of Moab; and I shall cause wine to cease from the winepresses: none shall tread with song; *their* song *shall be* no song.

34 The cry, from Heshbon *even* unto Elealeh, *and even* unto Jahaz, have they uttered their voice, from Zoar *even* unto Horonaim, *as* an heifer of three years old: for the waters of Nimrim shall also be destroyed.

35 Moreover I will cause to cease in Moab, saith the LORD, him that offereth upon *an* altar, and him that burneth incense to his gods.

36 Therefore my heart shall sound like flutes for Moab, and my heart shall sound like flutes for the men of Kirheres: because the riches *that* he hath gotten are perished.

37 For every head *shall be* bald, and every beard shaved: upon all the hands *shall be* cuttings, and upon all the loins sackcloth.

38 *There shall be* lamentation generally upon all the housetops of Moab, and in the streets thereof: for I have broken Moab like a vessel wherein *is* no pleasure, said the LORD.

39 They shall howl, *saying,* How is it broken down! how hath Moab turned the back with shame! so shall Moab be a derision and a dismaying to all them about him.

40 For thus hath the LORD said; Behold, he shall fly as an eagle, and shall spread his wings over Moab.

41 The cities are taken, and the strong holds are taken, and the mighty men's hearts in Moab at that day shall be as the heart of a woman in her pangs.

42 And Moab shall be destroyed from *being* a people, because he hath magnified *himself* against the LORD.

43 Fear, and the pit, and the snare, *shall be* upon thee, O inhabitant of Moab, said the LORD.

44 He that fleeth from the fear shall fall into the pit; and he that getteth up out of the pit shall be taken in the snare: for I will bring upon him, *even* upon Moab, the year of their visitation, said the LORD.

45 They that fled from the force stood under the shadow of Heshbon: because fire came forth out of Heshbon, and a flame from the midst of Sihon, and burned the corner of Moab, and the crown of the head of the rebellious sons.

46 Woe be unto thee, O Moab! the people of Chemosh have perished: for thy sons are taken prisoners into captivity, and thy daughters *are* captives.

47 Yet will I turn again the captivity of Moab in the last of the times, said the LORD. Thus far *is* the judgment of Moab.

Chapter 49

1 Concerning the Ammonites, thus hath the LORD said; Hath Israel no sons? hath he no heir? why *then* doth their king inherit Gad, and his people dwell in his cities?

2 Therefore, behold, the days come, said the LORD, that I will cause an alarm of war to be heard in Rabbah of the Ammonites; and it shall be *made* a desolate heap, and her cities shall be burned with fire: then shall Israel be heir unto them that were his heirs, said the LORD.

3 Howl, O Heshbon, for Ai is spoiled: cry, ye daughters of Rabbah, gird you with sackcloth; lament, and run to and fro by the hedges; for their king shall go into captivity, *and* his priests and his princes together.

4 Why gloriest thou in the valleys? Thy valley hath slipped, O backsliding daughter that trusted in her treasures, she that saith, Who shall come against me?

5 Behold, I bring fear upon thee, saith the Lord GOD of the hosts, from all sides; and ye shall be driven out every man right forth in the direction he is facing; and none shall gather up him that wandereth.

6 And afterward I will turn again the captivity of the sons of Ammon, said the LORD.

7 Concerning Edom, thus hath the LORD of the hosts said; Is there no more wisdom in Teman? Has the counsel of the wise perished? Is their wisdom corrupted?

8 Flee ye, turn back, hide in the deeps to remain, O inhabitants of Dedan; for I will bring the calamity of Esau upon him, at the time *that* I have to visit him.

9 If grapegatherers came against thee, would they not leave *some* gleaning grapes? If thieves by night, they will take what they have need of.

10 But I will make Esau bare, I will uncover his secret places, and he shall not be able to hide himself: his seed shall be destroyed, and his brethren, and his neighbours, and he shall no longer be.

11 Leave thy fatherless children, I will raise them; and thy widows shall trust in me.

12 For thus hath the LORD said; Behold, those who were not condemned to drink of the cup have assuredly drunken; and shalt thou be absolved of everything? Thou shalt not be absolved, but thou shalt surely drink *of it.*

13 For I have sworn by myself, said the LORD, that Bozrah shall become a desolation, a reproach, a waste, and a curse; and all the cities thereof shall be perpetual wastes.

14 I have heard the news, that from the LORD a messenger had been sent unto the Gentiles, *saying,* Gather ye together, and come against her, and rise up to the battle.

15 For, behold, I have placed thee as small among the Gentiles, *and* despised among men.

16 Thy arrogance hath deceived thee, *and* the pride of thine heart, O thou that dwellest in the clefts of the rock, that holdest the height of the mountain: though thou shouldest make thy nest as high as the eagle, I will bring thee down from thence, said the LORD.

17 Also Edom shall be a desolation: every one that goeth by it shall be astonished, and shall hiss at all the plagues thereof.

18 As in the overthrow of Sodom and Gomorrah and the neighbour *cities* thereof, said the LORD, no man shall abide there, neither shall a son of man dwell in it.

19 Behold, he shall come up like a lion from the swelling of Jordan to the strong habitation: for I will make rest and make him run from upon her, and he who *is* chosen shall I appoint over her; for who *is* like me? and who will appoint me the time? and who *is* that shepherd that will stand before me?

20 Therefore hear the counsel of the LORD, that he hath taken against Edom; and his thoughts, that he hath purposed against the inhabitants of Teman: Surely the least of the flock shall draw them out: surely he shall destroy their habitations with them.

21 The earth is moved at the noise of their fall, at the cry the noise thereof was heard in the Red sea.

22 Behold, he shall rise up and fly as the eagle, and spread his wings over Bozrah: and at that day shall the heart of the mighty men of Edom be as the heart of a woman in her pangs.

23 Concerning Damascus. Hamath is confounded, and Arpad: for they have heard bad news: they have melted in waters of feebleness; they cannot be reassured.

24 Damascus is waxed feeble, *and* turneth herself to flee, and fear hath seized on *her*: anguish and sorrows have taken her, as a woman in travail.

25 How did they not forgive the city of praise, the city of my joy!

26 Therefore her young men shall fall in her streets, and all the men of war shall be cut off in that day, said the LORD of the hosts.

27 And I will kindle a fire in the wall of Damascus, and it shall consume the houses of Benhadad.

28 Concerning Kedar, and concerning the kingdoms of Hazor, which Nebuchadrezzar king of Babylon did smite, thus hath the LORD said; Arise ye, go up to Kedar, and destroy the men of the east.

29 Their tents and their flocks shall they take away: they shall take to themselves their curtains, and all their vessels, and their camels; and they shall invoke fear on every side against them.

30 Flee, get you far off, dwell in the deeps that *ye* may stand, O ye inhabitants of Hazor, said the LORD; for Nebuchadrezzar king of Babylon hath taken counsel against you, and hath conceived a purpose against you.

31 Arise, get you up unto the wealthy nation, that dwelleth without care, saith the LORD, which have neither gates nor bars, *which* dwell alone.

32 And their camels shall be a booty, and the multitude of their cattle a spoil: and I will scatter them into all *the* winds, throwing them out unto the utmost corner; and from all their sides I will bring their ruin, said the LORD.

33 And Hazor shall be a dwelling for dragons, *and* a desolation for ever: there shall no man abide there, nor *any* son of man dwell in it.

34 The word of the LORD that came to Jeremiah the prophet regarding Elam in the beginning of the reign of Zedekiah king of Judah, saying,

35 Thus hath the LORD of the hosts said; Behold, I break the bow of Elam, the foundation of their might.

36 And upon Elam will I bring the four winds from the four quarters of heaven, and will scatter them toward all those winds; and there shall be no nation where the outcasts of Elam shall not come.

37 For I will cause Elam to fear before their enemies, and before them that seek their soul: and I will bring evil upon them, *even* my fierce anger, said the LORD; and I will send the sword after them, until I have consumed them:

38 And I will set my throne in Elam, and will destroy from thence the king and the princes, said the LORD.

39 But it shall come to pass in the last of the days, *that* I will turn again the captivity of Elam, said the LORD.

Chapter 50

1 The word that the LORD spoke against Babylon *and* against the land of the Chaldeans by the hand of Jeremiah the prophet.

2 Declare ye among the Gentiles, and publish, and set up a standard; publish, *and* conceal not: say, Babylon is taken, Bel is confounded, Merodach is broken in pieces; her idols are confounded, her images are broken in pieces.

3 For out of the north there cometh up a nation against her, which shall make her land desolate, and none shall dwell therein: they shall leave, they shall depart, both man and beast.

4 In those days, and in that time, saith the LORD, the sons of Israel shall come, they and the sons of Judah together, going and weeping: they shall go, and seek the LORD their God.

5 They shall ask the way to Zion, unto whence they shall turn their faces, *saying*, Come, and let us join ourselves to the LORD in an eternal covenant *that* shall never be forgotten.

6 My people have been lost sheep: their shepherds have caused them to go astray, they have turned them away *on* the mountains: they have gone from mountain to hill, they have forgotten their restingplace.

7 All that found them have devoured them: and their

221

adversaries said, We offend not, because they have sinned against the LORD, the habitation of justice, even the LORD, the hope of their fathers.

8 Flee out of the midst of Babylon, and go forth out of the land of the Chaldeans, and be as the meek in front of the flocks.

9 For, behold, I awake and cause to come up against Babylon an assembly of great nations from the north country: and from thence they shall set themselves in array against her; she shall be taken: their arrows *shall be* as of a mighty expert *one*, who shall not return in vain.

10 And the land of the Chaldeans shall be for a spoil: all that spoil her shall come forth full, saith the LORD.

11 Because ye were glad, because ye rejoiced destroying my heritage, because ye filled yourselves as a heifer on grass, and neighed like horses;

12 your mother was sore confounded; she that bore you was ashamed: see here the latter end of the Gentiles: wilderness, dry land, and desert.

13 Because of the wrath of the LORD *she* shall not be inhabited, but she shall be completely desolate: every one that goeth by Babylon shall be astonished, and hiss at all her plagues.

14 Put yourselves in array against Babylon round about: all ye that bend the bow, shoot at her, spare no arrows: for she hath sinned against the LORD.

15 Shout against her round about: she hath given her hand: her foundations are fallen, her walls are thrown down: for it *is* the vengeance of the LORD: take vengeance upon her; as she hath done, do unto her.

16 Cut off the sower from Babylon, and him that handleth the sickle in the time of harvest: for fear of the oppressing sword they shall turn every one to his people, and they shall flee every one to his own land.

17 Israel *has been like* scattered sheep; the lions have driven *him* away: first the king of Assyria hath devoured him; and last this Nebuchadrezzar king of Babylon hath broken his bones.

18 Therefore thus hath the LORD of the hosts, the God of Israel said; Behold, I visit the king of Babylon and his land, as I have visited the king of Assyria.

19 And I will bring Israel again to his habitation, and he shall feed on Carmel and Bashan, and his soul shall be satisfied upon mount Ephraim and Gilead.

20 In those days, and in that time, said the LORD, the iniquity of Israel shall be sought for, and *there shall be* none; and the sins of Judah, and they shall not be found: for I will pardon them whom I shall have left.

21 Go up against the land of Merathaim, *even* against it, and against the inhabitants of Pekod: waste and utterly destroy after them, said the LORD, and do according to all that I have commanded thee.

22 A sound of battle *is* in the land, and of great destruction.

23 How is the hammer of the whole earth cut asunder and broken! how is Babylon become a desolation among the Gentiles!

24 I have laid a snare for thee, and thou art also taken, O Babylon, and thou wast not aware: thou art found, and also caught, because thou hast provoked the LORD.

25 The LORD hath opened his treasury, and hath brought forth the vessels of his indignation: for this *is* the work of the Lord GOD of the hosts in the land of the Chaldeans.

26 Come against her from the ends *of the earth,* open her storehouses: cast her up as heaps, and destroy her utterly: let nothing of her be left.

27 Slay all her bullocks; let them go down to the slaughter: woe unto them! for their day is come, the time of their visitation.

28 The voice of them that flee and escape out of the land of Babylon, to declare in Zion the vengeance of the LORD our God, the vengeance of his temple.

29 Call together the archers against Babylon: all ye that bend the bow, camp against it round about; let none thereof escape: recompense her according to her work; according to all that she hath done, do unto her: for she hath become proud against the LORD, against the Holy One of Israel.

30 Therefore shall her young men fall in her streets, and all her men of war shall be cut off in that day, said the LORD.

31 Behold, I *am* against thee, O *thou* proud one, said the Lord GOD of the hosts: for thy day is come, the time *that* I will visit thee.

32 And the proud one shall stumble and fall, and have no one to raise him up: and I will kindle a fire in his cities, and it shall devour all round about him.

33 Thus hath the LORD of the hosts said; The sons of Israel and the sons of Judah *were* oppressed together: and all that took them captives held them fast; they refused to let them go.

34 Their Redeemer *is* strong; the LORD of the hosts *is* his name: he shall thoroughly plead their cause, that he may give rest to the land, and disquiet the inhabitants of Babylon.

35 A sword *is* upon the Chaldeans, said the LORD, and upon the inhabitants of Babylon, and upon her princes, and upon her wise *men*.

36 A sword *is* upon the fortune-tellers; and they shall be fools: a sword *is* upon her mighty men; and they shall be broken.

37 A sword *is* upon their horses, and upon their chariots, and upon all the mingled people that *are* in the midst of her; and they shall become as women: a sword *is* upon her treasures; and they shall be robbed.

38 A drought *is* upon her waters; and they shall be dried up: for it *is* the land of graven images, and they are become mad upon *their* idols.

39 Therefore the wild beasts of the desert with the wild beasts of the islands shall dwell *there*, and the owls shall dwell therein: and it shall be no more inhabited for ever; neither shall it be dwelt in from generation to generation.

40 As God overthrew Sodom and Gomorrah and the neighbour *cities* thereof, saith the LORD; *so* shall no man abide there, neither shall any son of man dwell therein.

41 Behold, a people cometh from the north, and a great nation, and many kings shall be raised up from the coasts of the earth.

42 They shall hold the bow and the lance: they *shall be* cruel, and will not show mercy: their voice shall roar like the sea, and they shall ride upon horses, *every one* put in array, like a man to the battle, against thee, O daughter of Babylon.

43 The king of Babylon hath heard the report of them, and his hands waxed feeble: anguish took hold of him, *and* pangs as of a woman in travail.

44 Behold, he shall come up like a lion from the swelling of Jordan unto the strong habitation: but I will rest, and will make him run from upon her: and he who shall be chosen I will appoint over her. For who *is* like me? and who will appoint me the time? and who *is* that shepherd that will stand before me?

45 Therefore hear ye the counsel of the LORD, that he hath taken against Babylon; and his thoughts, that he hath purposed against the land of the Chaldeans: Surely the least of the flock shall drag them out and they shall destroy their habitations with them.

46 At the noise of the taking of Babylon the earth was moved, and the cry was heard among the Gentiles.

Chapter 51

1 Thus hath the LORD said; Behold, I raise up against Babylon, and against her inhabitants that rise up against me from the heart, a destroying wind.

2 And I will send unto Babylon fanners, that shall fan her, and shall empty her land: for in the day of trouble they shall be against her round about.

3 *I shall say* to the archer that bendeth his bow, and unto him that lifteth himself up in his brigandine, Spare ye not her young men; destroy ye utterly all her host.

4 Thus the slain shall fall in the land of the Chaldeans, and *they that are* thrust through in her streets.

5 For Israel and Judah have not been made widows of their God, of the LORD of the hosts; though their land was filled with sin against the Holy One of Israel.

6 Flee out of the midst of Babylon, and deliver every man his soul: that ye not perish because of her iniquity; for this *is* the time of the LORD'S vengeance; he will render unto her a recompense.

7 Babylon *hath been* a golden cup in the LORD'S hand, that made all the earth drunken: the Gentiles have drunken of her wine; therefore the nations are mad.

8 Babylon is suddenly fallen and destroyed: howl for her; take balm for her pain, if so be she may be healed.

9 We applied *the medicine to* Babylon, but she is not healed: forsake her, and let us go every one into his own land: for her judgment is come unto heaven, and is lifted up *even* to the clouds.

10 The LORD hath brought our righteousness to light: come, and let us declare in Zion the work of the LORD our God.

11 Make bright the arrows; gather the shields: the LORD hath awakened the spirit of the kings of the Medes: for his thought *is* against Babylon, to destroy her; for it *is* vengeance of the LORD, the vengeance of his temple.

12 Set up the standard upon the walls of Babylon, make the watch strong, set up the watchmen, prepare the ambushes: for the LORD hath deliberated and shall put into effect that which he spoke against the inhabitants of Babylon.

13 O thou that dwellest among many waters, rich in treasures, thine end is come; the measure of thy covetousness.

14 The LORD of the hosts hath sworn by himself, *saying,* Surely I will fill thee with men, as with locusts; and they shall sing the song

of the winepress against thee.

15 He is the one who maketh the earth by his power, he upholdeth the world by his wisdom, and extendeth the heavens by his understanding;

16 he who giveth with *his* voice a multitude of waters from heaven; then he causeth the clouds to ascend from the ends of the earth: he maketh lightnings with the rain, and bringeth forth the wind out of his treasures.

17 Every man has become carnal and is without knowledge; let every founder be ashamed of the graven image: for his molten image *is* falsehood, and *there is* no breath in them.

18 They *are* vanity, the work of errors: in the time of their visitation they shall perish.

19 The portion of Jacob *is* not like them; for he *is* the Former of all things: and *Israel is* the rod of his inheritance: the LORD of the hosts *is* his name.

20 Thou *art* my hammer, O weapons of war: for with thee will I break in pieces the Gentiles, and with thee will I destroy kingdoms;

21 and with thee will I break in pieces the horse

and his rider; and with thee will I break in pieces the chariots and their riders;

22 with thee also will I break in pieces men and women; and with thee will I break in pieces old and young; and with thee will I break in pieces young men and virgins;

23 I will also break in pieces with thee the shepherd and his flock; and with thee will I break in pieces the husbandman and his yoke of oxen; and with thee will I break in pieces dukes and princes.

24 And I will render unto Babylon and to all the inhabitants of Chaldea all their evil that they have done in Zion in your sight, said the LORD.

25 Behold, I *am* against thee, O destroying mountain, said the LORD, which destroyest all the earth: and I will stretch out my hand upon thee, and roll thee down from the rocks, and will make thee a burnt mountain.

26 And they shall not take of thee a stone for a corner, nor a stone for foundations; but thou shalt be desolate for ever, said the LORD.

27 Set ye up a standard in the land, blow the trumpet among the Gentiles, pre-pare the nations against her, call together against her the kingdoms of Ararat, Minni, and Ashchenaz; appoint a captain against her; cause *the* horses to come up as raised up locusts.

28 Prepare the nations against her: the kings of Media, the captains thereof, and all the princes thereof, and all the land of their dominion.

29 And the land shall tremble and sorrow: for every thought of the LORD is confirmed against Babylon, to make the land of Babylon a desolation without an inhabitant.

30 The mighty men of Babylon have forborne to fight, they have remained in *their* holds: their might hath failed; they became as women: the *enemies* have burned her dwellingplaces; they have broken her bars.

31 One post shall run to meet another, and one messenger to meet another, to show the king of Babylon that his city is taken in all places,

32 And the fords were taken, and the reeds they have burned with fire, and the men of war were astounded.

33 For thus hath the LORD of the hosts, the God of Israel said; The daughter of Babylon *is* like a threshing-floor, *it is* now time to thresh her: yet a little while, and the time of her harvest shall come.

34 Nebuchadrezzar the king of Babylon hath devoured me, he hath crushed me, he hath made me an empty vessel, he hath swallowed me up like a dragon, he hath filled his belly with my delicates, he hath cast me out.

35 The violence against me and my flesh *be* upon Babylon, shall the inhabitant of Zion say; and my blood upon the inhabitants of Chaldea, shall Jerusalem say.

36 Therefore thus hath the LORD said; Behold, I judge thy cause, and shall take thy vengeance; and I will dry up her sea, and make her flowing *waters* dry.

37 And Babylon shall become heaps, a dwelling-place for dragons, an astonishment, and an hissing, without an inhabitant.

38 They shall roar together like lions: they shall roar as lions' whelps.

39 In their heat I will place their feasts *before them*, and I will make them drunken, that they may rejoice, and sleep an eternal sleep, and not wake, said the LORD.

40 I will bring them down like lambs to the slaughter, like rams with he goats.

41 How is Sheshach a prey! and how is she who was the praise of the whole earth taken! how is Babylon become an astonishment among the Gentiles!

42 The sea is come up upon Babylon: she is covered with the multitude of the waves thereof.

43 Her cities were devastated, the land dry and desert, a land wherein no man dwelleth, neither shall *any* son of man pass thereby.

44 And I will visit Bel himself in Babylon, and I will bring forth out of his mouth that which he hath swallowed up: and the Gentiles shall not flow together any more unto him: yea, the wall of Babylon shall fall.

45 Come out of the midst of her, my people, and save each one his life from the fierce anger of the LORD.

46 And lest your heart faint, and ye fear because of the news that shall be heard in the land; in one year shall the news come, and after that in the *next* year *shall come* the rumour, and *then shall come* the violence in the land, and the ruler over he who rules.

47 Therefore, behold, the days come, that I will visit the graven images of Babylon: and her whole land shall be ashamed, and all her dead shall fall in the midst of her.

48 Then the heavens and the earth, and all that *is* therein, shall sing praises over Babylon: for the destroyers shall come unto her from the north, said the LORD.

49 As Babylon *hath caused the* dead of Israel to fall, so because of Babylon *the* dead of all the earth fell.

50 Ye that have escaped the sword, go away, do not tarry: remember the LORD for many days, and remember Jerusalem.

51 We are ashamed, because we have heard the reproach: confusion hath covered our faces: for strangers are come against the sanctuaries of the LORD'S house.

52 Therefore, behold, the days come, said the LORD, that I will visit her graven images: and through all her *land the wounded* unto death shall groan.

53 Though Babylon should mount up to heaven, and though she should fortify her strength upon high, *yet* from me shall destroyers come unto her, said the LORD.

54 The sound of a cry *cometh* from Babylon, and great destruction from the land of the Chaldeans!

55 Because the LORD destroyeth Babylon, and taketh out of her the many thunders; her waves shall roar, like many waters shall be the sound of their voice:

56 Because the destroyer is come against her, *even* upon Babylon, and her mighty men are taken, their bow is broken: for the LORD God of recompenses shall surely requite.

57 And I will make drunk her princes, and her wise *men*, her captains, and her rulers, and her mighty men: and they shall sleep an eternal sleep, and shall not wake, saith the King, whose name *is* the LORD of the hosts.

58 Thus hath the LORD of the hosts said; The broad walls of Babylon shall be utterly cast down, and her high gates shall be burned with fire; and peoples and nations shall labour in vain in the fire *to save her*, and they shall become weary.

59 The word which Jeremiah the prophet sent to Seraiah the son of Neriah, the son of Maaseiah, when he went with Zedekiah the king of Judah into Babylon in the fourth year of his reign. And *this* Seraiah *was* the chief steward of the bedchambers.

60 So Jeremiah wrote in a book all the evil that should come upon Babylon, *even* all these words that are written against Babylon.

61 And Jeremiah said to Seraiah, When thou comest to Babylon, and shalt see, and shalt read all these things;

62 then shalt thou say, O LORD, thou hast spoken against this place, to cut it off, that none shall remain in it, neither man nor beast, but that it shall be desolate for ever.

63 And it shall be, when thou hast made an end of reading this book, *that* thou shalt bind a stone to it, and cast it into the midst of Euphrates:

64 And thou shalt say, Thus shall Babylon sink, and shall not rise from the evil that I will bring upon her: and they shall be overcome. Thus far *are* the words of Jeremiah.

Chapter 52

1 Zedekiah *was* twenty-one years old when he began to reign, and he reigned eleven years in Jerusalem. And his mother's name *was* Hamutal the daughter of Jeremiah of Libnah.

2 And he did *that which was* evil in the eyes of the LORD, according to all that Jehoiakim had done.

3 For because of the anger of the LORD against Jerusalem and Judah, until he had cast them out of his presence, Zedekiah rebelled against the king of Babylon.

4 Therefore it came to pass after nine years of his reign, in the tenth month, in the tenth *day* of the month, *that* Nebuchadrezzar king of Babylon came, he and all his army, against Jerusalem, and pitched camp against it, and built forts against it round about.

5 So the city was besieged unto the eleventh year of king Zedekiah.

6 And in the fourth month, in the ninth *day* of the month, the famine prevailed in the city, so that there was no bread for the people of the land.

7 Then the city was breached, and all the men of war fled, and went forth out of the city by night by the way of the gate between the two walls, which *was* by the king's garden, and they went by the way of the desert, even though the Chaldeans *were* by the city round about.

8 But the army of the Chaldeans pursued after the king, and took Zedekiah in the plains of Jericho; and all his army was scattered from him.

9 So they took the king, and caused him to come up unto the king of Babylon to Riblah in the land of Hamath; where he pronounced the sentence upon him.

10 And the king of Babylon slew the sons of Zedekiah before his eyes: he slew also all the princes of Judah in Riblah.

11 But he put out the eyes of Zedekiah and bound him in chains; and the king of Babylon caused him to be taken to Babylon, and put him in prison until the day of his death.

12 And in the fifth month, in the tenth *day* of the month, which *was* the nineteenth year of Nebuchadrezzar king of Babylon, came Nebuzaradan, captain of the guard, *which* served the king of Babylon, into Jerusalem,

13 and burned the house of the LORD, and the king's house; and all the houses of Jerusalem, and every great house he burned with fire:

14 And all the army of the Chaldeans, that *were* with the captain of the guard, destroyed all the walls of Jerusalem round about.

15 Then Nebuzaradan the captain of the guard carried away captive *certain* of the poor of the people, and the residue of the people that remained in the city, and the fugitives that had fled to the king of Babylon, and the rest of the multitude.

16 But Nebuzaradan the captain of the guard left *certain* of the poor of the land for vinedressers and for husbandmen.

17 Also the pillars of brass that *were* in the house of the LORD, and the bases, and the brazen sea that *was* in the house of the LORD, the Chaldeans broke, and carried all the brass of them to Babylon.

18 The caldrons also, and the shovels, and the snuffers, and the bowls, and the spoons, and all the vessels of brass wherewith they ministered, they took away.

19 And the basons, and the censers, and the bowls, and

the caldrons, and the candlesticks, and the spoons, and the cups; *that* which *was* of gold *in* gold, and *that* which *was* of silver *in* silver, took the captain of the guard away.

20 The two pillars, one sea, and twelve brazen bulls that *were* under the bases, which king Solomon had made in the house of the LORD: the brass of all these vessels could not be weighed.

21 And *concerning* the pillars, the height of one pillar *was* eighteen cubits; and a fillet of twelve cubits did compass it; and the thickness thereof *was* four fingers: *it was* hollow.

22 And a chapiter of brass *was* upon it; and the height of one chapiter *was* five cubits, with network and pomegranates upon the chapiters round about, all *of* brass. The second pillar also and the pomegranates *were* like unto these.

23 And there were ninety and six pomegranates on a side; *and* all the pomegranates upon the network *were* an hundred round about.

24 And the captain of the guard took Seraiah the chief priest, and Zephaniah the second priest, and the three keepers of the door:

25 He took also out of the city an eunuch, which had the charge of the men of war; and seven men of them that were near the king's person, which were found in the city; and the principal scribe of the host, who mustered the people of the land for war; and sixty men of the people of the land, that were found in the midst of the city.

26 So Nebuzaradan the captain of the guard took them, and brought them to the king of Babylon to Riblah.

27 And the king of Babylon smote them, and put them to death in Riblah in the land of Hamath. Thus Judah was carried away captive out of his own land.

28 This *is* the people whom Nebuchadrezzar carried away captive: in the seventh year three thousand and twenty-three Jews:

29 In the eighteenth year of Nebuchadrezzar he carried away captive from Jerusalem eight hundred thirty-two persons:

30 In the three and twentieth year of Nebuchadrezzar Nebuzaradan the captain of the guard carried away captive of the Jews seven hundred forty-five persons: all the persons *were* four thousand six hundred.

31 And it came to pass in the thirty-seventh year of the captivity of Jehoiachin king of Judah, in the twelfth month, in the twenty-fifth *day* of the month, *that* Evilmerodach king of Babylon in the *first* year of his reign lifted up the head of Jehoiachin king of Judah, and brought him forth out of prison,

32 and spoke kindly unto him, and set his seat above the seat of the kings that *were* with him in Babylon,

33 and changed his prison garments: and he did continually eat bread before him all the days of his life.

34 And *for* his diet, there was a continual diet given him of the king of Babylon, every thing in its day for all the *days* of his life, until the day of his death.

The Lamentations of Jeremiah

(Composed in Alphabetical Order as Hebrew Poetry)

Chapter 1

1 *Aleph* How doth the city sit solitary, *that was* full of people! The great one among the nations is become as a widow, the lady of provinces is become tributary.

2 *Beth* She weepeth sore in the night, and her tears *are* on her cheeks: among all her lovers she hath none to comfort *her*: all her friends have dealt treacherously with her, they are become her enemies.

3 *Gimel* Judah is gone into captivity because of the affliction, and because of the greatness of the servitude: she dwelleth among the Gentiles, she findeth no rest: all her persecutors overtook her between the straits.

4 *Daleth* The streets of Zion do mourn, because there are none to come to the solemnities: all her gates *are* destroyed: her priests sigh, her virgins are afflicted, and she *is* in bitterness.

5 *He* Her enemies have been made the head, those who hated her have been prospered; for the LORD hath afflicted her for the multitude of her rebellions: her children are gone into captivity before the enemy.

6 *Vau* And from the daughter of Zion all her beauty is departed: her princes are become like harts *that* find no pasture, and they are gone without strength before the pursuer.

7 *Zain* Jerusalem remembered the days of her affliction, and of her rebellions, and of all her desireable things that she had in the times of old, when her people fell into the hand of the enemy, and none did help her: the enemies saw her, *and* did mock at her sabbaths.

8 *Cheth* Jerusalem hath grievously sinned; therefore she is removed: all that honoured her despise her, because they have seen her nakedness: yea, she sigheth, and is turned backward.

9 *Teth* Her filthiness *is* in her skirts; she remembered not her latter end; therefore she came down surprisingly: she hath no comforter. O LORD, behold my affliction: for the enemy hath magnified *himself*.

10 *Jod* The enemy hath spread out his hand upon all her precious things: and *she* saw the Gentiles enter into her sanctuary, whom thou didst command *that* they should not enter into thy congregation.

11 *Caph* All her people sought their bread with sadness; they have given all their precious things for food to maintain life: see, O LORD, and consider; for I am *become* vile.

12 *Lamed Is it* nothing to you, all ye that pass by? behold, and see if there be any sorrow like unto my sorrow, which is come unto me, because the LORD hath afflicted *me* in the day of his fierce anger.

13 *Mem* From apon high he hath sent fire into my bones, and it prevaileth against them: he hath spread a net for my feet, he hath turned me back: he hath made me desolate *and* always with pain.

14 *Nun* The yoke of my rebellions is bound in his hand: they are wreathed, *and* come up upon my neck: he hath made my strength to fall, the Lord hath delivered me into *their* hands, *from whom* I am not able to rise up.

15 *Samech* The Lord hath trodden under foot all my mighty *men* in the midst of me: he hath called a company against me to crush my young men: the Lord hath trodden the virgin daughter of Judah, *as* in a winepress.

16 *Ain* For these *things* I weep; my eyes, my eyes stream with water, because the comforter that giveth rest unto my soul hath left me: my children are desolate, because the enemy prevailed.

17 *Pe* Zion spread forth her hands, and hath no comforter: the LORD gave a commandment against Jacob, that his enemies *should* beseige him: Jerusalem was an abomination in the midst of them.

18 *Tzaddi* The LORD is righteous; for ˙ have rebelled against his mouth: hear now, all the peoples, and see my sorrow: my virgins and my young men are gone into captivity.

19 *Koph* I called unto my lovers, *but* they have deceived me: my priests and my elders in the city perished seeking food to maintain their lives.

20 *Resh* Look, O LORD; for I *am* in distress: my bowels are troubled; my heart is turned within me; for I have grievously rebelled: abroad the sword bereaveth, at home *there is* as death.

21 *Schin* They have heard that I sigh, and there is no comforter for me: all my enemies have heard of my trouble; they are glad that thou hast done *it*. Thou hast brought the day *that* thou hast spoken of, but they shall be like unto me.

22 *Tau* Let all their wickedness come before thee; and do unto them, as thou hast done unto me for all my rebellions: for my sighs *are* many, and my heart *is* filled with pain.

Chapter 2

1 *Aleph* How hath the Lord darkened the daughter of Zion in his anger. He hath cast down from heaven unto the earth the beauty of Israel, and remembered not his footstool in the day of his anger!

2 *Beth* The Lord hath destroyed, and hath not forgiven; he hath destroyed in his wrath all the habitations of Jacob, he hath thrown down to the ground

235

LAMENTATIONS 2:11

the strong holds of the daughter of Judah; he hath polluted the kingdom and the princes thereof.

3 *Gimel* He hath cut off in *his* fierce anger all the horn of Israel: he hath caused his right hand to draw back in the presence of the enemy, and he burned in Jacob like a flaming fire, *which* devoureth round about.

4 *Daleth* He hath bent his bow like an enemy: he strengthened his right hand as an adversary, and slew everything of beauty that could be seen in the tent of the daughter of Zion: he poured out his fury like fire.

5 *He* The Lord was as an enemy: he hath destroyed Israel: he hath destroyed all her palaces: he hath dissipated his strong holds, and hath multiplied in the daughter of Judah mourning and lamentation.

6 *Vau* And he hath violently taken away his tabernacle, as *if it were of* a garden: he hath destroyed his places congregation: the LORD hath caused the solemnities and sabbaths to be forgotten in Zion, and hath rejected in the indignation of his anger the king and the priest.

7 *Zain* The Lord hath cast off his altar, he hath abhorred his sanctuary, he hath given up into the hand of the enemy the walls of her palaces; they have shouted in the house of the LORD, as in the day of a feast.

8 *Cheth* The LORD hath purposed to destroy the wall of the daughter of Zion: he hath stretched out the line, he hath not withdrawn his hand from destroying: therefore he made the rampart and the wall to lament; they were destroyed together.

9 *Teth* Her gates were thrown to the ground; he hath destroyed and broken her bars: her king and her princes *are carried off* among the Gentiles: there is no law; nor have her prophets found vision from the LORD.

10 *Jod* The elders of the daughter of Zion sat upon the ground, *and* are silent: they have cast up dust upon their heads; they have girded themselves with sackcloth: the daughters of Jerusalem hung their heads down to the ground.

11 *Caph* My eyes do fail with tears, my bowels are troubled, my liver is poured upon the earth, for the destruction of the daughter of my people; because the children and the sucklings faint in the streets of the city.

12 *Lamed* They said to their mothers, Where *is* the wheat and the wine? fainting as the dead in the streets of the city, pouring out their souls into their mothers' bosom.

13 *Mem* What witness shall I take to thee? Or unto whom shall I liken thee, O daughter of Jerusalem? Unto whom shall I compare thee, that I may comfort thee, O virgin daughter of Zion? for thy breach *is* as great as the sea: who shall heal thee?

14 *Nun* Thy prophets have preached vainity and foolishness unto thee: and they have not uncovered thine iniquity, to turn away thy captivity; but have preached unto thee vain prophecies and digressions.

15 *Samech* All that passed by clapped *their* hands over thee; and whistled and wagged their heads over the daughter of Jerusalem, *saying, Is* this the city that *men* called The perfection of beauty, The joy of the whole earth?

16 *Pe* All thine enemies opened their mouth regarding thee: they whistled and gnashed their teeth: they said, Swallow *her* up: certainly this *is* the day that we looked for; we have found it, we have seen *it*.

17 *Ain* The LORD hath done *that* which he had determined; he hath fulfilled his word that he had commanded from *the* time of old: he hath destroyed, and hath not forgiven: and he hath caused *thine* enemy to rejoice over thee, he hath raised up the horn of thine adversaries.

18 *Tsade* Their heart cried unto the Lord, O wall of the daughter of Zion, let tears run down like a river day and night: give thyself no rest; let not the apple of thine eye cease.

19 *Koph* Arise, cry out in the night: in the beginning of the watches; pour out thine heart like water before the face of the Lord: lift up thy hands toward him for the life of thy young children, that faint for hunger in the top of every street.

20 *Resh* Look, O LORD, and consider unto whom thou hast shaken thus. Shall the women eat their fruit, the little ones that they are bringing up? shall the priest and the prophet be slain in the sanctuary of the Lord?

21 *Schin* The young and the old lay on the ground in the streets: my virgins and my young men fell by the sword; thou hast slain *them* in the day of thine anger; thou hast killed, *and* hast not forgiven.

22 *Tau* Thou hast called as to a day of solemnity, my terrors from everywhere, so that in the day of the LORD'S anger none escaped nor remained: those that I have swaddled and brought up hath my enemy consumed.

Chapter 3

1 *Aleph* I *am* a man *that* seeth affliction in the rod of his wrath.

2 *Aleph* He hath led me, and brought *me into* darkness, but not *into* light.

3 *Aleph* Surely against me is he turned; he turneth his hand *against me* all the day.

4 *Beth* My flesh and my skin hath he made old; he hath broken my bones.

5 *Beth* He hath builded against me, and compassed *me* with gall and travail.

6 *Beth* He hath set me in dark places, as *they that be* dead for ever.

7 *Gimel* He hath hedged me about, that I cannot get out: he hath made my chain heavy.

8 *Gimel* Even when I cried and shouted, he shut out my prayer.

9 *Gimel* He hath enclosed my ways with hewn stone, he hath made my paths crooked.

10 *Daleth* He *was* unto me *as* a bear lying in wait, *and as* a lion in secret places.

11 *Daleth* He hath made my ways crooked, and pulled me in pieces: he hath made me desolate.

12 *Daleth* He hath bent his bow, and set me as a mark for the arrow.

13 *He* He hath caused the arrows of his quiver to enter into my kidneys.

14 *He* I was a derision to all my people; *and* their song every day.

15 *He* He hath filled me with bitterness, he hath made me drunken with wormwood.

16 *Vau* He hath broken my teeth with gravel stones, he hath covered me with ashes.

17 *Vau* My soul removed itself far from peace: I forgot about good.

18 *Vau* And I said, My strength and my hope of the LORD is perished.

19 *Zain* Remember my affliction and my misery, the wormwood and the gall.

20 *Zain* My soul shall have *them* still in remembrance, because it is humbled in me.

21 *Zain* This shall go down into my heart, therefore I shall wait.

22 *Chet* It is *of* the LORD'S mercies that we are not consumed, because his mercies never diminish.

23 *Chet* *They are* new every morning: great *is* thy faith.

24 *Chet* The LORD *is* my portion, saith my soul; therefore will I wait for him.

25 *Teth* The LORD *is* good unto them that wait in him, to the soul *that* seeketh him.

26 *Teth* *It is* good to wait quietly in the saving health of the LORD.

27 *Teth* *It is* good for the man if he bear the yoke from his youth.

28 *Jod* He shall sit alone and keep silence, because he hath borne *it* upon him.

29 *Jod* He shall put his mouth in the dust; if so be there may be hope.

30 *Jod* He shall turn *his* cheek unto him that smiteth him: he shall be filled with reproach.

31 *Caph* For the Lord will not cast off for ever:

32 *Caph* But though he cause grief, yet will he also have compassion according to the multitude of his mercies.

33 *Caph* For he doth not afflict nor grieve the children of men from his heart.

34 *Lamed* To crush under his feet all the prisoners of the earth,

35 *Lamed* To turn aside the right of a man before the face of the most High,

36 *Lamed* To subvert a man in his cause, the Lord approveth not.

37 *Mem* Who shall he be that saith, that something cometh which the Lord hath not sent?

38 *Mem* Out of the mouth of the most High proceedeth not evil and good?

39 *Mem* Why doth the living man have pain, the man in his sin?

40 *Nun* Let us search out our ways, and seek, and turn again to the LORD.

41 *Nun* Let us lift up our heart with *our* hands unto God in the heavens.

42 *Nun* We have rebelled and been disloyal: therefore thou hast not forgiven.

43 *Samech* Thou hast unfurled anger, and persecuted us: thou hast slain, thou hast not forgiven.

44 *Samech* Thou hast covered thyself with a cloud, that *our* prayer should not pass through.

45 *Samech* Thou hast made us *as* the offscouring and abomination in the midst of the peoples.

46 *Pe* All our enemies have opened their mouths upon us.

47 *Pe* Fear and a snare is come upon us, desolation and destruction.

48 *Pe* My eyes stream with rivers of water for the destruction of the daughter of my people.

49 *Ain* My eyes run down, and cease not, for there is no relief,

50 *Ain* Until the LORD look down, and behold from the heavens.

51 *Ain* My eyes maketh my soul sad, because of all the daughters of my city.

52 *Tzaddi* My enemies hunted me like a bird, without cause.

53 *Tzaddi* They bound up my life in the dungeon, and cast a stone upon me.

54 *Tzaddi* Waters flowed over my head; *then* I said, I am dead.

55 *Koph* I called upon thy name, O LORD, out of the low dungeon.

56 *Koph* Thou hast heard my voice: hide not thine ear at my cry, that I might breath.

57 *Koph* Thou drewest near in the day *that* I called upon thee: thou saidst, Fear not.

58 *Resh* O Lord, thou hast pleaded the cause of my soul; thou hast redeemed my life.

59 *Resh* O LORD, thou hast seen where I was wrong: plead thou my cause.

60 *Resh* Thou hast seen all their vengeance *and* all their imaginations against me.

61 *Schin* Thou hast heard their reproach, O LORD, *and* all their imaginations against me;

62 *Schin* The sayings of those that rose up against me, and their design against me all the day.

63 *Schin* Behold their sitting down, and their rising up; I *am* their music.

64 *Tau* Render unto them a recompense, O LORD, according to the work of their hands.

65 *Tau* Give them sorrow of heart, thy curse unto them.

66 *Tau* Persecute them in thy anger and cut them off from under the heavens, oh LORD.

Chapter 4

1 Aleph How is the gold become dim! *how* is the most fine gold changed! the stones of the sanctuary are scattered through the crossings of every street.

2 Beth The sons of Zion, precious and esteemed more than pure gold, how are they taken for earthen vessels, the work of the hands of the potter!

3 Gimel Even the sea monsters draw out the breast, they give suck to their young ones: the daughter of my people *is* cruel, like the ostriches in the wilderness.

4 Daleth The tongue of the sucking child cleaveth to the roof of his mouth for thirst: the young children ask for bread, and there was no one to break *it* unto them.

5 He They that did feed delicately are made desolate in the streets: they that were brought up in scarlet embrace dunghills.

6 Vau For the iniquity of the daughter of my people hath increased more than the sin of Sodom, that was overthrown as in a moment, and companies did not camp upon her.

7 Zain Her Nazarites were whiter than snow, they were more radiant than milk, their composure had more fire than the precious stones cut from sapphire:

8 Cheth Their visage is blacker than a coal; they are not known in the streets: their skin cleaveth to their bones; it is withered, it is dry like a stick.

9 Teth Those slain with the sword are better than *those* slain with hunger: for these pine away, stricken through for *want of* the fruits of the earth.

10 Jod The hands of the compassionate women have cooked their own children: they were their food in the destruction of the daughter of my people.

11 Caph The LORD hath accomplished his fury; he hath poured out his fierce anger, and hath kindled a fire in Zion, and it hath devoured the foundations thereof.

12 Lamed The kings of the earth, and all the inhabitants of the world, never believed that the adversary and the enemy should would enter in through the gates of Jerusalem.

13 Mem For the sins of her prophets, *and* the iniquities of her priests, that have shed the blood of the just in the midst of her,

14 Nun They have wandered blindly in the streets, they were polluted in blood, so that no one could touch their garments.

15 Samech They cried unto them, Depart ye; *it is* unclean; depart, depart, touch not: because they were contaminated; and *when they were* thrust through, they said among the Gentiles, They shall never dwell here again.

16 Pe The anger of the LORD hath separated them; he will never look upon them again. They respected not the countenance of the priests, nor did they have compassion on the elders.

17 Ain As for us, our eyes have failed in seeking our vain help: in our watching we have watched for people *that* cannot save *us*.

18 Tzaddi They hunt our steps, that we cannot walk in our streets: our end came nigh, our days were fulfilled; for our end is come.

19 Koph Our persecutors were swifter than the eagles of the heaven: they pursued us upon the mountains, they laid wait for us in the wilderness.

20 Resh The breath of our nostrils, the anointed of the LORD, was taken in their pits, of whom we had said, Under his shadow we shall live among the Gentiles.

21 Schin Rejoice and be glad, O daughter of Edom, that dwellest in the land of Uz; the cup also shall pass even unto thee: thou shalt be drunken, and shalt vomit.

22 Tau The punishment of thine iniquity is accomplished, O daughter of Zion; he will never cause thee to be carried away again: he will visit thine iniquity, O daughter of Edom; he will uncover thy sins.

Chapter 5

1 Remember, O LORD, what is come upon us: look, and behold our reproach.

2 Our inheritance is turned to strangers, our houses to aliens.

3 We are orphans without father, our mothers *are* as widows.

4 We have drunken our water for money; our wood is sold unto us.

5 Our necks *are* under persecution: we are become tired, *and* have no rest.

6 We have given the hand *to* the Egyptians, *and to* the Assyrians, to be satisfied with bread.

7 Our fathers have sinned, *and are* dead; and we have borne their chastisements.

8 Servants have ruled over us: there was none to deliver *us* out of their hand.

9 We got our bread with *the peril of* our lives because of the sword of the wilderness.

10 Our skin became black like an oven because of the terrible famine.

11 They ravished the women in Zion, *and* the virgins in the cities of Judah.

12 Princes were hanged up by their hand: the countenance of the elders was not honoured.

13 They took the young men to grind, and the children fell under the wood.

14 The elders have ceased from the gate, the young men from their music.

15 The joy of our heart is ceased; our dance is turned into mourning.

16 The crown is fallen *from* our head: woe now unto us, for we have sinned!

17 For this our heart is saddened; for these *things* our eyes are become dim.

18 Because of the mountain of Zion, which is desolate, the foxes walk upon it.

19 Thou, O LORD, remainest for ever; thy throne from generation to generation.

20 Why should thou forget us for ever, *and* forsake us for so long time?

21 Turn thou us unto thee, O LORD, and we shall be turned; renew our days as at the beginning.

22 For in stepping back thou hast rejected us; thou hast become very angry against us.

The Book of the Prophet
Ezekiel

Chapter 1

1 Now it came to pass at thirty years, in the fourth *month*, in the fifth *day* of the month, as I *was* among the captives by the river of Chebar, *that* the heavens were opened, and I saw visions of God.

2 In the fifth *day* of the month, which *was* the fifth year of king Jehoiachin's captivity,

3 the word of the LORD came *expressly* unto Ezekiel the priest, the son of Buzi, in the land of the Chaldeans by the river Chebar; and there the hand of the LORD came upon him.

4 And I looked, and, behold, a whirlwind came out of the north, and *a* great cloud, and a fire enfolding itself, and a brightness *was* about it, and out of the midst thereof as the colour of amber, out of the midst of the fire.

5 Also out of the midst thereof *came* the likeness of four living creatures. And this *was* their appearance; they had the likeness of man.

6 And every one had four faces, and every one had four wings.

7 And their feet *were* straight feet; and the sole of their feet *was* like the sole of a calf's foot: and they sparkled like the colour of highly burnished brass.

8 And *they had* the hands of a man under their wings on their four sides; and their faces and their wings on *all* four sides.

9 With their wings they joined one to another; they returned not when they went; they went every one straight in the direction they were facing.

10 And for the likeness of their faces was human faces; and lion faces, on the right side: and they four had ox faces on the left side; likewise they four had eagle faces.

11 Thus *were* their faces: and their wings *were* stretched upward; two *wings* of every one *were* joined one to another, and two covered their bodies.

12 And they went every one straight forward in the direction they were facing: wherever the Spirit directed them to go, they went; *and* they returned not when they went.

13 As for the likeness of the living creatures, their appearance *was* like burning coals of fire, *and* like the appearance of *lit* torches: the *fire* went up and down among the living creatures, and the brightness of the fire; and out of the fire went forth lightning.

14 And the living creatures ran and turned as the appearance of lightnings.

15 Now as I beheld the living creatures, behold a wheel upon the earth with his four rims by the living creatures.

16 The appearance of the wheels and their work *was* like unto the colour of a *stone of* Tarsis [*or beryl*]: and they four had one likeness: and their appearance and their workmanship

was as it were a wheel in the middle of a wheel.

17 When they went, they went upon their four sides: *and* they returned not when they went.

18 And their ribs were high and dreadful, and full of eyes round about them in all four.

19 And when the living creatures went, the wheels went with them: and when the living creatures were lifted up from the earth, the wheels were lifted up.

20 Wherever the spirit wished to go, they went; wherever the spirit directed them, the wheels also rose up after them: for the spirit of the living creatures *was* in the wheels.

21 When those went, *these* went; and when those stood, *these* stood; and when those were lifted up from the earth, the wheels were lifted up after them: for the spirit of the living creatures *was* in the wheels.

22 And over the heads of each living creature there appeared a heaven like a marvellous crystal, stretched forth over their heads above.

23 And under the heaven their wings *were* straight one toward the other: every one had two, and another two which covered their bodies.

24 And when they went, I heard the noise of their wings, like the noise of many waters, as the voice of the Almighty, when they went; the voice of the word, as the voice of an army. When they stood, they let down their wings.

25 And there was heard a voice from the heaven that *was* over their heads, when they stood, *and* had let down their wings.

26 And above the heaven that *was* over their heads *was* the figure of a throne, as the appearance of a sapphire stone: and upon the figure of the throne *was* a likeness as the appearance of a man seated upon it.

27 And I saw something that looked like the colour of amber, that appeared to have fire round about within it, which could be seen from his loins upward, and from his loins downward, I saw what looked like fire, and it had brightness round about

28 that looked like the bow of heaven that is in the clouds in the day of rain, so *was* the appearance of the brightness round about. This *was* the vision of the likeness of the glory of the LORD. And I saw it, and fell upon my face, and I heard a voice of one that spoke.

Chapter 2

1 And he said unto me, Son of man, stand upon thy feet, and I will speak with thee.

2 And spirit entered into me when he spoke unto me, and set me upon my feet, and I heard him that spoke unto me.

3 And he said unto me, Son of man, I send thee to the sons of Israel, to rebellious Gentiles that have rebelled against me: they and their fathers have rebelled against me, *even* unto this very day.

4 And to sons *that have* hard faces and strong hearts do I send thee; and thou shalt say unto them, Thus hath the Lord GOD said.

5 And they will not hear nor forbear, (for they *are* a rebellious house,) but they shall know that there hath been a prophet among them.

6 And thou, son of man, be not afraid of them, neither be afraid of their words, for they are rebels; though thou find thyself among thorns, and thy dwelling be with briers: be not afraid of their words, nor fear before them, for they are a rebellious house.

7 And thou shalt speak my words unto them, but they will not hear nor forbear: for they are rebels.

8 But thou, son of man, hear what I say unto thee; Be not *thou* rebellious like the rebellious house: open thy mouth, and eat what I give thee.

9 And I looked, and behold, *an* hand was sent unto me; and in it was *the* roll of a book;

10 and he spread it before me; and it *was* written within and without: and *there was* written therein lamentations, and mourning, and woes.

Chapter 3

1 And he said unto me, Son of man, eat what thou findest; eat this roll, and go speak unto the house of Israel.

2 So I opened my mouth, and he caused me to eat that roll.

3 And he said unto me, Son of man, cause thy belly to eat, and fill thy bowels with this roll that I give thee. I ate it an: it was in my mouth as sweet as honey.

4 Then he said unto me, Son of man, go and enter into the house of Israel, and speak with my words unto them.

5 For thou *art* not sent to a people of a profound speech nor of an hard language, *but* to the house of Israel;

6 not to many peoples of profound speech nor of hard language, whose words thou can not understand. Surely, had I sent thee to them, they would have hearkened unto thee.

7 But the house of Israel will not desire to hear; for they do not desire to hear me: for all the house of Israel *are* impudent and hardhearted.

8 Behold, I have made thy face strong against their faces, and thy forehead strong against their foreheads.

9 As diamond harder than flint have I made thy forehead: fear them not, neither be dismayed at their looks, though they *be* a rebellious house.

10 Moreover he said unto me, Son of man, all my words that I shall speak unto thee receive in thine heart, and hear with thine ears.

11 And go, and enter in among the captives, unto the sons of thy people, and thou shalt speak unto them, and tell them, Thus hath the Lord GOD said, They will not hear, nor forbear.

12 And the Spirit took me up, and I heard behind me a voice of great thunder of the blessed glory of the LORD *leaving* his place,

13 and the noise of the wings of the living creatures that touched one another, and the noise of the wheels over against them, and a noise of great thunder.

14 And the Spirit lifted me up, and took me away, and I went in bitterness, in the heat of my spirit; but the hand of the LORD was strong upon me.

15 And I came unto the captives at Telabib, that dwelt by the river of Chebar, and I sat where they sat, and remained there disheartened among them seven days.

16 And it came to pass at the end of the seven days, that the word of the LORD came unto me, saying,

17 Son of man, I have placed thee as a watchman unto the house of Israel: therefore thou shalt hear the word at my mouth, and give them warning from me.

18 When I say unto the wicked, Thou shalt surely die; and thou givest him no warning, nor speakest to warn the wicked from his wicked way, that he might live; the same wicked *man* shall die for his iniquity; but his blood will I require at thine hand.

19 Yet if thou warn the wicked, and he turn not from his wickedness, nor from his wicked way, he shall die for his iniquity; but thou hast delivered thy soul.

20 Again, When the righteous *man* doth turn from his righteousness, and commit iniquity, and I lay a stumblingblock before him, he shall die, because thou hast not given him warning; he shall die in his sin, and his righteousness which he hath done shall not be remembered; but his blood will I require at thine hand.

21 Nevertheless if thou warn the righteous *man*, that the righteous sin not, and he doth not sin, he shall surely live, because he is warned; also thou hast delivered thy soul.

22 And the hand of the LORD came upon me there; and he said unto me, Arise, go forth into the plain, and I will talk with thee there.

23 Then I arose, and went forth into the plain: and, behold, the glory of the LORD stood there, as the glory which I saw by the river of Chebar: and I fell on my face.

24 Then spirit entered into me, and set me upon my feet, and *he* spoke with me, and said unto me, Go, shut thyself within thine house.

25 And thou, O son of man, behold, they shall put bands upon thee, and shall bind thee with them, and thou shalt not go out among them:

26 And I will make thy tongue cleave to the roof of thy mouth, that thou shalt be dumb, and shalt not be to them a reprover: for they *are* a rebellious house.

27 But when I speak with thee, I will open thy mouth, and thou shalt say unto them, Thus hath the Lord GOD said; He that heareth, let him hear; and he that forbeareth, let him forbear: for they *are* a rebellious house.

Chapter 4

1 Thou also, son of man, take thee a tile, and lay it before thee, and portray upon it the city of Jerusalem:

2 And lay siege against it, and build a fort against it, and cast a mount against it; set the camp also against it, and set *battering* rams against it round about.

3 And take thou an iron pan, and set it *for* a wall of iron between thee and the city: and set thy face against it, and it shall be for an encompassment, and thou shalt lay siege against the *city*. This *shall be* a sign to the house of Israel.

4 Thou shalt sleep upon thy left side, and lay the iniquity of the house of Israel upon it: *according* to the number of the days that thou shalt lie upon it thou shalt bear their iniquity.

5 For I have summed up *for* thee the years of their iniquity, according to the number of the days, three hundred and ninety days: so shalt thou bear the iniquity of the house of Israel.

6 And when thou hast accomplished them, thou shalt sleep on thy right side *this* second time, and thou shalt bear the iniquity of the house of Judah forty days: *a* day for *a* year; I have appointed thee *each* day for *a* year.

7 Therefore thou shalt set thy face toward the siege of Jerusalem, and thine arm *shall be* uncovered, and thou shalt prophesy against her.

8 And, behold, I laced bands upon thee, and thou shalt not turn thee from one side to another, until thou hast ended the days *appointed thee* upon thy sides.

9 Take thou also unto thee wheat, and barley, and beans, and lentiles, and millet, and fitches, and put them in one vessel, and make thee bread thereof, *according* to the number of the days that thou shalt lie upon thy side, three hundred and ninety days shalt thou eat thereof.

10 And thy food which thou shalt eat *shall be* by weight, twenty shekels a day: from time to time shalt thou eat it.

11 Thou shalt drink also water by measure, the sixth part of an hin: from time to time shalt thou drink.

12 And thou shalt eat barley cakes baked under the ashes, and thou shalt bake it with dung that cometh out of man, in their sight.

13 And the LORD said, Even thus shall the sons of Israel eat their defiled bread among the Gentiles, where I will drive them.

14 Then said I, Ah Lord GOD! behold, my soul is not defiled: for from my youth up even until now have I not eaten of that which dieth of itself, or is torn in pieces; neither came there abominable flesh into my mouth.

15 Then he said unto me, Behold, I give thee cow's dung for man's dung, and thou shalt prepare thy bread therewith.

16 Moreover he said unto me, Son of man, behold, I break the sustenance of bread in Jerusalem: and they shall eat bread by weight, and with anguish; and they shall drink water by measure, and with terror:

17 For they shall lack bread and water, and terrorise one another, and faint because of their iniquity.

Chapter 5

1 And thou, son of man, take thee a sharp knife, take thee a barber's razor, and cause *it* to pass upon thine head and upon thy beard: then take thee balances to weigh, and divide the *hair*.

2 Thou shalt burn with fire a third part in the midst of the city, when the days of the siege are fulfilled: and thou shalt take a third part, *and* smite about it with a knife: and a third part thou shalt scatter in the wind;

and I will draw out a sword after them.

3 Thou shalt also take thereof a few in number, and bind them in the skirt of thy garment.

4 Then take of them again, and cast them into the midst of the fire, and burn them in the fire; *for* thereof shall a fire come forth into all the house of Israel.

5 Thus hath the Lord GOD said; This *is* Jerusalem: I have set her in the midst of the Gentiles and of the lands *that are* round about her.

6 And she hath changed my judgments and my statutes into wickedness more than the Gentiles, and more than the lands that *are* round about her: for they have disregarded my judgments and my commandments, and have not walked in them.

7 Therefore thus hath the Lord GOD said; Because *I* multiplied you more than the Gentiles that *are* round about you, ye have not walked in my commandments, neither have ye kept my laws. Ye have not even acted according to the judgments of the Gentiles that *are* round about you.

8 Therefore thus hath the Lord GOD said; Behold, I, even I, *am* against thee, and will execute judgments in the midst of thee in the sight of the Gentiles.

9 And I will do in thee that which I have not done, and whereunto I will not do any more the like, because of all thine abominations.

10 For the fathers shall eat the sons in the midst of thee, and the sons shall eat their fathers; and I will execute judgments in thee, and the whole remnant of thee will I scatter into all the winds.

11 Wherefore, *as* I live, said the Lord GOD; Surely, because thou hast defiled my sanctuary with all thy contaminations, and with all thine abominations, therefore will I also destroy *thee*; neither shall my eye forgive, neither will I have mercy.

12 A third part of thee shall die of pestilence, and shall be consumed with famine in the midst of thee: and a third part shall fall by the sword round about thee; and I will scatter a third part into all the winds, and I will draw out a sword after them.

13 Thus shall my anger be accomplished, and I will cause my fury to cease in them, and I will be comforted: and they shall know that I the LORD have spoken *it* in my zeal, when I have accomplished my fury in them.

14 And I will make thee a desert, and a reproach among the Gentiles that *are* round about thee, in the sight of all that pass by.

15 And thou shalt be a reproach and a dishonour, and a chastisement and a terror unto the Gentiles that *are* round about thee, when I shall execute judgments in thee in anger and in fury and in furious rebukes. I, the LORD, have spoken.

16 When I shall send upon them the evil arrows of famine, which shall be for *their* destruction, *and* which I will send to destroy you, then I will increase the famine upon you, and will destroy your sustenance of bread.

17 So will I send upon you famine and evil beasts that will destroy thee; and pestilence and blood shall pass through thee; and I will bring the sword upon thee. I, the LORD, have spoken.

Chapter 6

1 And the word of the LORD came unto me, saying,

2 Son of man, set thy face toward the mountains of Israel, and prophesy against them,

3 and thou shalt say, Ye mountains of Israel, hear the word of the Lord GOD; Thus hath the Lord GOD said to the mountains, and to the hills, to the rivers, and to the valleys; Behold, I, *even* I, bring a sword upon you, and I will destroy your high places.

4 And your altars shall be desolate, and your images of the sun shall be destroyed: and I will cause your dead to fall before your idols.

5 And I will lay the dead carcasses of the sons of Israel before their idols; and I will scatter your bones round about your altars.

6 In all your provinces the cities shall be laid waste, and the high places shall be desolate; that your altars may be laid waste and made desolate, and your idols shall be destroyed and shall cease, and your images of the sun shall be cut down, and your works shall be abolished.

7 And the slain shall fall in the midst of you, and ye shall know that I *am* the LORD.

8 Yet will I leave a remnant, that ye may have *some* that shall escape the sword among the Gentiles, when ye shall be scattered through the countries.

9 And they that escape of you shall remember me among the Gentiles where they shall be carried captives, because I am broken because of your whorish heart, which hath departed from me, and because of your eyes, which went a whoring after your idols: and they shall loathe themselves for the evils which they have committed in all their abominations.

10 And they shall know that I *am* the LORD, *and that* I have not said in vain that I would do this evil unto them.

11 Thus hath the Lord GOD said; Smite with thine hand, and stamp with thy foot, and say, Alas for all the abominations of the evils of the house of Israel! for they shall fall by the sword, by the famine, and by the pestilence.

12 He that is far off shall die of the pestilence; and he that is near shall fall by the sword; and he that remaineth and is besieged shall die by the famine: thus will I accomplish my fury in them.

13 Then shall ye know that I *am* the LORD, when their slain *men* shall be among their idols round about their altars, upon every high hill, in all the tops of the mountains, and under every green tree, and under every thick oak, the place where they did offer sweet savour to all their idols.

14 So will I stretch out my hand upon them, and make the land desolate, yea, more desolate than the wilderness toward Diblath, in all their habitations: and they shall know that I *am* the LORD.

Chapter 7

1 And the word of the LORD came unto me, saying,

2 and thou son of man, thus hath the Lord GOD said unto the land of Israel; The end, the end cometh upon the four corners of the land.

3 Now *shall be* the end upon thee, and I will send my anger upon thee, and will judge thee according to thy ways, and will recompense upon thee all thine abominations.

4 And my eye shall not forgive thee, neither will I have mercy: but I will recompense thy ways upon thee, and thine abominations shall be in the midst of thee: and ye shall know that I *am* the LORD.

5 Thus hath the Lord GOD said; An evil, behold, an evil is come.

6 An end is come, the end is come: it watcheth for thee; behold, it is come.

7 The morning cometh for thee, O thou that dwellest in the land: the time cometh, the day of is near, the day of trouble and it shall not be the echo of the mountains.

8 Now will I shortly pour out my fury upon thee, and accomplish my anger in thee: and I will judge thee according to thy ways, and place all thine abominations upon thee.

9 And my eye shall not forgive, neither will I have mercy: I will recompense thee according to thy ways and thine abominations shall be in the midst of thee; and ye shall know that I *am* the LORD that smiteth.

10 Behold the day, behold, it cometh: the morning is gone forth; the rod hath blossomed, pride hath budded.

11 Violence is risen up into a rod of wickedness: nothing *shall remain* of them, nor of their riches, nor of anything of theirs: neither *shall there be* lamentation for them.

12 The time is come, the day draweth near: let not the buyer rejoice, nor the seller mourn: for wrath *is* upon all the multitude thereof.

13 For the seller shall not return to that which is sold, although they remain alive: for the vision *is* touching the whole multitude thereof, and shall not be cancelled; neither shall any in the iniquity of his life strengthen himself.

14 They shall blow the trumpet, and make everything ready; but there *shall be* none to go forth to the battle: for my wrath *is* upon all the multitude thereof.

15 The sword *is* without, and the pestilence and the famine within: he that *is* in the field shall die with the sword; and he that *is* in the city, famine and pestilence shall devour him.

16 And they that escape of them shall be upon the mountains like doves of the valleys, all of them mourning, every one for his iniquity.

17 All hands shall be feeble, and all knees shall be weak *as* water.

18 They shall also gird *themselves* with sackcloth, and trembling shall cover them; and shame *shall be* upon all faces, and baldness upon all their heads.

19 They shall cast their silver in the streets, and their gold far from *them*: their silver and their gold shall not be able to deliver them in the day of the wrath of the LORD: they shall not satisfy their souls, neither fill their bowels: because it shall be the stumblingblock of their iniquity.

20 Because they turned the glory of his ornament into pride, and made in her the images of their abominations, of their statues: therefore have I set it far from them.

21 And I gave it into the hands of the strangers for a prey, and to the wicked of the earth for a spoil; and they shall pollute it.

22 My face will I turn also from them, and they shall pollute my secret *place*: for the destroyers shall enter into it, and defile it.

23 Make a chain: for the land is full of bloody judgments, and the city is full of violence.

24 Wherefore I will bring the worst of all the Gentiles, and they shall possess their houses: I will also cause the arrogance of the strong to cease; and

their sanctuaries shall be defiled.

25 A cutting off cometh; and they shall seek peace, and *there shall be* none.

26 Destruction shall come upon destruction, and rumour shall be upon rumour; then shall they seek an answer from the prophet; but the law shall perish from the priest, and counsel from the elders.

27 The king shall mourn, and the prince shall be clothed with desolation, and the hands of the people of the land shall be troubled: I will do unto them after their way, and according to their judgments will I judge them; and they shall know that I *am* the LORD.

Chapter 8

1 And it came to pass in the sixth year, in the sixth *month,* in the fifth *day* of the month, *as* I sat in my house, and the elders of Judah sat before me, that the hand of the Lord GOD fell there upon me.

2 And I saw, and behold a likeness as the appearance of fire: from the appearance of his loins downward, was fire; and from his loins upward, as the appearance of brightness, as the colour of amber.

3 And that likeness put forth his hand, and took me by the locks of my head; and the Spirit lifted me up between the heaven and the earth, and brought me in *the* visions of God to Jerusalem, to the door of the inner gate that looketh toward the north; where *was* the habitation of the image of jealousy, which provoketh to jealousy.

4 And, behold, the glory of the God of Israel *was* there, like the vision that I saw in the plain.

5 Then said he unto me, Son of man, lift up thine eyes now the way toward the north. So I lifted up my eyes the way toward the north, and behold northward at the gate of the altar this image of jealousy in the entry.

6 He said furthermore unto me, Son of man, seest thou what they do? *even* the great abominations that the house of Israel committeth here, to cause me to go far away from my sanctuary? but turn thee yet again, *and* thou shalt see greater abominations.

7 And he brought me to the entrance of the court; and when I looked, behold a hole in the wall.

8 Then said he unto me, Son of man, dig now in the wall: and when I had digged in the wall, behold a door.

9 And he said unto me, Go in, and see the wicked abominations that they do here.

10 So I went in and saw; and behold every form of serpent, and beasts; the abomination, and all the idols of the house of Israel, portrayed upon the wall round about.

11 And there stood before them seventy men of the elders of the house of Israel, and in the midst of them stood Jaazaniah the son of Shaphan, with every man his censer in his hand; and a thick cloud of incense went up.

12 Then said he unto me, Son of man, hast thou seen what the elders of the house of Israel do in the dark, every man in the chambers of his imagery? for they say, The LORD seeth us not; the LORD hath forsaken the earth.

13 He said also unto me, Turn thee yet again, *and* thou shalt see greater abominations that they do.

14 Then he brought me to the entrance of the door of the LORD'S house which *is* toward the north; and, behold, there sat women weeping for Tammuz.

15 Then said he unto me, Hast thou seen *this*, O son of man? turn thee yet again, *and* thou shalt see greater abominations than these.

16 And he brought me into the inner court of the LORD'S house, and, behold, at the entrance of the temple of the LORD, between the porch and the altar, *were* about twenty-five men, with their backs toward the temple of the LORD, and their faces toward the east; and they worshipped the sun toward the east.

17 Then he said unto me, Hast thou seen *this*, O son of man? Is it a light thing to the house of Judah that they commit the abominations which they commit here? For after they have filled the land with evil, and have returned to provoke me to anger; behold, they put the stench to my nose.

18 Therefore will I also deal in fury: my eye shall not forgive, neither will I have mercy: and they shall cry in my ears with a loud voice, *yet* will I not hear them.

Chapter 9

1 And he cried in my ears with a loud voice, saying, The visitors of the city have come, even every man *with* his destroying weapon in his hand.

2 And, behold, six men came from the way of the higher gate, which lieth toward the north, and every man *had* a slaughter weapon in his hand; and one man among them *was* clothed with linen, with a writer's inkhorn by his side: and they went in, and stood beside the brazen altar.

3 And the glory of the God of Israel went up from over the cherubim, whereupon he had been, to the threshold of the house. And he called to the man clothed with linen, which *had* the writer's inkhorn by his side;

4 and the LORD said unto him, Go through the midst of the city, through the midst of Jerusalem, and set a mark upon the foreheads of the men that sigh and that cry out because of all the abominations that are done in the midst of her.

5 And to the others he said in my hearing, Go ye after him through the city, and smite: let not your eye forgive, neither have mercy:

6 Slay *the* old, *the* young men and *the* virgins, *the* children, and *the* women: but come not near anyone upon whom *is* the mark; and ye must begin from my sanctuary. Then they began with *the* men, the elders, which *were* in front of the temple.

7 And he said unto them, Defile the house, and fill the courts with the slain: go ye forth. And they went forth, and slew in the city.

8 And it came to pass, after they had slain them, I was left, and I fell upon my face, and cried out, and said, Ah Lord GOD! wilt thou destroy all the remnant of Israel in thy pouring out of thy fury upon Jerusalem?

9 Then said he unto me, The iniquity of the house of Israel and Judah *is* exceeding great, and the land is full of blood, and the city full of perverseness: for they have said, The LORD hath forsaken the earth, and the LORD seeth not.

10 And as for me also, my eye shall not forgive, neither will I have mercy, *but* I will recompense their way upon their head.

11 And, behold, the man clothed with linen, which *had* the inkhorn by his side,

reported the matter, saying, I have done according to all thou hast commanded me.

Chapter 10

1 Then I looked, and, behold, above the heaven that was above the head of the cherubim there appeared over them as it were a sapphire stone, as the appearance of the likeness of a throne.

2 And he spoke to the man clothed with linen, and said, Go in between the wheels under the cherubim, and fill thine hand with coals of fire from between the cherubim, and scatter *them* over the city. And he went in my sight.

3 Now the cherubim stood on the right side of the house, when this man went in; and the cloud filled the inner court.

4 And the glory of the LORD had gone up from the cherubim to the threshold of the door; and the house was filled with the cloud, and the court was full of the brightness of the LORD'S glory.

5 And the thunder of the cherubim' wings was heard *even* to the outer court, as the voice of the Almighty God when he speaketh.

6 And it came to pass, *that* when he had commanded

the man clothed with linen, saying, Take fire from between the wheels, from between the cherubim; then he went in, and stood among the wheels.

7 And *one* cherubim stretched forth his hand from between the cherubim unto the fire that *was* between the cherubim, and took *thereof*, and put *it* into the hands of *him that was* clothed with linen: who took *it*, and went out.

8 And there appeared in the cherubim the form of a man's hand under their wings.

9 And when I looked, behold, four wheels by the cherubim, one wheel by each cherubim: and the colour of the wheels *was* as a stone of Tarsis [*or beryl*].

10 And *as for* their appearance, the four were the same, as if one were in the midst of another.

11 When they went, they went upon their four sides; they turned not as they went, but to the place where the first one went, they followed it; they turned not as they went.

12 And all their flesh, and their ribs, and their hands, and their wings, and the wheels, they were full of eyes round about in their four wheels.

13 To the wheels, it was shouted unto them in my hearing, Roll!

14 And every one had four faces: the first face *was the face* of a cherubim, and the second face *was the face* of a man, and the third the face of a lion, and the fourth the face of an eagle.

15 And the cherubim rose up. These *are* the living creatures that I saw by the river of Chebar.

16 And when the cherubim went, the wheels went with them: and when the cherubim lifted up their wings to mount up from the earth, the same wheels also turned not from beside them.

17 When they stood still, *these* stood still; and when they lifted up themselves, *these* lifted up themselves *also*: for the spirit of the living creatures *was* in them.

18 And the glory of the LORD departed from off the threshold of the house, and stood over the cherubim.

19 And the cherubim lifted up their wings, and mounted up from the earth in my sight: when they went out, the wheels also *were* in front of them, and they stood at the entrance of the east gate of the LORD'S house; and the glory of the God of Israel *was* over them above.

20 These *were* the living creatures that I saw under the God of Israel by the river of Chebar; and I knew that they *were* cherubim.

21 Each one had four faces, and each one four wings; and the likeness of the hands of a man *was* under their wings.

22 And the likeness of their faces *was* the same faces which I saw by the river of Chebar, their appearance and their being: each one went straight in the direction they were facing.

Chapter 11

1 And the Spirit lifted me up, and brought me through the east gate of the LORD'S house, which looketh eastward: and behold at the entrance of the gate twenty-five men; among whom I saw Jaazaniah the son of Azur, and Pelatiah the son of Benaiah, princes of the people.

2 Then said he unto me, Son of man, these *are* the men that devise mischief, and give wicked counsel in this city:

3 Which say, *It is* not near; let us build houses: this *city is* the caldron, and we *be* the flesh.

4 Therefore prophesy against them, prophesy, O son of man.

5 And the Spirit of the LORD fell upon me, and said unto me, Say; Thus hath the LORD said; Thus have ye said, O house of Israel: for I have understood the things that come up into your spirit.

6 Ye have multiplied your slain in this city, and ye have filled the streets thereof with the slain.

7 Therefore thus hath the Lord GOD said; Your slain whom ye have laid in the midst of it, they *are* the flesh, and this *city is* the caldron: but I will bring you forth out of the midst of it.

8 Ye have feared the sword; and I will bring a sword upon you, said the Lord GOD.

9 And I will bring you out of the midst thereof, and deliver you into the hands of strangers, and will execute judgments in you.

10 Ye shall fall by the sword; I will judge you in the border of Israel; and ye shall know that I *am* the LORD.

11 This *city* shall not be your caldron, neither shall ye be the flesh in the midst thereof; *but* I must judge you in the border of Israel: **12** And ye shall know that I *am* the LORD: for ye have not walked in my statutes, neither have ye acted *according to* my judgments, but according to the judgments of the Gentiles that *are* round about you. **13** And it came to pass, as I was prophesying, that Pelatiah the son of Benaiah died. Then I fell down upon my face, and cried with a loud voice, and said, Ah Lord GOD! wilt thou make a full end of the remnant of Israel?

14 And the word of the LORD came unto me, saying, **15** Son of man, thy brethren, *even* thy brethren, the men of thy kindred, and all the house of Israel together, *are* they unto whom the inhabitants of Jerusalem have said, Get you far from the LORD: unto us is this land given in possession.

16 Therefore say, Thus hath the Lord GOD said; Although I have cast them far off among the Gentiles, and although I have scattered them among the countries, yet will I be to them as a little sanctuary in the countries where they shall come. **17** Therefore say, Thus hath the Lord GOD said; I will even gather you from the peoples, and assemble you out of the countries where ye have been scattered, and I will give you the land of Israel.

18 And they shall come thither, and they shall remove all her contaminations and all her abominations from her. **19** And I will give them one heart, and I will put a new spirit within you; and I will take the stony heart out of their flesh, and will give them an heart of flesh: **20** That they may walk in my statutes, and keep my judgments, and fulfil them: and they shall be my people, and I will be their God.

21 But *as for them* whose heart walketh after the desire of their contaminations and of their abominations, I will recompense their way upon their own heads, said the Lord GOD.

22 Then did the cherubim lift up their wings, and the wheels after them; and the glory of the God of Israel *was* over them above. **23** And the glory of the LORD went up from the midst of the city, and stood upon the mountain which *is* on the east side of the city.

24 Afterwards the Spirit took me up, and brought me in a vision by the Spirit of God into the land of the Chaldeans, to the captives. So the vision that I had seen went up from me.

25 Then I spoke unto the captives all the words of the LORD that he had showed me.

Chapter 12

1 The word of the LORD also came unto me, saying,

2 Son of man, thou dwellest in the midst of a rebellious house, which have eyes to see, and see not; they have ears to hear, and hear not: for they *are* a rebellious house.

3 Therefore, thou son of man, prepare thee stuff for moving, and move by day in their sight; and thou shalt move from thy place to another place in their sight: they will not see for they are a rebellious house.

4 And thou shalt bring forth thy stuff by day in their sight, as stuff for moving: and thou shalt go forth in the evening in their sight, as they that go forth to not return.

5 Dig thou through the wall in their sight, and leave thereby.

6 In their sight shalt thou bear *it* upon *thy* shoulders, *and* carry *it* forth in the night: thou shalt cover thy face, and thou shalt not look at the land: for I have set thee *for* a sign unto the house of Israel.

7 And I did so as I was commanded: I brought forth my stuff by day, as stuff for a journey, and in the evening I digged through the wall with my hand; I brought *it* forth in the night, *and* I bare *it* upon *my* shoulder in their sight.

8 And in the morning came the word of the LORD unto me, saying,

9 Son of man, hath not the house of Israel, the rebellious house, said unto thee, What doest thou?

10 Say thou unto them, Thus hath the Lord GOD said; This burden *concerneth* the prince in Jerusalem, and all the house of Israel that *are* among them.

11 Say, I *am* your sign: like as I have done, so shall it be done unto them: when they go to another country they shall go in captivity.

12 And the prince that *is* among them shall be born upon *their* shoulders in the night, and they shall go forth: they shall dig through the wall to carry him out thereby: he shall cover his face, that he see not the land with *his* eyes.

13 But I will spread my net upon him, and he shall be taken in my snare: and I will cause him to be taken to Babylon *to* the land of the Chaldeans; yet shall he not see it, though he shall die there.

14 And I will scatter toward every wind all that *were* about him to help him, and all his companies; and I will draw out the sword after them.

15 And they shall know that I *am* the LORD, when I shall scatter them among the Gentiles, and disperse them in the countries.

16 But I will leave a few men of them from the sword, from the famine, and from the pestilence; that they may declare all their abominations among the Gentiles where they go; and they shall know that I *am* the LORD.

17 And the word of the LORD came to me, saying,

18 Son of man, eat thy bread with quaking, and drink thy water with trembling and with anxiety;

19 and say unto the people of the land, Thus hath the Lord GOD said regarding the inhabitants of Jerusalem, *and* the land of Israel; They shall eat their bread with anxiety, and drink their water with terror, that her land may be desolate from all that is therein, because of the violence of all them that dwell therein.

20 And the cities that are inhabited shall be laid waste, and the land shall be desolate; and ye shall know that I *am* the LORD.

21 And the word of the LORD came unto me, saying,

22 Son of man, what *is* that saying *that* ye have in the land of Israel that saith, The days shall be prolonged, and every vision shall fail?

23 Tell them therefore, Thus hath the Lord GOD said; I will make this saying to cease, and they shall not repeat this as a saying in Israel; but say unto them, Those days hath drawn nigh, and the fulfilment of every vision.

24 For there shall no longer be any vain vision or flattering divination within the house of Israel.

25 Because I, the LORD, will speak, and the word that I shall speak shall come to pass; it shall no longer be prolonged: for in your days, O rebellious house, I will speak the word, and will perform it, said the Lord GOD.

26 Again the word of the LORD came to me, saying,

27 Son of man, behold, *they of* the house of Israel say, The vision that he seeth *is* for many days *to come*, and he prophesieth of the times *that are* far off.

28 Therefore say unto them, Thus hath the Lord GOD said; All of my words shall not be prolonged any longer, but the word which I have spoken shall be done, said the Lord GOD.

Chapter 13

1 And the word of the LORD came unto me, saying,

2 Son of man, prophesy against the prophets of Israel that prophesy, and say thou unto them that prophesy out of their own hearts, Hear ye the word of the LORD;

3 thus hath the Lord GOD said; Woe unto the foolish prophets, that follow their own spirit, and have seen nothing!

4 O Israel, thy prophets are like the foxes in the deserts.

5 Ye have not gone up into the gaps, neither made up the hedge for the house of Israel to stand in the battle in the day of the LORD.

6 They have seen vanity and lying divination, saying, The LORD saith: and the LORD hath not sent them: and they have made *others* to wait for the word to be confirmed.

7 Have ye not seen a vain vision, and have ye not spoken a lying divination, whereas ye say, The LORD hath said *it*; albeit I have not spoken?

8 Therefore thus hath the Lord GOD said; Because ye have spoken vanity, and seen lies, therefore, behold, I *am* against you, said the Lord GOD.

9 And my hand shall be against the prophets that see vanity, and that divine lies: they shall not be in the assembly of my people, neither shall they be written in the book of the house of Israel, neither shall they return to the land of Israel; and ye shall know that I *am* the Lord GOD.

10 Therefore and because they have seduced my people, saying, Peace; and *there was* no peace; and one built up the wall, and, behold, others plastered it with loose mud:

11 Say unto them which plaster *it* with loose mud, that it shall fall: there shall be an overflowing rain; and

I shall send great hailstones that will cause it to fall; and a stormy wind shall rend *it*.

12 And behold, when the wall is fallen, it shall not be said unto you, Where *is* the mud wherewith ye have plastered *it*?

13 Therefore thus hath the Lord GOD said; I will cause a stormy wind to rend *it* in my fury; and there shall come an overflowing rain in my anger, and great hailstones in *my* wrath to consume *it*.

14 So will I break down the wall that ye have plastered with loose mud, and bring it down to the ground, and the foundation thereof shall be discovered, and it shall fall, and ye shall be consumed in the midst thereof: and ye shall know that I *am* the LORD.

15 Thus will I accomplish my wrath upon the wall, and upon them that have plastered it with loose mud, and will say unto you, The wall *is* no *more*, neither they that plastered it;

16 *to wit*, the prophets of Israel which prophesy concerning Jerusalem, and which see visions of peace for her, and *there is* no peace, said the Lord GOD.

17 Likewise, thou son of man, set thy face against the daughters of thy people, which prophesy out of their own heart; and prophesy thou against them,

18 And say, Thus hath the Lord GOD said; Woe to the *women* that sew pillows to all armholes, and make kerchiefs upon the head of every stature to hunt souls! Must ye hunt the souls of my people to maintain thus your own life?

19 And will ye profane me among my people for handfuls of barley and for pieces of bread, slaying the souls that should not die, and giving life to the souls that *should* not live, by your lying to my people that listen to the lie?

20 Therefore thus hath the Lord GOD said; Behold, I *am* against your pillows, with which ye hunt there the loose souls, and I will tear them from your arms, and will let the souls go, *even* the loose souls that ye hunt.

21 Your kerchiefs also will I tear, and deliver my people out of your hand, and they shall be no more in your hand to be hunted; and ye shall know that I *am* the LORD.

22 Because with lies ye have made the heart of the righteous sad, whom I have not made sad; and ye strengthen the hands of the wicked, that he should not leave his wicked way, encouraging him:

23 Therefore ye shall not see vanity, nor divine divinations any longer: for I will deliver my people out of your hand: and ye shall know that I *am* the LORD.

Chapter 14

1 Then came certain of the elders of Israel unto me, and sat before me.

2 And the word of the LORD came unto me, saying,

3 Son of man, these men have caused their uncleanness to come up over their heart, and *have* established the stumblingblock of their iniquity before their face: should I be enquired of at all by them?

4 Therefore speak unto them, and say unto them, Thus hath the Lord GOD said; Every man of the house of Israel that setteth up his idols in his heart, and hath established the stumblingblock of his iniquity before his face, and cometh to the prophet; I, the LORD, will answer him that cometh like this in the multitude of his idols;

5 that I may take the house of Israel in their own heart, because they are all estranged from me through their idols.

6 Therefore say unto the house of Israel, Thus hath the Lord GOD said; Repent, and cause them to repent from your idols; and turn away your faces from all your abominations.

7 For any man of the house of Israel, or of the strangers that sojourn in Israel, which hath separated himself from walking after me, and hath set up his idols in his heart, and hath established the stumblingblock of his iniquity before his face, and cometh to the prophet to enquire of him concerning me; I, the LORD, will answer him by myself:

8 And I will set my face against that man, and will set him up for a sign and for sayings, and I will cut him off from among my people; and ye shall know that I *am* the LORD.

9 And the prophet when he be deceived and speak a word, I the LORD have deceived that prophet, and I will stretch out my hand upon him, and will destroy him from among my people Israel.

10 And they shall bear the *punishment of* their iniquity: the iniquity of the prophet shall be even as the iniquity of him that seeketh *unto him*;

11 that the house of Israel may go no more astray from me, neither be polluted any more in all their rebellions; but that they may be my people, and I may be their God, said the Lord GOD.

12 The word of the LORD came again to me, saying,
13 Son of man, when the land sinneth against me by rebelling blatantly, and I stretch out my hand upon her, and break the staff of the bread thereof, and send famine upon her, and cut off man and beast out of her:
14 Though these three men, Noah, Daniel, and Job, were in the midst of her, they should deliver *but* their own souls by their righteousness, said the Lord GOD.
15 If I cause an evil beast to pass through the land, and destroy her, so that it be desolate, that there be no one to pass through because of the beast:
16 *Though* these three men *were* in the midst of her, *as* I live, said the Lord GOD, they shall deliver neither their sons nor their daughters; they only shall be delivered, and the land shall be destroyed.

17 Or *if* I bring a sword upon the land, and say, Sword, go through the land; so that I cut off man and beast out of her:
18 Though these three men *were* in the midst of her, *as* I live, said the Lord GOD, they shall deliver neither their sons nor their daughters, but they only shall be delivered themselves.
19 Or *if* I send a pestilence into that land, and pour out my fury upon her in blood, to cut off out of her man and beast:
20 Though Noah, Daniel, and Job, *were* in the midst of her, *as* I live, said the Lord GOD, they shall deliver neither son nor daughter; they shall *but* deliver their own souls by their righteousness.
21 Therefore thus hath the Lord GOD said; How much more if I send my four sore judgments against Jerusalem, the sword, and the famine, and the evil beast, and the pestilence, to cut off out of her man and beast?
22 Yet, behold, there shall be left a remnant in her, of whom shall be taken captive your sons and daughters: they shall be taken away: behold, they shall come forth unto you, and

ye shall see their way and their doings: and ye shall be comforted concerning the evil that I have brought upon Jerusalem, *even* concerning all that I have brought upon her.

23 And they shall comfort you, when ye see their ways and their doings: and ye shall know that I have not done without cause all that I have done in her, said the Lord GOD.

Chapter 15

1 And the word of the LORD came unto me, saying,

2 Son of man, What is the vine tree more than any tree? What is the branch among the trees of the forest?

3 Shall wood be taken from it to do a work? Will *men* take a peg from it to hang any vessel thereon?

4 Behold, it is cast into the fire for fuel; the fire devoureth both the ends of it, and the midst of it is burned. Is it meet for *any* work?

5 Behold, when it was whole, it was meet for no work: how much less afterward shall it be meet for *any* work, when the fire hath devoured it, and it is burned?

6 Therefore thus hath the Lord GOD said; As the vine tree among the trees of the forest, which I have given to the fire for fuel, so have I given over the inhabitants of Jerusalem.

7 And I will set my face against them; they came out of *one* fire, and *another* fire shall devour them; and ye shall know that I *am* the LORD, when I set my face against them.

8 And I will make the land desolate, because they have completely rebelled, said the Lord GOD.

Chapter 16

1 Again the word of the LORD came unto me, saying,

2 Son of man, notify Jerusalem of her abominations,

3 and say, Thus hath the Lord GOD said concerning Jerusalem; Thy habitation and thy race was of the land of Canaan; thy father *was* an Amorite, and thy mother an Hittite.

4 And *as for* thy nativity, in the day thou wast born thy navel was not cut, neither wast thou washed in water to supple *thee*; thou wast not salted at all, nor swaddled at all.

5 No eye pitied thee, to do any of these unto thee, to have mercy upon thee; but thou wast cast out in the open field, with little value given to thy life, in the day that thou wast born.

6 I passed by thee, and saw thee polluted in thine own blood, and I said unto thee, In thy blood thou shalt live; yea, I said unto thee, In thy blood thou shalt live.

7 In thousands, as the grass of the field, have I placed thee and thou wast increased and made great, and thou art come to be adorned with excellent ornaments: *thy* breasts were fashioned, and thy hair is grew; but thou *wast* naked and bare.

8 And I passed by thee, and looked upon thee, behold, thy time *was* the time of love; and I spread my mantle over thee, and covered thy shame; and I gave thee an oath, and entered into a covenant with thee, said the Lord GOD, and thou becamest mine;

9 and I washed thee with water, and washed away thy blood from upon thee, and I anointed thee with oil.

10 I clothed thee also with broidered work, and shod thee with badgers' skin, and I girded thee about with fine linen, and I clothed thee with silk.

11 I decked thee also with ornaments, and I put bracelets upon thy arms, and a chain on thy neck.

12 And I put nose rings upon thy nostrils, and earrings in thine ears, and a diadem of beauty upon thine head.

13 Thus wast thou decked with gold and silver; and thy raiment *was of* fine linen, and silk, and broidered work; thou didst eat fine flour of wheat, and honey, and oil: and thou wast made exceeding beautiful, and thou hast prospered even until thou hast reigned .

14 And thy renown went forth among the Gentiles for thy beauty: for it *was* perfect, because of my beauty which *I* placed upon thee, said the Lord GOD.

15 But thou didst trust in thine own beauty, and playedst the harlot because of thy renown, and pouredst out thy fornications on every one that passed by; thou wert his.

16 And of thy garments thou didst take, and madest altars of divers colours, and playedst the harlot thereupon: *the like* shall not come *again*, neither shall it be *so*.

17 Thou hast taken likewise the vessels of thy

beauty of my gold and of my silver, which I had given thee, and madest to thyself images of men, and didst commit whoredom with them,

18 And tookest thy garments of many colours, and coveredst them: and thou hast set my oil and my incense before them.

19 My bread also which I had given thee, the fine flour, and the oil, and the honey, *wherewith* I fed thee, thou hast even set it before them for a sweet savour: and *thus* it was, said the Lord GOD.

20 Moreover thou hast taken thy sons and thy daughters, whom thou hast borne unto me, and these hast thou sacrificed unto them to be devoured. *Is this* of thy whoredoms a small matter,

21 that thou hast sacrificed my children, and given them over to them that they might cause them to pass through *the fire* unto them?

22 And in all thine abominations and thy whoredoms hast thou not remembered the days of thy youth, when thou wast naked and bare? Thou wast polluted in thy blood.

23 And it came to pass after all thy wickedness, (woe, woe unto thee! said the Lord GOD;)

24 *that* thou hast also built unto thee an high place, and hast made thee an altar in every street.

25 Thou hast built thy altar at every head of every way, and hast made thy beauty abominable, and hast opened thy thighs to every one that passed by, and multiplied thy whoredoms.

26 Thou hast also committed fornication with the sons of Egypt, thy neighbours, great of flesh; and hast increased thy whoredoms, to provoke me to anger.

27 Behold, therefore I have stretched out my hand over thee, and have diminished thy liberty, and delivered thee unto the will of them that hate thee, the daughters of the Philistines, which are ashamed of thy lewd way.

28 Thou hast played the whore also with the sons of Assyria, because thou wast unsatiable; yea, thou hast played the harlot with them, and yet couldest not be satisfied.

29 Thou hast likewise multiplied thy fornication in the land of Canaan and of the Chaldeans; and yet thou wast not satisfied herewith.

30 How inconsistent is thy heart, said the Lord GOD, having done all these *things*, the work of a powerful harlot;

31 building thine altars at the head of every way, and making thine altars in every street! And thou hast not been as an harlot, in that thou scornest hire;

32 but *as* a wife that committeth adultery, *which* taketh strangers instead of her husband!

33 They give gifts to all whores: but thou givest thy gifts to all thy lovers, and givest them offerings, that they may come unto thee on every side for thy whoredom.

34 And in thee it is to the contrary from *other* women in thy whoredoms, and after thee there shall never be *whoredom like unto thine*: because in giving thy gifts when gifts are not given unto thee, it has been backwards.

35 Therefore, O harlot, hear the word of the LORD:

36 Thus hath the Lord GOD said; Because thy nakedness has been uncovered, and thy confusion has been manifested to thy lovers in thy whoredoms; and to the idols of thy abominations, and in the blood of thy children, which thou didst give unto them;

37 therefore, behold that I will gather all thy lovers, with whom thou hast taken pleasure, and all *them* that thou hast loved, with all *them* that thou hast hated; I will even gather them round about against thee, and will uncover thy nakedness unto them, that they may see all thy nakedness.

38 And *I* will judge thee by the laws regarding women who commit adultery, and those that shed blood; and I will give thee *away* in blood of fury and of jealousy.

39 And I will deliver thee into their hand, and they shall destroy thy high *place*, and shall break down thy altars: they shall strip thee also of thy clothes, and shall take the vessels of thy glory, and shall leave thee naked and bare.

40 They shall also bring up a company against thee, and they shall stone thee with stones, and thrust thee through with their swords.

41 And they shall burn thine houses with fire, and execute judgments upon thee in the sight of many women: and I will cause thee to cease from playing the harlot, and thou also shalt give no hire any more.

42 So will I make my fury toward thee to rest, and my jealousy shall depart from thee, and I will be quiet, and will no longer be angry.

43 Because thou hast not remembered the days of thy youth, but hast provoked me to anger in all this; therefore, behold I also have recompensed thy way upon *thine* head, said the Lord GOD: for thou hast not even thought regarding all thine abominations.

44 Behold, every one that maketh proverbs shall make *this* proverb regarding thee, saying, As *is* the mother, *so is* her daughter.

45 Thou *art* thy mother's daughter, that discarded her husband and her children; and thou *art* the sister of thy sisters, which discarded their husbands and their children: your mother *was* an Hittite, and your father an Amorite.

46 And thine elder sister *is* Samaria with her daughters, that dwell at thy left hand: and thy younger sister, that dwelleth at thy right hand, *is* Sodom with her daughters.

47 Yet thou hast not walked after their ways, nor done after their abomina-tions: but, as *if that were* a very little *thing*, thou wast corrupted more than they in all thy ways.

48 *As* I live, said the Lord GOD, Sodom thy sister hath never done, she nor her daughters, as thou hast done, thou and thy daughters.

49 Behold, this was the iniquity of thy sister Sodom, pride, fullness of bread, and abundance of idleness was in her and in her daughters, neither did she strengthen the hand of the afflicted and needy.

50 And they filled themselves with arrogance, and committed abomination before me: and when I saw it I took them away.

51 Neither hath Samaria committed half of thy sins; but thou hast multiplied thine abominations more than they, and hast justified thy sisters with all thine abominations which thou hast done.

52 Thou also, which hast judged thy sisters, bear thine own shame for thy sins that thou hast committed more abominable than they: they are more righteous than thou: yea, be thou confounded also, and bear thy shame, in that thou hast justified thy sisters.

53 When I shall turn their captivity, the captivity of Sodom and her daughters, and the captivity of Samaria and her daughters, then *will I release* the captivity of thy captives in the midst of them:

54 That thou mayest bear thine own shame, and mayest be confounded in all that thou hast done, in that thou art a comfort unto them.

55 When thy sisters, Sodom and her daughters, shall return to their first state, and Samaria and her daughters shall return to their first state, and thou and thy daughters shall return to your first state.

56 Sodom, thy sister was not mentioned by thy mouth in the time of thy pride,

57 before thy wickedness discovered itself, as at the time of the reproach of the daughters of Syria, and of all the daughters of the Philistines round about, which despise thee in everything.

58 Thou hast borne thy lewdness and thine abominations, said the LORD.

59 For thus hath the Lord GOD said; Will I deal with thee even as thou hast done, despising the oath to invalidate the covenant?

60 Nevertheless I will remember my covenant that I made with thee in the days of thy youth, and I will confirm unto thee an everlasting covenant.

61 Then thou shalt remember thy ways, and be ashamed, when thou shalt receive thy sisters, thine elder and thy younger: and I will give them unto thee for daughters, but not by thy covenant.

62 And I will confirm my covenant with thee; and thou shalt know that I *am* the LORD:

63 That thou mayest remember, and be confounded, and never open thy mouth any more because of thy shame, when I am pacified toward thee for all that thou hast done, said the Lord GOD.

Chapter 17

1 And the word of the LORD came unto me, saying,

2 Son of man, propose a figure, and compose a parable unto the house of Israel;

3 and say, Thus hath the Lord GOD said; A great eagle with great wings, and long members, full of feathers of divers colours, came unto Lebanon, and took the highest branch of the cedar:

4 He cropped off the principal shoot, and carried it

into a land of markets; he set it in the city of the merchants.

5 He took also of the seed of the land, and planted it in a fruitful field; he placed *it* by great waters, *and* set it *as* a willow tree.

6 And it grew, and became a vine of many branches, low of stature, whose branches looked at him, and the roots thereof were under him: so it became a vine, and brought forth branches, and shot forth sprigs.

7 There was also another great eagle with great wings and many feathers: and, behold, this vine did join her roots toward him, and extended her branches toward him, that he might water it by the furrows of her plantation.

8 It was planted in a good soil by many waters, that it might bring forth branches, and that it might bear fruit, that it might be a goodly vine.

9 Say thou, Thus hath the Lord GOD said; Shall it be prospered? Shall he not pull up the roots thereof, and destroy the fruit thereof, and let it wither? All of the leaves of her spring shall wither, even without great power or many people, plucking it up by the roots thereof.

10 Yea, behold, *being* planted, shall it be prospered? Shall it not utterly wither, when the east wind toucheth it? It shall wither in the furrows where it grew.

11 And the word of the LORD came unto me, saying,

12 Say now to the rebellious house, Know ye not what these *things mean*? Tell *them*, Behold, the king of Babylon is come to Jerusalem, and hath taken the king thereof, and the princes thereof, and led them with him to Babylon;

13 And hath taken of the seed of the kingdom, and made a covenant with him, and hath brought him to an oath: he hath also taken the mighty of the land:

14 That the kingdom might be cast down, that it might not lift itself up, *but* that it might keep his covenant and stay in her.

15 But he rebelled against him in sending his ambassadors unto Egypt, that they might give him horses and much people. Shall he be prospered, shall he escape that doeth such *things*? And shall he who broke the covenant be able to flee?

16 *As* I live, said the Lord GOD, surely in the place *where* the king *dwelleth* that made him king, whose oath he despised, and whose covenant he broke, *even* with him in the midst of Babylon he shall die.

17 And not with a mighty army, nor with a great company shall Pharaoh do anything for him in the battle, when they cast up mounts, and build forts to cut off many lives:

18 Seeing he despised the oath to invalidate the covenant, when, behold, he had given his hand, and hath done all these *things*, he shall not escape.

19 Therefore thus hath the Lord GOD said; *As* I live, surely my oath that he hath despised, and my covenant that he hath broken, even it will I turn upon his own head.

20 And I will spread my net upon him, and he shall be taken in my snare, and I will bring him to Babylon, and will enter into judgment with him there for his trespass with which he hath rebelled against me.

21 And all his fugitives with all his armies shall fall by the sword, and they that remain shall be scattered toward all winds: and ye shall know that I the LORD have spoken *it*.

22 Thus hath the Lord GOD said; I will also take of the highest branch of that high cedar, and will set *it up*; I will crop off from the principal branch a shoot, and will plant *it* upon the high and sublime mountain:

23 In the high mountain of Israel will I plant it: and it shall bring forth boughs, and bear fruit, and become a magnificent cedar: and under it shall dwell every fowl, everything that flieth shall dwell in the shadow of the branches thereof.

24 And all the trees of the field shall know that I the LORD have brought down the high tree, have exalted the low tree, have dried up the green tree, and have made the dry tree to flourish: I the LORD have spoken and have done *it*.

Chapter 18

1 The word of the LORD came unto me again, saying,

2 What mean ye, that ye use this saying concerning the land of Israel, saying, The fathers have eaten sour grapes, and the children's teeth are set on edge?

3 *As* I live, said the Lord GOD, ye shall never again have *reason* to use this saying in Israel.

4 Behold, all souls are mine; as the soul of the father, so also the soul of the son is mine: the soul that sinneth, it shall die.

5 But if a man be just, and do judgment and righteousness;

6 that he not eat upon the mountains, neither lift up his eyes to the idols of the house of Israel, neither defile his neighbour's wife, neither come near to the menstruous woman,

7 neither oppress any, *but* restore to the debtor his pledge, not commit robbery, give his bread to the hungry, and cover the naked with a garment,

8 neither lend at interest, neither take any increase, withdraw his hand from iniquity, execute true judgment between man and man,

9 walk in my statutes, and keep my rights, to do according to the truth; he *is* just, he shall surely live, said the Lord GOD.

10 If he beget a son *that is* a robber, a shedder of blood, and *that* doeth the like of *any* one of these *things*,

11 and that doeth not any of those *duties*, but on the other hand he doth eat upon the mountains, or defile his neighbour's wife,

12 oppress the poor and needy, commit robbery, restore not the pledge, or lift up his eyes to the idols, or make an abomination,

13 give forth upon usury, and take increase: shall he then live? He shall not live: he hath done all these abominations; he shall surely die; his blood shall be upon him.

14 But if he beget a son, that seeth all his father's sins which he hath done, and seeing them, doeth not according to them,

15 *that* he not eat upon the mountains, neither lift up his eyes to the idols of the house of Israel, nor defile his neighbour's wife,

16 neither oppress any, nor withhold the pledge, neither commit robbery, *but* give his bread to the hungry, and cover the naked with a garment,

17 take off his hand from *oppressing* the poor, not receive usury nor increase, act *according to* my rights, and walk in my statutes; he shall not die for the iniquity of his father, he shall surely live.

18 *As for* his father, because he cruelly oppressed, spoiled his brother by violence, and did *that* which *is* not good among his people, behold, even he shall die for his iniquity.

19 Yet if ye say, Why doth not the son bear the iniquity of the father? Because the son hath lived according to judgment and righteousness, *and* hath kept all my statutes, and hath done them, he shall surely live.

20 The soul that sinneth, it shall die. The son shall not bear the iniquity of the father, neither shall the father bear the iniquity of the son: the righteousness of the righteous shall be upon he *who is righteous*, and the wickedness of the wicked shall be upon he *who is wicked*.

21 But if the wicked will turn from all his sins that he hath committed, and keep all my statutes, and live according to judgment and righteousness, he shall surely live, he shall not die.

22 All his rebellions that he hath committed, they shall not be mentioned unto him: by his righteousness that he hath done he shall live.

23 Do I desire perchance the death of the wicked? said the Lord GOD, Shall he not live if he should leave his ways?

24 But if the righteous should leave his righteousness, and commit iniquity, *and* do according to all the abominations that the wicked *man* doeth, shall he live? All his righteousness that he hath done shall not be mentioned: by his rebellion in which he hath trespassed, and by his sin that he hath sinned, because of them shall he die.

25 And if ye say, The way of the Lord is not straight. Hear now, O house of Israel; Is my way not straight? Are not your ways crooked?

26 When a righteous *man* leaveth his righteousness, and committeth iniquity, he shall die in it; for his iniquity that he hath done shall he die.

27 Again, when the wicked *man* leaveth his wickedness that he hath committed, and liveth according to judgment and righteousness, he shall cause his soul to live.

28 Because he saw, and left all his rebellions that he hath committed, he shall surely live, he shall not die.

29 If even *now* the house of Israel should say, The way of the Lord is not straight. O house of Israel, are not my ways straight? Certainly your ways are not straight.

30 Therefore I will judge you, O house of Israel, every one according to his ways, said the Lord GOD. Repent, and turn *yourselves* from all your iniquities; so iniquity shall not be your ruin.

31 Cast away from you all your iniquities, whereby ye have rebelled; and make you a new heart and a new spirit: for why will ye die, O house of Israel?

32 For I desire not the death of him that dieth, said the Lord GOD: wherefore turn *yourselves*, and ye shall live.

Chapter 19

1 And take thou up a lamentation for the princes of Israel,

2 and thou shalt say, How hast thy mother, the lioness, lain down among the lions? She raised her whelps among the young lions.

3 And she brought up one of her whelps: it became a young lion, and it learned to catch the prey and to devour men.

4 The Gentiles also heard of him; he was taken in their trap, and they brought him with chains unto the land of Egypt.

5 Now when *she* saw that she had waited a long time, *and* her hope was being lost, then she took another of her whelps, *and* made him a young lion.

6 And he went up and down among the lions, he became a young lion, and learned to catch the prey, *and* devoured men.

7 And he knew their widows, and he laid waste their cities; and the land was desolate, and the fullness thereof, by the voice of his roaring.

8 Then the Gentiles set against him on every side from the provinces, and spread their net over him: he was taken in their pit.

9 And they put him in prison in chains, and brought him to the king of Babylon: they brought him into fortresses, that his voice should no more be heard upon the mountains of Israel.

10 Thy mother *was* like a vine in thy blood, planted by the waters: bearing fruit and spreading forth branches by reason of the many waters.

11 And she had strong rods for the sceptres of them that bare rule, and her stature was exalted among the thick branches, and she appeared in her height and with the multitude of her branches.

12 But she was plucked up in fury, she was cast down to the ground, and the east wind dried up her fruit: *her branches* were broken and she withered; fire consumed the rod of her strength.

13 And now she *is* planted in the wilderness, in a dry and thirsty ground.

14 And fire is gone out of the rod from her branches, *which* hath devoured her fruit, so that no strong rod *to be* a sceptre to rule hath remained in her. This *is* a lamentation, and shall be for a lamentation.

Chapter 20

1 And it came to pass in the seventh year, in the fifth *month*, the tenth *day* of the month, *that* certain of the elders of Israel came to enquire of the LORD, and sat before me.

2 Then came the word of the LORD unto me, saying,

3 Son of man, speak unto the elders of Israel, and say unto them, Thus hath the Lord GOD said; Are ye come to enquire of me? *As* I live, said the Lord GOD, I will not be enquired of by you.

4 Dost thou desire to judge them? Dost thou desire to judge them, son of man? Notify them of the abominations of their fathers:

5 And say unto them, Thus hath the Lord GOD said; In the day when I chose Israel, and lifted up my hand for the seed of the house of Jacob, and made myself known unto them in the land of Egypt, when I lifted up my hand unto them, saying, I *am* the LORD your God;

6 in the day *that* I lifted up my hand unto *them with an oath*, that I would bring them forth from the land of Egypt into a land that I had prepared for them, flowing with milk and honey, which *is* the most beautiful of all lands:

7 Then said I unto them, Cast ye away every one of you *all* worship of god fabricated by carnal appearance, and defile not yourselves with the idols of Egypt: I *am* the LORD your God.

8 But they rebelled against me, and did not desire to hearken unto me: they did not every one cast away the abominations of their eyes, neither did they forsake the idols of Egypt: then I said, I will pour out my fury upon them, to accomplish my anger against them in the midst of the land of Egypt.

9 With all this, I intervened for my name's sake, that it should not be polluted before the Gentiles, among whom they *were*, in whose sight I made myself known unto them, in bringing them forth out of the land of Egypt.

10 Therefore I took them out of the land of Egypt, and brought them into the wilderness;

11 and I gave them my statutes, and declared unto them my rights, *by* which the man that doeth them, shall live by them.

12 And I also gave them my sabbaths, to be a sign between me and them, that they might know that I *am* the LORD that sanctify them.

13 But the house of Israel rebelled against me in the wilderness: they walked not in my statutes, and they despised my rights, *by* which the man that doeth them, shall live by them; and my sabbaths they greatly polluted: therefore I said, I would pour out my fury upon them in the wilderness, to consume them.

14 But I intervened for my name's sake, that it should not be polluted before the Gentiles, in whose sight I brought them out.

15 Yet also I lifted up my hand unto them in the wilderness, *with an oath*, that I would not bring them into the land which I had given *them*, flowing with milk and honey, which *is* the most beautiful of all lands;

16 because they despised my rights, and walked not in my statutes, but polluted my sabbaths: for their heart went after their idols.

17 With all this, my eye spared them from destroying them, neither did I make an end of them in the wilderness.

18 But I said unto their children in the wilderness, Walk ye not in the statutes of your fathers, neither keep their laws, nor defile yourselves with their idols:

19 I *am* the LORD your God; walk in my statutes, and keep my rights, and do them;

20 and hallow my sabbaths; and they shall be a sign between me and you, that ye may know that I *am* the LORD your God.

21 Notwithstanding the children rebelled against me: they walked not in my statutes, neither kept my rights to do them, *by* which the man that doeth them, shall live by them; they polluted my sabbaths: then I said, I would pour out my fury upon them, to accomplish my anger against them in the wilderness.

22 Nevertheless I withdrew my hand, and intervened for my name's sake, that it should not be polluted in the sight of the Gentiles, in whose sight I brought them forth.

23 I lifted up my hand unto them also in the wilderness, *with an oath*, that I would scatter them among the Gentiles, and disperse them through the countries;

24 because they had not executed my rights, and had despised my statutes, and had polluted my sabbaths, and their eyes were after their fathers' idols.

25 For this reason I also gave them statutes *that were* not good, and rights by which they could not live;

26 and I polluted them in their offerings when they caused to pass through *the fire* all that openeth the womb, that I might make them desolate, to the end that they might know that I *am* the LORD.

27 Therefore, son of man, speak unto the house of Israel, and say unto them, Thus hath the Lord GOD said; Even in this your fathers have blasphemed me when they committed rebellion against me.

28 *For* when I had brought them into the land, *for* the which I lifted up my hand to give it to them, then they saw every high hill, and all the thick trees, and they offered there their sacrifices, and there they presented the provocation of their offerings: there *also* they made their sweet savour, and poured out there their drink offerings.

29 Then I said unto them, What *is* the high place whereunto ye go? And the name thereof is called Bamah unto this day.

30 Therefore say unto the house of Israel, Thus hath the Lord GOD said; Perchance are ye polluted after the manner of your fathers? and commit ye whoredom after their abominations?

31 For when ye offer your gifts, when ye make your sons to pass through the fire, ye pollute yourselves with all your idols, even unto this day: and shall I be enquired of by you, O house of Israel? As I live said the Lord GOD, I will not be enquired of by you.

32 And that which ye think shall not be at all, that ye say, We will be as the Gen tiles, as the families of the nations, to serve wood and stone.

33 *As* I live, said the Lord GOD, surely with a mighty hand, and with a stretched out arm, and with fury poured out, must I rule over you:

34 And I will bring you out from among the peoples, and will gather you out of the countries wherein ye are scattered, with a mighty hand, and with a stretched out arm, and with fury poured out.

35 And I will bring you into the wilderness of peoples, and there will I litigate with you face to face.

36 Like as I litigated with your fathers in the wilderness of the land of Egypt, so will I litigate with you, said the Lord GOD.

37 And I will cause you to pass under the rod, and I will bring you into the bond of the covenant:

38 And I will purge out from among you the rebels, and those that rebelled against me: I will take them out of the country where they have gone, and they shall not enter into the land of Israel: and ye shall know that I *am* the LORD.

39 As for you, O house of Israel, thus hath the Lord GOD said; Go ye, serve ye every one his idols, and hereafter *also*, if ye will not hearken unto me: but pollute ye my holy name no more with your gifts, and with your idols.

40 For in the mountain of my holiness, in the high mountain of Israel, said the Lord GOD, there shall all the house of Israel serve me, all of them in the land: there will I be pleased with them, and there will I require your offerings, and the firstfruits of your gifts, with all your sacred things.

41 I will accept you with your sweet savour, when I have brought you out from among the peoples, and gathered you out of the countries wherein ye have been scattered; and I will be sanctified in you in the eyes of the Gentiles.

42 And ye shall know that I *am* the LORD, when I shall bring you into the land of Israel, into the land *for* the which I lifted up my hand to give it to your fathers.

43 And there shall ye remember your ways, and all your doings, wherein ye have been defiled; and ye shall loathe yourselves in your own sight for all your evils that ye have committed.

44 And ye shall know that I *am* the LORD, when I have intervened with you for my name's sake, not according to your wicked ways, nor according to your corrupt doings, O ye house of Israel, said the Lord GOD.

45 And the word of the LORD came unto me, saying, **46** Son of man, set thy face toward the south, and drop *thy word* toward the south, and prophesy against the forest of the south field; **47** and thou shalt say to the forest of the south, Hear the word of the LORD; Thus hath the Lord GOD said; Behold, I kindle a fire in thee, which shall devour every green tree in thee, and every dry tree: the flame of the fire shall not be quenched, and all faces from the south to the north shall be burned therein. **48** And all flesh shall see that I the LORD have kindled it: it shall not be quenched. **49** Then said I, Ah Lord GOD! they say of me, Doth he not speak parables?

Chapter 21

1 And the word of the LORD came unto me, saying, **2** Son of man, set thy face against Jerusalem, and drop *my word* upon the sanctuaries, and prophesy over the land of Israel, **3** and thou shalt say to the land of Israel, Thus hath the LORD said; Behold, I *am* against thee, and will draw forth my sword out of his sheath, and will cut off from thee the righteous and the wicked. **4** Seeing then that I will cut off from thee the righteous and the wicked, therefore shall my sword go forth out of his sheath against all flesh from the south to the north: **5** That all flesh may know that I the LORD have drawn forth my sword out of his sheath: it shall not return any more. **6** Cry out therefore, thou son of man, with the breaking of *thy* loins; and with bitterness cry out before their eyes. **7** And it shall be, when they say unto thee, Wherefore criest thou? that thou shalt answer, For the tidings that come: and every heart shall melt, and all hands shall be feeble, and every spirit shall faint, and all knees shall be weak *as* water: behold, it cometh, and shall be brought to pass, said the Lord GOD. **8** And the word of the LORD came unto me, saying,

9 Son of man, prophesy, and say, Thus hath the LORD said; Say, A sword, a sword is sharpened, and also furbished:

10 It is sharpened to slay victims; it is furbished that it may glitter: should we then make mirth? it despiseth the rod of my son, *as* every tree.

11 And he hath given it to be furbished, that it may be handled: this sword is sharpened, and it is furbished, to give it into the hand of the slayer.

12 Cry and howl, son of man: for it shall be upon my people, it *shall be* upon all the princes of Israel: fear of the sword shall be upon my people: therefore smite the thigh;

13 because *it shall be* a trial. What shall be if it doth not despise the rod, said the Lord GOD.

14 Thou therefore, son of man, prophesy, and smite *thine* hands together, and let the sword be doubled the third time, the sword of the slain: this is the sword of great slaughter that shall pierce them.

15 I have set the fear of the sword in all their gates, that *their* heart may faint, and *their* ruins be multiplied: ah! *it is* made so that it might shine, *it is* prepared for the slaughter.

16 Go thee one way or other, *either* on the right hand, *or* on the left, wherever thy face *is* set.

17 I will also smite my hands together, and I will cause my fury to rest: I the LORD have spoken.

18 The word of the LORD came unto me again, saying,

19 Also, thou son of man, show two ways from whence the sword of the king of Babylon cometh: both shall come forth out of the same land: and draw an army; at the head of the way to the city thou shalt do this.

20 Show the way that the sword will come to Rabbath of the Ammonites, and to Judah against Jerusalem the defenced.

21 For the king of Babylon stood at the parting of the way, at the head of the two ways, to use divination: he made *his* arrows bright, he consulted with images, he looked in the liver.

22 The divination was to his right hand upon Jerusalem, to appoint captains, to open the mouth for the slaughter, to lift up the voice with shouting, to appoint *battering* rams against the gates, to cast a mount, *and* to build a fort.

23 And it shall be unto them as a false divination in their sight, to them that have sworn oaths: but he will call to remembrance the iniquity, that they may be taken.

24 Therefore thus hath the Lord GOD said; Because ye have made your iniquity to be remembered, manifesting your betrayals, and uncovering your sins in all your doings; for which ye are come to remembrance, ye shall be taken with the hand.

25 And thou, profane wicked prince of Israel, whose day is come in the time when the iniquity shall be brought to an end,

26 thus hath the Lord GOD said; Remove the diadem, and take off the crown: it shall no longer be like this: I will exalt the one that is low, and abase the one that is high.

27 I will overturn, overturn, overturn, it: and it shall be no *more*, until he come whose right it is; and I will give it *him*.

28 And thou, son of man, prophesy and say, Thus saith the Lord GOD concerning the Ammonites, and concerning their reproach; even say thou, The sword, the sword *is* drawn for the slaughter; *it is* furbished, to consume with brightness:

29 They prophesy vanity unto thee, they divine a lie unto thee, to give thee over among the necks of the wicked who are sentenced to death, whose day is come in the time when the iniquity shall be brought to an end.

30 Shall I cause *it* to return into his sheath? I must judge thee in the place where thou wast raised, in the land of where thou hast lived.

31 And I will pour out my indignation upon thee, I will blow against thee in the fire of my wrath, and deliver thee into the hand of fearful men *who are* skilful to destroy.

32 Thou shalt be for fuel to the fire; thy blood shall be in the midst of the land; thou shalt be no *more* remembered: for I the LORD have spoken.

Chapter 22

1 Moreover the word of the LORD came unto me, saying,

2 Now, thou son of man, wilt thou not judge, wilt

thou not judge the city that spilleth innocent blood and cause her to know all her abominations?

3 Then thou shalt say, Thus hath the Lord GOD said, City that sheddeth blood in the midst of thyself, that thy time may come, and that hath made idols against thyself to defile thyself!

4 In thy blood that thou hast shed thou hast sinned; and hast defiled thyself with thine idols which thou hast made; and thou hast caused thy days to draw near, and art come *even* unto thy years: therefore have I given thee in reproach unto the Gentiles, and in shame unto all the countries.

5 *Those that be* near, and *those that be* far from thee, shall mock thee, *which art* infamous *and* much vexed.

6 Behold, the princes of Israel, every one according to their power, were in thee to shed blood.

7 In thee have they despised father and mother: in the midst of thee have they dealt by oppression with the stranger: in thee have they vexed the fatherless and the widow.

8 Thou hast despised my holy things, and hast profaned my sabbaths.

9 In thee are men that carry tales to shed blood: and in thee they eat upon the mountains: in the midst of thee they commit lewdness.

10 In thee have they discovered their fathers' nakedness: in thee have they forced the unclean menstruous *woman.*

11 And one hath committed abomination with his neighbour's wife; and another hath lewdly defiled his daughter in law; and another in thee hath forced his sister, his father's daughter.

12 In thee have they taken gifts to shed blood; thou hast taken usury and increase, and thou hast greedily gained of thy neighbours by extortion, and hast forgotten me, said the Lord GOD.

13 Behold, therefore I have smitten my hand at thy dishonest gain which thou hast made, and at thy blood which hath been in the midst of thee.

14 Can thine heart endure, or can thine hands be strong, in the days that I shall deal with thee? I the LORD have spoken *it*, and will do *it*.

15 And I will scatter thee among the Gentiles, and

disperse thee in the countries, and will consume thy filthiness out of thee.

16 And thou shalt take thine inheritance in thyself in the sight of the Gentiles, and thou shalt know that I *am* the LORD.

17 And the word of the LORD came unto me, saying,

18 Son of man, the house of Israel is to me become dross: all they *are* brass, and tin, and iron, and lead, in the midst of the furnace; they are become the dross of silver.

19 Therefore thus hath the Lord GOD said; Because ye are all become dross, behold, therefore I will gather you into the midst of Jerusalem.

20 *As* they gather silver, and brass, and iron, and lead, and tin, into the midst of the furnace, to blow the fire upon it, to melt *it*; so will I gather *you* in my anger and in my fury, and I will cause *you* to rest, and melt you.

21 Yea, I will gather you, and blow upon you in the fire of my wrath, and ye shall be melted in the midst thereof.

22 As silver is melted in the midst of the furnace, so shall ye be melted in the midst thereof; and ye shall know that I the LORD have poured out my fury upon you.

23 And the word of the LORD came unto me, saying,

24 Son of man, say unto her, Thou *art* not clean land, nor *art thou* sprinkled with rain in the day of indignation.

25 *There is* a conspiracy of her prophets in the midst thereof, like a roaring lion ravening the prey; they have devoured souls; they have taken treasures and honour; they have made her many widows in the midst thereof.

26 Her priests have violated my law *by force*, and have profaned my holy things: they have made no difference between *the* holy and *the* profane, neither have they showed *the difference* between the unclean and the clean, and have hid their eyes from my sabbaths, and I am profaned among them.

27 Her princes in the midst thereof *are* like wolves ravening the prey, to shed blood, *and* to destroy souls, to follow their own greed.

28 And her prophets have plastered them *over* with loose mud, prophesying vanity, and divining lies unto them, saying, Thus hath the Lord GOD said, when the LORD hath not spoken.

29 The people of the land have used oppression, and exercised robbery, and have done violence unto the poor and needy: yea, they have oppressed the stranger wrongfully.

30 And I sought for a man among them, that should make up the hedge, and stand in the gap before me for the land, that I should not destroy it: but I found none.

31 Therefore have I poured out my indignation upon them; I have consumed them with the fire of my wrath: their own way have I recompensed upon their heads, said the Lord GOD.

Chapter 23

1 The word of the LORD came again unto me, saying,

2 Son of man, there were two women, the daughters of one mother:

3 And they committed whoredoms in Egypt; they committed whoredoms in their youth: there were their breasts pressed, and there they bruised the teats of their virginity.

4 And the names of them *were* Aholah the elder, and Aholibah her sister: and they were mine, and they bore sons and daughters. Thus *were* their names; Samaria *is* Aholah, and Jerusalem Aholibah.

5 And Aholah played the harlot when she was mine; and she fell in love with her lovers, the Assyrians *her* neighbours,

6 *which were* clothed with blue, captains and rulers, all of them desirable young men, horsemen riding upon horses.

7 Thus she committed her whoredoms with them, with all them *that were* the chosen men of Assyria, and with all whom she fell in love: with all their idols she defiled herself.

8 Neither left she her whoredoms of Egypt: for in her youth they lay with her, and they bruised the breasts of her virginity, and poured their whoredom upon her.

9 Therefore I have delivered her into the hand of her lovers, into the hand of the Assyrians, of whom she fell in love.

10 These uncovered her nakedness: they took her sons and her daughters, and slew her with the sword: and she became famous among women; for they had executed judgment upon her.

11 And when her sister Aholibah saw *this*, she was more corrupt in her inordinate love than she, and in her whoredoms more than her sister in *her* whoredoms.

12 She fell in love with the Assyrians *her* neighbours, captains and rulers clothed to perfection, horsemen riding upon horses, all of them desirable young men.

13 Then I saw that she was defiled, *that* they both *took* the same way,

14 and *that* she increased her whoredoms: for when she saw men painted upon the wall, the images of the Chaldeans painted in colour,

15 girded with girdles upon their loins, and mitres painted upon their heads, all of them looking like princes, after the manner of the men of Babylon, born in the land of the Chaldeans,

16 she fell in love with them as soon as she saw them with her eyes, and sent messengers unto them into Chaldea.

17 And the Babylonians came to her into the bed of love, and they defiled her with their whoredom, and she was polluted with them, and her soul was alienated from them.

18 So she uncovered her whoredoms, and uncovered her nakedness: then my soul was alienated from her, like as my soul was alienated from her sister.

19 Yet she multiplied her whoredoms, in calling to remembrance the days of her youth, wherein she had played the harlot in the land of Egypt.

20 For she doted upon their paramours, whose flesh *is as* the flesh of asses, and whose issue *is like* the issue of horses.

21 Thus thou calledst to remembrance the lewdness of thy youth, in bruising thy teats by the Egyptians for the breasts of thy youth.

22 Therefore, O Aholibah, thus hath the Lord GOD said; Behold, I will raise up thy lovers against thee, from whom thy desire is alienated, and I will bring them against thee on every side;

23 the Babylonians, and all the Chaldeans, rulers, and princes, and captains, *and* all the Assyrians with them: all of them desirable young men; all of them captains and rulers, great lords and renowned; all of them riding upon horses.

24 And they shall come against thee with chariots,

wagons, and wheels, and with a multitude of peoples, *which* shall set against thee buckler and shield and helmet round about: and I will set judgment before them, and they shall judge thee according to their laws.

25 And I will set my jealousy against thee, and they shall deal with thee in furor: they shall take away thy nose and thine ears; and what is left shall fall by the sword: they shall take thy sons and thy daughters; and thy remnant shall be devoured by the fire.

26 They shall also strip thee out of thy clothes, and take away the vessels of thy glory.

27 Thus will I make thy lewdness to cease from thee, and thy whoredom of the land of Egypt: so that thou shalt not lift up thine eyes unto them, nor remember Egypt any more.

28 For thus hath the Lord GOD said; Behold, I deliver thee into the hand *of them* whom thou hatest, into the hand *of them* from whom thy soul is alienated:

29 And they shall deal with thee hatefully, and shall take away all thy labour, and shall leave thee naked and bare: and the nakedness of thy whoredoms shall be uncovered, both thy lewdness and thy whoredoms.

30 I will do these *things* unto thee, because thou hast gone a whoring after the Gentiles, *and* because thou art polluted with their idols.

31 Thou hast walked in the way of thy sister; therefore will I put her cup into thine hand.

32 Thus hath the Lord GOD said; Thou shalt drink of thy sister's cup deep and large: the Gentiles shall laugh thee to scorn and hold thee in derision; it containeth much.

33 Thou shalt be filled with drunkenness and with pain, *because* of the cup of astonishment and desolation, *because* of the cup of thy sister Samaria.

34 Thou shalt even drink it and finish it, and thou shalt break the shards thereof, and pluck off thine own breasts: for I have spoken *it*, said the Lord GOD.

35 Therefore thus hath the Lord GOD said; Because thou hast forgotten me, and cast me behind thy back, therefore bear thou also thy lewdness and thy whoredoms.

36 And The LORD said unto me; Son of man, wilt thou

judge Aholah and Aholibah and declare unto them their abominations?

37 For they have committed adultery, and blood *is* on their hands, and with their idols have they committed adultery, and have even caused their sons, whom they bore unto me, to pass for them through *the fire*, to devour *them* .

38 Moreover this they have done unto me: they have defiled my sanctuary in the same day, and have profaned my sabbaths.

39 For when they had slain their children unto their idols, then they came the same day into my sanctuary to profane it; and, behold, thus have they done in the midst of my house.

40 And furthermore, that ye have sent for men to come from far, unto whom a messenger *was* sent; and, behold, they came: for the love of whom thou didst wash thyself, paintedst thy eyes, and deckedst thyself with ornaments,

41 and satest upon a stately bed, and a table prepared before it, whereupon thou hast set my incense and my oil.

42 And in her was heard a voice of a multitude at a feast: and with the men *of* *renown* were brought the Sabeans from the wilderness to multiply the men, and they put bracelets upon their hands, and crowns of glory upon their heads.

43 Then said I unto *her that was* old in adulteries, Now shalt thy whoredoms come to an end, and she *with them*;

44 for they have come to her, as those who come to a woman that playeth the harlot: so went they in unto Aholah and unto Aholibah, the lewd women.

45 Therefore righteous men shall judge them by the law of adulteresses, and after the law of women that shed blood; because they *are* adulteresses, and blood *is* on their hands.

46 For thus hath the Lord GOD said; I will bring up a company upon them, and will give them to be removed and spoiled.

47 And the company shall stone them with stones, and dispatch them with their swords; they shall slay their sons and their daughters, and burn up their houses with fire.

48 Thus will I cause the lust to cease out of the land, that all women may be taught not to do after your lewdness.

49 And they shall recompense your lust upon you, and ye shall bear the sins of your idols: and ye shall know that I *am* the Lord GOD.

Chapter 24

1 Again in the ninth year, in the tenth *month*, in the tenth *day* of the month, the word of the LORD came unto me, saying,

2 Son of man, write thee the name of the day, *even* of this same day: the king of Babylon laid siege against Jerusalem this same day.

3 And speak unto the house of rebellion by parable, and say unto them, Thus hath the Lord GOD said; Set on a pot, set *it* on, and also pour water into it:

4 Gather her pieces *of meat* into it, *even* every good piece, the thigh, and the shoulder; fill *it* with the choice bones.

5 Take the choice of the flock, and burn also the bones under it, *and* make it boil well, and let them seethe the bones of it therein.

6 For thus hath the Lord GOD said; Woe to the bloody city, to the pot whose scum *is* therein, and whose scum is not gone out of it! For her pieces, because of her pieces let it be removed; let no lot fall upon it.

7 For her blood is in the midst of her; she set it upon the top of a rock; she poured it not upon the ground, to cover it with dust;

8 that wrath might rise up to take vengeance; I have set her blood upon the high place of the rock, that it should not be covered.

9 Therefore thus hath the Lord GOD said; Woe to the bloody city! I will also make a great fire,

10 multiplying the wood, kindleling the fire, to consume the flesh, and to make the broth, and the bones shall be burned.

11 setting afterward the empty pot upon the coals thereof, that it may become *red* hot, and may burn, and *that* the filthiness of it may be molten in it, *that* the scum of it may be consumed.

12 In fraud she hath become weary, and her great scum went not forth out of her: her scum *shall be* in the fire.

13 In thy perverse filthiness *thou shalt die*: because I have cleansed thee, and thou didst not cleanse thyself from thy uncleanness, thou shalt never cleanse thyself again, until I have caused my fury to rest upon thee.

14 I, the LORD, have spoken: I came, and worked. I will not turn back, neither will I have mercy, neither will I repent; according to thy ways, and according to thy doings, shall they judge thee, said the Lord GOD.

15 And the word of the LORD came unto me, saying,

16 Son of man, behold, I take away from thee the desire of thine eyes by death: yet neither shalt thou mourn nor weep, neither shall thy tears run down.

17 Forbear to cry, make no mourning for the dead, bind thy turban upon thy head, and put on thy shoes upon thy feet, and cover not *thy* lips, and eat not the bread of comfort.

18 So I spoke unto the people in the morning: and at even my wife died; and I did in the morning as I was commanded.

19 And the people said unto me, Wilt thou not tell us what these *things are* to us, that thou doest *so*?

20 Then I answered them, The word of the LORD came unto me, saying,

21 Speak unto the house of Israel, Thus hath the Lord GOD said; Behold, I will profane my sanctuary, the glory of your strength, the desire of your eyes, and the gift of your soul; your sons and your daughters whom ye have left shall fall by the sword.

22 And ye shall do as I have done: ye shall not cover *your* lips, nor eat the bread of men.

23 And your turbans *shall be* upon your heads, and your shoes upon your feet: ye shall not mourn nor weep; but ye shall pine away for your iniquities, and cry out one with another.

24 Thus Ezekiel shall be unto you for a sign: according to all that he hath done shall ye do: and when this cometh, ye shall know that I *am* the Lord GOD.

25 Also, thou son of man, in the day when *I* take from them their strength, the joy of their glory, the desire of their eyes, and the care of their souls, their sons and their daughters,

26 that day *one that* escapeth shall come unto thee, to bring the news.

27 In that day shall thy mouth be opened *to speak* unto him which is escaped, and thou shalt speak, and be no more dumb: and thou shalt be a sign unto them; and they shall know that I *am* the LORD.

Chapter 25

1 The word of the LORD came again unto me, saying, *2* Son of man, set thy face against the sons of Ammon, and prophesy against them; *3* and say unto the sons of Ammon, Hear the word of the Lord GOD; Thus hath the Lord GOD said; Because thou saidst, Aha, *it is well*! upon my sanctuary, which was profaned; and upon the land of Israel, which it was made desolate; and upon the house of Judah, because they went into captivity; *4* behold, therefore I will deliver thee to the men of the east for a possession, and they shall set their palaces in thee, and pitch their tents in thee: they shall eat thy plantings, and they shall drink thy milk. *5* And I will make Rabbah a habitation for camels, and the sons of Ammon a resting place for sheep: and ye shall know that I *am* the LORD.

6 For thus hath the Lord GOD said; Because thou hast clapped *thine* hands, and stamped with the feet, and rejoiced in thy soul with all thy despite upon the land of Israel;

7 behold, therefore I will stretch out my hand upon thee, and will deliver thee unto the Gentiles as a spoil; and I will cut thee off from among the peoples, and I will destroy thee from among the countries: I will pluck thee out; and thou shalt know that I *am* the LORD.

8 Thus hath the Lord GOD said; Because Moab and Seir said, Behold, the house of the LORD *is* like unto all the Gentiles [*submitted to Babylon*];

9 therefore, behold, I will open the side of Moab from the cities, from his cities *which are* on his frontiers, the desirable lands of Bethjeshimoth, and Baalmeon, and Kiriathaim, *10* unto the sons of the east against the sons of Ammon, and will give them in possession, that the sons of Ammon may not be remembered any more among the Gentiles.

11 I will also execute judgments in Moab; and they shall know that I *am* the LORD.

12 Thus hath the Lord GOD spoken; Because of what Edom did when he took vengeance against the house of Judah, for they sinned greatly, and revenged themselves upon them;

13 therefore thus hath the Lord GOD said; I will also stretch out my hand upon Edom, and will cut off man and beast from her; and I will make her desolate from Teman; and *they of* Dedan shall fall by the sword.

14 And I will place my vengeance in Edom by the hand of my people Israel: and they shall do in Edom according to my anger and according to my fury; and they shall know my vengeance, said the Lord GOD.

15 Thus hath the Lord GOD said; Because the Palistinians have dealt by revenge, and have taken vengeance with a despiteful heart, to destroying because of perpetual enmity;

16 therefore thus hath the Lord GOD said; Behold, I stretch out my hand upon the Palestinians, and I will cut off the Cherethims, and destroy the remnant of the sea coast.

17 And I will execute great vengeance in them with furious rebukes; and they shall know that I *am* the LORD, when I shall give my vengeance in them.

Chapter 26

1 And it came to pass in the eleventh year, in the first *day* of the month, *that* the word of the LORD came unto me, saying,

2 Son of man, because Tyre hath said concerning Jerusalem, Aha, *it is well that* she is broken who is the gate of the peoples: she is turned unto me: I shall be filled; and she *shall be* deserted:

3 Therefore thus hath the Lord GOD said; Behold, I *am* against thee, O Tyre, and will cause many nations to come up against thee, as the sea causeth his waves to come up.

4 And they shall demolish the walls of Tyre, and destroy her towers: I will also scrape her dust from her, and make her like the top of a rock.

5 It shall be *a place for* the spreading of nets in the midst of the sea: for I have spoken, said the Lord GOD: and it shall be spoiled by the Gentiles.

6 And her daughters which *are* in the field shall be slain by the sword; and they shall know that I *am* the LORD.

7 For thus hath the Lord GOD said; Behold, I bring upon Tyre Nebuchadrezzar, king of Babylon, *a* king of kings, from the north, with horses, and with chariots, and with horsemen, and companies, and much people.

8 He shall slay with the sword thy daughters who *are* in the field: and he shall make a fort against thee, and cast a mount against thee, and lift up the buckler against thee.

9 And he shall set engines of war against thy walls, and with his hammers he shall break down thy towers.

10 By reason of the abundance of his horses their dust shall cover thee: thy walls shall shake at the noise of the horsemen, and of the wheels, and of the chariots, when he shall enter into thy gates, as men enter through breaches into a destroyed city.

11 With the hoofs of his horses shall he tread down all thy streets: he shall slay thy people by the sword, and the statues of thy strength shall fall to the ground.

12 And they shall steal thy riches, and make a spoil of thy merchandise: and they shall ruin thy walls, and destroy thy precious houses: and they shall lay thy stones and thy timber and thy dust in the midst of the waters.

13 And I will cause the noise of thy songs to cease; and the sound of thy harps shall no longer be heard.

14 And I will make thee like the top of a rock: thou shalt be *a place* to spread nets upon; thou shalt never be built again: for I the LORD have spoken, said the Lord GOD.

15 Thus hath the Lord GOD said to Tyre; Certainly the isles shall shake at the sound of thy fall, when the wounded shall cry, when the slaughter shall be made in the midst of thee.

16 Then all the princes of the sea shall come down from their thrones, and lay away their robes, and put off their broidered garments: they shall clothe themselves with trembling; they shall sit upon the ground, and shall tremble at *every* moment, and be astonished at thee.

17 And they shall take up a lamentation for thee, and say to thee, How didst thou perish, *that wast* inhabited in the seas? The renowned city, which wast strong in the sea, she and her inhabitants, which caused their terror *to be* on all those that dwell therein.

18 Now shall the isles tremble in the day of thy fall; yea, the isles that *are* in the sea shall be terrorised at thy end.

19 For thus hath the Lord GOD said; I shall make thee a desolate city, like the cities that are not inhabited; I shall cause the abyss to come up over thee, and the many waters shall cover thee.

20 And I shall bring thee down with them that descend into the grave, with the people of the age, and shall set thee in the lowest part of the earth, as the deserts of old, with them that go down to the grave, that thou be not inhabited again; and I shall set glory in the land of the living;

21 I will turn thee into nothing, and thou *shalt be* no *more*: though thou be sought for, yet shalt thou never be found again, said the Lord GOD.

Chapter 27

1 The word of the LORD came again unto me, saying,

2 Now, thou son of man, raise up lamentations upon Tyre.

3 And say unto Tyre, O thou that dwelleth at the ports of the sea, *which art* a merchant of the people for many isles, Thus hath the Lord GOD said; O Tyre, thou hast said, I *am* of perfect beauty.

4 In the heart of the seas are thy borders, thy builders have completed thy beauty.

5 They have made all thy *ship* boards of fir trees of Senir: they have taken cedars from Lebanon to make masts for thee.

6 *Of* the oaks of Bashan have they made thine oars; the company of the Ashurites have made thy benches *of* ivory, *brought* out of the isles of Chittim.

7 Of fine linen with broidered work from Egypt was thy curtain, that it might serve to be thy sail; of blue and purple from the isles of Elishah was thy pavilion.

8 The inhabitants of Zidon and Arvad were thy rowers: thy wise *men*, O Tyre, were in thee; they were thy pilots.

9 The elders of Gebal and the wise *men* thereof were in thee to repair thy breaches: all the galleys of the sea with their rowers were in thee to negotiate thy business dealings .

10 They of Persia and of Lud and of Africa were in thine army, thy men of war: they hanged the shield and helmet in thee; they gave thee thine honour.

11 The sons of Arvad with thine army *were* upon thy walls round about, and the Gammadims were in thy towers: they hanged their shields upon thy walls round about; they completed thy beauty.

12 Tarshish *was* thy market by reason of the multitude of all *thy* riches in silver, iron, tin, and lead, they traded in thy fairs.

13 Greece, Tubal, and Meshech, thy merchants, with the soul of men and with vessels of brass, they traded in thy fairs.

14 They of the house of Togarmah traded in thy fairs with horses and horsemen and mules.

15 The sons of Dedan *were* thy merchants; many isles *took* merchandise from thy hand: they brought thee *for* a present horns of ivory and peacocks.

16 Syria *was* thy merchant by reason of the multitude of the wares of thy making: they traded in thy fairs with rubies, and purple, and broidered work, and fine linen, and coral, and pearls.

17 Judah, and the land of Israel, they *were* thy merchants: they traded in thy market with wheat, Minnith, and Pannag, and honey, and oil, and balm.

18 Damascus *was* thy merchant in the multitude of the wares of thy making, for the abundance of all riches, with wine of Helbon, and white wool.

19 Dan also and Greece and Mozel traded in thy fairs: bright iron, cassia, and calamus.

20 Dedan *was* thy merchant in precious cloth for chariots.

21 Arabia, and all the princes of Kedar, merchants of thy strength in lambs, and rams, and he goats: in these *were they* thy merchants.

22 The merchants of Sheba and Raamah, they *were* thy merchants: they traded in thy fairs with chief of all spices, and with all precious stones, and gold.

23 Haran, and Canneh, and Eden, the merchants of Sheba, Asshur, *and* Chilmad, *were* in thy market.

24 These, thy merchants, negotiated with thee in all sorts *of things*: in blue robes, and broidered work, and in chests of rich apparel, bound with cords, and made of cedar, among thy merchandise.

25 The ships of Tarshish, thy squadrons, went forth on thy behalf: and thou wast full, and wast multiplied greatly in the midst of the seas.

26 In many waters they overcame thy rowers: the east wind hath broken thee in the midst of the seas.

27 Thy riches, and thy markets, thy business, thy rowers, and thy pilots, those that repair thy breaches, and the agents of thy business, and all thy men of war, that *are* in thee, with all thy company which *is* in the midst of thee, shall fall into the midst of the seas in the day of thy ruin.

28 The suburbs shall shake at the sound of the cry of thy pilots.

29 And all that handle the oar, the rowers, *and* all the pilots of the sea, shall come down from their ships, they shall stand upon the land;

30 and shall cause their voice to be heard upon thee, and shall cry bitterly, and shall cast up dust upon their heads, they shall wallow themselv s in the ashes:

31 And they shall pull out their hair for thee, and gird themselves with sackcloth, and they shall weep for thee with bitterness of soul *and* bitter wailings.

32 And in their wailing they shall take up a lamentation for thee, and lament over thee, *saying,* Who *is* like Tyre, like the destroyed in the midst of the sea?

33 When thy wares went forth out of the seas, thou filledst many peoples; thou didst enrich the kings of the earth with the multitude of thy riches and of thy contracts.

34 In the time *when* thou shalt be broken by the seas in the depths of the waters thy commerce and all thy company in the midst of thee shall fall.

35 All the inhabitants of the isles shall be astonished at thee, and their kings shall be sore afraid, they shall be troubled in *their* countenance.

36 The merchants among the peoples shall hiss at thee; thou shalt be a terror, and never *shalt be* any more.

Chapter 28

1 The word of the LORD came again unto me, saying,

2 Son of man, say unto the prince of Tyre, Thus hath the Lord GOD said; Because thine heart hath lifted *thee* up, and thou hast said, I *am* God, I sit *in* the seat of God, in the midst of the seas (yet thou *art* man, and not God); and thou hast set thine heart as the heart of God:

3 Behold, thou *art* wiser than Daniel; there is no secret that they can hide from thee:

4 With thy wisdom and with thine understanding thou hast gotten thee riches, and hast gotten gold and silver into thy treasures:

5 By the greatness of thy wisdom in thy trafficking thou hast multiplied thy riches, and thine heart is lifted up because of thy riches:

6 Therefore thus hath the Lord GOD said; Because thou hast set thine heart as the heart of God;

7 behold, therefore I will bring strangers upon thee, the strong ones of the Gentiles: and they shall draw their swords against the beauty of thy wisdom, and they shall defile thy brightness.

8 They shall bring thee down to the pit, and thou shalt die of the death of *them that are* slain in the midst of the seas.

9 Wilt thou yet say before him that slayeth thee, I *am* God? but thou *shalt be* a man, and not God, in the hand of him that slayeth thee.

10 Thou shalt die the death of the uncircumcised by the hand of strangers: for I have spoken, said the Lord GOD.

11 And the word of the LORD came unto me, saying,

12 Son of man, raise up lamentations upon the king of Tyre, and say unto him, Thus hath the Lord GOD said; Thou sealest up the sum *of perfection*, full of wisdom, and completed in beauty.

13 Thou hast been in Eden the garden of God; every precious stone *was* thy covering, the sardius, topaz, diamond, tuquoise, onyx, and beryl, the sapphire, ruby, and emerald, and gold: the works of thy tambourines and of thy pipes was prepared in thee in the day that thou wast created.

14 Thou, great cherubim, *wast* covered, and I placed thee; thou wast in the holy mountain of God; thou hast walked among stones of fire.

15 Thou *wast* perfect in all thy ways from the day that thou wast created, until iniquity was found in thee.

16 Because of the multitude of thy trafficking thou wast filled with iniquity, and thou didst sin: and *I* cast thee out of the mountain of God: and I cast thee unto evil from among the stones of fire, O cherubim *that wast* covered.

17 Thine heart lifted thee up because of thy beauty, thou hast corrupted thy wisdom by reason of thy brightness: I will cast thee to the earth; I will expose thee before the kings, that they may behold thee.

18 Thou hast defiled thy sanctuary by the multitude of thine iniquities, by the iniquity of thy trafficking; therefore I brought forth fire from the midst of thee, which hath consumed thee, and I brought thee to ashes upon the earth in the sight of all them that behold thee.

19 All they that knew thee from among the peoples shall marvel over thee: thou hast been *greatly* disturbed, and thou shalt not exist again forever.

20 And the word of the LORD came unto me, saying,

21 Son of man, set thy face against Zidon, and prophesy against her,

22 and say, Thus hath the Lord GOD said; Behold, I *am* against thee, O Zidon; and I will be glorified in the midst of thee: and they shall know that I *am* the LORD, when I shall have executed judgments in her, and shall be sanctified in her.

23 For I will send into her pestilence, and blood into her streets; and the dead shall fall in the midst of her, by the sword upon her on every side; and they shall know that I *am* the LORD.

24 And there shall no longer be a pricking brier unto the house of Israel, nor *any* thorn that causeth him pain, round about *them* of those that despise them; and they shall know that I *am* the Lord GOD.

25 Thus hath the Lord GOD said; When I shall have gathered the house of Israel from the peoples among whom they are scattered, and shall be sanctified in them in the eyes of the Gentiles, then shall they dwell in their land that I have given to my servant Jacob.

26 And they shall dwell safely therein, and shall build houses, and plant vineyards; yea, they shall dwell with confidence, when I have executed judgments in all those that spoil them round about them; and they shall know that I *am* the LORD their God.

Chapter 29

1 In the tenth year, in the tenth *month*, in the twelfth *day* of the month, the word of the LORD came unto me, saying,

2 Son of man, set thy face against Pharaoh king of Egypt, and prophesy against him, and against all Egypt:

3 Speak, and say, Thus hath the Lord GOD said; Behold, I *am* against thee, Pharaoh king of Egypt, the great dragon that lieth in the midst of his rivers, which hath said, My river *is* my own, and I have made *it* for myself.

4 But I will put hooks in thy jaws, and I will cause the fish of thy rivers to stick unto thy scales, and I will bring thee up out of the midst of thy rivers, and all the fish of thy rivers shall come out stuck onto thy scales.

5 And I will leave thee *thrown* into the wilderness, thee and all the fish of thy rivers: thou shalt fall upon the open fields; thou shalt not be brought together, nor gathered: I have given thee for food to the beasts of the field and to the fowls of the heaven.

6 And all the inhabitants of Egypt shall know that I *am* the LORD, because they have been a staff of reed to the house of Israel.

7 When they took hold of thee by thy hand, thou didst break, and rend all their shoulder: and when they leaned upon thee, thou brakest, and madest all their loins to come to nothing.

8 Therefore thus hath the Lord GOD said; Behold, I bring a sword upon thee, and will cut off man and beast out of thee.

9 And the land of Egypt shall be made desolate and waste; and they shall know that I *am* the LORD: because he hath said, The river *is* mine, and I have made *it*.

10 Behold, therefore I *am* against thee, and against thy rivers, and I will make the land of Egypt utterly waste *and* desolate, from the tower of Syene even unto the border of Ethiopia.

11 No foot of man shall pass through it, nor foot of beast shall pass through it, neither shall it be inhabited forty years.

12 And I will make the land of Egypt desolate in the midst of the countries *that are* desolate, and her cities among the cities *that are* laid waste shall be desolate forty years: and I will scatter the Egyptians among the nations, and will disperse them through the countries.

13 Yet thus hath the Lord GOD said; At the end of forty years will I gather the Egyptians from the peoples where they were scattered:

14 And I will turn to bring *again* the captives of Egypt, and will cause them to return *into* the land of Pathros, into the land of their habitation; and there they shall be a minor kingdom.

15 In comparison with the other kingdoms it shall be humble; neither shall it exalt itself any more above the nations: for I will diminish them, that they shall no more rule among the Gentiles.

16 And it shall be no more the confidence of the house of Israel, which bringeth *their* iniquity to remembrance, when they shall look after them: but they shall know that I *am* the Lord GOD.

17 And it came to pass in the seven and twentieth year, in the first *month*, in the first *day* of the month, the word of the LORD came unto me, saying,

18 Son of man, Nebuchadrezzar king of Babylon caused his army to serve a great service against Tyre: every head *was* made bald, and every shoulder *was* peeled: and yet neither he nor his army had wages of Tyre, for the service that he had served against her:

19 Therefore thus hath the Lord GOD said; Behold, I give the land of Egypt unto Nebuchadrezzar king of Babylon; and he shall take her multitude, and gather her spoil, and take her prey; and it shall be the wages for his army.

20 I have given him the land of Egypt *for* his labour wherewith he served against her, because they wrought for me, said the Lord GOD.

21 In that time will I cause the horn of the house of Israel to bud forth, and I will give thee the opening of the mouth in the midst of them; and they shall know that I *am* the LORD.

Chapter 30

1 And the word of the LORD came unto me, saying,

2 Son of man, prophesy and say, Thus hath the Lord GOD said; Howl ye, Woe of the day!

3 For the day *is* near, even the day of the LORD *is* near, a cloudy day; it shall be the time of the Gentiles.

4 And the sword shall come upon Egypt, and *great* fear shall be in Ethiopia, when the slain shall fall in Egypt, and they shall take away her multitude, and her foundations shall be destroyed.

5 Ethiopia, and Libya, and Lydia, and all the mingled people, and Chub, and the men of the land that is in league, shall fall with them by the sword.

6 Thus hath the LORD said; They also that uphold Egypt shall fall; and the pride of her power shall come down: from the tower of Syene shall they fall in it by the sword, said the Lord GOD.

7 And they shall be made desolate among the countries *that are* destroyed, and her cities shall be among the cities *that are* wasted.

8 And they shall know that I *am* the LORD, when I have set a fire in Egypt, and *when* all her helpers shall be broken.

9 In that time shall messengers go forth from me in ships to make the confident Ethiopians afraid, and great fear shall come upon them, as in the day of Egypt: for, behold, it cometh.

10 Thus hath the Lord GOD said; I will make the multitude of Egypt to cease by the hand of Nebuchadrezzar king of Babylon.

11 He and his people with him, the strongest of the Gentiles, shall be brought to destroy the land: and they shall draw their swords against Egypt, and fill the land with the slain.

12 And I will make the rivers dry, and deliver the land into the hand of the wicked: and I will destroy the land, and all that is therein, by the hand of strangers: I the LORD have spoken.

13 Thus hath the Lord GOD said; I will also destroy the images, and I will cause the idols of Menfis to cease; and there shall no longer be a prince of the land of Egypt: and I will put fear in the land of Egypt.

14 And I will make Pathros desolate, and will set fire in Tafnes, and will execute judgments in No [*Alexandria*].

15 And I will pour my fury upon Pelusio [*the people of the marsh*], the strength of Egypt; and I will cut off the multitude of No.

16 And I will set fire to Egypt: Pelusio shall have great pain, and No shall be rent asunder, and Menfis *shall have* distresses daily.

17 The young men of Heliopolis [*city of the sun*]

and of Pubasti [*the (cat) goddess Basht*] shall fall by the sword: and these *cities* shall go into captivity.

18 At Tehaphnehes also the day shall be darkened, when I shall break there the yokes of Egypt: and the pride of her strength shall cease in her: *as for her*, a cloud shall cover her, and the inhabitants of her villages shall go into captivity.

19 Thus will I execute judgments in Egypt: and they shall know that I *am* the LORD.

20 And it came to pass in the eleventh year, in the first *month*, in the seventh *day* of the month, *that* the word of the LORD came unto me, saying,

21 Son of man, I have broken the arm of Pharaoh king of Egypt; and, behold, it has not been bound up with medicine, to bind it that it might be made whole, to make it strong to hold the sword.

22 Therefore thus hath the Lord GOD said; Behold, I *am* against Pharaoh king of Egypt, and will break his arms, the strong, and that which was broken; and I will cause the sword to fall out of his hand.

23 And I will scatter the Egyptians among the Gentiles, and will disperse them through the countries.

24 And I will strengthen the arms of the king of Babylon, and put my sword in his hand: but I will break Pharaoh's arms, and he shall groan before him with the groanings of a *man* wounded unto death.

25 But I will strengthen the arms of the king of Babylon, and the arms of Pharaoh shall fall down; and they shall know that I *am* the LORD, when I place my sword into the hand of the king of Babylon, and he shall stretch it out upon the land of Egypt.

26 And I will scatter the Egyptians among the Gentiles, and disperse them among the countries; and they shall know that I *am* the LORD.

Chapter 31

1 And it came to pass in the eleventh year, in the third *month*, in the first *day* of the month, *that* the word of the LORD came unto me, saying,

2 Son of man, speak unto Pharaoh king of Egypt, and to his people; Whom art thou like in thy greatness?

3 Behold, the Assyrian *was* a cedar in Lebanon with fair branches, and with a shadowing shroud, and of an high stature; and his top was *highest* among the thick boughs.

4 The waters made him grow, the deep set him up on high; her rivers ran round his feet, and sent her flow to all the trees of the field.

5 Therefore his height was exalted above all the trees of the field, and his boughs were multiplied, and his branches became long because of his many waters, which he sent forth.

6 All the fowls of heaven made their nests in his boughs, and under his branches did all the beasts of the field bring forth their young, and under his shadow dwelt many Gentiles.

7 He made himself beautiful in his greatness, with the extension of his branches: for his root was by many waters.

8 The cedars in the garden of God did not cover him: the fir trees were not like his boughs, and the chestnut trees were not like his branches; nor any tree in the garden of God was like unto him in his beauty.

9 I have made him beautiful with the multitude of his branches: and all the trees of Eden, that *were* in the garden of God, envied him.

10 Therefore thus hath the Lord GOD said; Because thou hast lifted up thyself in height, and he hath shot up his top among the thick boughs, and his heart is lifted up in his height;

11 I have therefore delivered him into the hand of the strong one of the Gentiles; he shall surely deal with him: I have cut him down for his wickedness.

12 And strangers, the strong ones of the Gentiles, shall cut him down, and shall leave him: his branches shall fall upon the mountains and by all the valleys, and his boughs shall be broken by all the rivers of the land; and all the peoples of the earth shall go forth from his shadow, and shall leave him.

13 Upon his ruin shall all the fowls of the heaven remain, and all the beasts of the field shall be upon his branches:

14 To the end that none of all the trees by the waters exalt themselves for their height, neither shoot up their top among the thick boughs, neither in their branches shall all that drink waters stand up in their height: for they shall all be delivered unto death, to the lower parts of the earth, in the midst of the children of men, with them that go down to the grave.

15 Thus said the Lord GOD; In the day when he went down to hell I caused a mourning: I covered the deep for him, and I restrained the floods thereof, and the many waters were stayed: and I caused Lebanon to mourn for him, and all the trees of the field fainted.

16 I made the Gentiles to shake at the sound of his fall, when I cast him down to hell with them that descend into the grave: and all the choice trees of Eden, and the best of Lebanon, all that drink waters, shall be comforted in the lower parts of the earth.

17 They also went down into hell with him, with those *that were* slain with the sword; and *they that were* his arm, *that* dwelt under his shadow in the midst of the Gentiles.

18 To whom art thou thus like in glory and in greatness among the trees of Eden? Yet thou shalt thou be cut down with the trees of Eden unto the lower parts of the earth: thou shalt lie in the midst of the uncircumcised with *them that be* slain by the sword. This *is* Pharaoh and all his people, said the Lord GOD.

Chapter 32

1 And it came to pass in the twelfth year, in the twelfth month, in the first *day* of the month, *that* the word of the LORD came unto me, saying,

2 Son of man, raise up lamentations upon Pharaoh king of Egypt, and say unto him, Thou art like a young lion of the nations, and thou *art* as the whale in the seas, that driest up thy rivers, and troubledst the waters with thy feet, and foulest their streams.

3 Thus hath the Lord GOD said; I will therefore spread out my net over thee with a company of many peoples; and they shall bring thee up in my net.

4 Then will I leave thee upon the land, I will cast thee forth upon the open field, and will cause all the fowls of the heaven to remain upon thee, and I will fill the beasts of the whole earth with thee.

5 And I will lay thy flesh upon the mountains, and fill the valleys with thy height.

6 I will also water with thy blood the land wherein thou swimmest, *even* to the mountains; and the rivers shall be full of thee.

7 And when thou art dead, I will cover the heavens, and

make the stars thereof dark; I will cover the sun with a cloud, and the moon shall not give her light.

8 All the bright lights of heaven will I make dark because of thee, and set darkness upon thy land, said the Lord GOD.

9 I will also make the hearts of many peoples sad, when I shall bring thy destruction upon the Gentiles, into the countries which thou hast not known.

10 Yea, I will make many peoples amazed at thee, and their kings shall be horribly afraid because of thee, when I shall brandish my sword before them; and they shall tremble at *every* moment, every man for his own life, in the day of thy fall.

11 For thus hath the Lord GOD said; The sword of the king of Babylon shall come upon thee.

12 By the swords of the mighty will I cause thy people to fall: they *shall* all be the strong of the Gentiles: and they shall destroy the pride of Egypt, and all the multitude thereof shall be undone.

13 I will destroy also all the beasts thereof from upon the many waters; neither shall the foot of man, nor the hoofs of beasts foul them any more.

14 Then will I make their waters deepen, and cause their channels to run like oil, said the Lord GOD.

15 When I shall make the land of Egypt desolate, and the fullness of the land shall be taken away, when I shall smite all them that dwell therein, then shall they know that I *am* the LORD.

16 This *is* the lamentation, and they shall sing it: the daughters of the Gentiles shall sing it: they shall lament over Egypt, and over all her multitude, said the Lord GOD.

17 It came to pass also in the twelfth year, in the fifteenth *day* of the month, *that* the word of the LORD came unto me, saying,

18 Son of man, lament over the multitude of Egypt, and cast him down, and the habitations of the strong Gentiles, into the lower parts of the earth, with them that go down into the grave.

19 Because thou art so beautiful, go down, and be thou laid with the uncircumcised.

20 They shall fall in the midst of *them that are* slain by the sword: he is delivered to the sword: bring him and all his peoples.

21 The strong among the mighty shall speak to him out of the midst of hell with them that help him: they are gone down, they lie uncircumcised, slain by the sword.

22 Asshur *is* there and all his company: his graves *are* about him: all of them slain, fallen by the sword:

23 Whose graves are set in the sides of the pit, and his company is round about his grave: all of them slain, fallen by the sword, which caused terror in the land of the living.

24 There *is* Elam and all his multitude round about his grave, all of them slain, fallen by the sword, which are gone down uncircumcised into the lowest *parts* of the earth, because they spread their terror in the land of the living; yet have they borne their shame with them that go down to the grave.

25 They have set him a bed in the midst of the slain with all his multitude: his graves *are* round about him: all of them uncircumcised, slain by the sword: because they spread their terror in the land of the liv-

ing, yet have they borne their shame with them that go down to the pit: *he* was put in the midst of the dead.

26 There *is* Meshech, Tubal, and all his multitude: his graves *are* round about him: all of them uncircumcised, slain by the sword, because they had caused their terror in the land of the living.

27 And they shall not lie with the mighty *that are* fallen of the uncircumcised, which are gone down to hell with their weapons of war: and they have laid their swords under their heads, but their sins shall be upon their bones, because *they were* the terror of the mighty in the land of the living.

28 Yea, thou shalt be broken in the midst of the uncircumcised, and shalt lie with *them that are* slain with the sword.

29 There *is* Edom, his kings, and all his princes, which with their might are laid with *them that were* slain by the sword: they shall lie with the uncircumcised, and with them that go down to the pit.

30 There *be* the princes of the north, all of them, and all the Zidonians, which are gone down with the slain with their terror, ashamed of their might; and they lie uncircumcised with *them that be* slain by the sword, and bear their shame with them that go down to the pit.

31 Pharaoh shall see them, and shall be comforted over all his multitude, *even* Pharaoh and all his army slain by the sword, said the Lord GOD.

32 Because I have spread my terror in the land of the living: he shall also lay in the midst of the uncircumcised with *them that are* slain with the sword, *even* Pharaoh and all his multitude, said the Lord GOD.

Chapter 33

1 And the word of the LORD came unto me, saying,

2 Son of man, speak to the sons of thy people, and say unto them, When I bring *a* sword upon the land, and the people of the land take a man from *within* their borders, and set him up as a watchman:

3 and he should see the sword coming upon the land, *if* he should blow the shophar, and warn the people;

4 then whosoever heareth the sound of the shophar, and taketh not warning; and the coming of the sword should take him away, his blood shall be upon his own head.

5 He heard the sound of the shophar, and took not warning; his blood shall be upon him. But he that taketh warning shall deliver his soul.

6 But if the watchman should see the sword coming, and not blow the shophar, and the people be not warned; if the sword come, and take *any* person from among them, he is taken away because of his iniquity; but his blood will I require at the watchman's hand.

7 So thou, O son of man, I have set thee a watchman unto the house of Israel; therefore thou shalt hear the word at my mouth, and warn them from me.

8 When I say unto the wicked, O wicked *man*, thou shalt surely die; if thou dost not speak to warn the wicked from his way, that wicked *man* shall die for his sin; but his blood will I require at thine hand.

9 Nevertheless, if thou warn the wicked of his way to turn from it; if he do not turn from his way, he shall die for his iniquity; but thou hast delivered thy soul.

10 Therefore, O thou son of man, speak unto the house

of Israel; Thus ye speak, saying, Our transgressions and our sins *are* upon us, and we are consumed because of them. How should we then live?

11 Say unto them, *As* I live, said the Lord GOD, I do not desire the death of the wicked; but that the wicked turn from his way, and that he live: turn ye, turn ye from your evil ways; for why will ye die, O house of Israel?

12 And thou, son of man, say unto the sons of thy people, The righteousness of the righteous shall not deliver him the day that he rebels; and the wickedness of the wicked shall not impede him in the day that he turneth from his wickedness; and the righteous shall not be able to live by his righteousness *in* the day that he sinneth.

13 When I am saying to the righteous, Thou shalt shall surely live; and he trusting in his own righteousness committeth iniquity, all his righteousnesses shall not be remembered; but for his iniquity that he hath committed, he shall die for it.

14 And, when I am saying unto the wicked, Thou shalt surely die; if he turn from his sin, and do judgment and righteousness;

15 *if* the wicked restore the pledge, return that which he had robbed, walk in the statutes of life, without committing iniquity; he shall surely live, he shall not die.

16 None of his sins that he hath committed shall be mentioned unto him. Hath he done that which is lawful and right? He shall surely live.

17 Then the sons of thy people shall say, The way of the Lord is not straight: *but* their way is the one that is not straight.

18 When the righteous turneth from his righteousness, and committeth iniquity, he shall die thereby.

19 And when the wicked turneth from his wickedness, and doeth judgment and righteousness, he shall live thereby.

20 Yet ye say, The way of the Lord is not straight. O ye house of Israel, I will judge you every one after his ways.

21 And it came to pass in the twelfth year of our captivity, in the tenth *month*, in the fifth *day* of the month, *that* one that had escaped out of Jerusalem came unto me, saying, The city is smitten.

22 Now the hand of the LORD was upon me in the evening, before he that was escaped came; and had opened my mouth, until he came to me in the morning; and opened my mouth, and I was never dumb again.

23 And the word of the LORD came unto me, saying,

24 Son of man, they that inhabit these wastes in the land of Israel speak, saying, Abraham was one, and he possessed the land: but we *are* many; the land is given us for a possession.

25 Therefore say unto them, Thus hath the Lord GOD said; Ye eat with the blood, and lift up your eyes toward your idols, and shed blood: and shall ye possess this land?

26 Ye stand upon your sword, ye work abomination, and ye defile every one his neighbour's wife: and shall ye possess the land?

27 Thou shalt speak unto them like this, Thus hath the Lord GOD said; *As* I live, surely they that *are* in those wastes shall fall by the sword, and him that *is* in the open field will I give to the beasts to be devoured, and they that *be* in the forts

and in the caves shall die of the pestilence.

28 For I will make the land into desert and solitude, and the pride of her strength shall cease; and the mountains of Israel shall be desolate, that none shall pass through.

29 Then shall they know that I *am* the LORD, when I have made the land into solitude and desert because of all their abominations which they have committed.

30 And thou, son of man, the sons of thy people still are talking against thee by the walls and in the doors of the houses, and speak one to another, every one to his brother, saying, Come, I pray you, and hear what is the word that cometh forth from the LORD.

31 And they shall come unto thee as the people cometh, and they shall be before thee, my people, and they shall hear thy words, but they shall not do them: for with their mouth they flatter, *but* their heart goeth after their covetousness.

32 And, behold, thou *art* unto them as a singer of love *songs,* one that hath a good voice, and can sing well: and they shall hear thy words, but they will not do them.

33 But when this cometh to pass, (behold, it cometh,) then shall they know that a prophet hath been among them.

Chapter 34

1 And the word of the LORD came unto me, saying,

2 Son of man, prophesy against the shepherds of Israel, prophesy, and say unto the pastors, Thus hath the Lord GOD said; Woe *be* to the shepherds of Israel that do feed themselves! should not the shepherds feed the flocks?

3 Ye eat the milk, and ye clothe you with the wool, ye kill them that are fat: *but* ye feed not the flock.

4 Ye have not strengthened the weak, neither have ye healed that which was sick, neither have ye bound up *that which was* broken, neither have ye brought again that which was driven away, neither have ye sought that which was lost; but with force and with cruelty have ye ruled them;

5 and they are dispersed because *there is* no shepherd: and they became food to all the beasts of the field, and they were scattered.

6 My sheep *were* lost *and* wandered through all the mountains, and upon every high hill: yea, my flock was dispersed upon all the face of the earth, and there was no one to search for them or to require *anything* of them.

7 Therefore, ye shepherds, hear the word of the LORD;

8 *As* I live, said the Lord GOD, surely because my flock became a prey, and my flock became food to every beast of the field, without a pastor, neither did my shepherds search for my flock, but the shepherds fed themselves, and fed not my flock;

9 therefore, O ye pastors, hear the word of the LORD;

10 Thus hath the Lord GOD said; Behold, I *am* against the shepherds; and I will require my flock at their hand, and cause them to cease from feeding the flock; neither shall the shepherds feed themselves any more; for I will deliver my flock from their mouth, and they shall no longer be food for them.

11 For thus hath the Lord GOD said; Behold, I, *even* I, will both search and recognise my sheep.

12 As the shepherd recognizeth his flock in the day that he is among his sheep *that are* scattered; so will I recognise my sheep, and will deliver them out of all places where they have been scattered in the cloudy and dark day.

13 And I will bring them out from the peoples, and gather them from the countries, and will bring them to their own land, and feed them upon the mountains of Israel by the rivers, and in all the habitations of the country.

14 I will feed them in good pastures, and upon the high mountains of Israel shall their fold be: there shall they sleep in a good fold, and in fat pastures shall they be fed upon the mountains of Israel.

15 I will feed my flock, and I will cause them to have a fold, saith the Lord GOD.

16 I will seek that which was lost, and bring again that which was driven away, and will bind up *that which was* broken, and will strengthen that which was sick: but I will destroy the fat and the strong; I will feed them in judgment.

17 And *as for* you, O my flock, thus hath the Lord GOD said; Behold, I judge between sheep and sheep, between the rams and the he goats.

18 *Seemeth it* a small thing unto you that ye eat *of* the good pastures, but ye *also* tread down with your feet the residue of your pastures? and that *in* drinking of the deep waters, ye must also foul the residue with your feet?

19 And my sheep eat that which ye have trodden with your feet; and they drink that which ye have fouled with your feet.

20 Therefore thus hath the Lord GOD said unto them; Behold, I, *even* I, will judge between the fat sheep and between the lean sheep.

21 because ye have thrust with side and with shoulder, and pushed all the weak with your horns, until ye have scattered them outside.

22 I will save my flock, and they shall no more be a prey; and I will judge between sheep and sheep.

23 And I will raise up one shepherd over them, and he shall feed them, *even* my servant David; he shall feed them, and he shall be their shepherd.

24 And I the LORD will be their God, and my servant David a prince among them; I the LORD have spoken *it*.

25 And I will establish with them a covenant of peace, and will cause the evil beasts to cease out of the land: and they shall dwell safely in the wilderness, and sleep in the woods.

26 And I will give unto them, and to the places round about my hill, blessing; and I will cause the rain to come down in his season; they shall be rains of blessing.

27 And the tree of the field shall yield her fruit, and the earth shall yield her fruit, and they shall be safe in their land, and shall know that I *am* the LORD, when I have broken the bands of their yoke, and delivered them out of the hand of those that served themselves of them.

28 And they shall no longer be a prey to the Gentiles, neither shall the beast of the land devour them; but they shall dwell safely, and none shall make *them* afraid.

29 And I will raise up for them a Plant by name, and they shall no longer be consumed with hunger in the land, neither bear the shame of the Gentiles any more.

30 Thus shall they know that I the LORD their God *am* with them, and *that* they, *even* the house of Israel, *are* my people, said the Lord GOD.

31 And ye my flock, the flock of my pasture, *are* men, *and* I *am* your God, said the Lord GOD.

Chapter 35

1 Moreover the word of the LORD came unto me, saying,

2 Son of man, set thy face against mount Seir, and prophesy against him,

3 And say unto him, Thus saith the Lord GOD; Behold, O mount Seir, I *am* against thee, and I will stretch out my hand against thee, and I will make thee waste and solitary.

4 I will lay thy cities waste, and thou shalt be desolate, and thou shalt know that I *am* the LORD.

5 Because thou hast had perpetual enmities, and hast scattered the sons of Israel to the force of the sword in the time of their calamity, in the extremely evil time:

6 Therefore, *as* I live, said the Lord GOD, I will prepare thee unto blood, and blood shall pursue thee: and if thou hatest not blood, blood shall pursue thee.

7 And I will make mount Seir waste and solitary, and cut off from him he that passeth out and he that returneth.

8 And I will fill his mountains with his dead: and in

thy hills, and in thy valleys, and in all thy rivers, shall they fall that are slain with the sword.

9 I will make thee perpetual desolations, and thy cities shall never be restored: and ye shall know that I *am* the LORD.

10 Because thou hast said, These two nations and these two countries shall be mine, and we will possess them; whereas the LORD was there:

11 Therefore, *as* I live, said the Lord GOD, I will even do according to thine anger, and according to thine envy which thou hast used out of thy enmity against them; and I shall be known in them, when I judge thee.

12 A nd thou shalt know that I, the LORD, have heard all thy injuries which thou hast spoken against the mountains of Israel, saying, They are laid desolate, they are given us to devour.

13 Thus with your mouth ye have boasted against me, and have multiplied your words against me: I have heard *them*.

14 Thus hath the Lord GOD said; Thus shall the whole earth rejoice, *when* I shall make thee desolate.

15 As thou didst rejoice upon the inheritance of the house of Israel, because it was desolate, so will I do unto thee: thou shalt be desolate, O mount Seir, and all Idumea, *even* all of it: and they shall know that I *am* the LORD.

Chapter 36

1 Also, thou son of man, prophesy upon the mountains of Israel, and say, Ye mountains of Israel, hear the word of the LORD:

2 Thus hath the Lord GOD said; Because the enemy hath said regarding you, Aha, even the ancient high places are ours in possession:

3 Therefore prophesy and say, Thus hath the Lord GOD said; Because they have made *you* desolate, and swallowed you up on every side, that ye might be a possession unto the residue of the Gentiles, and ye are taken up in the lips of talkers, and *are* an infamy of the people:

4 Therefore, ye mountains of Israel, hear the word of the Lord GOD; Thus hath the Lord GOD said to the mountains, and to the hills, to the rivers, and to the valleys, to the ruins and the desolate wastes, and to the cities that are forsaken, which became a prey and derision to the residue of the Gentiles that *are* round about;

5 therefore thus hath the Lord GOD said; Surely in the fire of my jealousy have I spoken against the other Gentiles, and against all Idumea, which have disputed my land into their possession with the joy of all *their* heart, with despiteful desires, to cast it out for a prey.

6 Prophesy therefore upon the land of Israel, and say unto the mountains, and to the hills, to the rivers, and to the valleys, Thus hath the Lord GOD said; Behold, I have spoken in my jealousy and in my fury, because ye have borne the shame of the Gentiles:

7 Therefore thus hath the Lord GOD said; I have lifted up my hand, Surely the Gentiles that *are* about you, they shall bear their shame.

8 But ye, O mountains of Israel, ye shall shoot forth your branches, and yield your fruit to my people of Israel; for they are at hand to come.

9 For, behold, I *am* for you, and I will turn unto you, and ye shall be tilled and sown:

10 And I will multiply men upon you, all the house of Israel, *even* all of it: and the cities shall be inhabited, and the ruins shall be builded:

11 And I will multiply upon you man and beast; and they shall multiply and grow: and I will cause thee to dwell as was thy desire of old, and will do better *unto you* than at your beginnings: and ye shall know that I *am* the LORD.

12 Yea, I will cause men to walk upon you, *even* my people Israel; and they shall possess thee, and thou shalt be their inheritance, and thou shalt no more henceforth bereave them *of sons*.

13 Thus hath the Lord GOD said; Because they say of you, Thou *land that* devourest up men, and hast bereaved thy nations of sons;

14 therefore thou shalt devour men no more, neither bereave thy nations of sons any more, saith the Lord GOD.

15 Neither will I cause *men* to hear in thee the shame of the Gentiles any more, neither shalt thou bear the reproach of the peoples any more, neither shalt thou cause the sons of thy inhabitants to die any more, saith the Lord GOD.

16 And the word of the LORD came unto me, saying,

17 Son of man, the house of Israel which dwelleth in their land, have defiled it with their own ways and with their works: their way was before me as the uncleanness of a menstruous woman.

18 And I poured my fury upon them for the blood that they had shed upon the land, and for their idols *wherewith* they had polluted it:

19 And I scattered them among the Gentiles, and they were dispersed through the countries: according to their ways and according to their doings I judged them.

20 And when they entered unto the Gentiles, where they went, they profaned my holy name, when they said to them, These *are* the people of the LORD, and are gone forth out of his land.

21 And it has pained me to see my holy name profaned by the house of Israel among the Gentiles where they went.

22 Therefore say unto the house of Israel, Thus hath the Lord GOD said; I do not *this* for your sakes, O house of Israel, but for my holy name's sake, which ye have profaned among the Gentiles, where ye went.

23 And I will sanctify my great name, which was profaned among the Gentiles, which ye have profaned in the midst of them; and the Gentiles shall know that I *am* the LORD, said the Lord GOD, when I shall be sanctified in you before their eyes.

24 And I will take you from among the Gentiles, and gather you out of all countries, and will bring you into your own land.

25 And I will sprinkle clean water upon you, and ye shall be cleansed from all your filthiness, and from all your idols, will I cleanse you.

26 And I will give you a new heart, and a new spirit will I put within you: and I will take away the stony heart out of your flesh, and I will give you an heart of flesh.

27 And I will put my Spirit within you, and cause you to walk in my commandments, and ye shall keep my rights, and do *them*.

28 And ye shall dwell in the land that I gave to your fathers; and ye shall be my people, and I will be your God.

29 I will also keep you from all your uncleanness: and I will call to the wheat, and will multiply it, and lay no famine upon you.

30 I will multiply likewise the fruit of the trees, and the fruit of the fields, that ye shall receive no more reproach of famine among the Gentiles.

31 Then shall ye remember your own evil ways, and your doings that *were* not good, and shall loathe yourselves in your own sight for your iniquities and for your abominations.

32 Not for your sakes do I *this*, said the Lord GOD, be it known unto you: be ashamed and confounded for your iniquities, O house of Israel.

33 Thus said the Lord GOD; In the day that I shall have cleansed you from all your iniquities I will also cause *you* to dwell in the cities, and the wastes shall be builded.

34 And the desolate land shall be tilled, whereas it lay desolate in the sight of all that passed by;

35 who said, This desolate land used to be like the garden of Eden; and these waste and desolate and ruined cities used to be fortified.

36 And the Gentiles that are left round about you shall know that I the LORD built the ruined *places, and* planted that that was desolate: I the LORD have spoken *it*, and I will do *it*.

37 Thus hath the Lord GOD said; I will yet be enquired of by the house of Israel, to do *it* for them; I will multiply men like flocks.

38 As the holy sheep, as the sheep of Jerusalem in her solemn feasts; so shall the waste cities be filled with flocks of men: and they shall know that I *am* the LORD.

Chapter 37

1 And the hand of the LORD was upon me, and took me out in the Spirit of the LORD, and set me down in the midst of a field which *was* full of bones,

2 and caused me to pass by them round about: and, behold, *there were* very many upon the face of the field; and *they were* very dry.

3 And he said unto me, Son of man, can these bones live? And I answered, O Lord GOD, thou knowest.

4 Then he said unto me, Prophesy upon these bones, and say unto them, O ye dry bones, hear the word of the LORD.

5 Thus hath the Lord GOD said unto these bones; Behold, I will cause spirit to enter into you, and ye shall live:

6 And I will lay nerves upon you, and will bring up flesh upon you, and cover you with skin, and put spirit in you, and ye shall live; and ye shall know that I *am* the LORD.

7 So I prophesied as I was commanded: and as I prophesied, there was a thunder, and behold a shaking, and the bones came together, bone to his bone.

8 And I beheld, and behold nerves upon them and the flesh came up upon them, and the skin covered them above: but *there was* no spirit in them.

9 Then said he unto me, Prophesy unto the spirit, prophesy, son of man, and say to the spirit, Thus hath the Lord GOD said; Come from the four winds, O spirit, and breathe upon these slain, and they shall live.

10 And I prophesied as he commanded me, and the spirit entered into them, and they lived, and stood up upon their feet, an exceeding great army.

11 Then he said unto me, Son of man, all these bones are the house of Israel: be-

hold, they say, Our bones have dried, and our hope is lost, and in ourselves we are totally cut off.

12 Therefore prophesy and say unto them, Thus hath the Lord GOD said; Behold, O my people, I open your graves, and will cause you to come up out of your graves, and bring you into the land of Israel.

13 And ye shall know that I *am* the LORD, when I have opened your graves, O my people, and brought you up out of your graves,

14 and shall put my Spirit in you, and ye shall live, and I shall cause you to rest upon your *own* land: then shall ye know that I the LORD have spoken *it*, and performed *it*, said the LORD.

15 And the word of the LORD came again unto me, saying,

16 Thou, son of man, take thee one stick, and write upon it, To Judah, and to the sons of Israel his companions: then take another stick, and write upon it, To Joseph, the stick of Ephraim, and to all the house of Israel his companions:

17 And join them one to another, that they might become one; and they shall be one in thy hand.

18 And when the sons of thy people shall speak unto thee, saying, Wilt thou not show us what thou *meanest* by these?

19 Say unto them, Thus hath the Lord GOD said; Behold, I take the stick of Joseph, which *is* in the hand of Ephraim, and the tribes of Israel his fellows, and will put them with him, *even* with the stick of Judah, and make them one stick, and they shall be one in my hand.

20 And the sticks whereon thou writest shall be in thine hand before their eyes.

21 And thou shalt say unto them, Thus hath the Lord GOD said; Behold, I take the sons of Israel from among the Gentiles, where they be gone, and will gather them on every side, and bring them into their *own* land:

22 And I will make them one nation in the land in the mountains of Israel; and one king shall be king to them all: and they shall no longer be two nations, neither shall they be divided into two kingdoms any more at all:

23 Neither shall they defile themselves any more with their idols, nor with their abominations, nor with all their rebellions: but I will save them out of all their dwellingplaces, wherein they have sinned, and will cleanse them: so shall they be my people, and I will be their God.

24 And David my servant *shall be* king over them; and they all shall have one shepherd: they shall also walk within my rights, and keep my statutes, and do them.

25 And they shall dwell in the land that I have given unto Jacob my servant, wherein your fathers have dwelt; and they shall dwell therein, *even* they, and their children, and their children's children for ever: and my servant David *shall be* their prince for ever.

26 Moreover I will make a covenant of peace with them; it shall be an everlasting covenant with them: and I will plant them, and multiply them, and will set my sanctuary in the midst of them for evermore.

27 And my tabernacle shall be in them: yea, I will be their God, and they shall be my people.

28 And the Gentiles shall know that I the LORD do sanctify Israel, when my sanctuary shall be in the midst of them for evermore.

Chapter 38

1 And the word of the LORD came unto me, saying,

2 son of man, set thy face against Gog in *the* land of Magog, prince of the capital of Meshech and Tubal, and prophesy over him,

3 and say, Thus hath the Lord GOD said; Behold, I *come* unto thee, O Gog, prince of the capital of Meshech and Tubal:

4 And I will break thee, and put hooks into thy jaws, and I will bring thee forth, and all thine army, horses and horsemen, all of them clothed with all sorts *of armour, even* a great company *with* bucklers and shields, all of them handling swords:

5 Persia, Ethiopia, and Libya with them; all of them with shield and helmet:

6 Gomer, and all his companies; the house of Togarmah that dwelleth to the sides of the north, and all his companies: *and* many peoples with thee.

7 Be thou prepared, and prepare for thyself, thou, and all thy company that are assembled unto thee, and be thou a guard unto them.

8 After many days thou shalt be visited: at the end of years thou shalt come to the land broken by the sword, gathered out of many peoples, to the mountains of Israel, which have been always waste: but she is brought forth out of the nations, and they shall dwell safely all of them.

9 Thou shalt ascend and come like a storm, thou shalt be like a cloud to cover the land, thou, and all thy companies, and many peoples with thee.

10 Thus hath the Lord GOD said; It shall also come to pass in that day, that words shall rise up in thy heart, and thou shalt conceive an evil thought:

11 And thou shalt say, I will go up against the land of unwalled villages; I will go *against* those that are at rest, that dwell safely, all of them dwelling without walls, and having neither bars nor gates,

12 to take a spoil, and to take a prey; to turn thine hand upon the desolate places *that are now* inhabited, and upon the people *that are* gathered out of the Gentiles, which have gotten cattle and goods, that dwell in the navel of the land.

13 Sheba, and Dedan, and the merchants of Tarshish, with all the young lions thereof, shall say unto thee,

Art thou come to take a spoil? hast thou gathered thy company to take a prey? to carry away silver and gold, to take away cattle and goods, to take a great spoil?

14 Therefore, son of man, prophesy and say unto Gog, Thus hath the Lord GOD said; In that time when my people of Israel shall dwell securely, shalt thou not know *it*?

15 And thou shalt come from thy place out of the north parts, thou, and many peoples with thee, all of them riding upon horses, a great company, and a mighty army:

16 And thou shalt come up against my people of Israel, as a cloud to cover the land; it shall be at the end of the days, and *I* will bring thee upon my land, that the Gentiles may know me, when I shall be sanctified in thee, O Gog, before their eyes.

17 Thus hath the Lord GOD said; *Art* thou not he of whom I have spoken in days past by my servants the prophets of Israel, which prophesied in those times that I would have to bring thee upon them?

18 And it shall come to pass in that time, when Gog shall come against the land of Israel, said the Lord GOD, *that* my fury shall rise up in my anger.

19 For in my jealousy *and* in the fire of my wrath have I spoken, Surely in that day there shall be a great shaking upon the land of Israel;

20 so that the fishes of the sea, and the fowls of the heaven, and the beasts of the field, and every serpent that walketh by dragging *itself* upon the earth, and all the men that *are* upon the face of the earth, shall shake before my presence, and the mountains shall be ruined, and the stairs shall fall, and every wall shall fall to the ground.

21 And I will call for a sword against him through out all my mountains, said the Lord GOD: every man's sword shall be against his brother.

22 And I will litigate against him with pestilence and with blood; and I will rain upon him, and upon his companies, and upon the many peoples that *are* with him, an overflowing rain and great hailstones, fire and brimstone.

23 And I will be magnified and sanctified, and I will be known in the eyes of many

Gentiles, and they shall know that I *am* the LORD.

Chapter 39

1 Therefore, thou son of man, prophesy against Gog, and say, Thus hath the Lord GOD said; Behold, I *am* against thee, O Gog, prince of the capital of Meshech and Tubal:

2 And I will break thee, and leave but the sixth part of thee, and will cause thee to come up from the north parts, and will bring thee upon the mountains of Israel:

3 And I will smite thy bow out of thy left hand, and will cause thine arrows to fall out of thy right hand.

4 Thou shalt fall upon the mountains of Israel, thou, and all thy companies, and the peoples that *go* with thee: I have given thee unto every bird and unto everything that flies, and *to* the beasts of the field as food.

5 Thou shalt fall upon the open field: for I have spoken *it*, said the Lord GOD.

6 And I will send a fire on Magog, and among them that dwell securely in the isles: and they shall know that I *am* the LORD.

7 So will I make my holy name known in the midst of my people Israel; and I will not *let them* pollute my holy name any more: and the Gentiles shall know that I *am* the LORD, Holy in Israel.

8 Behold, it is come, and it is over, said the Lord GOD; this *is* the day whereof I have spoken.

9 And they that dwell in the cities of Israel shall go forth, and shall set on fire and burn weapons, and shields and bucklers, bows and arrows, and handstaves, and spears, and they shall burn them in *the* fire for seven years:

10 So that they shall take no wood out of the field, neither cut down *any* out of the forests; for they shall burn the weapons in the fire: and they shall spoil those that spoiled them, and rob those that robbed them, said the Lord GOD.

11 And it shall come to pass in that day, *that* I will give unto Gog a place there of graves in Israel, the valley of the passengers on the east of the sea: and it shall stop the *noses* of the passengers: and there shall they bury Gog and all his multitude: and they shall call *it* The valley of Hamongog.

12 And seven months shall the house of Israel be burying of them, that they may cleanse the land.

13 Yea, all the people of the land shall bury *them*; and it shall be to them a renown the day that I shall be glorified, said the Lord GOD.

14 And they shall take men out of continual employment, who shall go through the land with the passengers to bury those that remain upon the face of the earth, to cleanse it: after the end of seven months shall they search.

15 And the passengers *that* pass through the land, when *any* seeth a man's bone, then shall he set up a sign by it, until the buriers have buried it in the valley of Hamongog.

16 And also the name of the city *shall be* Hamonah. Thus shall they cleanse the land.

17 And, thou son of man, thus hath the Lord GOD said; Speak unto every bird, unto everything that flies, and to every beast of the field, Assemble yourselves, and come; gather yourselves on every side to my sacrifice that I do sacrifice for you, *even* a great sacrifice upon the mountains of Israel, that ye may eat flesh, and drink blood.

18 Ye shall eat the flesh of the mighty, and drink the blood of the princes of the earth, of rams, of lambs, and of he goats, of oxen, and of bulls, all of them fattened in Bashan.

19 And ye shall eat fat until ye be full, and drink blood until ye be drunken, of my sacrifice which I have sacrificed for you.

20 Thus ye shall be filled at my table with horses and strong chariots, and with all *the* men of war, said the Lord GOD.

21 And I will set my glory among the Gentiles, and all the Gentiles shall see my judgment that I have executed, and my hand that I have laid upon them.

22 So the house of Israel shall know that I *am* the LORD their God from that day and forward.

23 And the Gentiles shall know that the house of Israel went into captivity for their iniquity: because they rebelled against me, and I hid my face from them, and gave them into the hand of their enemies: so they all fell by the sword.

24 According to their uncleanness and according to their rebellions have I done unto them, and hid my face from them.

25 Therefore thus hath the Lord GOD said; Now will I

turn the captivity of Jacob, and have mercy upon the whole house of Israel, and will be jealous for my holy name.

26 After they shall feel their shame, and all their rebellion whereby they have rebelled against me, when they dwelt safely in their land, and none made *them* afraid.

27 When I bring them again from the peoples, and gather them out of their enemies' lands, and am sanctified in them in the sight of many Gentiles.

28 And they shall know that I *am* the LORD their God, when after causing them to be led into captivity among the Gentiles: I shall gather them unto their own land, without leaving any of them there any longer.

29 Neither will I hide my face any longer from them: for I will pour out my Spirit upon the house of Israel, said the Lord GOD.

Chapter 40

1 In the five and twentieth year of our captivity, in the beginning of the year, in the tenth *day* of the month, in the fourteenth year after that the city was smitten, in the selfsame day the hand of the LORD was upon me, and brought me there.

2 In the visions of God he brought me into the land of Israel, and set me upon a very high mountain, upon which *was* as the frame of a city to the south.

3 And he brought me there, and, behold, *there was* a man, whose appearance *was* like the appearance of brass, with a line of flax in his hand, and a measuring reed; and he stood in the gate.

4 And the man said unto me, Son of man, behold with thine eyes, and hear with thine ears, and set thine heart upon all that I show thee; for to the intent that I might show *them* unto thee *art* thou brought here: declare all that thou seest to the house of Israel.

5 And behold a wall on the outside of the house, and the measuring reed which that man had in his hand, was six cubits *long,* of a cubit and a hand breadth: so he measured the breadth of the building, one reed; and the height, one reed.

6 Then came he unto the gate which looketh toward the east, and went up the stairs thereof, and measured the post of the gate, *which was* one reed broad; and the other post *of the gate, which was* one reed broad.

7 And *every* chamber *was* one reed long, and one reed broad; and between the chambers *were* five cubits; and *every* post of the gate by the porch of the gate within *was* one reed.

8 He measured also the porch of the gate within, one reed.

9 Then measured he the entrance of the portal, eight cubits; and the posts thereof, two cubits; and the entrance of the portal within.

10 And the gate eastward *had* three chambers on each side, they three *were* of one measure: and the portals were also of one measure on each side.

11 And he measured the breadth of the entry of the gate, ten cubits; *and* the length of the portal, thirteen cubits.

12 The space also before the chambers *was* one cubit *on this side*, and the space *was* one cubit on that side: and the chambers *were* six cubits on this side, and six cubits on that side.

13 He measured then the gate from the roof of *one* chamber to the roof of an-other: the breadth *was* five and twenty cubits, door against door.

14 He also made the portals of sixty cubits, each portal of the court and of the portal all around.

15 And from the face of the gate of the entrance unto the face of the porch of the inner gate *were* fifty cubits.

16 And *there were* narrow windows in the chambers, and in their portals within the gate round about, and likewise in the arches: and the windows *were* round about inward: and upon *each* post *were* palm trees.

17 Then he brought me into the outer court, and, behold, *there were* chambers, and a pavement made for the court round about: thirty chambers *were* in that court.

18 And the lower pavement *was* paved to the side of the gates, in proportion to the length of the portals.

19 Then he measured the breadth from the forefront of the lower gate unto the forefront of the inner court without, an hundred cubits eastward and northward.

20 And the gate of the outer court that looked toward the north, he measured the length thereof, and the breadth thereof.

21 And the chambers thereof *were* three on this side and three on that side; and the posts thereof and the arches thereof were after the measure of the first gate: the length thereof *was* fifty cubits, and the breadth five and twenty cubits.

22 And their windows, and their arches, and their palm trees, *were* after the measure of the gate that looketh toward the east; and they went up unto it by seven steps; and the arches thereof *were* before them.

23 And the gate of the inner court *was* over against the gate toward the north, and toward the east; and he measured from gate to gate an hundred cubits.

24 After that he brought me toward the south, and behold a gate toward the south: and he measured the portals thereof and the arches thereof according to these measures.

25 And *there were* windows in it and in the arches thereof round about, like those windows: the length *was* fifty cubits, and the breadth five and twenty cubits.

26 And *there were* seven steps to go up to it, and the arches thereof *were* before them: and it had palm trees, one on this side, and another on that side, upon the posts thereof.

27 And *thus was the* gate in the inner court toward the south: and he measured from gate to gate toward the south an hundred cubits.

28 And he brought me to the inner court by the south gate: and he measured the south gate according to these measures;

29 and the chambers thereof, and the posts thereof, and the arches thereof, according to these measures: and *there were* windows in it and in the arches thereof round about: *it was* fifty cubits long, and five and twenty cubits broad.

30 And the arches round about *were* five and twenty cubits long, and five cubits broad.

31 And the arches thereof *went* into the court outside; with palm trees upon *each of* the posts thereof: and the going up to it *had* eight steps.

32 And he brought me into the inner court toward the east: and he measured the gate according to these measures.

33 And the chambers thereof, and the posts thereof, and the arches thereof, *were* according to these measures: and *there were* windows therein and in the arches thereof round about: *it was* fifty cubits long, and five and twenty cubits broad.

34 And the arches thereof *went* into the court outside; with palm trees upon *each of* the posts thereof, on this side, and on that side: and the going up to it *had* eight steps.

35 Then he brought me to the north gate, and measured *it* according to these measures;

36 The chambers thereof, the posts thereof, and the arches thereof, and the windows to it round about: the length *was* fifty cubits, and the breadth five and twenty cubits.

37 And the posts thereof *were* toward the outer court; with palm trees upon *each of* the posts thereof, on this side, and on that side: and the going up to it *had* eight steps.

38 And *there was* a chamber and the gate thereof with posts of portals, there shall they wash the burnt offering.

39 And in the porch of the gate *were* two tables on this side, and two tables on that side, to slay thereon the burnt offering and the atonement and the sacrifice for sin.

40 And to the outside of the steps, at the entry of the north gate, *were* two tables; and on the other side, which *was* at the porch of the gate, *were* two tables.

41 Four tables *were* on this side, and four tables on that side, by the side of this gate; eight tables, whereupon they slew *their sacrifices*.

42 And the four tables *were* of hewn stone for the burnt offering, of a cubit and an half long, and a cubit and an half broad, and one cubit high: whereupon also they laid the instruments wherewith they slew the burnt offering and the sacrifice.

43 And within *were* hooks, an hand broad, fastened round about: and upon the tables *was* the flesh of the offering.

44 And without the inner gate *were* the chambers of the singers in the inner court, which *was* at the side of the north gate; and they faced toward the south: one at the side of the east gate facing toward the north.

45 And he said unto me, This chamber facing toward the south, *shall be* for the priests, the keepers of the charge of the house.

46 And the chamber facing toward the north *shall be* for the priests, the keepers of the charge of the altar: these *are* the sons of Zadok which are called from the sons of Levi to minister to the LORD.

47 So he measured the court, an hundred cubits long, and an hundred cubits broad, foursquare; and the altar *that was* before the house.

48 And he brought me to the porch of the house, and measured *each* post of the porch, five cubits on this side, and five cubits on that side: and the breadth of the gate *was* three cubits on this side, and three cubits on that side.

49 The length of the porch *was* twenty cubits, and the breadth eleven cubits; into which they went in by steps: and *there were* pillars by the posts, one on this side, and another on that side.

Chapter 41

1 Afterward he brought me to the temple, and measured the posts, six cubits broad on the one side, and six cubits broad on the other side, *which was* the breadth of the arch.

2 And the breadth of *each* door *was* ten cubits; and the sides of the door *were* five cubits on the one side, and five cubits on the other side: and he measured the length thereof, forty cubits: and the breadth, twenty cubits.

3 Then went he inward, and measured *each* post of the door, two cubits; and the door, six cubits; and the breadth of the door, seven cubits.

4 So he measured the length thereof, twenty cubits; and the breadth, twenty cubits, before the temple: and he said unto me, This *is* the most holy *place.*

5 After he measured the wall of the house, six cubits; and the breadth of the chambers, four cubits, round about the house on every side.

6 And the chambers *were* one over another, and thirty and three by order; and they entered *supports* into the wall of the house round about, upon which the chambers might have hold, but they had not hold upon the wall of the house.

7 And *there was* an enlarging, and a winding about in the chambers to the highest *part*: for the winding about of the house *went* very high round about *inside* the house: therefore the house *had greater* breadth upward, and from the lowest chamber it rose to the highest by the one in the middle.

8 I saw also the height of the house round about: the foundations of the chambers *were* a full reed of six great cubits.

9 The thickness of the outside wall of the chambers *was* five cubits: and the space that was left of the chambers that *were* within.

10 And between the chambers *was* the wideness of twenty cubits round about the house on every side.

11 And the door of each chamber *was* toward the space that was left, one door toward the north, and another door toward the south: and the breadth of the space that was left *was* five cubits round about.

12 Now the building that *was* before the separate place to the side toward the west *was* seventy cubits broad; and the wall of the building *was* five cubits thick round about, and the length thereof ninety cubits.

13 So he measured the house, an hundred cubits long; and the separate place, and the building, with the walls thereof, an hundred cubits long;

14 Also the breadth of the face of the house, and of the separate place toward the south, an hundred cubits.

15 And he measured the length of the building over against the separate place which *was* behind it, and the chambers thereof on the one side and on the other side, an hundred cubits, with the inner temple, and the portals of the court.

16 The thresholds, and the narrow windows, and the chambers, three around about to the front, all covered with wood round about from the ground up to the windows, and the windows *were also* covered.

17 Above over the door, and unto the inner house, and without, and by all the wall round about within and without, he took measurements.

18 And *the wall* was decorated with cherubim and palm trees, so that a palm tree *was* between a cherub and a cherub; and *every* cherub had two faces;

19 So that the face of a man *was* toward the palm tree on the one side, and the face of a lion toward the palm tree on the other side, through all the house round about.

20 From the ground unto above the door *were* cherubim and palm trees made, and *upon* the entire wall of the temple.

21 Each post of the temple *was* squared, *and* the front of the sanctuary was as the other front.

22 The altar of wood *was* three cubits high, and the length thereof two cubits; and the corners thereof, and the surface thereof, and the walls thereof, *were* of wood: and he said unto me, This *is* the table that *is* before the LORD.

23 And the temple and the sanctuary had two doors.

24 And the doors had two leaves *apiece*, two turning leaves; two *leaves* for the one door, and two leaves for the other *door*.

25 And *there were* made on them, on the doors of the temple, cherubim and palm trees, like as *were* made upon the walls; and *there were* thick planks upon the face of the porch without.

26 And *there were* narrow windows and palm trees on the one side and on the other side, on the sides of the porch, and of the house, and upon the beams.

Chapter 42

1 Then he brought me forth into the outer court, the way toward the north: and he brought me into the chamber that *was* over against the space which *was* in front of the building toward the north.

2 In front of the north door the length *was* an hundred cubits, and the breadth *was* fifty cubits.

3 Over against the twenty *cubits* which *were* in the inner court, and over against the pavement which *was* in the outer court, *were* the chambers in three *stories*.

4 And in front of the chambers *was* a walk of ten cubits breadth inward, a way of one cubit; and their doors toward the north.

5 Now the upper chambers *were* shorter: for the galleries took away from the others, from the lower ones, and from the middle ones.

6 For they *were* in three *stories*, but had not pillars as the pillars of the courts: therefore they were narrower than the lowest and the middlemost from the ground.

7 And the wall that *was* without over against the chambers, toward the outer court in front of the chambers, *was* fifty cubits long. **8** For the length of the chambers that *were* in the outer court *was* fifty cubits: and, before the front of the temple *were* an hundred cubits.

9 And under these chambers *was* the entry *to the temple* on the east side, to enter in to it from the outer court.

10 All along the wall of the court toward the east, over against the separate place, and in front of the building *were* chambers.

11 And the way before them *was* like the appearance of the chambers which *were* toward the north, as long as they, *and* as broad as they: and all their goings out *were* both according to their fashions, and according to their doors.

12 And according to the doors of the chambers that *were* toward the south *was* a door in the head of the way, *even* the way directly in front of the wall toward the east, as one entereth into them.

13 Then said he unto me, The north chambers *and* the south chambers, which *are* before the separate place, they *are* holy chambers, where the priests that approach unto the LORD shall eat the holy offerings: there shall they lay the holy offerings, and the grain offering, and the atonement, and the sacrifice for sin; for the place *is* holy.

14 When the priests enter therein, then shall they not go out of the holy *place* into the outer court, but there they shall lay their garments wherein they minister; for they *are* holy; and shall put on other garments, and in this manner shall approach unto that which *is* of the people.

15 Now when he had made an end of measuring the inner house, he brought me forth by the way of the gate facing toward the east, and measured it round about. **16** He measured the east side with the measuring reed, five hundred reeds, with the measuring reed round about. **17** He measured the north side, five hundred reeds, with the measuring reed round about. **18** He measured the south side, five hundred reeds, with the measuring reed. **19** He turned about to the west side, *and* measured five hundred reeds with the measuring reed.

20 He measured it by the four sides: it had a wall round about, five hundred *reeds* long, and five hundred broad, to make a separation between the sanctuary and the profane place.

Chapter 43

1 Afterward he brought me to the gate, *even* the gate that looketh toward the east:

2 And, behold, the glory of the God of Israel that was coming from the east: and his noise *was* like the noise of many waters: and the earth shined with his glory.

3 And *it was* according to the appearance of the vision which I saw, *even* according to the vision that I saw when I came to destroy the city: and the visions *were* like the vision that I saw by the river Chebar; and I fell upon my face.

4 And the glory of the LORD came into the house by the way of the gate facing toward the east.

5 So the Spirit took me up, and brought me into the inner court; and, behold, the glory of the LORD filled the house.

6 And I heard *him* speaking unto me out of the house; and the man stood by me.

7 And he said unto me, Son of man, *this is* the place of my throne, and the place of the soles of my feet, wherein I will dwell in the midst of the sons of Israel for ever, and my holy name, shall the house of Israel no more defile, *neither* they, nor their kings, by their whoredom, nor by the carcasses of their kings in their altars.

8 In their setting of their threshold by my threshold, and their post by my post, and *a* wall between me and them, they have even defiled my holy name by their abominations that they have committed: wherefore I have consumed them in my anger.

9 Now let them put away their whoredom, and the carcasses of their kings, far from me, and I will dwell in the midst of them for ever.

10 Thou son of man, show this house to the house of Israel, that they may be ashamed of their iniquities: and let them understand the pattern.

11 And if they be ashamed of all that they have done, show them the form of the house, and the pattern thereof, and the goings out thereof, and the comings in thereof, and all the figures thereof, and all the descriptions thereof, and all the paintings thereof, and all the laws thereof: and write *it* in their sight, that they may keep the whole form thereof, and all the ordinances thereof, and do them.

12 This *is* the law of the house; Upon the top of the mountain *it shall be built*, the whole limit thereof round about *shall be* most holy. Behold, this *is* the law of the house.

13 And these *are* the measures of the altar in cubits: The cubit *is* a cubit and an hand breadth; the middle *rim*, one cubit, and the breadth a cubit, and the border thereof by the edge thereof round about of a span. This shall be the high bottom of the altar.

14 And from the middle *rim* of the ground *even* to the lower settle, two cubits, and the breadth one cubit; and from the lesser settle to the greater settle, four cubits, and the breadth a cubit.

15 So the altar, of four cubits; and above the altar, four horns.

16 And the altar *was* twelve *cubits* long, twelve broad, square on its four sides.

17 And the patio *was* fourteen *cubits* long and fourteen broad on all four sides;

and the border about it *was* half a cubit; and the middle which had a *rim* of a cubit on all sides; and its stairs were toward the east.

18 And he said unto me, Son of man, thus hath the Lord GOD said; These *are* the ordinances of the altar in the day when they shall make it, to offer burnt offerings thereon, and to sprinkle blood thereon.

19 And thou shalt give to the priests the Levites that be of the seed of Zadok, which approach unto me, to minister unto me, said the Lord GOD, a young bullock for atonement.

20 And thou shalt take of the blood thereof, and put *it* on the four horns of *the altar*, and on the four corners of the patio, and upon the border round about: thus shalt thou cleanse and purify it.

21 Then thou shalt take the bullock of the atonement, and burn it according to the law of the house, outside the sanctuary.

22 And on the second day thou shalt offer a he goat without blemish for atonement; and they shall purify the altar, as they did purify *it* with the bullock.

23 When thou hast made an end to the atonement,

thou shalt offer a young bullock without blemish, and a ram out of the flock without blemish.

24 And thou shalt offer them before the LORD, and the priests shall cast salt upon them, and they shall offer them up *for* a burnt offering unto the LORD.

25 Seven days shalt thou prepare every day a he goat in atonement: and a young bullock and a ram out of the flock, without blemish, shall they sacrifice.

26 Seven days shall they atone the altar and they shall cleanse it; and they shall extend their hands.

27 And when these days are expired, it shall be, *that* upon the eighth day, and *so* forward, the priests shall sacrifice your burnt offerings upon the altar, and your peace offerings; and I will accept you, said the Lord GOD.

Chapter 44

1 Then he brought me back toward the outer gate of the sanctuary which looketh toward the east; and it *was* shut.

2 Then said the LORD unto me; This gate shall be shut, it shall not be opened, and no man shall enter in by it; because the LORD, the God of Israel, hath entered in by it, therefore it shall be shut.

3 *It is* for the prince; the prince, he shall sit in it to eat bread before the LORD; he shall enter by the way of the porch of *that* gate, and shall go out by the way of the same.

4 Then he brought me toward the north gate in front of the house: and I looked, and, behold, the glory of the LORD filled the house of the LORD: and I fell upon my face.

5 And the LORD said unto me, Son of man, pay attention, and behold with thine eyes, and hear with thine ears all that I say unto thee concerning all the ordinances of the house of the LORD, and all the laws thereof; and pay attention to the entering in of the house, and to every going forth from the sanctuary.

6 And thou shalt say to the rebellious, *even* to the house of Israel, Thus hath the Lord GOD said; O ye house of Israel, let all your abominations cease.

7 In that ye have brought *into my sanctuary* strangers, uncircumcised in heart, and uncircumcised in flesh, to be in my sanctuary, to pollute it, *even* my house, when ye offer my bread, the fat and the blood, and they have broken my covenant because of all your abominations.

8 And ye have not kept the charge of my holy things: but ye have set keepers of my charge in my sanctuary for yourselves.

9 Thus hath the Lord GOD said; No son of a stranger, uncircumcised in heart, nor uncircumcised in flesh, shall enter into my sanctuary, of any sons of strangers that *are* among the sons of Israel.

10 And the Levites that are gone away far from me, when Israel went astray, which went astray away from me after their idols; they shall even bear their iniquity.

11 Yet they shall be ministers in my sanctuary, gatekeepers at the gates of the house, and servants in the house: they shall slay the burnt offering and the sacrifice for the people, and they shall stand before them to serve them.

12 Because they served them before their idols, and caused the house of Israel to fall into iniquity; therefore have I lifted up my hand regarding them, said the Lord GOD, that they shall bear their iniquity.

13 And they shall not come near unto me, to serve me as priests, nor to come near to any of my holy things, to my most holy things: but they shall bear their shame, and their abominations which they have committed.

14 But I will make them keepers of the charge of the house, for all the service thereof, and for all that shall be done therein.

15 But the priests the Levites, the sons of Zadok, that kept the charge of my sanctuary when the children of Israel went astray from me, they shall come near to me to minister unto me, and they shall stand before me to offer unto me the fat and the blood, said the Lord GOD:

16 They shall enter into my sanctuary, and they shall come near to my table, to minister unto me, and they shall keep my charge.

17 And it shall come to pass, *that* when they enter in at the gates of the inner court, they shall be clothed with linen garments; and no wool shall come upon them, whiles they minister in the gates of the inner court, and within.

18 They shall have linen bonnets upon their heads, and shall have linen breeches upon their loins; they shall not gird *themselves* with any thing that causeth sweat.

19 And when they go forth into the outer court, *even* into the outer court to the people, they shall put off their garments wherein they ministered, and lay them in the chambers of the sanctuary, and they shall put on other garments; and they shall not sanctify the people with their garments.

20 Neither shall they shave their heads, nor suffer their locks to grow long; they shall only cut their hair.

21 Neither shall any priest drink wine, when they enter into the inner court.

22 Neither shall they take for their wives a widow, nor her that is put away: but they shall take virgins of the seed of the house of Israel, or a widow that had a priest before.

23 And they shall teach my people *the difference* between the holy and profane, and teach them to discern between the clean and the unclean.

24 And in controversy they shall stand in judgment; *and* they shall judge it according to my rights: and they shall keep my laws and my statutes in all my *solemn* assemblies; and they shall hallow my sabbaths.

25 And they shall come near no dead person to defile themselves: but for father, or for mother, or for son, or for daughter, for brother, or for sister that hath had no husband, they may defile themselves.

26 And after he is cleansed, they shall reckon unto him seven days.

27 And in the day that he goeth into the sanctuary, unto the inner court, to minister in the sanctuary, he shall offer his atonem ent, said the Lord GOD.

28 And *this* shall be unto them for an inheritance: I shall be their inheritance: and ye shall give them no possession in Israel: I *am* their possession.

29 They shall eat the grain offering, and the *sacrifice for* atonement, and for sin, they shall eat; and every dedicated thing *unto God* in Israel shall be theirs.

30 And the first of all the firstfruits of all *things*, and every offering of all, of every *sort* of your offerings, shall be the priest's: ye shall also give unto the priest the first of your dough, that he may cause the blessing to rest in thine house.

31 The priests shall not eat of any thing that is dead of itself, or torn, whether it be fowl or beast.

Chapter 45

1 Moreover, when ye shall divide by lot the land for inheritance, ye shall separate a lot for the LORD of the land which ye shall consecrate: the length *shall be* the length of five and twenty thousand *reeds*, and the breadth *shall be* ten thousand. This *shall be* holy in all the borders thereof round about.

2 Of this there shall be for the sanctuary five hundred *in length*, with five hundred *in breadth*, square round about; and fifty cubits round about for the suburbs thereof.

3 And of this measure shalt thou measure the length of five and twenty thousand, and the breadth of ten thousand: and in it shall be the sanctuary *and* the most holy *place*.

4 The holy *portion* of the land shall be for the priests the ministers of the sanctuary, which are chosen to minister unto the LORD: and it shall be a place for their houses, and an holy place for the sanctuary.

5 And *another* five and twenty thousand of length, and the ten thousand of breadth, shall also the Levites, the ministers of the house, have for themselves, for a possession, with twenty chambers.

6 And ye shall appoint the possession of the city five thousand broad, and five and twenty thousand long, in front of that which was separated for the sanctuary; it shall be for the whole house of Israel.

7 And *the portion* of the prince shall be on the one side and on the other side of that which was separated for the sanctuary, and next to the possession of the city, in front of that which was separated for the sanctuary, and in front of the possession of the city, from the west corner westward, unto the east corner eastward: and the length *shall be* from one side to the other, from the west corner unto the east corner.

8 He shall have this land for possession in Israel: and my princes shall no longer oppress my people; but they shall give the land unto the house of Israel according to their tribes.

9 Thus hath the Lord GOD said; Let it suffice you, O princes of Israel: remove violence and spoil, and execute judgment and justice, take away your exactions from my people, said the Lord GOD.

10 Ye shall have just balances, and a just ephah, and a just bath.

11 The ephah and the bath shall be of one measure, that the bath may contain the tenth part of an homer, and the ephah the tenth part of an homer: the measure thereof shall be after the homer.

12 And the shekel *shall be* twenty gerahs: twenty shekels, with five and twenty shekels, and fifteen shekels, shall be your maneh.

13 This *is* the offering that ye shall offer; the sixth part of an ephah of an homer of wheat, and ye shall give the sixth part of an ephah of an homer of barley:

14 The ordinance concerning the oil *shall be that ye shall offer* a bath of oil, which is the tenth part of the cor, *which is* an homer of ten baths; for ten baths *are* an homer:

15 And one *female* lamb out of the flock, out of two hundred, out of the fat pastures of Israel; for a sacrifice, and for a burnt offering, and for peace offerings, to make atonement for you, said the Lord GOD.

16 All the people of the land shall give this oblation for the prince in Israel.

17 And it shall be the prince's part *to give* the burnt offering, and the sacrifice, and the drink offering, in the solemnities, and in the new moons, and in the sabbaths, in all the feasts of the house of Israel: he shall do the atonement, and the grain offering, and the burnt offering, and the peace offerings, to make atonement for the house of Israel.

18 Thus hath the Lord GOD said; In the first *month*, in the first *day* of the month, thou shalt take a young bullock, without blemish, and atone for the sanctuary:

19 And the priest shall take of the blood of the calf of the atonement, and put *it* upon the posts of the house, and upon the four corners of the patio of the altar, and upon the posts of the gate of the inner court.

20 And so thou shalt do *until* the seventh *day* of the month for every one that erreth, and for *him that is* deceived: so shall ye atone for the house.

21 In the first *month*, in the fourteenth day of the month, ye shall have the Passover, a feast of seven days; unleavened bread shall be eaten.

22 And upon that day shall the prince prepare for himself and for all the people of the land a calf *for* a sin offering.

23 And in *all* seven days of the solemnity he shall prepare a burnt offering to the LORD, seven calves and seven rams without blemish daily the seven days; and a he goat daily *for* a sin offering.

24 And he shall prepare a grain offering of an *ephah of fine flour* for a calf, and an ephah with every ram, and for every ephah an hin of oil.

25 In the seventh *month*, in the fifteenth day of the month, shall he do the like in the feast of the seven days, regarding the atonement, regarding the burnt offering, and regarding the grain offering, and regarding the oil.

Chapter 46

1 Thus hath the Lord GOD said; The gate of the inner court that looketh toward the east shall be shut the six working days; and the day of the sabbath it shall be opened, and in the same manner it shall be opened; the day of the new moon..

2 And the prince shall enter by the way of the porch of *that* gate without, and shall stand by the threshold of the gate, (while the priests shall prepare his burnt offering and his peace offerings), and he shall worship at the entrance of the gate: then he shall go forth; but the gate shall not be shut until the evening.

3 Likewise the people of the land shall worship at the door of this gate before the LORD in the sabbaths and in the new moons.

4 And the burnt offering that the prince shall offer unto the LORD in the day of the sabbath *shall be* six lambs without blemish, and a ram without blemish.

5 And the grain offering *shall be* an ephah *of fine flour* for each ram, and the grain offering for each lamb as he shall be able to give, and an hin of oil for each ephah.

6 But in the day of the new moon *it shall be* a young bullock, without blemish, and six lambs, and a ram: they shall be without blemish.

7 And he shall prepare a grain offering of an ephah *of fine flour* with the calf, and *another* ephah with each ram, and for the lambs according as his hand shall attain unto, and an hin of oil with each ephah.

8 And when the prince shall enter, he shall go in by the way of the porch of *that* gate, and he shall go forth by the *same* way thereof.

9 But when the people of the land shall come before the LORD in the solemn feasts, he that entereth in by the way of the north gate *to worship* shall go out by the way of the south gate; and he that entereth by the way of the south gate shall go forth by the way of the north gate: he shall not return by the way of the gate whereby he came in, but shall go forth opposite it.

10 And the prince, when they go in, he shall go in in the midst of them; and when they go forth, he shall go forth.

11 And in the feasts and in the solemnities the grain offering shall be an ephah *of fine flour* with each calf, and another ephah with *each* ram, and with the lambs as he is able to give, and an hin of oil with *each* ephah.

12 Now when the prince shall prepare a voluntary burnt offering or peace offerings voluntarily unto the LORD, they shall open him the gate that looketh toward the east, and he shall prepare his burnt offering and his peace offerings, as he doeth on the day of the sabbath: then he shall go forth; and after his going forth they shall shut the gate.

13 Thou shalt daily prepare a burnt offering unto the LORD *of* a lamb of the first year without blemish: thou shalt prepare it every morning.

14 And thou shalt prepare a grain offering with it every morning, the sixth part of an ephah *of fine flour*, and the third part of an hin of oil, to temper with the fine flour; *this shall be* a grain offering for the LORD continually by *a* perpetual ordinance.

15 Thus shall they prepare the lamb, and the grain offering, and the oil, every morning *for* a continual burnt offering.

16 Thus hath the Lord GOD said; If the prince give a gift of his inheritance unto any of his sons, it *shall be* theirs, the possession thereof *shall be* by inheritance.

17 But if he give a gift of his inheritance to one of his servants, then it shall be his until the year of liberty; when it shall return to the prince: but his inheritance shall be his sons' for them.

18 And the prince shall take nothing from the people's inheritance, that he not defraud them of their possession; *but* he shall give his sons inheritance out of his own possession: that my people be not scattered every man from his possession.

19 After he brought me through the entry, which *was* at the side of the gate, into the holy chambers of the priests, which looked toward the north: and, behold, there *was* a place on the two sides westward.

20 Then said he unto me, This *is* the place where the priests shall boil the *sacrifice for* sin and for the atonement, where they shall bake the grain offering; that they bear *them* not out into the outer court, to sanctify the people.

21 Then he brought me forth into the outer court, and caused me to pass by the four corners of the court; and, behold, in every corner of the court *there was* a patio.

22 In the four corners of the court *there were* patios joined of forty *cubits* long and thirty broad: these four corners *were* of one measure.

23 And *there was* a wall round about in them, round about them four, and *it was* made with fire places under the walls round about.

24 Then said he unto me, These *are* the quarters of the cooks, where the servers of the house shall cook the sacrifice of the people.

Chapter 47

1 Afterward he made me return to the entrance of the house; and, behold, waters issued out from under the threshold of the house eastward: for the forefront of the house *stood toward* the east, and the waters came down from under towards the right side of the house, to the south *side* of the altar.

2 Then he brought me out by the way of the north gate, and led me by the way outside the gate, outside to the way that looketh eastward; and, behold, there ran out waters on the right side.

3 And when the man went forth eastward, *he had* a line in his hand, and he measured a thousand cubits, and he brought me through the waters; the waters *were* to the ankles.

4 Again he measured a thousand, and brought me through the waters; the waters *were* to the knees. Again he measured a thousand, and brought me through; the waters *were* to the loins.

5 Afterward he measured a thousand; *and it was* a river that I could not pass over: for the waters were risen, a river that could not be passed over without swimming.

6 And he said unto me, Son of man, hast thou seen *this*? Then he brought me, and caused me to return to the brink of the river.

7 And as I turned, behold, at the bank of the river *were* very many trees on the one side and on the other.

8 Then he said unto me, These waters issue out toward the east country, and shall go down into the desert, and go into the sea: *which being* brought forth into the sea, the waters *of the sea* shall be healed.

9 And it shall come to pass, *that* every living soul, which swimmeth wherever these two rivers shall come, shall live: and there shall be a very great multitude of fish, because of these waters going there: for they shall be healed; and every thing shall live that shall enter into this river.

10 And it shall come to pass, *that* the fishermen shall stand next to it; and from Engedi even unto Eneglaim there shall be a *place* to spread forth nets; according to their kinds, their fish shall be as the fish of the great sea, exceeding many.

11 But the miry places thereof and the marshes thereof shall not be healed; they shall be given to salt.

12 And by the river upon the bank thereof, on this side and on that side, shall grow every *fruitful* tree for food, whose leaf shall not fall, neither shall the fruit thereof be lacking: it shall bring forth mature fruit in his months, because their waters come forth out of the sanctuary: and the fruit thereof shall be for food, and the leaf thereof for medicine.

13 Thus hath the Lord GOD said; This is the border, whereby ye shall divide the land in inheritance among to the twelve tribes of Israel: Joseph *shall have two* portions.

14 And ye shall inherit it, one as well as another: *concerning* that which I lifted up my hand that I must give it unto your fathers: therefore, this land shall fall unto you for inheritance.

15 And this *shall be* the border of the land toward the north side, from the great sea, the way of Hethlon, as men go to Zedad;

16 Hamath, Berothah, Sibraim, which *is* between the border of Damascus and the border of Hamath; Hazarhatticon, which *is* by the coast of Hauran.

17 And the border of the north shall be from the sea of Hazarenan to the border of Damascus to the north, and to the border of Hamath to the side of the north.

18 And to the east side through Hauran, and Damascus, and Gilead, and through the land of Israel to the Jordan, ye shall measure this from the border unto the east sea.

19 And to the south side southward, from Tamar *even* to the waters of strife; from Kadesh and the river to the great sea. And *this shall be* the south side southward.

20 And to the west side the great sea shall be the border straight unto Hamath. This *shall be* the west side.

21 So shall ye divide this land among you according to the tribes of Israel.

22 And it shall come to pass, *that* ye shall divide it by lot for an inheritance unto you, and to the strangers that sojourn among you, who have begotten sons among you: and they shall be unto you as native born among the sons of Israel; they shall have cast lots with you to inherit among the tribes of Israel.

23 And it shall come to pass, *that* in the tribe in which the stranger sojourneth, there shall ye give *him* his inheritance, said the Lord GOD.

Chapter 48

1 Now these *are* the names of the tribes. From the side of the north by the way of Hethlon, as one goeth to Hamath, Hazarenan, to the border of Damascus northward, to the coast of Hamath; Dan shall have a *portion,* his sides being to the east and to the west.

2 And next to the border of Dan, from the east side unto the side of the sea, Asher shall have a *portion.*
3 And next to the border of Asher, from the east side unto the side of the sea, a *portion for* Naphtali.
4 And next to the border of Naphtali, from the east side unto the side of the sea, a *portion for* Manasseh.
5 And next to the border of Manasseh, from the east side unto the side of the sea, a *portion for* Ephraim.
6 And next to the border of Ephraim, from the east side even unto the side of the sea, a *portion for* Reuben.
7 And next to the border of Reuben, from the east side unto the side of the sea, a *portion for* Judah.
8 And next to the border of Judah, from the east side unto the side of the sea, shall be the lot which ye shall set apart of five and twenty thousand *reeds in* breadth, and *in* length as one of the *other* portions; *that is,* from the east side unto the side of the sea: and the sanctuary shall be in the midst of it.
9 The lot that ye shall separate unto the LORD *shall be* of five and twenty thousand in length, and of ten thousand in breadth.
10 And from there shall be the holy lot of the priests; toward the north five and twenty thousand *reeds in length,* and toward the west ten thousand in breadth, and toward the east ten thousand in breadth, and toward the south five and twenty thousand in length: and the sanctuary of the LORD shall be in the midst thereof.
11 The priests that are sanctified of the sons of Zadok; which have kept my charge, which went not astray when the children of Israel went astray, as the Levites went astray.
12 They shall receive *by lot,* separated in the dividing of the land, the most holy part, next to the border of the Levites.
13 And the *portion* of the Levites, *shall be* in front the border of the priests, of five and twenty thousand *reeds* in length, and of ten thousand in breadth: all the length *shall be* five and twenty thousand, and the breadth ten thousand.
14 They shall not sell of it, neither exchange, nor transpose the firstfruits of the land: for *it is* consecrated unto the LORD.
15 And the five thousand *reeds,* that are left in the

breadth over against the five and twenty thousand, shall be profane, for the city, for dwelling, and for suburbs: and the city shall be in the midst thereof.

16 And these *shall be* the measures thereof; the north side four thousand and five hundred *reeds*, and the south side four thousand and five hundred, and on the east side four thousand and five hundred, and the west side four thousand and five hundred.

17 And the suburbs of the city shall be toward the north two hundred and fifty *reeds*, and toward the west two hundred and fifty.

18 And the residue in length over against the lot of the holy *portion shall be* ten thousand eastward, and ten thousand westward: which shall be *what is left* of the lot of the holy *portion*; it shall be for food unto them that serve the city.

19 And they that serve the city shall be from all the tribes of Israel.

20 All the lot of five and twenty thousand by five and twenty thousand square: ye shall separate by lot for the sanctuary, and for the possession of the city.

21 And the residue *shall be* for the prince, on the one side and on the other of the holy lot, and of the possession of the city, over against the five and twenty thousand *reeds* of the *holy* lot unto the east border, and westward over against the five and twenty thousand unto the west border, over against the *said* portions shall be of the prince: and it shall be a holy lot; and the sanctuary of the house *shall be* in the midst thereof.

22 Moreover from the possession of the Levites, and from the possession of the city, in the midst *shall be* that which belongeth to the prince, between the border of Judah and the border of Benjamin, shall be *the lot* of the prince.

23 As for the rest of the tribes, from the east side unto the side of the sea, Benjamin *shall have* a *portion*.

24 And next to the border of Benjamin, from the east side unto the side of the sea, Simeon *shall have* a *portion*.

25 And next to the border of Simeon, from the east side unto the side of the sea, Issachar a *portion*.

26 And next to the border of Issachar, from the east

side unto the side of the sea, Zebulun a *portion*.

27 And next to the border of Zebulun, from the east side unto the side of the sea, Gad a *portion*.

28 And next to the border of Gad, at the south side southward, the border shall be from Tamar unto the waters of strife, and *from* Kadesh, *and* the river unto the great sea.

29 This *is* the land which ye shall divide by lot unto the tribes of Israel for inheritance, and these *are* their portions, said the Lord GOD.

30 And these *are* the goings out of the city on the north side, four thousand and five hundred *reeds* by measure.

31 And the gates of the city *shall be* according to the names of the tribes of Israel: three gates northward; the gate of Reuben, one; the gate of Judah, another; the gate of Levi, another.

32 And at the east side four thousand and five hundred *reeds*: and three gates; the gate of Joseph, one; the gate of Benjamin, another; the gate of Dan, another.

33 And at the south side four thousand and five hundred *reeds* by measure: and three gates; the gate of Simeon, one; the gate of Issachar, another; the gate of Zebulun, another.

34 At the west side four thousand and five hundred *reeds*, and their three gates; the gate of Gad, one; the gate of Asher, another; the gate of Naphtali, another.

35 *It was* round about eighteen thousand *reeds*: and the name of the city from that day shall be, THE LORD IS HERE.

The Prophecy of
Daniel

Chapter 1

1 In the third year of the reign of Jehoiakim king of Judah came Nebuchadnezzar king of Babylon unto Jerusalem, and besieged it.

2 And the Lord gave Jehoiakim king of Judah into his hand, with part of the vessels of the house of God: which he carried into the land of Shinar to the house of his god; and he brought the vessels into the treasure house of his god.

3 And the king spoke unto Ashpenaz the prince of his eunuchs, that he should bring *certain* of the sons of Israel, of the royal lineage of the princes;

4 young men in whom *was* no blemish whatsoever, but good looking, and taught in all wisdom, and wise in knowledge, and of good understanding, and that *had* strength in them to stand in the king's palace; that they might be taught the letters and speech of the Chaldeans.

5 And the king appointed them a daily provision of the king's food, and of the wine which he drank: so nourishing them three years, that at the end thereof they might stand before the king.

6 Now among these, of the sons of Judah, were Daniel, Hananiah, Mishael, and Azariah:

7 Unto whom the prince of the eunuchs gave names: for he gave unto Daniel *the name* of Belteshazzar; and to Hananiah, of Shadrach; and to Mishael, of Meshach; and to Azariah, of Abednego.

8 And Daniel purposed in his heart that he would not defile himself with the portion of the king's food, nor

with the wine which he drank: therefore he requested of the prince of the eunuchs that he might not defile himself.

9 (And God brought Daniel into grace and good will with the prince of the eunuchs.)

10 And the prince of the eunuchs said unto Daniel, I fear my lord the king, who hath appointed your food and your drink: for when he shall see your faces more downcast than the *other* young men which *are* like unto you, then shall ye condemn my head before the king.

11 Then said Daniel to Melzar, whom the prince of the eunuchs had set over Daniel, Hananiah, Mishael, and Azariah,

12 Prove, now, with thy servants ten days; and let them give us vegetables to eat, and water to drink.

13 Then let our countenances be looked upon before thee, and the countenances of the young men that eat of the portion of the king's food: and as thou seest, deal with thy servants.

14 So he consented to them in this matter, and proved them ten days.

15 And at the end of ten days their countenances appeared fairer and fatter in flesh than the young men which did eat the portion of the king's food.

16 Thus Melzar took the portion of their food, and the wine that they should drink; and gave them vegetables.

17 And unto these four young men, God gave them knowledge and intelligence in all letters and science: furthermore Daniel had understanding in all visions and dreams.

18 Now at the end of the days after which the king had said he should bring them in, the prince of the eunuchs brought them in before Nebuchadnezzar.

19 And the king communed with them; and among them all was found none like Daniel, Hananiah, Mishael, and Azariah: and *therefore* they stood before the king.

20 And in all matters of wisdom *and* intelligence, that the king enquired of them, he found them ten times better than all the magicians *and* astrologers that *were* in all his realm.

21 And Daniel continued *even* unto the first year of king Cyrus.

Chapter 2

1 And in the second year of the reign of Nebuchadnezzar Nebuchadnezzar dreamed dreams, wherewith his spirit was troubled, and his sleep fled from him. *2* Then the king commanded to call magicians, astrologers, enchanters, and Chaldeans, that they might show the king his dreams. So they came and presented themselves before the king. *3* And the king said unto them, I have dreamed *a* dream, and my spirit was troubled to know the dream. *4* Then spoke the Chaldeans to the king in Syriack, O king, live for ever: tell thy servants the dream, and we will show the interpretation. *5* The king answered and said to the Chaldeans, The thing is gone from my *memory*: if ye will not make known unto me the dream, with the interpretation thereof, ye shall be cut in pieces, and your houses shall be made a dunghill. *6* But if ye show the dream, and the interpretation thereof, ye shall receive of me gifts and rewards and great honour: therefore show me the dream, and the interpretation thereof.

7 They answered the second time and said, Let the king tell his servants the dream, and we will show the interpretation of it. *8* The king answered and said, I know of certainty that ye would gain time, because ye see the thing is gone from my memory. *9* But if ye will not make known unto me the dream, *there is but* one decree for you: for ye certainly prepare lying and corrupt words to speak before me, until the time be changed: therefore tell me the dream, and I shall know that ye can show me the interpretation thereof. *10* The Chaldeans answered before the king, and said, There is not a man upon the earth that can show the king's matter: furthermore *there is* no king, prince, nor lord, *that* asked such a thing of any magician, or astrologer, or Chaldean. *11* Finally, the thing that the king requireth is singular, and there is none other that can show it before the king, except the angels *of God*, whose dwelling is not with flesh. *12* For this cause the king was angry and very furious, and commanded to destroy all the wise *men* of Babylon.

13 And the decree went forth and the wise *men* were taken to be slain; and they sought Daniel and his fellows to kill them.

14 Then Daniel spoke with counsel and wisdom to Arioch the captain of the king's guard, which was gone forth to slay the wise *men* of Babylon:

15 He spoke and said to Arioch the king's captain, What is the reason for which this decree has gone forth from the king with such haste? Then Arioch made the thing known to Daniel.

16 And Daniel went in, and asked the king that he give him time, and that he would show the king the interpretation.

17 Then Daniel went to his house, and made the thing known to Hananiah, Mishael, and Azariah, his companions;

18 to petition mercies of the God of heaven concerning this mystery; and that Daniel and his fellows should not perish with the rest of the wise *men* of Babylon.

19 Then the mystery was revealed unto Daniel in a night vision; for which Daniel blessed the God of heaven.

20 And Daniel spoke and said, Blessed be the name of God from age to age: for wisdom and might are his:

21 And it is he that changeth the times and the opportunities: he removeth kings, and setteth up kings: he giveth wisdom unto the wise, and knowledge to them that know understanding:

22 He revealeth that which is deep and hidden: he knoweth what *is* in darkness, and the light dwelleth with him.

23 Unto thee, O thou God of my fathers, do I confess and give thee praise, that thou hast given me wisdom and might, and now hast shown me what we asked of thee: for thou hast shown us the king's matter.

24 After this Daniel went in unto Arioch, whom the king had ordained to destroy the wise *men* of Babylon: he went and said thus unto him; Destroy not the wise *men* of Babylon: bring me in before the king, and I will show unto the king the interpretation.

25 Then Arioch brought in Daniel before the king in haste, and said thus unto him, I have found a man of the captives of Judah, that will make known unto the king the interpretation.

26 The king answered and said to Daniel, whose name *was* Belteshazzar, Art thou able to make me understand the dream which I have seen, and the interpretation thereof?

27 Daniel answered in the presence of the king, and said, The mystery which the king demandeth cannot be shown unto the king by wise *men*, astrologers, magicians, nor fortune-tellers.

28 But there is *a* God in the heavens, who revealeth the mysteries, and he hath made known to the king Nebuchadnezzar what shall happen at the end of days. Thy dream, and the visions of thy head upon thy bed, is this:

29 Thou, O king, in thy bed, thy thoughts rose up to know what should come to pass in the future: and he that revealeth the mysteries showed thee what shall come to pass.

30 And unto me this mystery has been revealed, not for *any* wisdom that is in me, more than in all those living, but that I notify the interpretation to the king, and that thou mightest understand the thoughts of thy heart.

31 Thou, O king, sawest, and behold a great image. This image, which was very large, and whose glory was very sublime, stood before thee; and the form thereof *was* terrible.

32 The head of this image *was* of fine gold, his breasts and his arms of silver, his belly and his thighs of brass,

33 his legs of iron, his feet part of iron and part of baked clay.

34 Thou sawest, until a stone was cut out, not with hands, which smote the image upon his feet *that were* of iron and baked clay, and broke them to pieces.

35 Then was the iron, the baked clay, the brass, the silver, and the gold, broken to pieces together, and became like the chaff of the summer threshingfloors; and the wind carried them away, that no place was found for them again: and the stone that smote the image was made into a great mountain that filled the whole earth.

36 This *is* the dream; and we will tell the interpretation thereof before the king.

37 Thou, O king, *art* king of kings: for the God of heaven hath given thee the kingdom, the power, and the strength, and the majesty.

38 And everything that is inhabited by children of men, beasts of the field, and fowls of the heaven, hath *he* given into thine hand, and hath made thee ruler over them all. Thou *art* this head of gold.

39 And after thee shall arise another kingdom inferior to thee, and another third kingdom of brass, which shall bear rule over all the land.

40 And the fourth kingdom shall be strong as iron: and as iron breaketh in pieces and subdueth all *things*: and as iron that breaketh all these things, shall it break in pieces and bruise.

41 And whereas thou sawest the feet and toes, part of baked potters' clay, and part of iron, the kingdom shall be divisive; but there shall be in it *some* of the strength of the iron, such as thou sawest the iron mixed with baked clay.

42 And *as* the toes of the feet *were* part of iron, and part of baked clay, *so* the kingdom shall be partly strong, and partly fragile.

43 Concerning that which thou sawest, the iron mixed with baked clay, they shall mingle themselves with the seed of men: but they shall not cleave one to another, even as iron doth not mix with clay.

44 And in the days of those kings the God of heaven shall raise up a kingdom which eternally shall never become corrupted: and this kingdom shall not be left to another people, *but* it shall break in pieces and consume all these kingdoms, and it shall stand for ever.

45 In the manner which thou sawest that out of the mountain was cut one stone, not with hands, and that it broke in pieces the iron, the brass, the clay, the silver, and the gold; the great God hath shown the king what shall come to pass hereafter: and the dream *is* true, and the interpretation thereof sure.

46 Then the king Nebuchadnezzar fell upon his face, and humbled himself before Daniel, and commanded that they should sacrifice presents and sweet odours unto him.

47 The king answered unto Daniel, and said, Certainly the God *that is* your God *is* God of gods, and the Lord of the kings, and the revealer of the mysteries, seeing thou couldest reveal this mystery.

48 Then the king magnified Daniel, and gave him many

and great gifts, and made him governor over the whole province of Babylon, and prince of the governors over all the wise *men* of Babylon.

49 And Daniel requested of the king, and he set Shadrach, Meshach, and Abednego, over the affairs of the province of Babylon: but Daniel *was* at the gate of the king.

Chapter 3

1 Nebuchadnezzar the king made a statue of gold, whose height *was* sixty cubits, *and* the breadth thereof six cubits: he set it up in the plain of Dura, in the province of Babylon.

2 Then Nebuchadnezzar the king sent to gather together the great *ones*, the assistants and captains, the judges, the treasurers, those of the council, presidents, and all the governors of the provinces, to come to the dedication of the statue which Nebuchadnezzar the king had raised up.

3 Then the great *ones*, the assistants and captains, the judges, the treasurers, those of the council, presidents, and all the governors of the provinces, were gathered together unto the dedication of the statue that Nebuchadnezzar the king

had raised up; and they stood before the statue that Nebuchadnezzar the king had raised up.

4 Then an herald cried aloud, To you it is commanded, O people, nations, and languages,

5 *That* when ye hear the sound of the cornet, flute, harp, sackbut, psaltery, dulcimer, and of every musical instrument, ye *are to* fall down and worship the statue of gold that Nebuchadnezzar the king hath raised up:

6 And whosoever falleth not down and worshippeth shall the same hour be cast into the midst of a burning fiery furnace.

7 Therefore, when all the peoples heard the sound of the cornet, flute, harp, sackbut, psaltery, and every musical instrument, all the peoples, nations, and languages, fell down *and* worshipped the statue of gold that Nebuchadnezzar the king had raised up.

8 Wherefore at that time certain Chaldeans came near, and accused the Jews.

9 They spoke and said to the king Nebuchadnezzar, O king, live for ever.

10 Thou, O king, hast made a law that every man

upon hearing the sound of the cornet, flute, harp, sackbut, psaltery, and dulcimer, and every musical instrument, shall fall down and worship the statue of gold:

11 And whosoever falleth not down and worshippeth, *that* he should be cast into the midst of a burning fiery furnace.

12 There are certain Jews whom thou hast set over the affairs of the province of Babylon, Shadrach, Meshach, and Abednego; these men, O king, have not regarded thee: they do not worship thy gods, nor *do they* worship the statue of gold which thou hast raised up.

13 Then Nebuchadnezzar in *his* rage and fury commanded to bring Shadrach, Meshach, and Abednego. Then they brought these men before the king.

14 Nebuchadnezzar spoke and said unto them, *Is it* true, O Shadrach, Meshach, and Abednego, that ye do not honour my gods, nor worship the statue of gold which I have set up?

15 Now, are ye ready when ye hear the sound of the cornet, flute, harp, sackbut, psaltery, and dulcimer, and of every musical instrument, to fall down and worship the statue which I made? For if ye worship not, ye shall be cast the same hour into the midst of a burning fiery furnace; and who *is* that god that shall deliver you out of my hands?

16 Shadrach, Meshach, and Abednego, answered and said to king Nebuchadnezzar, We *are* not careful to answer thee in this matter.

17 Behold, our God whom we serve is able to deliver us from the burning fiery furnace, and he will deliver *us* out of thine hand, O king.

18 But if not, be it known unto thee, O king, that we will not serve thy god, nor honour the statue which thou hast raised up.

19 Then was Nebuchadnezzar full of fury, and the form of his visage was changed against Shadrach, Meshach, and Abednego: *therefore* he spoke, and commanded that they should heat the furnace seven times more than it was wont to be heated.

20 And he commanded the most mighty men that *were* in his army to bind Shadrach, Meshach, and Abednego, *and* to cast *them* into the burning fiery furnace.

21 Then these men were bound in their coats, their undergarments, and their hats, and their *other* garments, and were cast into the midst of the burning fiery furnace.

22 Therefore because the king's commandment was urgent, and the furnace exceeding hot, the flame of the fire slew those men that took up Shadrach, Meshach, and Abednego.

23 And these three men, Shadrach, Meshach, and Abednego, fell down bound into the midst of the burning fiery furnace.

24 Then Nebuchadnezzar the king was astonished, and rose up in haste, *and* spoke, and said unto his counsellors, Did we not cast three men bound into the midst of the fire? They answered and said unto the king, True, O king.

25 He answered and said, Behold, I see four men loose, walking in the midst of the fire, and they have no hurt; and the form of the fourth is like the Son of God.

26 Then Nebuchadnezzar came near to the mouth of the burning fiery furnace, *and* spoke, and said, Shadrach, Meshach, and Abednego, ye servants of the most high God, come forth, and come *hither.* Then Shadrach, Meshach, and Abednego, came forth of the midst of the fire.

27 And the great ones, the governors, and the captains, and the king's counsellors, gathered together to see these men, upon whose bodies the fire had no power, nor was an hair of their head singed, neither were their coats changed, nor the smell of fire had passed on them.

28 *Then* Nebuchadnezzar spoke, and said, Blessed *be* the God of these, of Shadrach, Meshach, and Abednego, who hath sent his angel, and delivered his servants that trusted in him, and have changed the king's word, and yielded their bodies, that they might not serve nor worship any god, except their own God.

29 Therefore I make a decree, That every people, nation, or language, which speak blasphemy against the God of Shadrach, Meshach, and Abednego, shall be cut in pieces, and their houses shall be made a dunghill: because there is no other god that can deliver after this sort.

30 Then the king promoted Shadrach, Meshach, and Abednego, in the province of Babylon.

Chapter 4

1 King Nebuchadnezzar, to all the peoples, nations, and languages, that dwell in all the earth; Peace be multiplied unto you.

2 The signs and wonders that the high God hath wrought with me, are such that I must publish them.

3 How great *are* his signs! and how mighty *are* his wonders! his kingdom *is* an everlasting kingdom, and his dominion *is* from generation to generation.

4 I Nebuchadnezzar was quiet in my house, and flourishing in my palace:

5 I saw a dream which made me afraid, and the imaginations and visions of my head troubled me in my bed.

6 Therefore made I a decree to bring in all the wise *men* of Babylon before me, that they might show me the interpretation of the dream.

7 Then came in the magicians, the astrologers, the Chaldeans, and the fortune-tellers: and I told the dream before them; but they never showed me the interpretation thereof.

8 But at the last Daniel came in before me, whose name is Belteshazzar, who when I name him it seemeth to me that I name my god, and in whom *is* the spirit of the holy angels *of God*: and before him I told the dream, *saying,*

9 Belteshazzar, prince of the wise *men, now that* I have understood that the spirit of the holy angels *of God is* in thee, and that no mystery is hidden from thee, tell me the visions of my dream that I have seen, and the interpretation thereof.

10 Thus *were* the visions of my head in my bed; It seemed that I saw a tree in the midst of the earth, and the height thereof was great.

11 The tree grew, and made itself strong, and the height thereof reached unto heaven, and the sight thereof to the end of all the earth:

12 His leaves *were* fair, and his fruit abundant, and in him *was* food for all: underneath him the beasts of the field lay down in the shadow thereof, and in his branches dwelt the fowls of the heaven, and all flesh was fed of him.

13 I saw in the visions of my head upon my bed, and, behold, one who was a watchman and holy descended from heaven;

14 He cried aloud, and said thus, Hew down the tree, and cut off his branches, shake off his leaves, and scatter his fruit: let the beasts get away from under it, and the fowls from his branches:

15 Nevertheless leave the stump of his roots in the earth, even with a band of iron and of brass shall he be bound in the green grass of the field; and let him be wet with the dew of heaven, and *let* his portion *be* with the beasts in the grass of the earth:

16 Let his heart be changed from a man's heart, and let a beast's heart be given unto him; and let seven times pass over him.

17 By sentence of the watchmen is the matter *resolved*, and the case by the word of the holy ones: to the intent that the living may know that the most High taketh rule over the kingdom of men, and giveth it to whomsoever he will, and setteth up over it the man who is the lowest.

18 I, king Nebuchadnezzar, saw this dream. Now thou, O Belteshazzar, shalt declare the interpretation thereof, forasmuch as all the wise *men* of my kingdom could never show me the interpretation thereof: but thou *art* able; for the spirit of the holy angels *of God is* in thee.

19 Then Daniel, whose name *was* Belteshazzar, was silent for almost one hour, and his thoughts troubled him. *Then* the king spoke, and said, Belteshazzar, let not the dream, or the interpretation thereof, trouble thee. Belteshazzar answered and said, My lord, the dream *be* to thine enemies, and the interpretation thereof to them that wish thee evil.

20 The tree that thou sawest, which grew, and made himself strong, whose height reached unto the heaven, and the sight thereof to all the earth;

21 whose leaves *were* fair, and his fruit abundant, and in him *was* food for all; under whom the beasts of the field dwelt, and in whose branches the fowls of the heaven dwelt:

22 It *is* thou, O king, that grew and made thyself strong: for thy greatness hath grown, and hath reached unto heaven, and thy dominion to the end of the earth.

23 And regarding that which the king saw, one who was a watchman and holy who came down from heaven, and said, Hew the tree down, and destroy it; yet leave the stump of the roots thereof in the earth, and with a band of iron and of brass *let it remain bound* in the green grass of the field; and let it be wet with the dew of heaven, and *let* his portion *be* with the beasts of the field, until seven times pass over him: **24** This *is* the interpretation, O king, and this *is* the decree of the most High, which is come upon my lord the king:

25 That they shall drive thee from among men, and thy dwelling shall be with the beasts of the field, and they shall feed thee with grass of the field as the oxen, and with the dew of heaven shalt thou be bathed, and seven times shall pass over thee, until thou shalt understand that the most High taketh rule over the kingdom of men, and that he shall give it to whomsoever he will.

26 And whereas they commanded to leave the stump of the tree roots in the earth; thy kingdom shall remain sure unto thee, that thou shalt understand that the rule *is* in the heavens.

27 Therefore, O king, approve my counsel, and redeem thy sins with righteousness, and thine iniquities with mercies unto the poor: behold the medicine for thy sin.

28 All this came upon the king Nebuchadnezzar.

29 At the end of twelve months as he was walking upon the palace of the kingdom of Babylon,

30 the king spoke, and said, Is this not the great Babylon, that I have built for *the* house of the kingdom, by the might of my power, and for the glory of my greatness?

31 The word was yet in the king's mouth, when there fell a voice from heaven, *saying,* O king Nebuchadnezzar, to thee it is spoken; The kingdom is departed from thee;

32 and they drive thee from among men, and thy dwelling *shall be* with the beasts of the field; and they shall feed thee as the oxen, and seven times shall pass over thee, until thou know that the most High taketh rule in the kingdom of men, and giveth it to whomsoever he will.

33 The same hour was the word fulfilled upon Nebuchadnezzar: and he was driven from among men, and did eat grass as the oxen, and his body was bathed with the dew of heaven, until his hair grew like eagles' *feathers*, and his nails like birds' *claws*.

34 But at the end of the time I Nebuchadnezzar lifted up my eyes unto heaven, and my understanding was returned unto me, and I blessed the most High, and I praised and glorified him that liveth for ever, whose dominion *is* an everlasting dominion, and his kingdom *is* through all ages:

35 And all the inhabitants of the earth *are* counted as nothing: and in the army of heaven, and in the inhabitants of the earth, he doeth according to his will: nor is their anyone who can interfere with his hand, and say unto him, What doest thou?

36 In the same time my reason was returned unto me; and I turned to the majesty of my kingdom; my dignity and greatness returned unto me; and my governors and my great *ones* sought me; and I was restored in my kingdom, and more *excellent* greatness was added unto me.

37 Now I, Nebuchadnezzar, praise and build up and glorify the King of heaven, because all his works *are* truth, and his ways judgment: and those that walk with arrogance he is able to humble.

Chapter 5

1 Belshazzar the king made a great banquet to a thousand of his lords, and against the thousand he drank wine.

2 Belshazzar, under the influence of the wine, commanded that they bring the vessels of gold and of silver which Nebuchadnezzar his father had brought from the Temple of Jerusalem; that the king, and his princes, his wives, and his concubines, might drink with them.

3 Then they brought the vessels of gold that they had brought from the Temple of the House of God which *was* in Jerusalem; and the king, and his princes, his wives, and his concubines, drank with them.

4 They drank wine, and praised the gods of gold, and of silver, of brass, of iron, of wood, and of stone.

5 In that same hour came forth some fingers of *a* man's hand, and wrote in front of the candlestick upon the plaster of the wall of the king's palace: and the king saw the palm of the hand that wrote.

6 Then the king became pale, and his thoughts troubled him, and the girdings of his loins were unloosed, and his knees smote one against another.

7 The king cried in *a* loud voice that they bring in the magicians, the Chaldeans, and the fortune-tellers. The king spoke, and said to the wise *men* of Babylon, Whosoever shall read this writing, and show me the interpretation thereof, shall be clothed with purple, and *have* a chain of gold about his neck, and shall be the third ruler in the kingdom.

8 Then came in all the king's wise *men*: but they could not read the writing, nor make known to the king the interpretation thereof.

9 Then was king Belshazzar greatly troubled, and his colour was changed, and his princes were upset.

10 *Now* the queen, by reason of the words of the king and of his princes, came into the banquet room. The queen spoke and said, O king, live for ever: let not thy thoughts trouble thee, nor let thy *countenance* be pale:

11 There is a man in thy kingdom, in whom *lives* the spirit of the holy angels *of God*; and in the days of thy father light and intelligence and wisdom, like the knowledge of the angels, was found in him; whom the king Nebuchadnezzar, thy father, made prince over all the magicians, astrologers, Chaldeans, *and* fortune-tellers: *thus did* thy father, the king,

12 because Daniel, whom the king named Beltechazzar, was found to have a more excellent spirit, and greater knowledge and understanding interpreting dreams, unravelling questions, and dissolving doubts. Now let Daniel be called, and he will show *thee* the interpretation.

13 Then Daniel was brought in before the king. *And* the king spoke and said unto Daniel, *Art* thou that Daniel, which *art* of the sons of the captivity of Judah, whom my father brought out of Judea?

14 I have heard of thee, that the spirit of the holy angels *of God* is in thee, and *that* light and understanding and greater wisdom was found in thee.

15 And now the wise *men*, the astrologers, have been

brought in before me, that they should read this writing, and make known unto me the interpretation thereof: but they could not show the interpretation of the thing:

16 And I have heard of thee, that thou canst declare that which is in doubt, and unravel difficulties: now if thou canst read this writing, and show me the interpretation thereof, thou shalt be clothed with purple, and *have* a chain of gold about thy neck, and shalt be the third ruler in the kingdom.

17 Then Daniel answered and said before the king, Let thy gifts be for thyself, and give thy rewards to another; yet I will read the writing unto the king, and show him the interpretation.

18 O thou king, the most high God gave Nebuchadnezzar thy father the kingdom, and the greatness, and the glory, and the magnificence:

19 And by the greatness that he gave him, all the peo nations, and languages, trembled and feared before him: whom he would he slew; and whom he would he kept alive; and whom he would he set up; and whom he would he humbled.

20 But when his heart made itself arrogant, and his spirit hardened itself in pride, he was deposed from the throne of his kingdom, and they took his glory from him:

21 And he was driven from among the sons of men; and his heart was put with the beasts, and his dwelling *was* with the wild asses: they made him eat grass like an ox, and his body was bathed with the dew of heaven; until he understood that the most high God taketh rule of the kingdom of men, and *that* he appointeth over it whomsoever he will.

22 And thou his son, O Belshazzar, hast not humbled thine heart, though thou knewest all this;

23 but hast lifted up thyself against the Lord of heaven; and they have brought the vessels of his house before thee, and thou, and thy princes, thy wives, and thy concubines, have drunk wine in them; furthermore, thou hast praised gods of silver, and of gold, of brass, of iron, of wood, and of stone, which see not, nor hear, nor know: and the God in whose hand *is* thy soul, and whose *are* all thy ways, thou hast never honoured:

24 Then from his presence was sent the palm of the hand that sculpted this writing.

25 And the writing that he sculpted is, MENE, MENE, TEKEL, UPHARSIN.

26 This *is* the interpretation of the thing: MENE; God hath audited thy kingdom, and finished it.

27 TEKEL; Thou art weighed in the balances, and art found wanting.

28 PERES; Thy kingdom has been broken, and is given to the Medes and Persians.

29 Then commanded Belshazzar, and they clothed Daniel with purple, and *put* a chain of gold about his neck, and made a proclamation concerning him, that he should be the third ruler in the kingdom.

30 That same night Belshazzar the king of the Chaldeans was slain.

31 And Darius the Median took the kingdom, being sixty-two years old.

Chapter 6

1 It pleased Darius to set over the kingdom an hundred and twenty governors, who should be in all the kingdom;

2 and over these three presidents; of whom Daniel *was* first: that the governors might give accounts unto them, and the king should not be bothered.

3 Then this Daniel was preferred above these governors and presidents, because an over abundance of *the* Spirit *was* in him; and the king thought to set him over the whole kingdom.

4 Then the presidents and governors looked for occasions against Daniel on behalf of the kingdom; but they could find no occasion or fault; because he was faithful, and no vice nor fault was found in him.

5 Then said these men, We shall never find any occasion against this Daniel, except we find *it* against him in the law of his God.

6 Then these governors and presidents assembled together before the king, and said thus unto him, King Darius, live for ever.

7 All the presidents of the kingdom, magistrates, governors, great *ones* and captains, have agreed in common accord to promote a royal decree, and to confirm it, that whosoever shall ask a petition of any God or man for thirty days, save of thee, O king, he shall be cast into the den of lions.

8 Now, O king, confirm the decree, and sign the writing, that it not be moved, according to the law of Media and of Persia, which does not change.

9 Therefore king Darius signed the writing and the decree.

10 Now when Daniel knew that the writing was signed, he entered into his house; and with the windows open toward Jerusalem in his dining chamber, he knelt three times a day, and prayed, and gave thanks before his God, as he was used to doing before.

11 Then these men assembled, and found Daniel praying and making supplication before his God.

12 Then they went, and spoke before the king concerning the royal decree; Hast thou not confirmed a decree, that whosoever shall ask *a petition* of any God or man within thirty days, save of thee, O king, shall be cast into the den of lions? The king answered and said, The thing *is* true, according to the law of the Media and Persia, which does not change.

13 Then they answered and said before the king, That Daniel, which *is* of the sons of the captivity of the Jews, hath not regarded thee, O king, nor the decree that thou hast confirmed, but maketh his petition three times a day.

14 When the king, heard the matter, it weighed very heavy upon him, and *he* set *his* heart on Daniel to deliver him: and he laboured until the going down of the sun to deliver him.

15 Then those men assembled near the king, and said unto the king, Know, O king, that this is the law of Media and of Persia: No decree nor statute which the king hath confirmed may be moved.

16 Then the king commanded, and they brought Daniel, and cast *him* into the den of lions. *Now* the king, speaking unto Daniel, said, Thy God whom thou servest continually, *may* he deliver thee.

17 And a stone was brought, and laid upon the mouth of the den; and the king sealed it with his own signet *ring*, and with the signet *ring* of his princes; that the agreement concerning Daniel might not be changed.

18 Then the king went to his palace, and lay down without eating: neither were instruments of music brought before him: and his sleep fled from him.

19 Therefore, the king arose very early in the morning at dawn, and went in haste unto the den of lions.

20 And when he came to the den, he cried loudly with a sad voice unto Daniel: *and* the king, in speaking to Daniel said, Daniel, servant of the living God, has thy God, whom thou servest continually, been able to deliver thee from the lions?

21 Then said Daniel unto the king, O king, live for ever.

22 My God hath sent his angel, who shut the lions' mouths, that they do me no evil: because before him righteousness was found in me; and even before thee, O king, have I done no corruption.

23 Then was the king exceeding glad because of him, and commanded that they should take Daniel up out of the den. So Daniel was taken up out of the den, and no injury was found upon him, because he believed in his God.

24 And the king commanded, and they brought those men who had accused Daniel, and they cast *them* into the den of lions,

them, their children, and their wives; and even before they reached the bottom of the den, the lions had the mastery of them, and broke all their bones in pieces.

25 Then king Darius wrote unto all the peoples, nations, and tongues, that dwell in all the earth; Peace be multiplied unto you.

26 On my behalf is a statute put into effect, That in all the dominion of my kingdom everyone tremble at the presence of the God of Daniel: for he *is* the Living God, and endureth for all ages, and his kingdom *is such* that it shall never come apart, and his dominion *shall be even* unto the end:

27 That saves and frees, and makes signs and wonders in heaven and in earth, who delivered Daniel from the power of the lions.

28 So this Daniel was prospered during the reign of Darius, and during the reign of Cyrus, *the* Persian.

Chapter 7

1 In the first year of Belshazzar king of Babylon, Daniel saw a dream and visions of his head upon his bed: then he wrote the dream, *and* penned the sum of the matters.

2 Daniel spoke and said, I saw in my vision by night, and, behold, the four winds of the heaven fought the great sea.

3 And four great beasts came up from the sea, different one from another.

4 The first *was* like a lion, and had eagle's wings: I beheld until the its wings were plucked off, and it was removed from the earth, and it stood up on its feet as a man, and a man's heart was given to it.

5 And behold the second beast, like unto a bear, which went off to one side, and *it had* three ribs between its teeth: and thus was said unto it, Arise, devour much flesh.

6 After this I beheld, and behold another, like a tiger, which had upon the back of it four wings of a fowl; this beast had also four heads; and power was given to it.

7 After this I saw in the night visions, and behold the fourth beast, dreadful and terrible, and exceedingly strong; and it had great iron teeth: it devoured and broke in pieces, and trod down that which was left with the feet of it: and it was very different from all the beasts that had been before her; and it had ten horns.

8 As I was considering the horns, behold, there came up among them another little horn, before whom three of the first horns were plucked up *by the roots*: and, behold, in this horn were eyes like the eyes of man, and a mouth speaking grand things.

9 I beheld until thrones were placed, and an Elder of great age did sit, whose garment *was* white as snow, and the hair of his head like pure wool: his throne *a* flame of fire, his wheels burning fire.

10 A river of fire issued and came forth from before him: thousands of thousands served him, and millions of millions stood before him: the Judge sat down, and the books were opened.

11 I beheld then because of the voice of the great words which the horn spoke: I beheld *even* until the beast was slain, and its body was undone, and given over to be burned in the fire.

12 They had also taken from the other beasts their rule: because their lives had been prolonged until a certain time.

13 I saw in the vision of the night, and, behold, in the clouds of heaven like a Son of man that came, and drew nigh unto the Elder of great age, and they brought him near before him.

14 And he gave him dominion, and glory, and kingdom; and all the peoples, nations, and tongues served him: his dominion *is* an eternal dominion, which shall not pass away, and his Kingdom such that it shall never be corrupted.

15 My spirit was troubled, I Daniel, in the midst of my body, and the visions of my head astonished me.

16 I came near unto one of them that stood by, and asked him the truth of all this. So he told me, and made me know the interpretation of the things.

17 These great beasts, which are four, *are* four kings, *which* shall arise in of the earth.

18 And they shall take the kingdom of the Holy *One who is* most High, and possess the kingdom until the age, and until the age of the ages.

19 Then I had the desire to know the truth regarding the fourth beast, which was so different from all the others, exceeding dreadful, whose teeth were of iron, and his nails of brass;

which devoured and broke in pieces, and trod down that which was left with its feet;

20 also regarding the ten horns that *were* in its head, and *of* the other which came up, and before whom three fell; and that same horn had eyes, and *a* mouth that spoke very grand things, whose appearance was greater than his fellows.

21 I saw that this horn made war against the saints, and overcame them;

22 until such time as the Elder of great age came, and the judgment was given unto the saints of the most High; and the time came, and the saints possessed the Kingdom.

23 Thus he said, The fourth beast shall be a fourth king in earth, which shall be greater than all the other kingdoms, and shall devour the whole earth, and shall tread it down, and break it in pieces.

24 And the ten horns *signify* that of this kingdom ten kings shall arise: and another shall rise after them; and he shall be greater than the first *kings*, and he shall bring down three kings.

25 And he shall speak *great* words against the most

High, and shall break down the saints of the most High, and think to move the times and the law: and they shall be given into his hand until *a* time and times and the half [*or dividing*] of a time.

26 And the Judge shall sit, and they shall take away his dominion, to destroy and to cast out unto the end;

27 and that the kingdom and the dominion, and the majesty of the kingdoms under the whole heaven, be given to the holy people of the most High, His Kingdom *shall be* an eternal Kingdom, and all the dominions shall serve him and hear *him*.

28 Up unto here was the end of the word. I, Daniel, was very troubled in my thoughts, and my countenance changed in me: but I kept the word in my heart.

Chapter 8

1 In the third year of the reign of king Belshazzar a vision appeared unto me, Daniel, after that *vision* which had appeared unto me before.

2 And I saw in *the* vision; (and it came to pass, when I saw it, that I *was* at Shushan, which is *the* head of the kingdom in the province of Persia); so that I saw in that vision, being by the river of Ulai,

3 and I lifted up my eyes, and saw, and, behold, a ram was standing before the river, which had two horns: and even though they were high, the one *was* higher than the other, and the higher one came up last.

4 I saw that the ram smote with the horns to the west, to the north, and to the south; and that no beast could stand before him, nor could anyone escape from his hand; but he did according to his will, and made himself great.

5 And as I was considering, behold, an he goat came from the west upon the face of the whole earth, and touched not the earth: and the goat *had* a notable horn between his eyes.

6 And he came to the ram that had the two horns, which *I* had seen standing before the river, and ran against him in the fury of his power.

7 And I saw him come close unto the ram, and he rose up against him, and smote him, and broke his two horns: because the ram did not have the strength to stand before him, therefore he cast him down to the

369 **DANIEL 8:19**

ground, and trod him un-
der: and there was no one
to deliver the ram out of his
hand.

8 And the he goat made
himself very great: and
when he was at his great-
est strength, that great
horn was broken; and in its
place came up another four
marvellous ones toward the
four winds of heaven.

9 And out of the first of
them came forth a little
horn, which grew much to-
ward the south, and toward
the east, and toward the desirable *land*.

10 And it magnified itself
unto the host of heaven;
and it cast down *part* of
the host and of the stars to
the ground, and trod them
under.

11 Even *against* the em-
peror of the host did he
magnify himself, and by
him the daily *sacrifice* was
taken away, and the place
of his sanctuary was cast
to *the* earth.

12 And the host was given
over by reason of the prevarication upon the daily
sacrifice; and he cast the
truth to the ground; and he
did *whatsoever he would*,
and prospered.

13 Then I heard one saint
speaking, and another
saint said unto the one

which spoke, How long
shall the vision of the daily
sacrifice last, and the prevarication of desolation that
places *both* the sanctuary
and the host to be trodden
under foot?

14 And he said unto me,
Unto two thousand and
three hundred *days of*
evening and morning; then
shall the sanctuary be
justified.

15 And it came to pass, as
I, Daniel, was considering
the vision, and seeking to
understand it, behold,
there stood before me the
likeness of a man.

16 And I heard a man's
voice between *the banks of
the* Ulai, which called, and
said, Gabriel, teach this
man the vision.

17 So he came near where
I stood: and with his coming, I was afraid, and fell
upon my face: and he said
unto me, Understand, O
son of man: for at the time
appointed *by God* shall the
vision be fulfilled.

18 Now as he was speaking with me, I fell into a
deep sleep on the ground
upon my face: and he
touched me, and changed
my state.

19 And he said, Behold, I
will show thee that *which* is
to come in the last end of

the wrath: for at the time appointed *this* shall be fulfilled.

20 The ram which thou sawest having *two* horns *are* the kings of Media and Persia.

21 And the he goat *is* the king of Grecia: and the great horn that he *had* between his eyes *is* the first king.

22 Now that being broken, whereas four stood up in its place, *means that* four kingdoms shall stand up out of the nation, but not in his strength.

23 And at the end of their empire, when the prevaricators are come to the full, a king of arrogant countenance, and expert in *casting* doubts, shall raise *himself* up.

24 And his power shall be strengthened, but not by his own power: and he shall destroy marvellously, and shall prosper, and do *according to his will*, and shall destroy the mighty and the people of the saints.

25 And with his understanding he shall cause the deceit in his hand to prosper; and he shall magnify *himself* in his heart, and by peace he shall destroy many: he shall also stand up against the Prince of princes; and without hand he shall be broken.

26 And the vision of the evening and the morning which was told *is* true: wherefore shut thou up the vision; for it *shall be* for many days.

27 And I Daniel was broken, and was sick *certain* days; and after I rose up, I did the king's business; but I was astonished at the vision, and there was no one who could understand it.

Chapter 9

1 In the first year of Darius the son of Ahasuerus, of the seed of the Medes, who was made king over the realm of the Chaldeans;

2 in the first year of his reign, I Daniel saw diligently in the books the number of the years, of which the LORD spoke unto Jeremiah the prophet, which would conclude the desolation of Jerusalem in seventy years.

3 And I turned my face unto the Lord God, seeking him in prayer and supplication, in fasting, and sackcloth, and ashes:

4 And I prayed unto the LORD my God, and made my confession, and said, Now O Lord, *thou* great God who is worthy to be feared, who keepeth the covenant and the mercy with those that love thee, and keep thy commandments;

5 we have sinned, we have committed iniquity, we have done wickedly, and we have been rebels, and we have departed from thy commandments and from thy judgments.

6 We have not hearkened unto thy servants the prophets, which spoke in thy name to our kings, and to our princes, to our fathers, and to all the people of the land.

7 O Lord, the righteousness *belongeth* unto thee, but unto us the confusion of face, as at this day; to the men of Judah, and to the inhabitants of Jerusalem, and unto all Israel, *that are* near, and *that are* far off, through all the lands where thou hast driven them, because of their rebellion with which they have rebelled against thee.

8 O Lord, to us *belongeth* confusion of face, to our kings, to our princes, and to our fathers, because we have sinned against thee.

9 Of the Lord our God is *the ability* to have mercy and to forgive, even though *we* have rebelled against him;

10 and have not listened to the voice of the LORD our God, to walk by his laws, which he set before us by the hand of his servants the prophets.

11 And all Israel transposed thy law, departing by not hearing thy voice; by which the curse has fallen upon us, and the oath that *is* written in the law of Moses, the servant of God, because we have sinned against him.

12 And he hath confirmed his words, which he spoke over us, and over our judges that governed us, by bringing upon us such a great evil: that *such* hath never been done under the whole heaven as hath been done upon Jerusalem.

13 As *it is* written in the law of Moses, all this evil is come upon us: and we never sought the face of the LORD our God, that we might be converted from our iniquities, and understand thy truth.

14 And the LORD hastened upon the chastisement, and brought it upon us: for the LORD our God *is* just in all his works which he hath done: for we did not listen to his voice.

15 And now, O Lord our God, who hast brought thy people forth out of the land of Egypt with a mighty hand, and hast won for thyself a very clear name, as appeareth unto this day; we have sinned, we have done wickedly.

16 O Lord, according to all thy righteousness, let thine anger and thy fury be turned away from thy city Jerusalem, thy holy mountain: because for our sins, and for the iniquities of our fathers, Jerusalem and all thy people is given in reproach to all *that are* about us.

17 Now therefore, O our God, hear the prayer of thy servant, and his supplications, and cause thy face to shine upon thy sanctuary that is made desolate, by the Lord.

18 O my God, incline thine ear, and hear; open thine eyes, and behold our desolations, and the city which is called by thy name: for we do not present our supplications before thee *confiding* in our righteousnesses, but in thy many mercies.

19 O Lord, hear; O Lord, forgive; O Lord, hearken and do; defer not, for thine own sake, O my God: for thy city and thy people are called by thy name.

20 And whiles I *was* speaking, and praying, and confessing my sin and the sin of my people Israel, and presenting my supplication before the LORD my God for the holy mountain of my God;

21 while I *was* yet speaking in prayer, and that man Gabriel, whom I had seen in the vision at the beginning, flying swiftly, touched me about the time of the evening sacrifice.

22 And he caused me to understand, and spoke with me, and said, O Daniel, I am now come forth to cause thee to understand the interpretation.

23 At the beginning of thy supplications the word went forth, and I have come to teach it unto thee; for thou *art a man* greatly beloved: therefore understand the word, and understand the vision.

24 Seventy weeks are determined [*Heb. Cut*] upon thy people and upon thy holy city, to finish the prevarication, and to conclude the sin, and to atone the iniquity, and to bring in the righteousness of the ages, and seal the vision and the prophecy, and to anoint the Holy of Holies.

25 Know therefore and understand, *that* from the going forth of the word to cause *the people* to return and to build Jerusalem unto the Messiah Prince, *there shall be* seven weeks, and sixty-two weeks: *while* the street shall be built again, and the wall, *even* in troublous times.

26 And after the sixty-two weeks the Messiah shall be killed, and shall have nothing: (and the ruling people that shall come shall destroy the city and the sanctuary; whose end *shall be as* a flood, until at the end of the war it shall be cut off *with* desolation.)

27 In one week (they are now seventy) he shall confirm the covenant by many: and at the midst of the week he shall cause the sacrifice and the oblation to cease, and because of the many abominations desolation shall come, even until perfect death shall be poured out upon the abominable *people*.

Chapter 10

1 In the third year of Cyrus king of Persia the Word was revealed unto Daniel, whose name *was called* Belteshazzar; and the Word *was* true, but the time appointed *was* long: and he understood the word, and had intelligence in the vision.

2 In those days I, Daniel, was mourning three weeks of days.

3 I ate no pleasant bread, neither came flesh nor wine in my mouth, neither did I anoint myself at all, until the three weeks of days were fulfilled.

4 And in the four and twentieth day of the first month, as I was by the side of the great river, which *is* Hiddekel;

5 and lifting up my eyes, I saw, and behold a man clothed in linens, whose loins *were* girded with very pure gold:

6 His body *was* like the *stone of* Tarsis [*turquoise*], and his face as a *bolt of* lightning, and his eyes as lamps of fire, and his arms and his feet like in colour to brilliant brass, and the voice of his words like the voice of *an* army.

7 And only I, Daniel, saw that vision: for the men that were with me saw not the vision; but a great fear fell upon them, and they fled and hid themselves.

8 Therefore I was left alone, and saw this great vision, and there remained no strength in me: for my strength was turned into dismay, and I retained no strength.

9 Yet I heard the voice of his words: and when I heard the voice of his words, then was I placed into a deep sleep on my face, and my face *was* toward the ground.

10 And, behold, a hand touched me, and caused me to move upon my knees and *upon* the palms of my hands.

11 And he said unto me, Daniel, O man greatly beloved, pay attention to the words that I shall speak unto thee, and stand up upon thy feet: for I am sent now unto thee. And as he was speaking this with me, I was trembling.

12 And he said unto me, Fear not, Daniel: for from the first day that thou didst give thy heart to understand, and to afflict thy soul before thy God, thy words were heard, and I am come because of thy words.

13 But the prince of the kingdom of Persia withstood me twenty-one days: and behold, Michael, one of the chief princes, came to help me; and I remained there with the kings of Persia.

14 Now I am come to make thee know what shall befall thy people in the latter days: for there shall still *be* vision for *several* days.

15 And as he was speaking such words unto me, I looked toward the ground, and became dumb.

16 And, behold, *one* like the similitude of *the* son of man touched my lips: then I opened my mouth, and spoke, and said unto him that stood before me, O my Lord, by the vision my sorrows are turned upon me, and I have retained no strength.

17 For how can the servant of my Lord talk with my Lord? for as for me, for in that instant I had no more strength in me, neither was there any breath left in me.

18 Then there came again and touched me *one* like the appearance of a man, and he comforted me,

19 and said, O man greatly beloved, fear not: peace *be* unto thee, be of good cheer, and be well. And as he spoke unto me, I was strengthened, and said, Let my Lord speak; for thou hast strengthened me.

20 Then said he, Knowest thou why I have come unto thee? Because now I must return to fight with the prince of the Persians: and when I am gone forth, next the prince of Grecia shall come.

21 But I will interpret unto thee that which is written

in the scripture of truth: and *there is* none that holdeth with me in these *things*, but Michael your prince.

Chapter 11

1 And in the first year of Darius the Mede, I stood to encourage and to strengthen him.

2 And now will I show thee the truth. Behold, there shall yet be three kings in Persia; and the fourth shall obtain far greater riches than *they* all: and by his strengthening himself with his riches he shall stir up all against the realm of Grecia.

3 And a valiant king shall stand up, that shall rule over *a* great dominion, and do according to his will.

4 But when he is reigning, his kingdom shall be broken, and shall be divided by the four winds of heaven; and not to his posterity, nor according to his dominion by which he ruled: for his kingdom shall be plucked up, even for others beside those.

5 And the king of the south, and of his principalities, shall make himself strong; and he shall exceed him, and make himself powerful; his dominion *shall be* a great dominion.

6 But at the end of *some* years they shall join themselves together; for the king's daughter of the south shall come to the king of the north to make an agreement: but she shall not retain the power of the arm; neither shall he stand, nor his arm: for she shall be given up, and they that brought her, and he that begat her, and those that were for her in *this* time.

7 But of the new shoot from her roots shall *one* stand up upon his throne, and shall come unto the army, and shall enter into the fortress of the king of the north, and do in them *according to his will*, and shall prevail:

8 And even their gods, with their princes, with their precious vessels of silver and of gold, shall be taken captive in Egypt; and for *some* years he shall maintain himself against the king of the north.

9 Thus shall the king of the south enter into the kingdom, and return to his own land.

10 But the sons of that one shall be stirred up, and shall assemble a multitude of great armies: and shall come in great haste, and overflow, and pass through, and turn, and come with wrath unto his fortress.

11 Therefore the king of the south shall become furious, and shall come forth and fight with him, *even* with the king of the north: and he shall put a great multitude into *the* field; but all that multitude shall be given into his hand.

12 Therefore the multitude shall be filled with pride, his heart shall be lifted up; and he shall cast down many thousands: but he shall not prevail.

13 And the king of the north shall put another multitude, greater than the former in *the* field, and at the end of a time of some years shall come in great haste with a great army and with much riches.

14 But in those times many shall stand up against the king of the south: and sons of robbers of thy people shall raise themselves up to establish the vision; but they shall fall.

15 So the king of the north shall come, and cast up a mount, and shall take the strong cities: and the arms of the south shall not withstand, neither his chosen people, neither shall there be *any* fortress that can withstand.

16 And he that cometh against him shall do according to his own will, and there shall be no one that can stand before him: and he shall stand in the glorious land, which by his hand shall be consumed.

17 He shall then set his face to come with the strength of his whole kingdom, and shall do upright things with him; and he shall give him a daughter of *his* women to persuade her: but she shall not stand, neither be for him.

18 After this he shall turn his face unto the isles, and shall take many: but a prince shall cause him to cease his affront; and shall even turn his reproach upon him.

19 Then he shall turn his face toward the fortresses of his own land: but he shall stumble and fall, and not appear again.

20 Then shall succeed in his throne a taker of taxes *who shall be the* Glory of the Kingdom: but within few days he shall be broken, neither in anger, nor in battle.

21 And a vile *person* shall succeed in his place, to whom they shall not give the honour of the Kingdom: nevertheless he shall come in with peace, and obtain the kingdom by flatteries.

22 And with the arms they shall be overflown of a flood before him, and shall be broken; yea, also the prince of the covenant.

23 And after the union made with him he shall work deceit: and shall rise, and shall overcome with few people.

24 With the province in peace and in abundance, he shall enter and do *that* which his fathers have never done, nor his fathers' fathers; he shall distribute prey, and spoil, and riches to his soldiers: and against the fortresses he shall forecast his devices, even for *a* time.

25 And he shall stir up his forces and his heart against the king of the south with a great army; and the king of the south shall move to the war with a great and mighty army; but he shall not prevail: for they shall betray him.

26 Even those that ate his bread, shall break him, and his army shall be destroyed: and many shall fall down slain.

27 And the heart of both these kings *shall be* to do evil, and at the same table they shall speak lies; but it shall not prosper: for the time appointed is not yet come.

28 Then shall he return into his land with great riches; and his heart *shall be* against the holy covenant; and he shall do *exploits*, and return to his own land.

29 At the time appointed he shall turn toward the south; but the latter *coming* shall not be as the former.

30 For the ships of Chittim shall come against him: therefore he shall be grieved, and return, and have indignation against the holy covenant: so shall he do; he shall even return, and think of those that have forsaken the holy covenant.

31 And arms shall be placed on his behalf, and they shall pollute the sanctuary of strength, and shall take away the daily *sacrifice*, and they shall place the abomination that maketh desolate.

32 And with flatteries shall he cause to sin those that violate the covenant: but the people that do know their God shall be strong, and do *exploits*.

33 And the wise among the people shall give wisdom to many: yet they shall fall by the sword, and by fire, by captivity, and by spoil, for *some* days.

34 And in their fall, they shall be helped with a little help: but many shall cleave to them with flatteries.

35 And *some* of the wise shall fall to be purged, and cleaned, and made white, *even* to the time of the end: because even for this *there is* time appointed.

36 And the king shall do according to his will; and he shall exalt himself, and magnify himself above every god, and shall speak marvels against the God of gods, and shall prosper until the indignation be accomplished: for the determination has been made.

37 Neither shall he care for the God of his fathers, nor the love of women, nor care for any god: for he shall magnify himself above all.

38 But in his place shall he honour the god of fortresses [*Ala Mahozim*]: *a* god whom his fathers knew not: he shall honour it with gold, and silver, and precious stones, and with things of great price.

39 And with the *people of* the strange god that he shall know, he shall make strong fortresses, increase their glory; and cause them to rule over many, and shall divide the land for gain.

40 But at the end of the time the king of the south shall lock horns with him: and the king of the north shall raise up a storm against him, with chariots, and with horsemen, and with many ships; and he shall enter into the lands, and shall overflow and pass over.

41 He shall come to the glorious land, and many *provinces* shall fall: but these shall escape out of his hand, *even* Edom, and Moab, and the first of the sons of Ammon.

42 He shall stretch forth his hand to the lands: and the land of Egypt shall not escape.

43 And he shall take over the treasures of gold and of silver, and of all the precious things of Egypt, of Libya, and Ethiopia where he passes.

44 But tidings out of the east and out of the north shall trouble him: therefore he shall go forth with great fury to destroy, and to kill many.

45 And he shall plant the tents of his palace between the seas, in the desirable mountain of the Sanctuary; and he shall come to his end, and shall have no one to help him.

Chapter 12

1 And at that time shall Michael stand up, the great prince who is for the sons of thy people: and it shall be a time of trouble, such as never was since there were people until now: but in that time thy people shall escape, all those that are found written in the book.

2 And many of them that sleep in the dust of the earth shall be awakened, some for eternal life, and some for shame *and* everlasting confusion.

3 And they that understand shall shine as the brightness of the firmament; and they that teach righteousness *to* the multitude as the stars in perpetual eternity.

4 But thou, O Daniel, shut up the words, and seal the book until the time of the end: many shall pass by, and knowledge shall be multiplied.

5 Then I Daniel looked, and, behold, another two who stood, one on this side of the bank of the river, and the other on that side of the bank of the river.

6 And *one* said to the Man clothed in linens, who *was* upon the waters of the river, When *shall be* the end of these wonders?

7 And I heard the Man clothed in linens, who *was* upon the waters of the river, who raised his right hand and his left hand unto heaven, and swore by the Living one in the ages, that *it shall be* for *a* time, times, and an half; and when the scattering of the power of the holy people shall be finished, all these *things* shall be fulfilled.

8 And I heard, but I did not understand: then I said, O my Lord, what *is* the fulfilment of these things?

9 And he said, Go thy way, Daniel: for these words *are* closed up and sealed until the time of the fulfilment.

10 Many shall be purified, and made white, and purged; but *the* wicked shall get worse: and none of the wicked shall understand; but the wise shall understand.

11 And from the time *that* the daily *sacrifice* is taken away until the abomination of desolation, *there shall be* a thousand two hundred and ninety days.

12 Blessed *is* he that waiteth, and cometh unto one thousand three hundred and thirty-five days.

13 And thou shall go to the end, and shalt rest, and thou shalt raise up in thy lot at the end of the days.

The Prophecies of
Hosea

Chapter 1

1 The word of the LORD that came unto Hosea, the son of Beeri, in the days of Uzziah, Jotham, Ahaz, *and* Hezekiah, kings of Judah, and in the days of Jeroboam the son of Joash, king of Israel.

2 The beginning of the word of the LORD with Hosea. And the LORD said to Hosea, Go, take unto thee a wife of whoredoms and children of whoredoms: for the land shall give itself over to whoredom *by* departing from the LORD.

3 So he went and took Gomer the daughter of Diblaim; which conceived, and bare him a son.

4 And the LORD said unto him, Call his name Jezreel; for yet a little *while*, and I will visit the blood of Jezreel upon the house of Jehu, and will cause the kingdom of the house of Israel to cease.

5 And it shall come to pass in that day, that I will break the bow of Israel in the valley of Jezreel.

6 And she conceived again, and bare a daughter. And *God* said unto him, Call her name Loruhamah: for I will never again have mercy upon the house of Israel; but I will utterly forget them.

7 But I will have mercy upon the house of Judah, and will save them in the LORD their God, and will not save them by bow, by sword, by battle, by horses, nor by horsemen.

8 And after she had weaned Loruhamah, she conceived, and bare a son.

9 Then said *God*, Call his name Loammi: for ye *are* not my people, and I will not be your *God*.

10 With all *this*, the number of the sons of Israel shall be as the sand of the sea, which cannot be measured nor numbered; and it shall come to pass, *that* in the place where it was said unto them, Ye *are* not my people, *there* it shall be said unto them, *Ye are* the sons of the living God.

11 And the sons of Judah and the sons of Israel shall be congregated together, and they shall raise up for themselves one head, and they shall rise up from the land: for the day of Jezreel *is* great.

Chapter 2

1 Say ye unto your brethren, Ammi; and to your sisters, Ruhamah.

2 Contend with your mother, contend: for she *is* not my wife, neither *am* I her husband: let her therefore remove her whoredoms from her face, and her adulteries from between her breasts;

3 lest I strip her naked, and set her as in the day that she was born, and make her as a wilderness, and set her like a dry land, and slay her with thirst.

4 Neither will I have mercy upon her sons; for they *are* the sons of whoredoms.

5 For their mother hath played the harlot: she that conceived them hath been shamed: for she said, I will go after my lovers, that give *me* my bread and my water, my wool and my flax, my oil and my drink.

6 Therefore, behold, I will hedge up thy way with thorns, and make a wall, that she shall not find her paths.

7 And she shall follow after her lovers, but she shall not overtake them; and she shall seek *them*, but shall not find *them*: then shall she say, I will go and return to my first husband; for then *was it* better with me than now.

8 For she did not recognise that I gave her the wheat, and the wine, and the oil, and multiplied unto them the silver and the gold, *with which* they made Baal.

9 Therefore will I return, and take away my wheat in the time thereof, and my wine in the season thereof, and will recover my wool and my flax that *I* had given to cover her nakedness.

10 And now *I* will uncover her folly in the sight of her lovers, and none shall deliver her out of my hand.

11 I will also cause all her mirth to cease, her feast,

her new moon, and her sabbath, and all her festivities.
12 And I will cause her vine
and her fig tree to be cut
down, of which she hath
said, These *are* my wages
that my lovers have given
me: and I will reduce them
to a thicket, and the beasts
of the field shall eat them.
13 And I will visit upon her
the times of the Baals, unto
whom she burned incense,
and she adorned herself
with her earrings and her
jewels, and she went after
her lovers, oblivious of me,
saith the LORD.

14 Therefore, behold, I will
induce her, and bring her
into the wilderness, and
speak unto her heart.
15 And I will give her vineyards from thence, and the
valley of Achor for a door of
hope: and she shall sing
there, as in the days of her
youth, and as in the day
when she came up out of
the land of Egypt.
16 And it shall be in that
time, saith the LORD, *that*
thou shalt call me My Husband; and shalt call me no
more Baali.
17 For I will take away the
names of Baals out of her
mouth, and they shall no
more be remembered by
their name.

18 And in that time I will
make a covenant for them
with the beasts of the field,
and with the fowls of the
heaven, and *with* the serpents of the earth: and I will
break *the* bow and *the*
sword and *the* battle of the
earth, and will cause them
to sleep safely.
19 And I will betroth thee
unto me for ever; yea, I will
betroth thee unto me in
righteousness, and in judgment, and in mercy.
20 I will even betroth thee
unto me in faith: and thou
shalt know the LORD.
21 And it shall come to
pass in that day, I will respond, saith the LORD, I will
respond to the heavens,
and they shall respond to
the earth;
22 and the earth shall respond to the wheat, and the
wine, and the oil; and they
shall respond to Jezreel.
23 And I will sow her unto
me in the earth; and I will
have mercy upon Loruha-
mah, [*her that had not obtained mercy*]; and I will say
to Loammi, [*them which
were not my people*], Thou
art my people; and he shall
say, *Thou art* my God.

Chapter 3

1 Then said the LORD unto me again, Go, love a woman beloved of *her* friend, yet an adulteress, according to the love of the LORD toward the sons of Israel, who look to other gods, and love flagons of wine.

2 So I bought her for myself for fifteen *pieces* of silver, and a homer and a half of barley:

3 And I said unto her, Thou shalt abide for me many days; thou shalt not play the harlot, and thou shalt not be for *another* man: so *will* I also *be* for thee.

4 For the sons of Israel shall abide many days without king, and without Lord, and without sacrifice, and without image, and *without* teraphim:

5 Afterward shall the sons of Israel return, and they shall seek the LORD their God, and David their king; and they shall fear the LORD and his goodness in the end of the days.

Chapter 4

1 Hear *the* word of the LORD, *ye* sons of Israel: for the LORD contendeth with the inhabitants of the land, because *there is* no truth, nor mercy, nor knowledge of God in the earth.

2 By swearing, and lying, and killing, and stealing, and committing adultery, they prevailed, and blood toucheth blood.

3 Therefore shall the earth mourn, and every one that dwelleth therein shall be cut off, with the beasts of the field, and the fowls of heaven; and even the fishes of the sea shall be caught.

4 Certainly man *does* not contend *with* nor reprehend man: for thy people *are* as they that resist the priest.

5 Therefore shalt thou fall in the day, and the prophet also shall fall with thee by night, and I will cut off thy mother.

6 My people were cut off, because they lacked wisdom: because thou hast rejected wisdom, I will cast thee out of the priesthood: *seeing* thou hast forgotten the law of thy God, I will also forget thy sons.

7 According to their greatness, so did they sin against me: *therefore* will I change their honour into shame.

8 They eat up the sin of my people, and in their iniquity they raise up their soul.

9 The people shall become like the priest: and I will

visit his ways upon him, and they shall reward him according to his doings.

10 For they shall eat, and not be satisfied: they shall commit whoredom, and shall not increase: because they have quit showing hospitality unto the LORD.

11 Whoredom and wine and new wine take away the heart.

12 My people ask counsel of their wooden *idol*, and their stick declareth unto them: for the spirit of whoredoms hath caused *them* to err, and they have gone a whoring under their gods.

13 They sacrifice upon the tops of the mountains, and burn incense upon the hills, under oaks and poplars and elms, that had good shade: therefore your daughters shall commit whoredom, and your daughters-in-law shall commit adultery.

14 I will not visit upon your daughters when they commit whoredom, nor upon your daughters-in-law when they commit adultery: for they offer with whores, and they sacrifice with harlots: therefore the people without understanding shall fall.

15 Though thou, Israel, play the harlot, *yet* let not Judah sin; and come not ye unto Gilgal, neither go ye up to Bethaven, nor swear, The LORD liveth.

16 For Israel hath turned away as a wild heifer: shall the LORD now feed them as rams in a large place?

17 Ephraim *is* given over to idols: leave him.

18 Their drink has become corrupted: they have committed whoredom continually: her princes love gifts, shamefully.

19 The wind hath bound her up in her wings, and they shall be ashamed because of their sacrifices.

Chapter 5

1 Hear ye this, O priests; and hearken, ye house of Israel; and give ye ear, O house of the king; because the judgment *is* for you, for ye have been a snare in Mizpah, and a net spread over Tabor.

2 And in killing sacrifices ye have descended into the depths; therefore, I *shall be* the correction of them all.

3 I know Ephraim, and Israel is not hid from me: for now, O Ephraim, thou committest whoredom, *and* Israel is defiled.

4 They will not think about returning unto their God: for the spirit of whoredoms *is* in the midst of them, and they do not know the LORD.

5 And the pride of Israel doth testify to his face: therefore shall Israel and Ephraim fall in their iniquity; Judah also shall fall with them.

6 They shall go with their flocks and with their herds seeking the LORD; but they shall not find *him*; he hath withdrawn himself from them.

7 They have rebelled against the LORD: for they have begotten strange children: now shall a month devour them with their portions.

8 Blow ye the shophar in Gibeah, *and* the trumpet in Ramah; sound the drum in Bethaven; after thee, O Benjamin.

9 Ephraim shall be made desolate *in* the day of chastisement: in the tribes of Israel I made known *my* truth.

10 The princes of Judah were like them that move the boundaries: *therefore* I will pour out my wrath upon them like water.

11 Ephraim *is* oppressed *and* broken in judgment, because he wanted to walk after commandments.

12 Therefore *will* I *be* unto Ephraim as a moth, and to the house of Judah as rottenness.

13 And Ephraim shall see his sickness, and Judah his wound, *then* Ephraim shall go to the Assyrian, and shall send to king Jareb: yet he shall not be able to heal you, nor cure you of your wound.

14 For I *will be* unto Ephraim as a lion, and as a young lion to the house of Judah: I, *even* I, will tear and go away; I will take away, and there shall be no one *left* to escape.

15 I will go *and* return to my place, until they acknowledge their sin, and seek my face: in their affliction they will seek me early.

Chapter 6

1 Come, and let us return unto the LORD: for he hath torn, and he will heal us; he hath smitten, and he will bind us up.

2 After two days he shall give us life: in the third day he will resurrect us, and we shall live in his sight.

3 And we shall know, and follow on in knowing the LORD: his going forth is prepared as the dawn; and he shall come unto us as the rain, as the latter *and* former rain unto the earth.

4 O Ephraim, what shall I do unto thee? O Judah, what shall I do unto thee? Your mercy *is* as a morning cloud, and as the early dew it goeth away.

5 Therefore have I hewed *them* by the prophets; I have slain them by the words of my mouth: that thy righteousness *be* as the light *that* goeth forth.

6 For I desired mercy, and not sacrifice; and the knowledge of God more than burnt offerings.

7 But they have transposed the covenant as of men: there have they rebelled against me.

8 Gilead *is* a city of them that work iniquity, *and is* polluted with blood.

9 And as troops of robbers wait for a man, *so* the council of priests murder in the way by common accord: for they put the abomination into effect.

10 I saw uncleanness in the house of Israel: there Ephraim played the harlot, Israel defiled herself.

11 Also, Judah, placed *a* plant in thee, when I had turned the captivity of my people.

Chapter 7

1 When I was healing Israel, the iniquity of Ephraim was uncovered, and the wickedness of Samaria: for they worked deceit; and the thief cometh in, *and* the troop of robbers spoileth without.

2 And they consider not in their hearts *that* I remember all their wickedness: now their own doings have beset them about; they are before my face.

3 They make the king glad with their wickedness, and the princes with their lies.

4 They *are* all adulterers, as an oven heated by the baker, *who* shall cease from waking after he hath kneaded the dough, until it be leavened.

5 In the day of our king the princes have made *him* sick with *a* wineskin; he stretched out his hand with the scorners.

6 For they have made ready their heart like an oven, whiles they lie in wait: their baker sleepeth all the night; in the morning it burneth as a flaming fire.

7 They are all hot as an oven, and have devoured their judges; all their kings are fallen: *there is* none among them that calleth unto me.

8 Ephraim, he hath mixed himself among the peoples; Ephraim is a cake not turned.

9 Strangers have devoured his strength, and he knoweth *it* not: yea, gray hairs are here and there upon him, yet he understandeth not.

10 And the pride of Israel shall testify to his face: and they have not returned to the LORD their God, nor have they sought him with all this.

11 Ephraim also was like a deceived dove, without understanding: they shall call to Egypt, they shall go to Assyria.

12 When they shall go, I will spread my net upon them; I will bring them down as the fowls of the heaven; I will chastise them according to what has been heard in their congregations.

13 Woe unto them! for they have fled from me: destruction upon them! because they have rebelled against me: *though* I have redeemed them, yet they have spoken lies against me.

14 And they have not cried unto me with their heart, when they howled upon their beds: they congregated themselves for the wheat and the wine, *and* they rebelled against me.

15 Though I have bound *and* strengthened their arms, yet do they imagine evil against me.

16 They returned, *but* not to the most High: they were like a deceitful bow: their princes fell by the sword for the arrogance of their tongue: this *shall be* their derision in the land of Egypt.

Chapter 8

1 *Set* the shophar to thy mouth. *He shall come* as an eagle against the house of the LORD, because they have transgressed my covenant, and rebelled against my law.

2 Israel shall cry unto me, My God, we have known thee.

3 Israel hath cast off the good: the enemy shall pursue him.

4 They have reigned, but not by me: they have made dominion, and I knew *it* not: of their silver and their gold have they made themselves idols, that they may be cut off.

5 Thy calf, O Samaria, hath cast *thee* off; my anger has been kindled against them, until they could no longer be absolved.

6 For it is of Israel: and *a* workman made it; who is not God: because the calf of Samaria shall be broken in pieces.

7 For they have sown the wind, and they shall reap the whirlwind: they shall have no harvest: the fruit shall yield no meal: if so be it yield, the strangers shall swallow it up.

8 Israel shall be swallowed up: soon shall they be among the Gentiles as a vessel wherein *is* no pleasure.

9 For they are gone up to Assyria, a wild ass *thinking* only of himself: Ephraim hath hired lovers.

10 Even though they hire the Gentiles, now will I gather them, and they shall sorrow a little for the burden of the king and of the princes.

11 Because Ephraim hath multiplied altars for sin, he hath had altars for sin.

12 I have written to him the great things of my law, *but* they were counted as strange things.

13 In the sacrifices of my gifts they sacrificed flesh, and did eat; *but* the LORD accepteth them not; now will he remember their iniquity, and visit their sins: they shall return to Egypt.

14 For Israel hath forgotten his Maker, and hath built temples; and Judah hath multiplied fenced cities: but I will send a fire upon his cities, and it shall devour the palaces thereof.

Chapter 9

1 Rejoice not, O Israel, for joy, as the peoples: for thou hast gone a whoring from thy God, thou hast loved the *salary of an harlot* upon every threshing floor.

2 The threshing floor and the winepress shall not feed them, and the new wine shall fail in her.

3 They shall not remain in the land of the LORD; but Ephraim shall return to Egypt, and to Assyria where they shall eat unclean food.

4 They shall not pour out wine unto the LORD, neither shall he take pleasure in their sacrifices: as the bread of mourners *shall they be* unto them; all that eat thereof shall be polluted: for their bread shall not enter into the house of the LORD because of their soul.

5 What will ye do in the solemn day, and *in* the day of the feast of the LORD?

6 For, behold, they have left because of the destruction: Egypt shall gather them up, Memphis shall bury them:

nettles shall possess in inheritance that which is desirable of their silver: thorns *shall grow up* in their dwellings.

7 The days of visitation are come, the days of recompense are come; Israel shall know *it*: the prophet *is* a fool, the spiritual man *is* a fool, for the multitude of thine iniquity, and *the* great hatred.

8 The watchman of Ephraim regarding my God, the prophet, *is a* snare of *a* fowler in all his ways, hatred in the house of his God.

9 They have arrived at the depths, they have corrupted *themselves* as in the days of Gibeah: *therefore* he will remember their iniquity, he will visit their sin.

10 I found Israel like grapes in the wilderness; I saw your fathers as the early fruit of the fig tree in her beginning: *but* they went in unto Baalpeor, and separated themselves unto shame; and made themselves as abominable as that which they loved.

11 *As for* Ephraim, their glory shall fly away like a bird, from the birth, even from the womb, and from the conception.

12 Though they bring up their children, yet will I bereave them, *that there shall* not *be* a man *left*: yea, woe also to them when I depart from them!

13 Ephraim, as I saw Tyre, *is* planted in a pleasant place: but Ephraim shall bring forth his children to the murderer.

14 Give them, O LORD: that which thou must give them; give them a miscarrying womb and dry breasts.

15 All their wickedness *was* in Gilgal: for there I took a dislike to them: for the wickedness of their doings I will drive them out of my house, I will never love them again: all their princes *are* disloyal.

16 Ephraim was smitten, their root is dried up, they shall bear no more fruit: yea, though they bring forth, yet will I slay *even* the desirable *fruit* of their womb.

17 My God will cast them away, because they did not hearken unto him: and they shall be wanderers among the Gentiles.

Chapter 10

1 Israel *is* an empty vine. Shall he bring forth fruit unto himself? According to the multiplication of his fruit he hath multiplied altars; according to the goodness of his land they have bettered their statues.

2 Their heart has wandered; now shall they be convinced: he shall break down their altars, he shall destroy their statues.

3 For now they shall say, We have no king, because we feared not the LORD; what then should a king do to us?

4 They have spoken words, swearing falsely in making a covenant: thus judgment springeth up as hemlock in the furrows of the field.

5 The inhabitants of Samaria shall fear because of the calves of Bethaven: for the people thereof shall mourn because of the calf, and the priests thereof *that* rejoiced on it, for the glory thereof, which shall be made to vanish away.

6 It shall be also carried unto Assyria *for* a present to king Jareb: Ephraim shall be ashamed, and Israel shall be confused at his own counsel.

7 *As for* Samaria, her king is cut off as the foam upon the surface of the waters.

8 And the altars of Aven shall be destroyed, the sin of Israel: the thorn and the thistle shall grow upon their altars; and they shall say to the mountains, Cover us; and to the hills, Fall on us.

9 O Israel, thou hast sinned from the days of Gibeah: there they stood: the battle in Gibeah against the children of iniquity did not overtake them.

10 And I shall chastise them as I desire; and *the* peoples shall gather themselves over them, when they shall be bound in their two furrows.

11 Ephraim *is* an heifer *that is* taught, *and* loveth to tread out *the wheat*; but I shall pass over upon her fair neck: I will make Ephraim to bear *the yoke*; Judah shall plow, *and* Jacob shall break his clods.

12 Sow yourselves unto righteousness, reap yourselves unto mercy; break up your fallow ground: for *it is* the time to seek the LORD, until he come and teach you righteousness.

13 Ye have plowed wickedness, ye have reaped iniquity; ye shall eat the fruit of lies: because thou didst trust in thy way, *and* in the multitude of thy mighty men.

14 Therefore, in thy peoples a tumult shall arise, and all thy fortresses shall be destroyed, as Shalman destroyed Betharbel in the day of battle: the mother

was dashed in pieces upon
her children.
15 So shall Bethel do unto
you because of your great
wickedness: in the morning
shall the king of Israel utterly be cut off.

Chapter 11

1 When Israel *was* a boy, I
loved him, and called my
son out of Egypt.
2 *As* they called them, so
they went from them: they
sacrificed unto Baalim, and
burned incense to graven
images.
3 Even with all this I guided
the feet of *this* same
Ephraim, taking them by
their arms; but they knew
not that I cared for them.
4 I drew them with human
cords, with bands of love:
and I was to them as they
that raise the yoke from
upon their cheeks, and I fed
them.
5 He shall not return into
the land of Egypt, but the
Assyrian shall be his king,
because they refused to be
converted.
6 And the sword shall fall
upon his cities, and shall
consume his villages, and
devour *them*, because of
their own counsels.
7 Meanwhile, my people
adhere to the rebellion
against me: though they
call unto me upon High,

absolutely none at all wish
to exalt me.
8 How must I leave thee,
Ephraim? *how* shall I give
thee up, Israel? how could
I make thee as Admah? nor
set thee as Zeboim? my
heart churns within me, all
my compassion is inflamed.
9 I will not execute the
fierceness of my anger, I will
not return to destroy
Ephraim: for I *am* God, and
not man; the Holy One in
the midst of thee: and I will
not enter into the city.
10 They shall walk after the
LORD: he shall roar like a
lion: when he shall roar,
then the sons shall come
trembling from the west.
11 As a bird they shall
move speedily out of Egypt,
and as a dove out of the
land of Assyria: and I will
place them in their houses,
saith the LORD.
12 Ephraim compasseth
me about with lies, and the
house of Israel with deceit:
but Judah yet ruleth with
God, and is faithful with the
saints.

Chapter 12

1 Ephraim feedeth on wind,
and followeth after the east
wind: he daily increaseth
lies and desolation; because
they made a covenant with
the Assyrians, and *the* oil
is carried into Egypt.

2 The LORD hath also a controversy with Judah to visit Jacob according to his ways; according to his doings will he recompense him.

3 He took his brother by the heel in the womb, and with his strength he overcame the angel:

4 Yea, he overcame the angel, and prevailed: he wept, and made supplication unto him: he found him *in* Bethel, and there he spoke with us;

5 But the LORD is God of the hosts; the LORD *is* his memorial.

6 Therefore be thou converted unto thy God: keep mercy and judgment, and in thy God wait continually.

7 *He is* a merchant who hath the balances of deceit in his hand: he loveth to oppress.

8 And Ephraim said, Surely I have become rich, I have found riches for myself: no one shall find iniquity in me, nor sin in all my labours.

9 But I *am* the LORD thy God from the land of Egypt; I will yet make thee to dwell in tents, as in the days of the solemn feast.

10 I have also spoken by the prophets, and I have multiplied visions, and used similitudes, by the ministry of the prophets.

11 Is Gilead iniquity? surely they are vanity: they sacrifice bullocks in Gilgal; yea, their altars *are* as heaps in the furrows of the fields.

12 But Jacob fled into the land of Aram, and Israel served for *his* wife, and for *his* wife he was a pastor.

13 And by *a* prophet the LORD brought Israel out of Egypt, and by *a* prophet was he preserved.

14 Ephraim provoked *God* to anger with bitterness: therefore his blood shall be spilled upon him, and his reproach shall his Lord repay unto him.

Chapter 13

1 When Ephraim spoke *everyone* feared, he was exalted in Israel; but he sinned in Baal, and died.

2 And now they have added to their sin, and of their silver they have made molten images according to their own understanding, idols, all of it the work of the craftsmen: they say of them, Let the men that sacrifice kiss the calves.

3 Therefore they shall be as the morning mist, and as the early dew that passeth away, as the chaff *that* is driven with the whirlwind out of the threshing floor, and as the smoke out of the chimney.

4 Yet I *am* the LORD thy God from the land of Egypt, therefore thou shalt know no God other than me; nor any other saviour but me.

5 I knew thee in the wilderness, in the dry land.

6 In their pastures, they filled themselves; they were satisfied, and their heart was exalted; for this reason they have forgotten me.

7 Therefore I will be unto them as a lion: as a tiger in the way will I observe *them*:

8 I will meet them as a bear *that is bereaved of her whelps*, and will rend the veil of their heart, and there will I devour them like a lion: the wild beast shall tear them apart.

9 O Israel, thou hast caused thyself to become lost; but in me *is* thine help.

10 Where is thy king, that may save thee with all thy cities? and thy judges of whom thou saidst, Give me a king and princes?

11 I gave thee a king in my anger, and took *him* away in my wrath.

12 The iniquity of Ephraim *is* bound up; his sin *is* hid.

13 The sorrows of a travailing woman shall come upon him: he *is* an unwise son; for a long time now he should not have stopped short at the very breaking forth of birth.

14 I will ransom them from the power of the grave; I will redeem them from death: O death, I will be thy end; O grave, I will be thy destruction: repentance shall be hid from my eyes.

15 Though he be fruitful among *his* brethren, the east wind shall come, the wind of the LORD shall come up from the wilderness, and his spring shall become dry, and his fountain shall be dried up: he shall spoil the treasure of all the vessels of desire.

16 Samaria shall become desolate; for she hath rebelled against her God: they shall fall by the sword: their infants shall be dashed in pieces, and their women with child shall be ripped open.

Chapter 14

1 O Israel, become converted unto the LORD thy God; for thou hast fallen by thine iniquity.

2 Take with you words, and be converted unto the LORD: say unto him, Take away all iniquity, and receive *us* graciously: so will we render the calves of our lips.

3 Asshur shall not save us; we will not ride upon horses: neither will we say any more to the work of our hands, *Ye are* our gods: for in thee the fatherless findeth mercy.

4 I will heal their rebellion, I will love them freely: for my anger is turned away from them.

5 I will be as the dew unto Israel: he shall flourish as the lily, and cast forth his roots as Lebanon.

6 His branches shall spread, and his glory shall be as the olive tree, and his smell as Lebanon.

7 They that shall sit under his shadow shall return; they shall be given life *as the* wheat, and they shall flourish as the vine: the scent thereof *shall be* as the wine of Lebanon.

8 Ephraim *shall then say*, What have I to do any more with idols? I will hear *him*, and gaze upon him: I *will be unto him* like a green fir tree; of me shall thy fruit be found.

9 Who *is* wise that he might understand this? and prudent, that he might know this? for the ways of the LORD *are* right, and the just shall walk in them: but the rebellious shall fall therein.

The Prophecy of

Joel

Chapter 1

1 The word of the LORD that went to Joel the son of Pethuel.

2 Hear this, ye old men, and give ear, all ye inhabitants of the earth. Hath this been in your days, or even in the days of your fathers?

3 Tell ye your children of it, and *let* your children *tell* their children, and their children another generation.

4 That which the palmerworm hath left hath the locust eaten; and that which the locust hath left hath the cankerworm eaten; and that which the cankerworm hath left hath the caterpillar eaten.

5 Awake, ye drunkards, and weep; and howl, all ye drinkers of wine, because of the new wine; for it is cut off from your mouth.

6 For a people has come up upon my land, strong, and without number, whose teeth *are* the teeth of a lion, and he hath the molars of a *great* lion.

7 He hath laid my vine waste, and barked my fig tree: he hath made it clean bare, and cast *it* away; the branches thereof are made white.

8 Lament like a young woman girded with sackcloth for the husband of her youth.

9 The grain offering and the drink offering of the house of the LORD hath perished; the priests, the LORD'S ministers, mourn.

10 The field was destroyed, the land mourneth; for the wheat was destroyed: the new wine was dried up, the oil perished.

11 Be ye ashamed, O ye husbandmen; howl, O ye

vinedressers, for the wheat and for the barley; because the harvest of the field is lost.

12 The vine has dried up, and the fig tree hath perished; the pomegranate tree, the palm tree also, and the apple tree, *even* all the trees of the field, have withered: therefore joy has withered away from the sons of men.

13 Gird yourselves, and lament, ye priests: howl, ye ministers of the altar: come, lie all night in sackcloth, ye ministers of my God: for the grain offering and the drink offering is taken away from the house of your God.

14 Sanctify ye a fast, call a solemn assembly, gather the elders *and* all the inhabitants of the earth *into* the house of the LORD your God, and cry unto the LORD.

15 Alas for the day! for the day of the LORD *is* at hand, and as a destruction from the Almighty shall it come.

16 Is not the food cut off before our eyes, *yea*, joy and gladness from the house of our God?

17 The seed has rotted under their clods, the storehouses were laid desolate, the barns were destroyed; for the wheat is withered.

18 How do the beasts groan! the herds of cattle are perplexed, because they have no pasture; *yea*, the flocks of sheep are also made desolate.

19 O LORD, to thee will I cry: for *the* fire hath devoured the pastures of the wilderness, and *the* flame hath burned all the trees of the field.

20 The beasts of the field cry also unto thee: for the rivers of waters are dried up, and *the* fire hath devoured the meadows of the wilderness.

Chapter 2

1 Blow ye the shophar in Zion, and sound an alarm in my holy mountain: let all the inhabitants of the earth tremble: for the day of the LORD cometh, for *it is* nigh at hand;

2 A day of darkness and of gloominess, a day of clouds and of shadow, that spreadeth itself upon the mountains as the dawn: a people great and strong; there hath not been ever the like, neither shall be any more after him, *even* to the years of many generations.

3 A fire devoureth before him; and behind him a flame burneth: the earth *is* as the garden of Eden before him, and behind him a desolate wilderness; yea, and no one shall escape him.

4 His appearance *is* as the appearance of horses; and as horsemen, so shall they run.

5 Like the thunder of chariots shall they leap over the tops of mountains, like the noise of a flame of fire that devoureth the stubble, as a strong people set in battle array.

6 Before him the peoples shall fear: all faces shall go pale.

7 They shall run like mighty men; they shall climb the wall like men of war; and they shall march every one in his ways, and they shall not break his ranks:

8 No one shall crowd his companion; they shall walk every one in his path: and *even* falling upon the sword, they shall not be wounded.

9 They shall go through the city; they shall run upon the wall, they shall climb up upon the houses; they shall enter in at the windows like a thief.

10 The earth shall quake before him; the heavens shall tremble: the sun and the moon shall go dark, and the stars shall withdraw their shining:

11 And the LORD shall utter his voice before his army: for many are his camps and strong, that execute his word: for the day of the LORD *is* great, and very terrible; and who can abide it?

12 Therefore also now, saith the LORD, turn ye unto me with all your heart, and with fasting, and with weeping, and with mourning:

13 And rend your heart, and not your garments, and turn unto the LORD your God: for he *is* gracious and merciful, slow to anger, and great in mercy, and he doth repent of chastisement.

14 Who knoweth *if* he will return and repent, and leave a blessing behind him; *even* a grain offering and a drink offering unto the LORD your God?

15 Blow the shophar in Zion, sanctify a fast, call a solemn assembly:

16 Gather the people, sanctify the meeting, assemble the elders, gather the children, and those that suck the breasts: let the bridegroom go forth of his chamber, and the bride out of her closet.

17 Let the priests, the ministers of the LORD, weep between the porch and the altar, and let them say, Forgive thy people, O LORD, and give not thine heritage to reproach, that the Gentiles should rule over her: wherefore should they say among the people, Where *is* their God?

18 Then will the LORD be jealous for his earth, and forgive his people.
19 Yea, the LORD will answer and say unto his people, Behold, I will send you bread, and new wine, and oil, and ye shall be satisfied therewith: and I will no longer make you a reproach among the Gentiles.
20 But I will remove far off from you he of the north *wind*, and will drive him into a land barren and desolate, his face shall be toward the east sea, and his end unto the western sea, and he shall exhale his foul odour, and he shall decompose, because he hath lifted himself up.
21 Fear not, O land; be glad and rejoice: for the LORD hath done great things.
22 Be not afraid, ye animals of the field: for the pastures of the wilderness shall become green again, for the trees shall bear their fruit, the fig tree and the vine shall give their fruits.

23 Ye also, children of Zion, be glad and rejoice in the LORD your God: for he hath given you the former rain moderately, and he will cause to come down for you the rain, the former rain, and the latter rain *as* in the beginning.
24 And the floors shall be full of wheat, and the vats shall overflow with wine and oil.
25 And I will restore to you the years that the caterpillar hath eaten, the locust, and the cankerworm, and the palmerworm, my great army which I sent among you.
26 And ye shall eat in plenty, and be satisfied, and praise the name of the LORD your God, that hath dealt wondrously with you: and my people shall never again be ashamed.
27 And ye shall know that I *am* in the midst of Israel, and *that* I *am* the LORD your God, and *there is* none other: and my people shall never be ashamed.
28 And it shall come to pass after this, *that* I will pour out my Spirit upon all flesh; and your sons and your daughters shall prophesy, your old men shall dream dreams, your young men shall see visions:

29 And even upon the servants and upon the handmaids in those days will I pour out my spirit.

30 And I will show wonders in the heaven and in the earth, blood, and fire, and pillars of smoke.

31 The sun shall be turned into darkness, and the moon into blood, before the great and the terrible day of the LORD come.

32 And it shall come to pass, *that* whosoever shall call on the name of the LORD shall escape: for in mount Zion and in Jerusalem shall be salvation, as the LORD hath said, and in those who are left, to whom the LORD shall have called.

Chapter 3

1 For, behold, in those days, and in that time, when I shall cause the captivity of Judah and Jerusalem to end,

2 I will gather together all the Gentiles, and will cause them to descend into the valley of Jehoshaphat, and there I will enter into judgment with them because of my people and of my heritage Israel, whom they scattered among the nations, and parted my land.

3 And they have cast lots for my people; and have given a boy for an harlot, and sold a girl for wine, that they might drink.

4 Yea, and what have ye to do with me, O Tyre, and Zidon, and all the coasts of Palestine? will ye render me a recompense? and if ye recompense me, swiftly *and* speedily I will return your recompense upon your own head;

5 Because ye have taken my silver and my gold, and have carried into your temples my precious and beautiful things;

6 and ye have sold the children of Judah and the children of Jerusalem unto the Grecians, that ye might remove them far from their border.

7 Behold, I will raise them out of the place where ye have sold them, and will return your recompense upon your own head:

8 And I will sell your sons and your daughters into the hand of the children of Judah, and they shall sell them to the Sabeans, to a people far off: for the LORD hath spoken *it*.

9 Proclaim ye this among the Gentiles; Prepare war, wake up the mighty men, let all the men of war draw near; let them come up:

10 Beat your plowshares into swords, and your

pruninghooks into spears: let the weak say, I *am* strong.

11 Assemble yourselves, and come, all ye Gentiles, and gather yourselves together round about: thither cause thy mighty ones to come down, O LORD.

12 Let the Gentiles be wakened, and come up to the valley of Jehoshaphat: for there will I sit to judge all the Gentiles round about.

13 Put ye in the sickle, for the harvest is ripe: come, get you down; for the press is full, the vats overflow; for their wickedness *is* great.

14 Multitudes, multitudes in the valley of decision: for the day of the LORD *is* near in the valley of decision.

15 The sun and the moon shall be darkened, and the stars shall withdraw their shining.

16 The LORD also shall roar out of Zion, and utter his voice from Jerusalem; and the heavens and the earth shall shake: but the LORD *will be* the hope of his people, and the strength of the sons of Israel.

17 So shall ye know that I *am* the LORD your God, that I inhabit Zion, the mountain of my holiness: then shall Jerusalem be holy, and there shall no strangers pass through her any more.

18 And it shall come to pass in that day, *that* the mountains shall drop down new wine, and the hills shall flow with milk, and all the rivers of Judah shall flow with waters, and a fountain shall come forth of the house of the LORD, and shall water the valley of Shittim.

19 Egypt shall be a desolation, and Edom shall be a desolate wilderness, for the violence *against* the children of Judah, because they have shed innocent blood in their land.

20 But Judah shall dwell for ever, and Jerusalem from generation to generation.

21 For I will cleanse the blood *of those whom* I have not cleansed: for the LORD dwelleth in Zion.

The Prophet

Amos

Chapter 1

1 The words of Amos, who was among the pastors of Tekoa, which he saw concerning Israel in the days of Uzziah king of Judah, and in the days of Jeroboam the son of Joash king of Israel, two years before the earthquake.
2 And he said, The LORD will roar from Zion, and utter his voice from Jerusalem; and the habitations of the pastors shall be destroyed, and the top of Carmel shall wither.
3 Thus hath the LORD said; For three transgressions of Damascus, and for the fourth, I will not convert her; because they have threshed Gilead with threshing instruments of iron:

4 But I will send a fire into the house of Hazael, which shall devour the palaces of Benhadad.
5 I will break also the bar of Damascus, and cut off the inhabitants of the plain of Aven, and him that holdeth the sceptre from the house of Eden: and the people of Syria shall go into captivity unto Kir.

6 Thus hath the LORD said; For three transgressions of Gaza, and for the fourth, I will not convert her; because they carried away captive the whole captivity, to deliver *them* up to Edom:
7 But I will send a fire in the wall of Gaza, which shall devour the palaces thereof:
8 And I will cut off the inhabitants of Ashdod, and

him that holdeth the
sceptre from Ashkelon, and
I will turn my hand against
Ekron: and the remnant of
the Palestinians shall perish, said the Lord GOD.

9 Thus hath the LORD said;
For three transgressions of
Tyre, and for the fourth, I
will not convert her; be-
cause they delivered up the
whole captivity to Edom,
and remembered not the
brotherly covenant:
10 But I will send fire in
the wall of Tyre, which
shall devour the palaces
thereof.

11 Thus hath the LORD
said; For three transgressions of Edom, and for the
fourth, I will not convert
her; because she did pur-
sue her brother with the
sword, and did cast off all
mercy, and with her anger
she did steal from him per-
petually, and she kept her
wrath for ever:
12 But I will send fire in
Teman, which shall devour
the palaces of Bozrah.

13 Thus saith the LORD;
For three transgressions of
the children of Ammon, and
for the fourth, I will not convert her; because they have
ripped off the mountains of

Gilead, that they might enlarge their border:
14 But I will kindle fire in
the wall of Rabbah, and it
shall devour the palaces
thereof, *as* with shouting in
the day of battle, *as* with a
tempest in the day of the
whirlwind:
15 And their king shall go
into captivity, he and his
princes together, said the
LORD.

Chapter 2

1 Thus hath the LORD said;
For three transgressions of
Moab, and for the fourth, I
will not convert her; be-
cause she burned the bones
of the king of Edom into
lime:
2 But I will send fire in
Moab, and it shall devour
the palaces of Kerioth: and
Moab shall die in tumult,
with shouting, *and* with the
sound of the shophar:
3 And I will cut off the judge
from the midst thereof, and
will slay all the princes
thereof with him, said the
LORD.

4 Thus hath the LORD said;
For three transgressions of
Judah, and for the fourth,
I will not convert her; because they have despised
the law of the LORD, and
have not kept his statutes,
and their lies caused them

to err, after the which their fathers have walked:

5 But I will send fire in Judah, and it shall devour the palaces of Jerusalem.

6 Thus hath the LORD said; For three transgressions of Israel, and for the fourth, I will not convert her; because they sold the righteous for silver, and the poor for a pair of shoes;

7 desiring that there be dust of the earth upon the head of the poor, and to twist the way of the humble: and the man and his father have gone in unto the *same* maid, profaning my holy name:

8 And they lay *themselves* down upon clothes laid to pledge by every altar, and they drink the wine of the condemned *in* the house of their god.

9 Yet I destroyed the Amorite before them, whose height *was* like the height of the cedars, and he *was* strong as an oak; yet I destroyed his fruit above, and his roots beneath.

10 Also I brought you up from the land of Egypt, and led you forty years through the wilderness, that you might possess the land of the Amorite.

11 And I raised up of your sons for prophets, and of your young men for Nazarites. *Is it* not even thus, O ye sons of Israel? said the LORD.

12 But ye gave the Nazarites wine to drink; and commanded the prophets, saying, Prophesy not.

13 Behold, I will press you in your place, as a cart is pressed *that is* full of sheaves.

14 Therefore the flight shall perish from the swift, and the strong shall not strengthen his force, neither shall the mighty deliver his soul:

15 Neither shall he stand that handleth the bow; and *he that is* swift of foot shall not escape: neither shall he that rideth the horse save his life.

16 And *he that is* strong among the mighty shall flee away naked in that day, said the LORD.

Chapter 3

1 Hear this word that the LORD hath spoken against you, O sons of Israel, against the whole family which I brought up from the land of Egypt, saying,

2 You only have I known of all the families of the earth: therefore I will visit all your iniquities against you.

3 Can two walk together, except they be agreed?

4 Will a lion roar in the forest, when he hath no prey? will a young lion cry out of his den, if he have taken nothing?

5 Can a bird fall in a snare upon the earth, without a fowler? Shall the snare rise up from the earth, and have taken nothing at all?

6 Shall the shophar be blown in the city, and the people not be afraid? shall there be any evil in the city which the LORD hath not done?

7 Because the Lord GOD will do nothing, unless he reveal his secret to his servants the prophets.

8 The lion hath roared, who will not fear? the Lord GOD hath spoken, who can but prophesy?

9 Publish upon the palaces of Ashdod, and upon the palaces of the land of Egypt, and say, Assemble yourselves upon the mountains of Samaria, and behold the great oppression in the midst thereof, and the *great* violence in the midst thereof.

10 For they know not to do right, said the LORD, storing up violence and robbery in their palaces.

11 Therefore thus said the Lord GOD; An adversary *there shall be* even round about the land; and he shall bring down thy strength from thee, and thy palaces shall be spoiled.

12 Thus hath the LORD said; As the pastor taketh out of the mouth of the lion two legs, or a piece of an ear; so shall the children of Israel escape that dwell in Samaria in the corner of the bed, and at the border of the couch.

13 Hear ye, and protest in the house of Jacob, said the Lord GOD, the God of the hosts,

14 that in the day that I shall visit the rebellions of Israel upon him, I will also visit upon the altars of Bethel: and the horns of the altar shall be cut off, and fall to the ground.

15 And I will smite the winter house with the summer house; and the houses of ivory shall perish, and many houses shall be cut off, said the LORD.

Chapter 4

1 Hear this word, ye cows of Bashan, that *are* in the mountain of Samaria, which oppress the poor, which crush the needy, which say to their masters, Bring, and let us drink.

2 The Lord GOD hath sworn by his holiness, that, behold, the days shall come upon you, that he will take you away with hooks, and your posterity in fishing boats.

3 And ye shall go forth by the breaches one after another; and ye shall be cast out of the palace, saith the LORD.

4 Go to Bethel, and transgress; at Gilgal increase the rebellion; and bring your sacrifices early *in the morning, and* your tithes every three years:

5 And offer a sacrifice of praise with leaven, and proclaim *and* publish the free *will* offerings: for this is the way you like it, O ye sons of Israel, said the Lord GOD.

6 I also have given you cleanness of teeth in all your cities, and want of bread in all your places: yet ye have not returned unto me, said the LORD.

7 And also I have withheld the rain from you, when *there were* yet three months to the harvest: and I caused it to rain upon one city, and caused it not to rain upon another city: one piece was rained upon, and the piece whereupon it rained not withered.

8 So two *or* three cities wandered unto one city, to drink water; but they were not satisfied: yet ye have not returned unto me, said the LORD.

9 I have smitten you with *the* east wind and with *the* caterpillar: your many gardens and your vineyards and your fig trees and your olive trees were devoured by the locust: yet ye have never returned unto me, said the LORD.

10 I have sent among you the pestilence in the way to Egypt: your young men have I slain with the sword, and have taken away your horses; and I have made the stink of your camps to come up unto your nostrils: and ye never returned unto me, said the LORD.

11 I have overthrown *some* of you, as God overthrew Sodom and Gomorrah, and ye were as a firebrand plucked out of the fire: and ye never returned unto me, said the LORD.

12 Therefore thus will I do unto thee, O Israel: *and* because I must do this unto thee, prepare to meet thy God, O Israel.

13 For, behold, he that formeth the mountains, and createth the wind, and declareth unto man what *is* his thought, that maketh the darkness into morning, and treadeth above the high

places of the earth, The
LORD, The God of the hosts,
is his name.
Chapter 5
1 Hear ye this word, because I raise up a lamentation upon you, O house of
Israel.

2 The virgin of Israel has
fallen; she shall not be able
to rise again: she was forsaken upon her land; *there
is* none to raise her up.

3 For thus hath the Lord
GOD said; The city that sent
out a thousand shall have
a hundred left, and that
which sent forth a hundred
shall have ten, in the house
of Israel.

4 But thus hath the LORD
said unto the house of Israel, Seek ye me, and ye
shall live:

5 But seek not Bethel, nor
enter into Gilgal, and pass
not to Beersheba: for Gilgal
shall surely go into captivity, and Bethel shall come
to nought.

6 Seek the LORD, and ye
shall live; lest he break out
like fire in the house of Joseph, and devour *it*, and
there be none to quench *it*
in Bethel.

7 Ye who turn judgment to
wormwood, and leave off
doing righteousness in the
earth,

8 look unto him that
maketh the seven stars and
Orion, and turneth the
shadow of death into the
morning, and maketh the
day dark with night: that
calleth for the waters of the
sea, and poureth them out
upon the face of the earth:
The LORD *is* his name:

9 That strengtheneth the
spoiler against the strong,
so that the spoiler shall
come against the fortress.

10 They hate him that
rebuketh in the gate, and
they abhor him that
speaketh uprightly.

11 Forasmuch therefore as
your treading *is* upon the
poor, and ye take from him
burdens of wheat: ye have
built houses of hewn stone,
but ye shall not dwell in
them; ye have planted
pleasant vineyards, but ye
shall not drink wine of
them.

12 For I have known of your
many rebellions and your
great sins that afflict the
just, and take a bribe, and
turn aside the poor in the
gate *from their right*.

13 Therefore the prudent
shall keep silence in that
time; for it *is* an evil time.

14 Seek that which is good,
and not that which is evil,
that ye may live: and so the

LORD, the God of the hosts, shall be with you, as ye have spoken.

15 Hate the evil, and love the good, and establish judgment in the gate: it may be that the LORD God of the hosts will be gracious unto the remnant of Joseph.

16 Therefore the LORD, *the* God of the hosts, the Lord, said this; Wailing *shall be* in all streets; and they shall say in all the highways, Alas! alas! and they shall call the husbandman to mourning, and such as are skilful of lamentation to wailing.

17 And in all vineyards *shall be* wailing: for I will pass through the midst of thee, said the LORD.

18 Woe unto you that desire the day of the LORD! to what end *is* it for you? the day of the LORD *shall be* darkness, and not light.

19 As if a man did flee from a lion, and a bear met him; or went into the house, and leaned his hand on the wall, and a serpent bit him.

20 *Shall* not the day of the LORD *be* darkness, and not light? even very dark, and no brightness in it?

21 I hate, I despise your solemnities, and I will not savor your assemblies.

22 Though ye offer me *your* burnt offerings and your grain offerings, I will not accept *them*: neither will I regard the peace offerings of your fat beasts.

23 Take thou away from me the noise of thy songs; for I will not hear the melody of thy instruments.

24 But let judgment run down as waters, and righteousness as a mighty stream.

25 Perchance did you offer me any sacrifices and offerings in the wilderness in forty years, O house of Israel?

26 But ye have offered unto Sicut your king, and unto Chiun your idols, the star of your gods which ye made.

27 Therefore will I cause you to go into captivity beyond Damascus, said the LORD, whose name *is* The God of the hosts.

Chapter 6

1 Woe to them *that are* at ease in Zion, and to them that trust in the mountain of Samaria, *which are* named principals among the same nations which shall come upon them, O house of Israel!

2 Pass ye unto Calneh, and see; and from thence go ye to Hamath the great: then go down to Gath of the Palestinians: *be they* better than these kingdoms? or their border greater than your border?

3 Ye that put far away the evil day, and cause the seat of iniquity to come near;

4 that lie upon beds of ivory, and stretch themselves upon their couches, and eat the lambs out of the flock, and the calves out of the midst of the stall;

5 that chant to the sound of the flute, *and* invent to themselves instruments of music, like David;

6 that drink wine in bowls, and anoint themselves with the chief ointments: but they are not grieved for the affliction of Joseph.

7 Therefore now shall they go captive with the first that go captive, and the banquet of them that stretched themselves *upon their couches* shall be removed.

8 The Lord GOD hath sworn by himself, the LORD God of the hosts said, I abhor the grandeur of Jacob, and hate his palaces: therefore will I give the city with all that is therein over to the enemy.

9 And it shall come to pass, if there remain ten men in one house, that they shall die.

10 And their uncle shall take each one, and burn them to bring out the bones out of the house, and shall say unto him that *is* by the sides of the house, *Is there* yet *any* with thee? and he shall say, No. Then shall he say, Hold thy tongue: for we may not make mention of the name of the LORD.

11 For, behold, the LORD shall command, and he will smite the great house with breaches, and the little house with clefts.

12 Shall horses run upon the rocks? will *one* plow *there* with oxen? why have ye turned judgment into gall, and the fruit of righteousness into hemlock?

13 Ye which rejoice in a thing of nought, which say, Have we not taken to us horns by our own strength?

14 But, behold, I will raise up against you Gentiles, O house of Israel, said the LORD God of the hosts; and they shall afflict you from the entering in of Hemath unto the river of the wilderness.

Chapter 7

1 Thus hath the Lord GOD showed unto me; and, behold, he formed grasshoppers in the beginning of the shooting up of the latter hay; and, behold that the latter *hay grew* after the king's reapings.

2 And it came to pass, *that* when they had come to an end of eating the grass of the land, then I said, O Lord GOD, forgive, I beseech thee: who shall lift up Jacob? for he *is* small.

3 The LORD repented of this: It shall not be, said the LORD.

4 *Afterward* the Lord GOD showed me this: And, behold, the Lord GOD called to judge by fire, and it devoured the great deep, and did eat up the inheritance.

5 Then said I, O Lord GOD, cease, I beseech thee: who shall raise up Jacob? for he *is* small.

6 The LORD repented of this: This also shall not be, said the Lord GOD.

7 Thus he showed me: and, behold, the Lord stood upon a wall *made* by a plumbline, with a plumbline in his hand.

8 And the LORD said unto me, Amos, what seest thou? And I said, A plumbline. Then said the Lord, Behold, I set a plumbline in the midst of my people Israel: I will not again pass over them any more:

9 And the altars of Isaac shall be destroyed, and the sanctuaries of Israel shall be laid waste; and I will rise upon the house of Jeroboam with the sword.

10 Then Amaziah the priest of Bethel sent to Jeroboam king of Israel, saying, Amos hath conspired against thee in the midst of the house of Israel: the land is not able to bear all his words.

11 For thus hath Amos said, Jeroboam shall die by the sword, and Israel shall surely be led away captive out of their own land.

12 And Amaziah said unto Amos, O thou seer, go, flee thee away into the land of Judah, and eat thy bread there, and prophesy there:

13 But do not prophesy any more in Bethel: for it *is* the king's sanctuary, and the head of the kingdom.

14 Then answered Amos, and said to Amaziah, I am not a prophet, neither am I a prophet's son; but I am an herdsman, and a gatherer of sycamore fruit:

15 And the LORD took me as I followed the flock, and the LORD said unto me, Go, prophesy unto my people Israel.

16 Now therefore hear thou the word of the LORD: Thou sayest, Prophesy not against Israel, and drop not *thy word* against the house of Isaac.

17 Therefore thus hath the LORD said; Thy wife shall be an harlot in the city, and thy sons and thy daughters shall fall by the sword, and thy land shall be divided by lots; and thou shalt die in a polluted land: and Israel shall surely go into captivity from his land.

Chapter 8

1 Thus hath the Lord GOD showed unto me: and behold a basket of summer fruit.

2 And he said, Amos, what seest thou? And I said, A basket of summer fruit. Then said the LORD unto me, The end is come upon my people of Israel; I will not again pass over them any more.

3 And the cantors of the temple shall howl in that day, said the Lord GOD: *there shall be* many dead bodies in every place; they shall cast *them* forth with silence.

4 Hear this, O ye that swallow up the needy, and cut off the poor of the land,

5 saying, When the month is over, we will sell the wheat; and after the end of the week we will open *the storehouse* of bread, mak-

ing the ephah small, and the shekel great, and falsifying the balances by deceit;

6 that we may buy the poor for money, and the needy for a pair of shoes; *yea,* and sell the refuse of the wheat.

7 The LORD hath sworn by the excellency of Jacob, Surely I will never forget any of their works.

8 Shall not the land tremble for this, and every one mourn that dwelleth therein? and it shall all rise up as a flood; and it shall be cast out and sunk, as the river of Egypt.

9 And it shall come to pass in that day, said the Lord GOD, that I will cause the sun to go down at noon, and I will cover the earth with darkness in the clear day:

10 And I will turn your feasts into mourning, and all your songs into lamentation; and I will cause sackcloth to be brought up upon all loins, and baldness upon every head; and I will make it as the mourning of an only *son,* and the end thereof as a bitter day.

11 Behold, *the* days come, said the Lord GOD, that I will send a famine to the earth, not a famine of bread, nor a thirst for water, but of hearing *the* words of the LORD:

12 And they shall wander from sea to sea, and from the north even to the east, they shall run to and fro to seek *the* word of the LORD, and shall not find *it*.

13 In that day shall the fair virgins and young men faint for thirst.

14 They that swear by the sin of Samaria, and say, As thy God of Dan liveth; and, As the way of Beersheba liveth; even they shall fall, and never rise up again.

Chapter 9

1 I saw the Lord standing upon the altar: and he said, Smite the threshold, and shake the doors: and cut the head of them all into pieces; and I will slay the last of them with the sword: there shall be none of them *left* to flee away, or to escape.

2 Though they dig unto hell, thence shall my hand take them; though they climb up to heaven, thence will I bring them down:

3 And though they hide themselves in the top of Carmel, I will search and take them out thence; and though they hide from my sight in the bottom of the sea, thence will I command the serpent, and he shall bite them:

4 And though they go into captivity before their enemies, thence will I command the sword, and it shall slay them: and I will set my eyes upon them for evil, and not for good.

5 The Lord GOD of the hosts *is* he that toucheth the earth, and it shall melt, and all that dwell therein shall mourn: and it shall all rise up like *a* river; and shall be sunk, as the river of Egypt.

6 He that built his degrees in the heaven, and hath founded his gathering upon the earth; he that calleth the waters of the sea, and poureth them out upon the face of the earth: The LORD *is* his name.

7 O sons of Israel, *Are* ye not as children of the Ethiopians unto me, said the LORD? Have not I brought up Israel out of the land of Egypt? and the Palestinians from Caphtor, and the Syrians from Kir?

8 Behold, the eyes of the Lord GOD *are* against the sinful kingdom, and I will destroy it from off the face of the earth; saving that I will not utterly destroy the house of Jacob, said the LORD.

9 For, behold, I will command, and I will cause the house of Israel to be sifted among all the Gentiles, like as *the grain* is sifted in a sieve, yet shall not the least grain fall to the earth.

10 All the sinners of my people shall die by the sword, which say, For our sake the evil shall not come near nor overtake us.

11 In that day will I raise up the tabernacle of David that is fallen, and close up the breaches thereof; and I will raise up his ruins, and I will build it as in the days of old:

12 That they which are called by my name, may possess the remnant of Edom, and all the Gentiles, said the LORD that doeth this.

13 Behold, the days come, saith the LORD, that the plowman shall catch up with the reaper, and the treader of grapes with him that soweth seed; and the mountains shall drop new wine, and all the hills shall melt.

14 And I will turn the captivity of my people of Israel, and they shall build the waste cities, and inhabit *them*; and they shall plant vineyards, and drink the wine thereof; they shall also make gardens, and eat the fruit of them.

15 For I will plant them upon their land, and they shall no more be pulled up out of their land which I have given them, said the LORD thy God.

The Prophecy of
Obadiah

Chapter 1

1 The vision of Obadiah. Thus hath the Lord GOD said concerning Edom; We have heard the message from the LORD, and *a* messenger is sent to the Gentiles, Arise ye, and let us rise up against her in battle.

2 Behold, I have made thee small among the Gentiles: thou *shalt be* greatly humbled.

3 The pride of thine heart hath deceived thee, thou that dwellest in the clefts of the rock, whose habitation *is* high; that saith in his heart, Who shall bring me down to the ground?

4 Though thou exalt *thyself* as the eagle, and though thou set thy nest among the stars, from there I will bring thee down, said the LORD.

5 Did thieves come to thee, or robbers by night? (how art thou destroyed!) would they not have stolen until they had enough? if the grapegatherers came to thee, would they not leave *some* grapes?

6 How were *the things* of Esau searched out! His hidden things were sought after!

7 All the men of thy confederacy have brought thee *even* to the border: the men that were at peace with thee have deceived thee, *and* prevailed against thee; *they that eat* thy bread have laid a wound under thee: *there is* no understanding in this.

8 Shall I not in that day, said the LORD, even destroy the wise *men* out of Edom, and prudence out of the mount of Esau?

9 And thy mighty *men*, O Teman, shall be dismayed, because every man shall be cut off from the mount of Esau by the slaughter.

10 For *thy* violence against thy brother Jacob shame shall cover thee, and thou shalt be cut off for ever.

11 In the day that thou stoodest on the other side, in the day that the strangers carried away captive his forces, and foreigners entered into his gates, and cast lots upon Jerusalem, even thou *wast* as one of them.

12 But thou shouldest not have looked on the day of thy brother in the day that he became a stranger; neither shouldest thou have rejoiced over the children of Judah in the day they were lost; neither shouldest thou have spoken proudly in the day of distress.

13 Thou shouldest not have entered into the gate of my people in the day of their calamity; yea, thou shouldest not have looked on their affliction in the day of their calamity, nor have laid *hands* on their substance in the day of their calamity;

14 neither shouldest thou have stood in the crossway, to kill those of his that did escape; neither shouldest thou have delivered up those of his that did remain in the day of distress.

15 For the day of the LORD *is* near upon all *the* Gentiles: as thou hast done, it shall be done unto thee: thy reward shall return upon thine own head.

16 For as ye have drunk upon my holy mountain, *so* shall all the Gentiles drink continually, yea, they shall drink, and they shall swallow down, and they shall be as though they had not been.

17 But in the mount Zion shall be deliverance, and it shall be holiness; and the house of Jacob shall possess their possessions.

18 And the house of Jacob shall be a fire, and the house of Joseph a flame, and the house of Esau for stubble, and they shall kindle in them, and devour them; and there shall not be *any* remaining of the house of Esau; for the LORD hath spoken *it*.

19 And *they of* the south shall possess the mount of Esau; and the plains of the Palestinians: and they shall also possess the fields of Ephraim, and the fields of Samaria: and Benjamin *shall possess* Gilead.

20 And the captives of this host of the sons of Israel *shall possess* that of the Canaanites, *even* unto Zarephath; and the captives of Jerusalem, who *shall be* in Sepharad, shall possess the cities of the south.

21 And saviours shall come up unto mount Zion to judge the mount of Esau; and the kingdom shall be the LORD'S.

The Prophecy of

Jonah

Chapter 1

1 Now the word of the LORD came unto Jonah the son of Amittai, saying,

2 Arise, go to Nineveh, that great city, and cry against it; for their wickedness is come up before me.

3 But Jonah rose up to flee unto Tarshish from the presence of the LORD, and went down to Joppa; and he found a ship going to Tarshish: so he paid the fare thereof, and went down into it, to go with them unto Tarshish *fleeing* from the presence of the LORD.

4 But the LORD caused a great wind to rise up in the sea, and there was a mighty tempest in the sea, so that the ship thought she would be broken.

5 And the mariners were afraid, and everyone called unto his god, and they cast forth the vessels that *were* in the ship into the sea, to lighten *it* of them. But Jonah was gone down into the sides of the ship; and he lay, and was fast asleep.

6 So the shipmaster came to him, and said unto him, What meanest thou, O sleeper? arise, call upon thy God, if so be that he will have compassion upon us, that we perish not.

7 And they said every one to his fellow, Come, and let us cast lots, that we may know for whose cause this evil *is* upon us. So they cast lots, and the lot fell upon Jonah.

8 Then said they unto him, Tell us, we pray thee, why this evil *is come* upon us; What *is* thine occupation? and whence comest thou? what *is* thy country? and of what people *art* thou?

9 And he said unto them, I *am* an Hebrew; and I fear the LORD, God of the heavens, which hath made the sea and the dry *land*.

10 Then were the men exceedingly afraid, and said unto him, Why hast thou done this? For the men knew that he fled from the presence of the LORD, because he had told them.

11 Then said they unto him, What shall we do unto thee, that the sea may be calm unto us? for the sea rose *higher*, and was wroth.

12 And he said unto them, Take me up, and cast me forth into the sea; so shall the sea be calm unto you: for I know that for my sake this great tempest *is* upon you.

13 Nevertheless the men rowed hard to turn the ship to land; but they could not: for the sea rose *higher*, and was wroth against them.

14 And they cried unto the LORD, and said, We beseech thee, O LORD, we beseech thee, let us not perish for the soul of this man, and lay not upon us innocent blood: for thou, O LORD, hast done as it pleased thee.

15 So they took up Jonah, and cast him forth into the sea: and the sea ceased from her raging.

16 Then the men feared the LORD exceedingly, and offered a sacrifice unto the LORD, and made vows.

17 Now the LORD had prepared a great fish to swallow up Jonah. And Jonah was in the belly of the fish three days and three nights.

Chapter 2

1 Then Jonah prayed unto the LORD his God out of the fish's belly,

2 And said, I cried by reason of my tribulation unto the LORD, and he heard me; out of the belly of hell I cried, *and* thou heardest my voice.

3 For thou hadst cast me into the deep, in the midst of the seas; and the floods compassed me about: all thy billows and thy waves passed over me.

4 Then I said, I am cast out of thy sight; yet I will see thy holy temple again.

5 The waters compassed me about, *even* to the soul: the depth closed me round about, the weeds were wrapped about my head.

6 I descended to the roots of the mountains; the earth *put* her bars about me for ever: yet thou hast brought up my life out of the grave, O LORD my God.

7 When my soul fainted within me I remembered the LORD: and my prayer entered in unto thee in thy holy temple.

8 They that observe lying vanities forsake his mercy.

9 But I will sacrifice unto thee with the voice of

thanksgiving; I will pay *that* that I have vowed, that saving cometh of the LORD.

10 And the LORD spoke unto the fish, and it vomited out Jonah upon the dry *land.*

Chapter 3

1 And the word of the LORD came unto Jonah the second time, saying,

2 Arise, go unto Nineveh, that great city, and preach unto it the preaching that I bid thee.

3 So Jonah arose, and went unto Nineveh, according to the word of the LORD. Now Nineveh was an exceeding great city of three days' journey.

4 And Jonah began to enter into the city a day's journey, and he cried, and said, Yet forty days, and Nineveh shall be destroyed.

5 So the people of Nineveh believed God, and proclaimed a fast, and put on sackcloth, from the greatest of them even to the least of them.

6 For word came unto the king of Nineveh, and he arose from his throne, and he threw his robe from him, and covered *himself* with sackcloth, and sat in ashes.

7 And he caused *it* to be proclaimed and published through Nineveh by the decree of the king and his nobles, saying, Let neither man nor beast, herd nor flock, taste any thing: let them not feed, nor drink water:

8 But let man and beast be covered with sackcloth, and cry mightily unto God: yea, let them turn every one from his evil way, and from the violence that *is* in their hands.

9 Who can tell *if* God will turn and repent, and turn away from his fierce anger, that we perish not?

10 And God saw their works, because they turned from their evil way; and he repented of the evil, that he had said that he would do unto them; and he did *it* not.

Chapter 4

1 But it displeased Jonah exceedingly, and he was very angry.

2 And he prayed unto the LORD, and said, I pray thee, O LORD, *was* this not what I said, when I was yet in my country? Therefore I hastened to flee unto Tarshish: for I knew that thou *art* a gracious God, and full of compassion, slow to anger, and of great mercy, and repentest when thou art come to take punishment.

3 Therefore now, O LORD, take, I beseech thee, my life

from me; for I would rather die than live.

4 Then said the LORD, Art thou so angry?

5 And Jonah went out of the city, and sat towards the east side of the city, and there made him a booth, and sat under it in the shade, until he might see what would become of the city.

6 And the LORD God prepared a gourd, and made *it* to come up over Jonah, that it might be a shadow over his head, to deliver him from his evil. So Jonah was exceeding glad for the gourd.

7 But God *also* prepared a worm when the morning rose the next day, and it smote the gourd *so* that it withered.

8 And it came to pass, when the sun arose, that God prepared a vehement east wind; and the sun beat upon the head of Jonah, that he fainted, and wished in his soul to die, and said, *It is* better for me to die than to live.

9 And God said to Jonah, Art thou so angry for the gourd? And he said, I do well to be angry, *even* unto death.

10 Then said the LORD, Thou hast had pity on the gourd, for the which thou hast not laboured, neither madest it grow; which came up in a night, and perished in a night:

11 And shall I not spare Nineveh, that great city, wherein are more than one hundred twenty thousand persons that cannot discern between their right hand and their left hand; and many animals?

The Prophecy of

Micah

Chapter 1

1 The word of the LORD that came to Micah the Morasthite in the days of Jotham, Ahaz, *and* Hezekiah, kings of Judah, which he saw concerning Samaria and Jerusalem.

2 Hear, all ye peoples; hearken, O earth, and all that therein is: and the Lord GOD, the Lord from his holy temple shall be *a* witness against you.

3 For, behold, the LORD cometh forth out of his place, and will come down, and tread upon the high places of the earth.

4 And the mountains shall melt under him, and the valleys shall be split, as wax before the fire, *and* as the waters *that* run down a steep place.

5 All this for the rebellion of Jacob, and for the sins of the house of Israel. What *is* the rebellion of Jacob? *is it* not Samaria? and what *are* the high places of Judah? *are they* not Jerusalem?

6 Therefore I will make Samaria into heaps in the field, into a land of vineyards: and I will scatter her stones throughout the valley, and I will uncover her foundations.

7 And all her graven images shall be broken to pieces, and all her gifts shall be burned in the fire, and all her idols will I destroy: for she gathered *it* of the gifts of harlots, and they shall return unto gifts of harlots.

8 Therefore I will wail and howl, I will go stripped and naked: I will make a wailing like the dragons, and mourning as the owls.

9 For her wound *is* painful; for it is come unto Judah; it is come unto the gate of my people, *even* to Jerusalem.

10 Declare ye *it* not in Gath, weep ye little: roll thyself in the dust for the house of Aphrah.

11 Pass ye away naked with shame, thou inhabitant of Saphir: the inhabitant of Zaanan came not forth in the mourning of Bethezel; he shall receive of you for his lateness.

12 For the inhabitant of Maroth was pained because of good: therefore evil came down from the LORD unto the gate of Jerusalem.

13 O thou inhabitant of Lachish, hitch the chariot to dromedaries: for thou *wert* the beginning of the sin to the daughter of Zion: for in thee the rebellions of Israel were invented.

14 Therefore shalt thou give gifts to Moreshethgath: the houses of Achzib *shall be* a lie to the kings of Israel.

15 Yet will I bring an heir unto thee, O inhabitant of Mareshah: the glory of Israel shall come unto Adullam.

16 Make thee bald, and shave thee for the children of thy delight; enlarge thy baldness as the eagle; for they are gone into captivity from thee.

Chapter 2

1 Woe to them that devise iniquity, and fabricate evil upon their beds! when the morning is light, they put it into effect, because they have power in their hands.

2 And they coveted fields, and stole them; and houses, and took *them* away: so they oppressed the man and his house, even the man and his heritage.

3 Therefore thus hath the LORD said; Behold, against this family do I devise an evil, from which ye shall not remove your necks; neither shall ye walk haughtily: for the time shall be evil.

4 In that time shall *one* take up a saying against you, and lament with a doleful lamentation, *and* say, We have been utterly destroyed: he hath changed the portion of my people: how hath he taken our fields! He hath given and *divided our fields unto others*.

5 Therefore thou shalt have no one to cast a cord by lot in the congregation of the LORD.

6 Prophesy ye not, *say they to* them that prophesy: Do not prophesy unto them *that* they are to understand shame.

7 O *thou that* calleth thyself the house of Jacob, is the spirit of the LORD shortened? *are* these his doings? do not my words do good to him that walketh uprightly?

8 He who yesterday *was* my people is risen up as an

enemy: ye pull off the robe with the garment from them that pass by, as those who return from war.

9 The women of my people have ye cast out from their pleasant houses; from their children have ye taken away my continual praise.

10 Arise ye, and depart; for this *is* not *your* rest: because it is polluted, it has become corrupted, and with a great corruption.

11 If there be one walking in the spirit of falsehood he shall lie, *saying,* I will prophesy unto thee of wine and of strong drink; he shall even be the prophet of this people.

12 I will surely assemble, O Jacob, all of thee; I will surely gather the remnant of Israel; I will put them together as the sheep of Bozrah, as *the* flock in the midst of their fold: they shall make great noise by reason of *the multitude of* men.

13 *The* breaker shall go up before them: they shall break through, and pass through the gate, and go out by it: and their king shall pass before them, the LORD at the head of them.

Chapter 3

1 And I said, Hear, I pray you, O princes of Jacob, and ye heads of the house of Israel; *did* it not *pertain* to you to know that which is right?

2 Who hate the good, and love the evil; who steal their skin from off them, and their flesh from off their bones;

3 and eat the flesh of my people, and flay their skin from off them; and they break their bones, and chop them in pieces, as for the pot, and as flesh within the caldron.

4 Then shall they cry unto the LORD, but he will not respond to them: he will even hide his face from them at that time, because of their evil doings.

5 Thus hath the LORD said concerning the prophets that make my people err, that bite with their teeth, and cry, Peace; and he that putteth not into their mouths, they even prepare war against him.

6 Therefore the vision shall be made night unto you, and darkness unto those that divine; and the sun shall go down over the prophets, and the day shall be dark over them.

7 Then shall the prophets be ashamed, and the diviners confounded: yea, they shall all cover their lips; because *they shall have* no answer from God.

8 But truly I am full of power by the Spirit of the LORD, and of judgment, and of might, to declare unto Jacob his rebellion, and to Israel his sin.

9 Now hear this, ye heads of the house of Jacob, and captains of the house of Israel, that abhor judgment, and pervert all equity;

10 that build up Zion with blood, and Jerusalem with iniquity;

11 The heads thereof judge for reward, and the priests thereof teach for hire, and the prophets thereof divine for money: yet they come near unto the LORD, and say, *Is* not the LORD among us? No evil can come upon us.

12 Therefore for your sake Zion shall be plowed *as* a field, and Jerusalem shall become heaps of ruins, and the mountain of the house as the high places of the forest.

Chapter 4

1 But it shall come to pass in the last of the times, *that* the mountain of the house of the LORD shall be established as the top of the mountains, and higher than all the hills; and peoples shall flow unto it.

2 And many Gentiles shall come, and say, Come, and let us go up to the mountain of the LORD, and to the house of the God of Jacob; and he will teach us of his ways, and we will walk in his paths: for the law shall go forth from Zion, and the word of the LORD from Jerusalem.

3 And he shall judge among many peoples, and correct strong nations even afar off; and they shall beat their swords into plowshares, and their spears into pruninghooks: nation shall not lift up a sword against nation, neither shall they train for war any more.

4 But each one shall sit under their vine and under their fig tree; and none shall make *them* afraid: for the mouth of the LORD of the hosts hath spoken *it*.

5 Even if all the peoples should walk every one in the name of their gods, with all this we will walk in the name of the LORD our God for ever and eternally.

6 In that day, saith the LORD, will I assemble her that is lame, and I will gather her that is driven out, and her that I have afflicted;

7 and I will make her that is lame to be heirs, and her that was cast off a strong nation: and the LORD shall reign over them in the mount of Zion from now, and for evermore.

8 And thou, O tower of the flock, the strong hold of the daughter of Zion shall come unto thee; and the dominion shall come first, the kingdom, to the daughter of Jerusalem.

9 Now why dost thou cry out aloud? *is there* no king in thee? is thy counsellor perished? for pangs have taken thee as a woman in travail.

10 Be in pain, and labour to bring forth, O daughter of Zion, like a woman in travail: for now shalt thou go forth out of the city, and thou shalt dwell in the field, and thou shalt go *even* to Babylon; there shalt thou be delivered; there the LORD shall redeem thee from the hand of thine enemies.

11 But now many nations are gathered against thee, that say, Let her be defiled, and let our eyes see our desire *carried out* upon Zion.

12 But they knew not the thoughts of the LORD, neither understood they his counsel; by which he gathered them as sheaves onto the *threshing* floor.

13 Arise and thresh, O daughter of Zion: for I will make thine horn iron, and I will make thy hoofs brass: and thou shalt break in pieces many peoples: and thou shalt consecrate their spoil unto the LORD, and their riches unto the Lord of the whole earth.

Chapter 5

1 Now thou shalt be besieged by armies, O daughter of *the* army: he shall lay siege against us: they shall smite the judge of Israel with a rod upon the cheek.

2 But thou, Bethlehem Ephratah, *though* thou be little among the thousands of Judah, *yet* out of thee shall he come forth unto me *that is* to be Lord in Israel; and his goings forth *are* from the beginning, from the days of the ages.

3 Therefore will he give them up, until the time *that* she which travaileth hath brought forth: then the remnant of his brethren shall return with the sons of Israel.

4 And he shall stand and feed in the strength of the

LORD, in the majesty of the name of the LORD his God; and they shall abide: for now shall he be great unto the ends of the earth.

5 And he shall be *our* peace, when the Assyrian shall come into our land: and when he shall tread in our palaces, then shall we raise against him seven shepherds, and eight principal men.

6 And they shall waste the land of Assyria with the blade, and the land of Nimrod with their swords: and he shall deliver *us* from the Assyrian, when he cometh against our land, and when he treadeth *within* our borders.

7 And the remnant of Jacob shall be in the midst of many peoples, as the dew of the LORD, as the rains upon the grass, which did not expect *a* man, nor did they expect the sons of men.

8 And the remnant of Jacob shall be among the Gentiles in the midst of many peoples as a lion among the beasts of the forest, as a young lion among the flocks of sheep: who, if he go through, and treadeth down, and teareth in pieces, and there are none that can escape.

9 Thine hand shall be lifted up upon thine enemies, and all thine adversaries shall be cut off.

10 And it shall come to pass in that day, said the LORD, that I will cause thy horses to be killed out of the midst of thee, and I will cause thy chariots to be destroyed:

11 And I will cause all the cities of thy land to be destroyed, and I will cause all thy fortresses to be destroyed:

12 And I will cause the witchcrafts to be destroyed by thy hand; and no *more* soothsayers shall be found in thee:

13 And I will cause thy graven images and thy images to be destroyed out of the midst of thee; and never again shalt thou worship the work of thine hands.

14 And I will pluck up thy groves out of the midst of thee: so will I destroy thy cities.

15 And I will execute vengeance in anger and fury in the Gentiles who have not heard.

Chapter 6

1 Hear ye now what the LORD saith; Arise, contend thou with the mountains, and let the hills hear thy voice.

2 Hear ye, O mountains, the LORD'S controversy, and ye strong foundations of the earth: for the LORD hath a controversy with his people, and he will reprove Israel.

3 O my people, what have I done unto thee? and wherein have I wearied thee? testify against me.

4 For I brought thee up out of the land of Egypt, and redeemed thee out of the house of servants; and I sent before thee Moses, Aaron, and Miriam.

5 O my people, remember now what Balak king of Moab consulted, and what Balaam the son of Beor answered him from Shittim unto Gilgal; that ye may know the righteousness of the LORD.

6 With what shall I present myself before the LORD, *and how* shall I worship the high God? shall I come before him with burnt offerings, with calves of a year old?

7 Will the LORD be pleased with thousands of rams, *or* with ten thousand of rivers of oil? shall I give my firstborn *for* my rebellion, the fruit of my bowels *for* the sin of my soul?

8 He hath declared unto thee, O man, what *is* good; and what the LORD requireth of thee: only to do *right* judgment, and to love mercy, and to humble thyself to walk with thy God.

9 The LORD'S voice crieth unto the city, and *the man of* wisdom shall see thy name: hear ye the rod, and who hath established it.

10 Are there yet the treasures of wickedness in the house of the wicked, and the scant measure *that is* abominable?

11 Can I be pure with false balances, and with a bag of deceitful weights?

12 With which their rich men are full of violence, and the inhabitants thereof have spoken lies, and their tongue *is* deceitful in their mouth.

13 Therefore also have I made *thee* weak in smiting thee, in making *thee* desolate because of thy sins.

14 Thou shalt eat, but not be satisfied; and thy casting down *shall be* in the midst of thee; and thou shalt take, but shalt not be saved; and *that* which thou savest, I will give it up to the sword.

15 Thou shalt sow, but thou shalt not reap; thou shalt tread the olives, but thou shalt not anoint thee with the oil; and sweet wine, but shalt not drink the wine.

16 For the statutes of Omri have been kept, and all the works of the house of Ahab, and ye have walked in their counsels; that I should make thee a desolation, and the inhabitants thereof an hissing: therefore ye shall bear the reproach of my people.

Chapter 7

1 Woe is me! for I am as when they have gathered the summer *fruits*, as the grapegleanings of the vintage: *there is* no cluster to eat: my soul desired the firstripe fruit.

2 The merciful *man* of the earth is missing: and *there is* none upright among men: they all lie in wait for blood; they hunt every man his brother with a net.

3 To complete the evil with their hands, the prince demandeth, and the judge *judgeth* for a reward; and the great *man* speaketh the desires of his heart: and they confirm it.

4 The best of them *is* as a brier: the most upright *as* a thorn hedge: the day of thy watchmen, thy visitation, cometh; now shall be their confusion.

5 Believe ye not in a friend, trust ye not in a prince: from her that lieth at thy side, take care, open not thy mouth.

6 For the son dishonoureth the father, the daughter riseth up against her mother, the daughter in law against her mother in law; and a man's enemies *are* those of his own house.

7 Therefore I will wait for the LORD; I will wait for the God of my saving health: my God will hear me.

8 Rejoice not against me, O my enemy: for if I have fallen, I shall arise; if I sit in darkness, the LORD *is* my light.

9 I will bear the indignation of the LORD, because I have sinned against him, until he hath judged my cause, and executed my judgment: he will bring me forth to the light, *and* I shall behold his righteousness.

10 Then *she that is* my enemy shall see *it*, and shame shall cover her which said unto me, Where is the LORD thy God? my eyes shall behold her: now shall she be trodden down as the mire of the streets.

11 In the day that thy walls shall be built unto thee, *in* that day shall the decree [*of thy slavery*] be far removed.

12 *In* that day *also* he shall come even to thee from Assyria, and *from* the fortified cities, and from the fortress even to the river, and from sea to sea, and *from* mountain to mountain.

13 And the land with them that dwell therein shall be made desolate, for the fruit of their doings.

14 Feed thy people with thy rod, the flock of thine heritage, which dwell only *in* the mountain, in the midst of Carmel: let them feed *in* Bashan and Gilead, as in the time of old.

15 I will show you marvellous *things* as in the day when thou camest out of Egypt.

16 The Gentiles shall see and be ashamed at all thy mighty acts: they shall lay *their* hand upon *their* mouth, their ears shall become deaf.

17 They shall lick the dust like a serpent, as the serpents of the earth, they shall tremble in their holes: they shall be filled with fear of the LORD our God, and shall *also* fear thee.

18 Who *is* a God like unto thee, that pardoneth iniquity, and passeth over the rebellion with the remnant of his heritage? He did not retain his anger for ever, because he delighteth *in* mercy.

19 He will turn again, he will have mercy on us; he will subdue our iniquities; and will cast all our sins into the depths of the sea.

20 Thou wilt perform the truth to Jacob, *and* the mercy to Abraham, which thou hast sworn unto our fathers from the times of old.

The Prophet
Nahum

Chapter 1

1 The burden of Nineveh. The book of the vision of Nahum the Elkoshite.

2 God *is* jealous, and the LORD revengeth; the LORD revengeth, and *is* furious; the LORD will take vengeance on his adversaries, and he reserveth *wrath* for his enemies.

3 The LORD *is* slow to anger, and great in power, and will not at all treat the guilty as though they were innocent: the LORD whose way *is* in the whirlwind and in the storm, and the clouds *are* the dust of his feet.

4 He reprehendeth the sea, and maketh it dry, and drieth up all the rivers: Bashan was destroyed, and Carmel, and the flower of Lebanon was destroyed.

5 The mountains quake at him, and the hills melt, and the earth is burned at his presence, yea, the world, and all that dwell therein.

6 Who can stand before his indignation? and who can abide in the fierceness of his anger? his fury is poured out like fire, and the rocks are thrown down by him.

7 The LORD *is* good, a strong hold in the day of trouble; and he knoweth them that trust in him.

8 But with an overrunning flood he will make an utter end of his place, and darkness shall pursue his enemies.

9 What do ye imagine against the LORD? he will make an utter end: he will not hold back the tribulation the second time.

10 For while *they be* entwined together *as* thorns, and while the drunkards shall be drinking, they shall be devoured as stubble full of dryness.

11 He hath come out of thee, that hath imagined evil against the LORD, a wicked counsellor.

12 Thus hath the LORD said; For much rest that they have, and though they be many, yet thus shall they be cut down, and *he* shall pass through. Though I have afflicted thee, I will afflict thee no more.

13 For now will I break his yoke from off thee, and will burst thy bonds in sunder.

14 And the LORD shall give a commandment concerning thee, *that* no one else of thy name ever be sown: out of the house of thy god will I cut off the graven image and the molten image; I will make it thy grave; because thou wert vile.

15 Behold upon the mountains the feet of him that bringeth good tidings, of him that publisheth peace! O Judah, keep thy solemn feasts, perform thy vows: for the wicked shall no more pass through thee; he is utterly cut off.

Chapter 2

1 The destroyer is risen up against thee: keep the fortress, watch the way, make *thy* loins strong, fortify *thy* power mightily.

2 For the LORD shall restore the glory of Jacob as the glory of Israel: for the emptiers have emptied them out, and marred their vine branches.

3 The shield of his valiant ones shall be red, the men of *his* army *are* in scarlet: the chariot *as* fire of torches; *in* the day which shall be made ready, the fir trees shall be terribly shaken.

4 The chariots shall rage in the streets, they shall flow through the streets: their faces like torches, they shall run like the lightnings.

5 He shall remember his valiant ones: they shall stumble in their walk when they make haste to their wall, and the covering shall be prepared.

6 The gates of the rivers shall be opened, and the palace shall be destroyed.

7 And the queen shall be taken captive, they shall order her to go up, and her maids shall take *her*, mourning as with the voice of doves, beating upon their breasts.

8 And Nineveh was of old like a pool of water: but *now* they flee away. Stand,

stand, *shall they cry*; but none looketh *back*.

9 Take ye the spoil of silver, take the spoil of gold: for *there is* no end of the riches; honour, more than all the desirable furniture.

10 She is empty, and worn out, and is in pieces,: and the heart melted, the knees smite together, and much pain *is* in the kidneys, and the faces of them all gather blackness.

11 What of the dwelling of the lions, and of the feeding place of the young lions, where the lion and the lioness walked, *and* the lion's whelps, and none made *them* afraid?

12 The lion did tear in pieces enough for his whelps, and strangled for his lionesses, and filled his holes with prey, and his dens with robbery.

13 Behold, I *speak* unto thee, saith the LORD of the hosts, and I will burn and *reduce* thy chariots into smoke, and the sword shall devour thy young lions: and I will cut off thy robbery from the earth, and the voice of thy ambassadors shall never be heard again.

Chapter 3

1 Woe to the bloody city! it *is* full of lies *and* robbery; stealing departeth not *from* her!

2 The noise of *the* whip, and the noise of the rattling of the wheels, and of the prancing horses, and of the jumping chariots *shall be heard in thee.*

3 The horseman lifteth up both the bright sword and the glittering spear: and *there is* a multitude of slain, and a great number of carcasses; and *there* shall be no end of *their* corpses; they stumble upon their corpses:

4 Because of the multitude of the whoredoms of the harlot of beautiful grace, the mistress of witchcrafts, that selleth the Gentiles *in slavery* through her whoredoms, and peoples through her witchcrafts.

5 Here I *am* against thee, saith the LORD of the hosts; and I will uncover thy skirts upon thy face, and I will show the Gentiles thy nakedness, and the kingdoms thy shame.

6 And I will cast abominable filth upon thee, and make thee vile, and will set thee as dung.

7 And it shall come to pass, *that* all they that look upon thee shall flee from thee, and say, Nineveh is laid waste: who will bemoan her? whence shall I seek comforters for thee?

8 Art thou better than populous No, that was situated among the rivers, *that had* the waters round about it, whose rampart *was* the sea, *and* her wall *was* from the sea?

9 Ethiopia was thy strength and Egypt with no limit; Put and Libia went to thy aid.

10 Yet *was* she carried away, she went into captivity: her young children also were dashed in pieces at the top of all the streets: and they cast lots for her honourable men, and all her nobles were bound in chains.

11 Thou also shalt be drunken: thou shalt be encompassed, thou also shalt seek strength because of the enemy.

12 All thy strong holds *are like* fig trees with the firstripe figs: if they be shaken, they even fall into the mouth of the eater.

13 Behold, thy people in the midst of thee *shall be like* women: the gates of thy land shall be set wide open unto thine enemies: the fire shall devour thy bars.

14 Draw thee waters for the siege, fortify thy strong holds: go into clay, and tread the morter, make strong the brickkiln.

15 There shall the fire devour thee; the sword shall cut thee off, it shall eat thee up like the cankerworm: make thyself many as the cankerworm, make thyself many as the locusts.

16 Thou hast multiplied thy merchants above the stars of heaven: the cankerworm spoileth, and flieth away.

17 Thy princes *shall be* as the locusts, and thy captains as the great grasshoppers, which camp in the hedges in the cold day, *but* when the sun ariseth they flee away, and it is not known where they were.

18 Thy shepherds have slumbered, O king of Assyria: thy valiant ones are at rest: thy people scattered themselves upon the mountains, and there is no one to unite *them*.

19 *There is* no cure for thy destruction; thy wound is grievous: all that hear thy story shall clap their hands over thee: for upon whom hath not thy wickedness passed continually?

The Prophet
Habakkuk

Chapter 1

1 The burden which Habakkuk the prophet did see.

2 O LORD, how long shall I cry, and thou wilt not hear; and raise my voice unto thee because of the violence, and thou wilt not save?

3 Why dost thou cause me to see iniquity, and cause *me* to behold grievance and destruction and violence before me: in addition to those that raise up strife and contention?

4 Therefore the law is weakened, and the judgment doth not go forth true: for the wicked doth compass about the righteous; therefore wrong judgment proceedeth.

5 Behold ye among the Gentiles, and regard, and wonder marvellously: for a work shall be done in your days, *which* ye will not believe, though it be told *you*.

6 For, behold, I raise up the Chaldeans, *that* bitter and hasty nation, which march through the breadth of the earth, to possess the dwellingplaces *that are* not theirs.

7 She *is* terrible and dreadful: from she herself shall go forth their rights and their grandeur.

8 Their horses shall be swifter than tigers, and are sharper than the evening wolves: and their horsemen shall multiply themselves, and their horsemen shall come from far; they shall fly as eagles *that* hasten to eat.

9 All of her shall come all for the prey: before their faces an east wind, and they shall gather the captives as the sand.

10 And he shall scoff at the kings, and the princes shall be a scorn unto him: he shall deride every fortress, and shall heap dust, and take it.

11 Then shall he become arrogant *against God*, and he shall pass ahead, and offend, *imputing* this his power unto his god.

12 *Art* thou not from the beginning, O LORD my God, my Holy One? we shall not die O LORD, thou hast ordained him for judgment; and thou hast established him strong for chastisement.

13 *Thou art* of purer eyes than to behold evil, and canst not·look on iniquity: wherefore lookest thou upon them that deal treacherously, *and* holdest thy tongue when the wicked devoureth *the man that is* more righteous than he?

14 And makest men as the fishes of the sea, as reptiles *that have* no lord?

15 He shall take up all of them with *his* hook, he shall catch them in his net, and gather them in his drag: therefore he shall rejoice and be glad.

16 Therefore he shall sacrifice unto his net, and burn incense unto his drag; because by them his portion *is* fat, and his food plenteous.

17 Shall he therefore empty his net, or have pity to *stop* slaying Gentiles continually?

Chapter 2

1 I will stand upon my watch, and affirm my foot upon the fortress, and will watch to see what he will say in me, and what I shall answer to my question.

2 And the LORD answered me, and said, Write the vision, and make *it* plain upon tables, that he may run that readeth it.

3 For the vision *is* yet for an appointed time, but at the end it shall speak, and not lie: though it tarry, wait for it; because it will surely come, wait for it.

4 Behold, he whose soul is not upright in him *will* become filled with pride: but the just in his faith shall live.

5 Even more than he who is given over to wine, *the* transposer, the proud man shall not remain, who enlargeth his desire as a graveyard, and *is* as death, and cannot be satisfied, but gathered unto him all the Gentiles, and heapeth unto him all the peoples:

6 Shall not all these take up a parable against him, and a taunting proverb against him, and say, Woe to him that multiplied *that which was* not his! And *for* how long would he pile thick clay upon himself?

7 Shall they not rise up suddenly that shall bite thee, and awake those that shall take thy place, and thou shalt be for a prey unto them?

8 Because thou hast spoiled many nations, all the other peoples shall spoil thee; because of human blood, and *for* the robberies of the land, of the cities, and of all that dwell therein.

9 Woe to him that coveteth ill gotten gain for his house, that he may set his nest on high, that he may escape from the power of evil!

10 Thou hast taken shameful counsel for thy house by cutting off many peoples, and hast sinned against thy life.

11 For the stone shall cry out from the wall, and the beam out of the timber shall answer it.

12 Woe to him that buildeth the city with blood, and foundeth the village with iniquity!

13 *Is* this not of the LORD of the hosts? Therefore the peoples shall labour for the fire, and the Gentiles shall weary themselves in vain.

14 For the earth shall be filled with the knowledge of the glory of the LORD, as the waters cover the sea.

15 Woe unto him that giveth his neighbours drink, that puttest thy bottle to *them*, and makest *them* drunken also, that thou mayest look on their nakedness!

16 Thou hast filled thyself with dishonour instead of honour: drink thou also, and thy foreskin shall be uncovered: the cup of the LORD'S right hand shall be turned unto thee, and shameful vomit *shall fall* upon thy glory.

17 For the violence of Lebanon shall fall upon thee, and the destruction of the *wild* beasts shall break thee, because of the human blood, and of the robbery of the land, of the cities, and of all that dwell therein.

18 What profiteth the graven image that the maker thereof hath sculpted; the molten image, that teacheth lies, so that in making dumb images the maker trusteth in his work?

19 Woe unto him that saith to the wood, Awake; to the dumb stone, Arise! Can it ever teach? Behold, it *is* laid over with gold and silver, and *there is* no breath at all within it.

20 But the LORD *is* in his holy temple: let all the earth keep silence before him.

Chapter 3

1 A prayer of Habakkuk the prophet, because of all the ignorance.

2 O LORD, I have heard thy word, *and* was afraid: O LORD, revive thy work in the midst of the times, in the midst of the times make it known; in wrath remember mercy.

3 God shall come from Teman, and the Holy *One* from mount Paran. Selah. His glory covered the heavens, and the earth was filled with his praise.

4 And *his* brightness was as the light; he had horns *coming* out of his hand: and there *was* hidden his strength.

5 Before his face went mortality, and burning coals went forth from his feet.

6 He stood, and measured the earth: he beheld, and drove out the Gentiles; and the ancient mountains crumbled, the ancient hills; the ways of the world did bow unto him.

7 I saw the tents of Cushan as nothing: *and* the curtains of the land of Midian did tremble.

8 Oh LORD, wast thou displeased against the rivers? *was* thine anger against the rivers? *was* thy wrath even against the sea, when thou didst ride upon thine horses *and* thy chariots of saving health?

9 Thy bow was entirely uncovered, and the oaths unto the tribes, eternal word, when thou didst divide the earth with rivers.

10 The mountains saw thee, *and* they trembled: the overflowing of the waters passed by: the abyss uttered his voice, the deep lifted up his hands.

11 The sun *and* the moon stood still in their habitation: at the light of thine arrows they went, *and* at the shining of thy glittering spear.

12 Thou didst tread upon the land in wrath, thou didst thresh the Gentiles in anger.

13 Thou wentest forth to save thy people, to save with thine anointed; thou didst shatter the head of the house of the wicked, by uncovering the foundation unto the neck. Selah.

14 Thou didst strike through with his staffs the heads of his villages: who as a whirlwind attempted to scatter me: their pride *was* as to devour the poor secretly.

15 Thou didst make a way through the sea for thine horses, *through* the heap of great waters.

16 When I heard, my belly trembled; my lips quivered at the voice: rottenness entered into my bones, and I trembled in my seat, that I might rest in the day of trouble: when he cometh up unto the people to destroy them.

17 Because the fig tree shall not blossom, neither *shall* fruit *be* on the vines; the labour of the olive shall lie, and the cultivated fields shall yield no food; the sheep shall be cut off from the fold, and *there shall be* no herd in the stalls:

18 Yet I will rejoice in the LORD, I will joy in the God of my saving health.

19 The LORD God *is* my strength, and he will make my feet like hinds' *feet*, and upon my high places he will cause me to walk victorious in my instruments of music.

Zephaniah

Chapter 1

1 The word of the LORD which went unto Zephaniah the son of Cushi, the son of Gedaliah, the son of Amariah, the son of Hizkiah, in the days of Josiah the son of Amon, king of Judah.

2 I will utterly destroy all things from off the face of the earth, saith the LORD.

3 I will destroy the men and the beasts; I will destroy the fowls of the heaven, and the fisnes of the sea, and the wicked shall stumble; and I will cut off men from upon the face of the earth, saith the LORD.

4 And I will extend my hand over Judah, and over all the inhabitants of Jerusalem; and I will cut off the remnant of Baal from this place, *and* the name of their religious *persons* with *their* priests;

5 and them that worship the host of heaven upon the housetops; and them that worship swearing by the LORD and by their king;

6 and them that have turned back from following the LORD; and *those* that did not seek the LORD, nor enquired about him.

7 Be silent before the presence of the Lord GOD: for the day of the LORD *is* at hand: for the LORD hath prepared a sacrifice, he hath bid his guests.

8 And it shall come to pass in the day of the LORD'S sacrifice, that I will make a visitation upon the princes, and upon the king's children, and upon all such as are clothed with strange apparel.

9 In the same day I will also make a visitation upon all those that leap over the door, which fill their masters' houses with robbery and deceit.

10 And it shall come to pass in that day, saith the

LORD, *that there shall be* the noise of a cry from the fish gate, and an howling from the school, and a great destruction from the hills.

11 Howl, ye inhabitants of Maktesh, for all the merchant people are cut down; all they that bear *ye* silver are cut off.

12 And it shall come to pass at that time, *that* I will search Jerusalem with candles, and make a visitation upon the men that are settled on their lees: that say in their heart, The LORD will not do good, neither will he do evil.

13 Therefore their goods shall become a spoil, and their houses a desolation: they shall build houses, but not inhabit *them*; and they shall plant vineyards, but not drink the wine thereof.

14 The great day of the LORD *is* near, *it is* near, and hasteneth greatly, the bitter voice of the day of the LORD: the mighty man shall cry there.

15 That day *is* a day of wrath, a day of trouble and distress, a day of wasteness and desolation, a day of darkness and gloominess, a day of cl uds and thick darkness,

16 A day of the trumpet and alarm upon the strong cities, and upon the high towers.

17 And I will bring distress upon men, that they shall walk like blind men, because they have sinned against the LORD: and their blood shall be poured out as dust, and their flesh as the dung.

18 Neither their silver nor their gold shall be able to deliver them in the day of the LORD'S wrath; but the whole earth shall be devoured by the fire of his jealousy: for he shall make even a speedy riddance of all them that dwell in the earth.

Chapter 2

1 Search yourselves and one another, O unfriendly people;

2 before the decree is executed, *before* the day pass as the chaff, before the fierce anger of the LORD come upon you, before the day of the LORD'S anger come upon you.

3 Seek ye the LORD, all ye humble of the earth, which have wrought his judgment; seek righteousness, seek humility: it may be ye shall be kept in the day of the LORD'S anger.

4 For Gaza shall be forsaken, and Ashkelon a desolation: they shall spoil Ashdod at the noon day, and Ekron shall be rooted up.

5 Woe unto the inhabitants of the sea coast, the people of the Cherethites! the word of the LORD *is* against you; O Canaan, the land of the Palistinians, I will cause thee to be destroyed until there shall be no inhabitant *left*.

6 And the sea coast shall be dwellings *and* cottages for pastors, and sheepfolds.

7 And the coast shall be for the remnant of the house of Judah; they shall feed thereupon: in the houses of Ashkelon shall they sleep for the night: for the LORD their God shall visit them, and return their captives.

8 I have heard the reproaches of Moab, and the revilings of the sons of Ammon, whereby they have dishonoured my people, and magnified *themselves* over their border.

9 Therefore *as* I live, said the LORD of the hosts, *the* God of Israel, Surely Moab shall be as Sodom, and the sons of Ammon as Gomorrah, *even* a field of nettles, and saltpits, and a perpetual desolation: the remnant of my people shall spoil them, and the remnant of my Gentiles shall inherit them.

10 This shall come upon them for their pride, because they have reproached and magnified *themselves* against the people of the LORD of the hosts.

11 The LORD *shall be* terrible against them: for he will weaken all the gods of the earth; and each one from his place shall worship him, *even* all the isles of the Gentiles.

12 Ye Ethiopians also, ye *shall be* slain by my sword.

13 And he will stretch out his hand over the north *wind*, and destroy Assyria; and will make Nineveh a desolation, *and* dry like a wilderness.

14 And flocks shall lie down in the midst of her, all the beasts of the Gentiles: both the cormorant and the bittern shall lodge in her thresholds; *their* voice shall sing in the windows; desolation *shall be* in the gates: for her cedar *work* shall be uncovered.

15 This *is* the rejoicing city that dwelt carelessly, that said in her heart, I *am*, and *there is* none beside me: how is she become a desolation, a place for beasts to lie down in! every one that passeth by her shall hiss, *and* wag his hand.

Chapter 3

1 Woe to her that is filthy and polluted, to the oppressing city!

2 She obeyed not the voice; she received not correction; she trusted not in the LORD; she drew not near to her God.

3 Her princes within her *are* roaring lions; her judges *are* evening wolves; they leave not a bone for tomorrow.

4 Her prophets *are* light *and* treacherous persons: her priests have polluted the sanctuary, they have falsefied the law.

5 The just LORD *is* in the midst thereof; he will not do iniquity: every morning doth he bring his judgment to light, he faileth not; but the unjust knoweth no shame.

6 I have caused *the* Gentiles to be cut off: their castles are desolate; I made their streets waste, until none passeth by: their cities are destroyed, so that there is no man *left*, there is no inhabitant.

7 Saying, Surely *now* thou wilt fear me, thou wilt receive chastisement; so thy dwelling shall not be thrown down, all of which I visited upon her: but they rose early, *and* corrupted all their doings.

8 Therefore wait ye for me, said the LORD, until the day that I rise up to the prey: for my judgment *is* to gather *the* Gentiles, that I may assemble the kingdoms, to pour upon them my indignation, *even* all my fierce anger: for all the earth shall be devoured with the fire of my jealousy.

9 For then will I restore to the peoples the pure language, that they may all call upon the name of the LORD, to serve him with one consent.

10 From beyond the rivers of Ethiopia my suppliants, *even* the daughter of my dispersed, shall bring me an offering.

11 In that day shalt thou not be ashamed for any of thy doings, wherein thou hast rebelled against me: for then I will take away out of the midst of thee them that rejoice in thy pride, and thou shalt no more be haughty because of the mountain of my holiness.

12 I will also leave in the midst of thee a poor and humble people, and they shall wait in the name of the LORD.

13 The remnant of Israel shall not do iniquity, nor speak lies; neither shall a deceitful tongue be found in their mouth: for they shall be fed and lie down, and none shall make *them* afraid.

14 Sing, O daughter of Zion; *shout with* jubilee O Israel; be glad and rejoice with all thy heart, O daughter of Jerusalem.

15 The LORD hath taken away thy judgments, he hath cast out thine enemy: the LORD *is* king of Israel in the midst of thee: thou shalt not see evil any more.

16 In that time it shall be said to Jerusalem, Fear thou not: *and to* Zion, Let not thine hands be slack.

17 The LORD thy God in the midst of thee *is* mighty; he will save, he will rejoice over thee with joy; he will rest in his love, he will joy over thee with singing.

18 I will gather *them that are* weary because of the *long* time, *who* are thine, *unto whom* her confusion *was* a burden.

19 Behold, at that time I will undo all that afflict thee: and I will save her that is lame, and gather her that was driven out; and I will make them a praise and of *good* reputation in every land where they have been put to shame.

20 At that time will I bring you *again,* even in the time that I gather you: for I will give you as fame and as praise among all peoples of the earth, when I shall return your captives before your eyes, saith the LORD.

The Prophet

Haggai

Chapter 1

1 In the second year of Darius the king, in the sixth month, in the first day of the month, came the word of the LORD by *the* hand of Haggai the prophet unto Zerubbabel the son of Shealtiel, governor of Judah, and to Joshua the son of Josedech, the high priest, saying,

2 Thus speaketh the LORD of the hosts, saying, This people say, The time is not yet come; the time to build the house of the LORD.

3 Then came the word of the LORD by the hand of Haggai the prophet, saying,

4 Do you have time, all of you, to dwell in your panelled houses, and this house *is* deserted?

5 Now therefore thus hath the LORD of the hosts said; Consider your ways.

6 Ye have sown much, and bring in little; ye eat, but ye are not filled; ye drink, but ye are not satisfied; ye clothe yourselves, but you are not warm; and he that is an hireling receiveth his wages in a bag with holes.

7 Thus hath the LORD of the hosts said; Consider your ways.

8 Go up to the mountain, and bring wood, and build the house; and I will place my will in her, and I will be glorified, said the LORD.

9 Ye look for much, and find little; and *when* ye lock it up at home, I shall blow upon it. Why? said the LORD of the hosts. Because my house is deserted, and ye run every one of you unto his *own* house.

10 Therefore the rain of the heavens over you is held back, and the earth has held back her fruits.

11 And I called for a drought upon this land, and upon the mountains, and upon the wheat, and upon the wine, and upon the oil, and upon *that* which the earth bringeth forth, and upon the men, and upon the beasts, and upon every labour of hands.

12 Then Zerubbabel the son of Shealtiel, and Joshua the son of Josedech, the high priest, with all the remnant of the people, did hear the voice of the LORD their God, and the words of Haggai the prophet, as the LORD their God had sent him, and the people did fear before the LORD.

13 Then spake Haggai the ambassador of the LORD in the embassy of the LORD unto the people, saying, I *am* with you, said the LORD.

14 And the LORD woke up the spirit of Zerubbabel the son of Shealtiel, governor of Judah, and the spirit of Joshua the son of Josedech, the high priest, and the spirit of all the remnant of the people; and they came and did work in the house of the LORD of the hosts, their God,

15 in the four and twentieth day of the sixth month, in the second year of Darius the king.

Chapter 2

1 In the seventh *month*, in the one and twentieth *day* of the month, came the word of the LORD by the hand of the prophet Haggai, saying,

2 Speak now to Zerubbabel the son of Shealtiel, governor of Judah, and to Joshua the son of Josedech, the high priest, and to the remnant of the people, saying,

3 Who *is* left among you that saw this house in her first glory? and how do ye see her now? *Is* she not as nothing before your eyes?

4 Yet now be strong, O Zerubbabel, said the LORD; and be strong, O Joshua, son of Josedech, the high priest; and be strong, all ye people of this land, said the LORD, and work: for I *am* with you, said the LORD of the hosts:

5 The word that I covenanted with you when ye came out of Egypt, and my Spirit is in the midst of you: fear ye not.

6 For thus hath the LORD of the hosts said; Yet even once, and I will shake the heavens, and the earth, and the sea, and the dry *land*;

7 and I will shake all the Gentiles, and the desire of all the Gentiles shall come:

and I will fill this house with glory, said the LORD of the hosts.

8 The silver *is* mine, and the gold *is* mine, said the LORD of the hosts.

9 The glory of this latter house shall be greater than of the former, said the LORD of the hosts: and in this place will I give peace, said the LORD of the hosts.

10 In the four and twentieth *day* of the ninth *month*, in the second year of Darius, came the word of the LORD by the hand of Haggai the prophet, saying,

11 Thus hath the LORD of the hosts said; Ask now the priests *concerning* the law, saying,

12 If one bear holy flesh in the skirt of his garment, and with his skirt do touch bread, or pottage, or wine, or oil, or any food, shall it be *made* holy? And the priests answered and said, No.

13 Then said Haggai, If *one that is* unclean by a dead body touch any of these, shall it be unclean? And the priests answered and said, It shall be unclean.

14 Then answered Haggai, and said, So *is* this people, and so *is* this nation before me, said the LORD; and so

is every work of their hands; and all that they offer here *is* unclean.

15 And now, I pray you, consider in your heart from this day forth, from before a stone was laid upon a stone in the temple of the LORD:

16 Since these *things* were, when *one* came to an heap of twenty *measures*, there were *but* ten: when *one* came to the pressfat for to draw out fifty *vessels* out of the press, there were *but* twenty.

17 I smote you with *the* east wind and with mildew and with hail in all the labours of your hands; yet ye *turned* not to me, said the LORD.

18 Consider now in your heart from this day forth, from the four and twentieth day of the ninth *month*, *even* from the day that the foundation of the LORD'S temple was laid, put your heart into *it*.

19 Is the seed yet in the barn? yea, as yet the vine, and the fig tree, and the pomegranate, and the olive tree, hath not brought forth: yet from this day will I bless *you*.

20 And the word of the LORD came the second time unto Haggai in the four and twentieth *day* of the month, saying,

21 Speak to Zerubbabel, governor of Judah, saying, I cause the heavens and the earth to shake;

22 and I will overthrow the throne of the kingdoms, and I will destroy the strength of the kingdom of the Gentiles; and I will overthrow the chariot, and those that ride in them; and the horses and their riders shall come down, every one by the sword of his brother.

23 In that day, said the LORD of the hosts, will I take thee, O Zerubbabel, my servant, the son of Shealtiel, said the LORD, and will make thee as a signet ring: for I have chosen thee, saith the LORD of the hosts.

The Prophet
Zechariah

Chapter 1

1 In the eighth month, in the second year of Darius, came the word of the LORD unto the prophet Zechariah, the son of Berechiah, the son of Iddo, saying,

2 The LORD hath been sore displeased with your fathers.

3 Therefore thou shalt say unto them, Thus hath the LORD of the hosts said; Turn ye unto me, said the LORD of the hosts, and I will turn unto you, said the LORD of the hosts.

4 Be ye not as your fathers, unto whom the former prophets have cried, saying, Thus hath the LORD of the hosts said; Turn ye now from your evil ways, and *from* your evil doings: but they did not hear, nor hearken unto me, said the LORD.

5 Your fathers, where *are* they? and the prophets, do they live for ever?

6 But my words and my statutes, which I commanded my servants the prophets, did they not take hold of your fathers? Therefore they returned *from captivity* and said, Like as the LORD of the hosts thought to do unto us, according to our ways, and according to our doings, so hath he dealt with us.

7 Upon the four and twentieth day of the eleventh month, which *is* the month Sebat, in the second year of Darius, came the word of the LORD unto the prophet Zechariah, the son of Berechiah, the son of Iddo, saying,

8 I saw by night, and behold a man riding upon a red horse, and he stood among the myrtle trees that *were* in the bottom; and behind him *were there* red horses, speckled, and white.

9 Then said I, O my lord, what *are* these? And the angel that talked with me said unto me, I will show thee who these *be*.

10 And the man that stood among the myrtle trees answered and said, These *are they* whom the LORD hath sent to walk to and fro through the earth.

11 And they answered the angel of the LORD that stood among the myrtle trees, and said, We have walked to and fro through the land, and, behold, all the earth sitteth still, and is at rest.

12 Then the angel of the LORD answered and said, O LORD of the hosts, when wilt thou have mercy on Jerusalem and on the cities of Judah, against which thou hast had indignation these seventy years?

13 And the LORD answered good words unto the angel that talked with me, words of consolation.

14 So the angel that communed with me said unto me, Cry thou, saying, Thus saith the LORD of the hosts; I am jealous for Jerusalem and for Zion with a great jealousy.

15 And I am very sore displeased with the Gentiles *that are* at ease: for I was but a little displeased, and they helped forward the affliction.

16 Therefore thus hath the LORD said; I am returned to Jerusalem with mercies: my house shall be built in her, saith the LORD of the hosts, and a line shall be stretched forth upon Jerusalem.

17 Cry yet, saying, Thus saith the LORD of the hosts; My cities through abundance of good shall yet be widened; and the LORD shall yet comfort Zion, and shall yet choose Jerusalem.

18 Then I lifted up my eyes, and saw, and behold four horns.

19 And I said unto the angel that talked with me, What *are* these? And he answered me, These *are* the horns which have scattered Judah, Israel, and Jerusalem.

20 And the LORD showed me four carpenters.

21 Then I said, What *do* these come to do? And he spake, saying, These *are* the horns which have scattered Judah, so that no one did lift up his head: but these are come to cause them to tremble, to cut down the horns of the Gentiles, which lifted up *their* horn over the land of Judah to scatter it.

Chapter 2

1 I lifted up my eyes again, and looked, and behold a man with a measuring line in his hand.

2 Then said I, Where goest thou? And he said unto me, To measure Jerusalem, to see what *is* the breadth thereof, and what *is* the length thereof.

3 And, behold, the angel that talked with me went forth, and another angel went out to meet him,

4 and said unto him, Run, speak to this young man, saying, Jerusalem shall be inhabited without walls for the multitude of men and beasts in the midst of her:

5 For I, saith the LORD, will be unto her a wall of fire round about, and will be the glory in the midst of her.

6 Ho, ho, *come forth*, and flee from the land of the north, saith the LORD: for I have spread you abroad by the four winds of the heavens, saith the LORD.

7 O Zion, that dwellest *with* the daughter of Babylon, thou must escape.

8 For thus hath the LORD of the hosts said; After the glory he shall send me unto the Gentiles which spoiled you: for he that toucheth you toucheth the apple of his eye.

9 For, behold, I raise my hand regarding them, and they shall be a spoil to their servants: and ye shall know that the LORD of the hosts hath sent me.

10 Sing and rejoice, O daughter of Zion: for, behold, I come, and I will dwell in the midst of thee, said the LORD.

11 And many Gentiles shall join themselves unto the LORD in that day, and shall be my people: and I will dwell in the midst of thee, and then thou shalt know that the LORD of the hosts hath sent me unto thee.

12 And the LORD shall possess Judah his portion in the holy land, and shall still choose Jerusalem.

13 Be silent, O all flesh, before the LORD: for he is raised up out of his holy habitation.

Chapter 3

1 And he showed me Joshua the high priest standing before the angel of the LORD, and Satan standing at his right hand to resist him.

2 And the LORD said unto Satan, The LORD reprehend thee, O Satan; even the LORD that hath chosen Jerusalem reprehend thee: *is* not this a brand plucked out of the fire?

3 Now Joshua was clothed with filthy garments, and stood before the angel.

4 And *the angel* answered and spake unto those that stood before him, saying, Take away the filthy garments from him. And unto him he said, Behold, I have caused thine iniquity to pass from thee, and I have caused thee to be clothed with new raiment.

5 And I said, Let them set a clean mitre upon his head. So they set a clean mitre upon his head, and clothed him with garments. And the angel of the LORD stood by.

6 And the angel of the LORD protested unto Joshua, saying,

7 Thus saith the LORD of the hosts; If thou wilt walk in my ways, and if thou wilt keep my charge, then thou shalt also govern my house, and shalt also keep my courts, and I will give thee *a* place among these that are here.

8 Hear now, O Joshua the high priest, thou, and thy fellows that sit before thee: for they *are* men of wonder. Behold, I bring forth my servant the BRANCH.

9 For behold the stone that I have laid before Joshua; upon one stone *there are* seven eyes: behold, I will engrave his labour, saith the LORD of the hosts, and I will remove the iniquity of the land in one day.

10 In that day, saith the LORD of the hosts, every one of you shall call his neighbour under his vine and under *his* fig tree.

Chapter 4

1 And the angel that talked with me came again, and waked me, as a man that is wakened out of his sleep,

2 and said unto me, What seest thou? And I said, I have looked, and behold a candlestick all *of* gold, with a bowl upon the top of it, and his seven lamps upon the candlestick, and seven pipes for the lamps, which *are* upon the top thereof:

3 And two olive trees over it, one upon the right hand *side* of the bowl, and the other upon the left hand *side* thereof.

4 So I answered and spoke to the angel that talked with me, saying, What *is* this, my lord?

5 Then the angel that talked with me answered and said unto me, Knowest thou not what this is? And I said, No, my lord.

6 Then he answered and spoke unto me, saying, This

is the word of the LORD unto Zerubbabel, saying, Not by might, nor by power, but by my Spirit, said the LORD of the hosts.

7 Who *art* thou, O great mountain before Zerubabel? *Thou shalt be reduced to* a plain: and he shall bring forth the headstone *thereof with* shoutings, *crying*, Grace, grace unto it.

8 And the word of the LORD came unto me, saying,

9 The hands of Zerubbabel shall lay the foundation of this house; his hands shall also finish it; and thou shalt know that the LORD of the hosts hath sent me unto you.

10 For who hath despised the day of small *beginnings*? for they shall rejoice, and shall see the plummet in the hand of Zerubbabel. Those seven *are* the eyes of the LORD, which run to and fro through the whole earth.

11 Then I spoke and said unto him, What *are* these two olive trees upon the right hand *side* of the candlestick and upon the left hand *side* thereof?

12 And I spoke the second time, and said unto him, What *be these* two olive branches which through the two golden pipes empty the golden *oil* out of themselves?

13 And he answered me and said, Knowest thou not what these *be*? And I said, No, my lord.

14 Then said he, These two sons of oil *are* those that stand by the Lord of the whole earth.

Chapter 5

1 Then I turned, and lifted up my eyes, and looked, and behold a flying roll.

2 And he said unto me, What seest thou? And I answered, I see a flying roll; the length thereof *is* twenty cubits, and the breadth thereof ten cubits.

3 Then said he unto me, This *is* the curse that goeth forth over the face of the whole earth: for every one that stealeth (as it *is written* on one side of the *roll*) shall be destroyed; and every one that sweareth (as it *is written* on the other side of the *roll*) shall be destroyed.

4 I brought it forth, said the LORD of the hosts, and it shall enter into the house of the thief, and into the house of him that sweareth falsely by my name: and it shall remain in the midst of his house, and shall consume it with the timber thereof and the stones thereof.

5 Then the angel that talked with me went forth, and said unto me, Lift up now thine eyes, and see what *is* this that goeth forth.

6 And I said, What *is* it? And he said, This *is* an ephah *to measure wheat* that goeth forth. He said moreover, This *is* their iniquity in all the earth.

7 And, behold, they lifted up a talent of lead: and a woman was sitting in the midst of that ephah.

8 And he said, This *is* wickedness. And he cast her into the midst of the ephah; and he cast the weight of lead upon the mouth thereof.

9 Then I lifted up my eyes, and looked, and, behold, there came out two women, and the wind *was* in their wings; for they had wings like the wings of a stork: and they lifted up the ephah between the earth and the heavens.

10 Then I said to the angel that talked with me, Where do these bear the ephah?

11 And he said unto me, To build it an house in the land of Shinar: and it shall be established, and set there upon her own base.

Chapter 6

1 And I turned, and lifted up my eyes, and looked, and, behold, there came four chariots out from between two mountains; and those mountains *were* of brass.

2 In the first chariot *were* red horses; and in the second chariot black horses;

3 in the third chariot white horses; and in the fourth chariot grisled and bay horses.

4 Then I answered and said unto the angel that talked with me, What *is* this, my lord?

5 And the angel answered and said unto me, These *are* the four spirits of the heavens, which go forth from standing before the Lord of all the earth.

6 The one with the black horses went forth towards the north country; and the white went forth after them; and the grisled went forth toward the south country.

7 And the bay went forth, and sought to go that they might walk to and fro through the earth: and he said, Get you hence, walk to and fro through the earth. So they walked to and fro through the earth.

8 Then he called me, and spoke unto me, saying, Be-

452

hold, those that went toward the north country have quieted my spirit in the north country.

9 And the word of the LORD came unto me, saying,

10 Take of *them of that returned from* the captivity, *of the lineage* of Heldai, of Tobijah, and of Jedaiah, and come thou the same day, and go into the house of Josiah the son of Zephaniah, which are come from Babylon.

11 Thou shalt take silver and gold, and make crowns, and set *them* upon the head of Joshua the son of Josedech, the high priest;

12 and speak unto him, saying, Thus spoke the LORD of the hosts, saying, Behold the man whose name *is* The BRANCH; and he shall grow up out of his place, and he shall build the temple of the LORD:

13 Even he shall build the temple of the LORD; and he shall bear the glory, and shall sit and rule upon his throne; and he shall be a priest upon his throne: and the counsel of peace shall be between them both.

14 And Helem, and Tobijah, and Jedaiah, and Hen the son of Zephaniah, shall have crowns for *a* memorial in the temple of the LORD.

15 And they *that are* far off shall come and build in the temple of the LORD, and ye shall know that the LORD of the hosts hath sent me unto you. And *this* shall come to pass, if ye will obediently hear the voice of the LORD our God.

Chapter 7

1 And it came to pass in the fourth year of king Darius, *that* the word of the LORD came unto Zechariah in the fourth *day* of the ninth month, *even* in Chisleu;

2 when they had sent unto the house of God Sherezer and Regemmelech, and their men, to pray before the LORD,

3 *and* to speak unto the priests which *were* in the house of the LORD of the hosts, and to the prophets, saying, Should we weep in the fifth month? Should we do abstinance as we have done these so many years?

4 Then came the word of the LORD of the hosts unto me, saying,

5 Speak unto all the people of the land, and to the priests, saying, When ye fasted and mourned in the fifth and seventh *month*, even those seventy years,

did ye at all fast unto me,
even to me?

6 And when ye did eat, and
when ye did drink, did not
ye eat *for yourselves*, and
drink *for yourselves*?

7 Are these not the words
which the LORD hath pub-
lished by the former prophets, when Jerusalem was
inhabited and quiet, and
the cities thereof round
about her, and *when* the
south and the plain were
inhabited?

8 And the word of the LORD
came unto Zechariah, saying,

9 Thus hath the LORD of
the hosts spoken, saying,
Execute true judgment, and
show mercy and compas-
sion every man to his
brother:

10 And oppress not the
widow, nor the fatherless,
the stranger, nor the poor;
and let none of you imag-
ine evil against his brother
in your heart.

11 But they refused to
hearken, and pulled away
the shoulder, and stopped
their ears, that they should
not hear.

12 Yea, they made their
hearts *as* an adamant
stone, lest they should hear
the law, and the words
which the LORD of the hosts
hath sent by his Spirit by
the hand of the former

prophets: therefore came a
great wrath from the LORD
of the hosts.

13 Therefore it is come to
pass, *that* as he cried, and
they would not hear; so
they cried, and I would not
hear, saith the LORD of the
hosts:

14 But I scattered them
with a whirlwind among all
the Gentiles whom they
knew not. Thus the land was
desolate after them, that no
man passed through nor
returned: for they laid the
desireable land desolate.

Chapter 8

1 Again the word of the
LORD of the hosts came *to
me*, saying,

2 Thus hath the LORD of
the hosts said; I was jealous for Zion with great jealousy, and I was jealous for
her with great fury.

3 Thus hath the LORD said;
I will restore Zion, and will
dwell in the midst of
Jerusalem: and Jerusalem
shall be called City of truth;
and the mountain of the
LORD of the hosts, the
mountain of holiness.

4 Thus hath the LORD of
the hosts said; There shall
yet old men and old women
dwell in the streets of
Jerusalem, and each one
with his staff in his hand for
the multitude of the days.

5 And the streets of the city shall be full of boys and girls, who shall play in them.

6 Thus saith the LORD of the hosts; If this should appear difficult in the eyes of the remnant of this people in these days, should it also be difficult in my eyes? saith the LORD of the hosts.

7 Thus hath the LORD of the hosts said; Behold, I will save my people of the land of the east, and of the land where the sun setteth;

8 and I will bring them, and they shall dwell in the midst of Jerusalem: and they shall be my people, and I will be their God, in truth and in righteousness.

9 Thus hath the LORD of the hosts said; Let your hands be strong, ye that hear in these days these words by the mouth of the prophets, from the day *that* the foundation of the house of the LORD of the hosts was laid, that the temple might be built.

10 For before these days there was no hire for man, nor any hire for beast; neither *was there any* peace to him that went out or came in because of the affliction: for I set all men every one against his neighbour.

11 But now I *will* not *do* unto the residue of this people as in the former days, said the LORD of the hosts.

12 For the seed of peace *shall remain*; the vine shall give her fruit, and the ground shall give her fruit, and the heavens shall give their dew; and I will cause the remnant of this people to possess all this.

13 And it shall come to pass, *that* as ye were a curse among the Gentiles, O house of Judah, and house of Israel; so will I save you, that ye might be a blessing: fear not, *but* let your hands be strong.

14 For thus hath the LORD of the hosts said; As I thought to punish you, when your fathers provoked me to wrath, said the LORD of the hosts, and I repented not:

15 So again have I thought in these days to do well unto Jerusalem and to the house of Judah: fear ye not.

16 These *are* the things that ye shall do; Speak ye every man the truth to his neighbour; execute the judgment of truth and peace in your gates:

17 And let none of you imagine evil in your hearts against his neighbour; and love no false oath: for all these *are things* that I hate, said the LORD.

18 And the word of the LORD of the hosts came unto me, saying,

19 Thus hath the LORD of the hosts said; The fast of the fourth *month*, and the fast of the fifth, and the fast of the seventh, and the fast of the tenth, shall be to the house of Judah joy and gladness, and cheerful feasts; therefore love the truth and peace.

20 Thus hath the LORD of the hosts said; *It shall* yet *come to pass*, that there shall come people, and the inhabitants of many cities:

21 And the inhabitants of one *city* shall go to another, saying, Let us go to pray before the LORD, and to seek the LORD of the hosts. [*And the other will respond:*] I will go also.

22 Yea, many peoples and strong nations shall come to seek the LORD of the hosts in Jerusalem, and to pray before the LORD.

23 Thus hath the LORD of the hosts said; In those days *it shall come to pass*, that ten men of all the languages of the Gentiles, shall take hold of the skirt of him that is a Jew, saying, We will go with you: for we have heard *that* God *is* with you.

Chapter 9

1 The burden of the word of the LORD against the land of Hadrach, and of Damascus his rest: because the eyes of the men, and of all the tribes of Israel, *are turned* toward the LORD.

2 And Hamath also shall come to an end in her; Tyre, and Zidon, though it be very wise.

3 And Tyre did build herself a strong hold, and heaped up silver as the dust, and fine gold as the mire of the streets.

4 Behold, the Lord will empoverish her, and he will smite her power in the sea; and she shall be devoured with fire.

5 Ashkelon shall see *it*, and fear; Gaza also *shall see it*, and be very sorrowful, and Ekron; for her hope shall be confounded; and the king shall perish from Gaza, and Ashkelon shall not be inhabited.

6 And a stranger shall dwell in Ashdod, and I will cut off the pride of the Philistines.

7 And I will take away his blood out of his mouth, and his abominations from between his teeth: but some of them shall remain for our God, and they shall be as captains in Judah, and Ekron as the Jebusite.

8 And I will be the defence and firm support to my house from him that cometh and goeth: and no oppressor shall pass through them any more: for now have I seen with my eyes.

9 Rejoice greatly, O daughter of Zion; *shout with* jubilee, O daughter of Jerusalem: behold, thy King shall come unto thee: just, and a salviour; humble, and riding upon an ass, even upon a colt the foal of an ass.

10 And I will cut off the chariot from Ephraim, and the horse from Jerusalem, and the battle bow shall be broken: and he shall speak peace unto the Gentiles: and his dominion *shall be* from sea *even* to sea, and from the river *even* to the ends of the earth.

11 As for thee also, by the blood of thy covenant I have taken thy prisoners out of the pit wherein *is* no water.
12 Return to the strong hold, ye prisoners of hope: even today do I declare *that* I will render double unto thee;
13 For I have bent Judah for me *as a* bow, and I made Ephraim his arrow, and I will raise up thy sons, O Zion, against thy sons, O Greece, and make thee as the sword of a mighty man.
14 And the LORD shall be seen over them, and his arrow shall go forth as the lightning: and the Lord GOD shall blow the shophar, and shall go forth as *the* whirlwinds of the south.
15 The LORD of the hosts shall defend them; and they shall devour, and subdue with sling stones; and they shall drink, *and* make a noise as though *drunk* with wine; and they shall be filled like bowls, *and* as the corners of the altar.
16 And the LORD their God shall save them in that day as a flock of his people: for they *shall be as* the stones of a crown, lifted up as an ensign upon his land.
17 For how great *is* his goodness, and how great *is* his beauty! The wheat shall make the young men cheerful, and the wine the maids.

Chapter 10

1 Ask ye of the LORD rain in the time of the latter rain; *so* the LORD shall make lightnings, and shall give you abundant rain, and grass in the field to each one.
2 For the idols have spoken vanity, and the diviners

have seen a lie, and have told vain dreams; they comfort in vain: therefore they went their way like sheep, they were humbled, because *there was* no shepherd.

3 My anger is kindled against the pastors, and I will visit the he goats: for the LORD of the hosts shall visit his flock, the house of Judah, and shall make them as his horse of honour in the battle.

4 Out of him shall come the corner, out of him the nail, out of him the battle bow, out of him also every oppressor.

5 And they shall be as mighty *men*, which tread down *their enemies* in the mire of the streets in the battle: and they shall fight, because the LORD *shall be* with them, and the riders on horses shall be confounded.

6 For I will strengthen the house of Judah, and I will keep the house of Joseph, and I will cause them to return; for I shall have compassion upon them: and they shall be as though I had not cast them off: for I *am* the LORD their God, and will hear them.

7 And *they of* Ephraim shall be like a mighty *man*,

and their heart shall rejoice as through wine: yea, their children shall also see *it*, and be glad; their heart shall rejoice in the LORD.

8 I will hiss for them, and gather them; for I have redeemed them: and they shall be multiplied as they were multiplied.

9 *It was* good that I planted them among the peoples: even in far countries there shall be mention made of me; and they shall live with their children, and turn again.

10 I will bring them again also out of the land of Egypt, and gather them out of Assyria; and I will bring them into the land of Gilead and Lebanon; and *place* shall not be found for them.

11 And the tribulation shall pass through the sea, and shall smite the waves in the sea, and all the deeps of the river shall dry up: and the pride of Assyria shall be brought down, and the sceptre of Egypt shall be lost.

12 And I will strengthen them in the LORD; and they shall walk up and down in his name, saith the LORD.

Chapter 11

1 Open thy doors, O Lebanon, that the fire may devour thy cedars.

2 Howl, fir tree; for the cedar is fallen; because the magnificent are cut down: howl, O ye oaks of Bashan; for the strong mountain is brought down.

3 *There is* a voice of the howling of the pastors; for their magnificence is destroyed: a voice of the roaring of young lions; for the pride of the Jordan is destroyed.

4 Thus hath the LORD my God said; Feed the flock of the slaughter;

5 whose buyers slayed them, and held themselves not guilty: and he that sold them said, Blessed *be* the LORD; for I am rich: and not even their own shepherds had compassion on them.

6 Therefore I will no longer pity the inhabitants of the land, saith the LORD: but, behold, I will deliver the men every one into his neighbour's hand, and into the hand of his king: and they shall smite the land, and I will not deliver *them* out of their hands.

7 And I will feed the flock of slaughter, *even* you, O poor of the flock.

For I took unto me two staves; the one I named Beauty, and the other Bands; and I fed the flock.

8 Three shepherds also I cut off in one month; and my soul was in anguish for them, and their soul also abhorred me.

9 Then I said, I will not feed you *any longer*; the one that dieth, let it die; and the one that is to be lost, let it be lost; and let the rest eat every one the flesh of another.

10 And I took my staff, *even* Beauty, and cut it asunder, that I might break my covenant which I had made with all the peoples.

11 And it was broken in that day: and so the poor of the flock that look unto me knew that it *was* the word of the LORD.

12 And I said unto them, If ye think good, give *me* my wages; and if not, forbear. So they weighed for my wages thirty *pieces* of silver.

13 And the LORD said unto me, Cast it unto the treasury: a goodly price that I was appraised at by them. And I took the thirty *pieces* of silver, and cast them in the house of the LORD unto the treasury.

14 Then I cut asunder my other staff, *even* Bands,

that I might break the brotherhood between Judah and Israel.

15 And the LORD said unto me, Take unto thee yet the instruments of a foolish shepherd.

16 For, behold, I raise up a shepherd in the land, *which* shall not visit those that are lost, neither shall seek the young one, nor heal the one that is broken, nor carry the one that is tired: but he shall eat the flesh of the fat, and tear their hoofs in pieces.

17 Woe to the useless pastor that leaveth the flock! the sword *shall be* upon his arm, and upon his right eye: his arm shall be completely dried up, and his right eye shall be utterly darkened.

Chapter 12

1 The burden of the word of the LORD upon Israel, said the LORD, who stretcheth forth the heavens, and layeth the foundation of the earth, and formeth the spirit of man within him.

2 Behold, I place Jerusalem as *a* cup of poison unto all the peoples round about, and also unto Judah *who* shall be in the siege against Jerusalem.

3 And it shall be that in that day I will make Jerusalem a burdensome stone unto all peoples: all that burden themselves with it shall be cut in pieces, and all the Gentiles of the earth shall gather themselves together against her.

4 In that day, said the LORD, I will smite every horse with astonishment, and his rider with madness: but I will open my eyes upon the house of Judah, and will smite every horse of the peoples with blindness.

5 And the captains of Judah shall say in their heart, My strength *is* the inhabitants of Jerusalem in the LORD of the hosts their God.

6 In that day I will make the captains of Judah like an hearth of fire among the wood, and like a torch of fire among *the* sheaves; and they shall devour all the peoples round about, on the right hand and on the left: and Jerusalem shall be inhabited again in her own place, *even* in Jerusalem.

7 And the LORD shall keep the tents of Judah *as* in the beginning, so that the glory of the house of David and of the inhabitants of Jerusalem shall not *cause* *those of* Judah to magnify *themselves.*

8 In that day shall the LORD defend the inhabitants of Jerusalem; and he that is weak among them in that time shall be as David; and the house of David *shall be* as God, as the angel of the LORD before them.

9 And it shall come to pass in that day, *that* I will seek to destroy all the Gentiles that come against Jerusalem.

10 And I will pour upon the house of David, and upon the inhabitants of Jerusalem, *the* Spirit of grace and of prayer: and they shall look upon me whom they have pierced, and they shall mourn over him, as one mourneth for *his* only *son,* afflicting themselves over him, as one doth afflict himself over *his* firstborn.

11 In that day shall there be a great mourning in Jerusalem, as the mourning of Hadadrimmon in the valley of Megiddon.

12 And the land shall mourn, every family apart; the family of the house of David apart, and their wives apart; the family of the house of Nathan apart, and their wives apart;

13 The family of the house of Levi apart, and their wives apart; the family of Shimei apart, and their wives apart;

14 All the families that remain, every family apart, and their wives apart.

Chapter 13

1 In that time there shall be an open fountain for the house of David and for the inhabitants of Jerusalem against sin and against uncleanness.

2 And it shall come to pass in that day, saith the LORD of the hosts, *that* I will cut off the names of the idols out of the land, and they shall no longer be remembered: and also I will cause the prophets and the spirit of uncleaness to be cut off out of the land.

3 And it shall come to pass, *that* when anyone else shall prophesy, then his father and his mother that begat him shall say unto him, Thou shalt not live; for thou speakest lies in the name of the LORD: and his father and his mother that begat him shall thrust him through when he prophesieth.

4 And it shall come to pass in that time, *that* the prophets shall be ashamed every one of his vision, when he hath prophesied; neither shall they wear a rough garment to deceive:

5 But he shall say, I *am* no prophet, I *am* an husbandman of the land; for I learned this from the man from my youth.

6 And *they* shall ask him, What *are* these wounds in thine hands? Then he shall answer, *Those* with which I was wounded *in* the house of my friends.

7 Awake, O sword, upon the pastor, and upon the man *that is* my fellow, said the LORD of the hosts: smite the shepherd, and the sheep shall be scattered: and I will turn my hand upon the little ones.

8 And it shall come to pass, *that* in all the land, said the LORD, two parts therein shall be cut off in her *and* shall be lost; but the third shall be left therein.

9 And I will put the third part into the fire, and will refine them as silver is refined, and will try them as gold is tried: He shall call on my name, and I will hear him: I will say, My people: and he shall say, The LORD *is* my God.

Chapter 14

1 Behold, the day of the LORD cometh, and thy spoil shall be divided in the midst of thee.

2 For I will gather all the Gentiles against Jerusalem in battle; and the city shall be taken, and the houses rifled, and the women ravished; and half of the city shall go forth into captivity, but the remnant of the people shall not be cut off from the city.

3 Then shall the LORD go forth, and fight against those Gentiles, as when he fought in the day of battle.

4 And his feet shall stand in that day upon the mount of Olives, which *is* before Jerusalem on the east, and the mount of Olives shall cleave in the midst thereof toward the east and toward the west, *making* a very great valley; and half of the mountain shall remove toward the north, and half of it toward the south.

5 And ye shall flee to the valley of the mountains; for the valley of the mountains shall reach unto Azal: yea, ye shall flee, like as ye fled from before the earthquake in the days of Uzziah king of Judah: and the LORD my God shall come, *and* all his saints with him.

6 And it shall come to pass in that day, *that* the light shall not be clear, *nor* dark: **7** But it shall be one day which *is* known to the LORD, not day, nor night: but it shall come to pass, *that* at evening time there shall be light.

8 And it shall be in that day, *that* living waters shall go out from Jerusalem; half of them toward the eastern sea, and half of them toward the western sea: in summer and in winter shall it be. **9** And the LORD shall be king over all the earth: in that day shall the LORD be one, and his name one. **10** All the land shall become a plain from Geba to Rimmon south of Jerusalem: and she shall be lifted up, and inhabited in her place, from Benjamin's gate unto the place of the first gate, unto the gate of the corners, and *from* the tower of Hananeel unto the king's winepresses. **11** And *men* shall dwell in it, and it shall never be anathama again; but Jerusalem shall be safely inhabited. **12** And this shall be the plague wherewith the LORD will smite all the peoples that fought against Jerusalem; Their flesh shall consume away while they stand upon their feet, and their eyes shall consume away in their holes, and their tongue shall consume away in their mouth.

13 And it shall come to pass in that day, *that* a great destruction from the LORD shall be in them; for they shall lay hold every one on the hand of his neighbour, and his hand shall rise up against the hand of his neighbour. **14** And Judah also shall fight against Jerusalem; and the wealth of all the Gentiles round about shall be gathered together, gold, and silver, and apparel, in great abundance. **15** And so shall be the plague of the horse, of the mule, of the camel, and of the ass, and of all the beasts that were in the armies. **16** And every one that is left of all the nations which came against Jerusalem shall even go up from year to year to worship the King, the LORD of the hosts, and to celebrate the feast of the tabernacles. **17** And it shall be, *that* whosoever will not come up of *all* the families of the earth unto Jerusalem to worship the King, the LORD of the hosts, even upon them shall be no rain.

18 And if the family of Egypt go not up, and come not, there shall be no *rain* upon them; *instead* there shall be the plague, wherewith the LORD will smite the Gentiles that come not up to celebrate the feast of the tabernacles.

19 This shall be *the punishment* of the sin of Egypt, and of the sin of all the Gentiles that come not up to celebrate the feast of the tabernacles.

20 In that day shall there be *written* upon the bells of the horses, HOLINESS UNTO THE LORD; and the pots in the LORD'S house shall be like the bowls before the altar.

21 Yea, every pot in Jerusalem and in Judah shall be holiness unto the LORD of the hosts: and all they that sacrifice shall come and take of them, and cook therein: and in that time there shall be no more merchandizing in the house of the LORD of the hosts.

The Prophecy of
Malachi

Chapter 1

1 The burden of the word of the LORD against Israel by the hand of Malachi.

2 I have loved you, said the LORD. Yet ye say, Wherein hast thou loved us? *Was* not Esau Jacob's brother? said the LORD: yet I loved Jacob,

3 and I rejected Esau, and laid his mountains and his heritage waste for the dragons of the wilderness.

4 When Edom saith, We are impoverished, but we will return and build the desolate places; thus hath the LORD of the hosts said, They shall build, but I will throw down; and they shall call them, The province of wickedness, and, The people against whom the LORD hath indignation for ever.

5 And your eyes shall see, and ye shall say, The LORD will be magnified over the province of Israel.

6 The son honoureth *his* father, and the servant his master: if then I *be* a father, where *is* my honour? and if I *be* a master, where *is* my fear? said the LORD of the hosts unto you, O priests, that despise my name. And ye say, Wherein have we despised thy name?

7 Ye offer polluted bread upon my altar; and ye say, Wherein have we polluted thee? In that ye say, We die of hunger in the service of the LORD.

8 And when ye offer the blind *animal* for sacrifice, *is it* not evil? Likewise when ye offer the lame and sick, *is it* not evil? offer it now unto thy prince; will he be pleased with thee, or accept thy person? said the LORD of the hosts.

9 And now, therefore, beseech the face of God, and he will have compassion on us: this hath come by your hand: will he regard your persons? said the LORD of the hosts.

10 Who *is there* even among you that would shut

465   MALACHI 2:7

the doors or tend *the fire* on my altar for free. I have no pleasure in you, said the LORD of the hosts, neither will the offering from your hand be agreeable unto me.

11 For from the rising of the sun even unto the going down of the same my name is great among the Gentiles; and in every place incense is offered unto my name, and a clean offering: for my name *is* great among the Gentiles, said the LORD of the hosts.

12 And ye have profaned it when ye say, We die of hunger at the service of the LORD; and when ye speak that his food is contemptible.

13 And ye say, Behold, what a weariness *it is*! and ye have rejected it, said the LORD of the hosts; and ye brought *that which was* stolen, or lame, or sick; and presented an offering: should this be acceptable unto me by your hand? said the LORD.

14 But cursed *be* the deceiver, which hath in his flock a male, and voweth, and sacrificeth unto the Lord a corrupt thing: for I *am* a great King, saith the LORD of the hosts, and my name *is* formidable among the Gentiles.

Chapter 2

1 And now, O ye priests, this commandment *is* for you.

2 If ye will not hear, and if ye will not lay *it* to heart, to give glory unto my name, said the LORD of the hosts, I will send a curse upon you, and I will curse your blessings: yea, I have cursed them already, because ye do not lay *it* to heart.

3 Behold, I reprehend *your* seed, and spread the dung upon your faces, *even* the dung of your solemnities; and ye shall be removed with it.

4 And ye shall know that I have sent this commandment unto you, that my covenant might be with Levi, said the LORD of the hosts.

5 My covenant was with him of life and peace; and I gave them to him *for* the fear wherewith he feared me, and was broken before my name.

6 The law of truth was in his mouth, and iniquity was not found in his lips: he walked with me in peace and righteousness, and did turn many away from iniquity.

7 For the priest's lips keep wisdom, and they seek the

law at his mouth: for he *is* an angel of the LORD of the hosts.

8 But ye are departed out of the way; ye have caused many to stumble in the law; ye have corrupted the covenant of Levi, said the LORD of the hosts.

9 Therefore have I also made you contemptible and base before all the people, according as ye have not kept my ways, but have been partial in the law.

10 Have we not all one father? hath not one God created us? why do we despise every man his brother, by breaking the covenant of our fathers?

11 Judah hath dealt treacherously, and an abomination hath been committed in Israel and in Jerusalem; for Judah hath profaned the holiness of the LORD, by loving, and marrying the daughter of a strange god.

12 The LORD will cut off the man that doeth this, the master and the scholar, out of the tabernacles of Jacob, and him that offereth an offering unto the LORD of the hosts.

13 And once again ye shall cover the altar of the LORD with tears, with weeping, and with crying out, for I shall not even look at the offering any more, to receive *a* free will offering from your hand.

14 Yet ye say, Why? Because the LORD hath been witness between thee and the wife of thy youth, against whom thou hast dealt treacherously: yet she *is* thy companion, and the wife of thy covenant.

15 And did not he make one, having in himself abundance of *the* Spirit? And why one? That he might seek offspring of God. Therefore take heed to your spirit, and let none deal treacherously against the wife of his youth.

16 He that rejecteth her, sending her away, said the LORD God of Israel, covereth the iniquity with his garment, said the LORD of the hosts: therefore take heed in your spirit, and do not be treacherous.

17 Ye have wearied the LORD with your words. Yet ye say, Wherein have we wearied *him*? When ye say, Every one that doeth evil pleaseth the LORD, and he delighteth in them; or, Where *is* the God of judgment?

Chapter 3

1 Behold, I send my messenger, and he shall prepare the way before me: and the Lord, whom ye seek, shall suddenly come to his temple, and the angel of the covenant, whom ye desire: behold, he cometh, said the LORD of the hosts.

2 But who may abide the time of his coming? and who shall stand when he appeareth? for he *shall be* like a refiner's fire, and like fullers' soap:

3 And he shall sit to refine and to purify the silver: for he shall purify the sons of Levi, and purge them as gold and silver, that they may offer unto the LORD an offering in righteousness.

4 Then shall the offering of Judah and Jerusalem be pleasant unto the LORD, as in the days of old, and as in former years.

5 And I will come near unto you for judgment; and I will be a swift witness against the sorcerers, and against the adulterers, and against false swearers, and against those that oppress the hireling in *his* wages, the widow, and the fatherless, and that turn aside the stranger *from his right*, and fear not me, said the LORD of the hosts.

6 For I *am* the LORD, I have not changed; therefore ye sons of Jacob have not been consumed.

7 Even from the days of your fathers ye had departed from my ordinances, and had never kept *them*. Return unto me, and I will return unto you, said the LORD of the hosts. But ye said, Wherein shall we return?

8 Will a man rob God? Yet ye have robbed me. But ye say, Wherein have we robbed thee? In the tithes and the offerings.

9 Ye *are* cursed with a curse: for ye, *even* this whole nation, have robbed me.

10 Bring ye all the tithes into the storehouse, and there shall be food in my house, and prove me now in this, said the LORD of the hosts, if I will not open you the windows of heaven, and pour you out a blessing, that *there shall* not *be room* enough *to receive it.*

11 And I will reprehend the devourer for your sakes, and he shall not destroy the fruits of the ground; neither shall the vine in the field abort, said the LORD of the hosts.

12 And all the Gentiles shall call you blessed: for ye

shall be a delightsome land, said the LORD of the hosts.

13 Your words have prevailed against me, saith the LORD. Yet ye say, What have we spoken against thee?

14 Ye have said, It *is* vain to serve God: and what profit *is it* that we have kept his law, and that we walk mournfully before the LORD of the hosts?

15 We say, therefore, now, that blessed are the proud, and even that they that work wickedness are prospered; yea, *they that* tempted God have escaped.

16 Then they that feared the LORD spoke one to another: and the LORD hearkened, and heard *it*, and a book of remembrance was written before him for them that feared the LORD, and for those that think in his name.

17 And they shall be mine, said the LORD of the hosts, in that day when I make up my jewels; and I will spare them, as a man spareth his own son that serveth him.

18 Therefore become ye converted, and ye shall make a difference between the just and the wicked, between him that serveth God and him that did not serve him.

Chapter 4

1 For, behold, the day cometh, that shall burn as an oven; and all the proud, yea, and all that do wickedly, shall be stubble: and the day that cometh shall burn them up, said the LORD of the hosts, that it shall leave them neither root nor branch.

2 But unto you that fear my name shall the Sun of righteousness be born, and in his wings *he shall bring* saving health; and ye shall go forth, and jump like calves of the herd.

3 And ye shall tread down the wicked; for they shall be ashes under the soles of your feet in the day that I make, said the LORD of the hosts.

4 Remember ye the law of Moses my servant, which I commanded unto him in Horeb; statutes and my rights over all Israel.

5 Behold, I send you Elijah the prophet before the coming of the great and terrible day of the LORD:

6 And he shall convert the heart of the fathers to the sons, and the heart of the sons to the fathers, lest I come and smite the earth with destruction.

Dictionary

of Proper Names

Aaron - illuminated.

Abednego - servant of Nebo.

Abraham - father of a great multitude.

Achbor - rat.

Achor - trouble or anguish.

Achzib - a stream that only flows in the season for rains; lie, deception.

Adbeel - servant of God.

Admah - fortress of earth, red earth.

Adrammelech - magnificence of the King (?) or King of fire (?).

Adullam - place of rest; righteousness of the people.

Africa - Phut (bow).

Ahab - brother of the father; uncle.

Ahasuerus - protector of the land, king; probably Xerxes.

Ahaz - possessor, sustained.

Ahikam - my brother riseth up; or a brother is revealed.

Aholah - she who possesses a tabernacle (her own dwelling).

Aholibah - I put my tabernacle in her (dwelling of her father).

Ai - pile of ruins.

Aiath - ruins.

Alexandria - of Alexander (he who defends man).

Amariah - The LORD said.

Amaziah - The LORD hath power; or The LORD strengtheneth.

Amittai - measureth up to the truth.

Ammi - my people.

Ammon - belongeth to the people; or son of my people; worker.

Amos - he who beareth a burden.

Amorite - mountaineer.

Amoz - strong.

Anathoth - answers to prayer.

Aphrah - dust.

Ar of Moab - the capital of Moab.

Arabian - a person from Arabia (desert); also Arab (to ambush).

Aram - Syria; high, exalted.

Ararat - mountainous area of Armenia.

Ariel - lion of God, or fire of God; city where David lived.

Arioch - as a lion, venerable.

Armenia - the fall of the curse; or the curse backwards.

Arnon - swift, impetuous.

Aroer - enclosed, ruins (?).

Arpad - place of rest, encampment.

Arphad - same as Arpad.

Arvad - refuge.

Asa - physician.

Asaph - collector.

Ashchenaz - a man as sprinkled; fire as scattered; son of Gomer, grandson of Japheth (Gen. 10:3).

Ashdod - a strong place.

Asher - blessed, happy.

Ashkelon - oak, migration (?).

Ashpenaz - I will make prominent the sprinkled.

Ashur - graceful one; Fig. pride, arrogance.

Assyria - level, plain; land of Ashur.

Aven - vanity, iniquity.

Azariah - the LORD keeps *me*; or the LORD *is my* help.

Azecah - ploughed.

Azel - decline, slope; foot of the mountains.

Azriel - my help is God.

Azur - or Azzur, helper.

Baal - lord, owner, possessor; pagan god.

Baali - my lord (Baal).

Baalis - son of rejoicing; or lord of joy.

Baalmeon - lord of the habitation, or of the dwelling.

Baalpeor - the lord of the opening; idol of Moab with which Baalam caused Israel to sin.

Baasha - impudent, wicked.

Babylon - Babel, confusion

Bajith - house, temple.

Balaam - stranger, lord of the people, ruin.

Baladan - he gave a son.

Balak - empty, waster, devastator.

Bamah - high place.

Baruch - blessed.

Bashan - soft and fertile land.

Beerelim - well of oaks , or well of palms.

Beeri - man of the well; or man that bringeth forth *the word*.

Beersheba - well of the oath.

Bel - lord; another name for Nimrod, Adonis, Baal, Tamuz, or Marduk; the god of Babylon.

Belshazzar - Bel preserve the king.

Belteshazzar - leader of the lord; or preserve his life.

Benaiah - who the LORD hath made; or the LORD maketh; or the LORD buildeth.

Benhadad - son of Hadad (powerful).

Benjamin - son of the right hand; Fig. fortunate.

Berechiah - The LORD is blessing.

Berothah - Berothai, food, wells.

Betharbel - house of the court of God; or house of the ambush of God.

Bethaven - house of iniquity, of vanity, of idols.

Bethdiblathaim - house of the two fig cakes.

Bethel - house of God.

Bethezel - house on the side; or house in decline.

Bethgamul - house of he that is weaned.

Bethhaccerem - house of the vineyard.

Bethjeshimoth - place of desolations.

Bethlehem - place of food; or house of bread.

Bethmeon - house of habitation (of Baal).

Bethshemesh - house of the sun.

Beulah - married.

Bozrah - sheepfold, fortified place.

Buz - contempt.

Buzi - my contempt.

Calneh - fortress of Anu (babylonian god); city of Assyria founded by Nimrod.

Calno - same as Calneh.

Canaan - lowlands, desirable.

Canneh - upright, distinguished.

Caphtor - cup, or chalice.

Carchemish - fortress of Chemosh (pagan god); city of the Hittites.

Careah - bald.

Carmel - fruitful garden.

Chaldea - land of spiritism.

Chaldeans - inhabitants of Chaldea, an important province of Babylon.

Chebar - gathering; Nahr Malca (royal canal, or artificial river) made by Nebuchadnezzar.

Chemosh - subduer; fire, hearth; pagan god of the Moabites.

Cherethites - executioners.

Chilmad - region between Arabia and Assyria.

Chimham - their *unfulfilled* longing; may refer to the inn of Bethlehem given by David to Chimham the follower or son of Barzillai the Gileadite.

Chisleu - the ninth month (corresponds to Nov. - Dec.).

Chittim - or Kittim, Cyprus; Fig. west or Westerners.

Chiun - Saturn; Renphan, pagan practices having to do with a star (of six points) which invaded Israel from the time of the apostasy of Solomon.

Coniah - abbreviated form of Jeconiah.

Cushan - black

Cushi - Ethiopian (black).

Cyrus - possess thou the throne, or the sun.

Damascus - the weaver of sackcloth is silent.

Dan - judge.

Daniel - God is judge, or judge placed by God.

Darius - preserver.

David - beloved.

Dedan - low country, Arabian people.

Delaiah - The LORD has saved him, or whom the LORD set free.

Diblaim - double embrace; two cakes.

Diblath - circle.

Dibon - perdition, wasting.

Dimon - same as Dibon.

Dumah - silence.

Dura - circle, fence.

Ebedmelec - servant of the king.
Eden - wellbeing, delight.
Edom - red; Fig. doers of their own thing.
Eglaim - two wells.
Egypt - black; Fig. the flesh and the world.
Ekron - erradicate, uproot.
Elam - eternal land, or eternity.
Elasah - whom God hath made.
Elealeh - where God ascendeth.
Eliakim - Whom God establisheth.
Elijah - my God is the LORD, or God Himself.
Elishah - God of the coming (one).
Elishama - my God heareth; or whom God heareth.
Elnathan - gift from God.
Emmanuel - God with us.
Eneglaim - fountain of the two calves.
Engedi - fountain of Gad (kids).
Ephah - measurement (to measure grain) of aprox. 37 liters; equal to the *bath* for liquids.
Ephai - overcast, gloomy.
Ephraim - double ash heap; place of double fruitfulness.
Ephratah - ash heap; place of fruitfulness.
Esarhaddon - Ashur hath given a brother.
Esau - hairy.
Ethiopia - region of faces burnt by the sun.

Eufrates - abundant, fertile (?).
Evilmerodach - man of merodach; son of Nebuchadnezzar.
Ezekiel - God is strong.

Gabriel - God is powerful; or man of God.
Gad - the seer, lot, fortune; many.
Galilee - circuit, district.
Gallim - heaps.
Gareb - bare spot.
Gath - winepress.
Gaza - the strong *place*.
Geba - hill.
Gebal - border, or chain of hills.
Gebim - cisterns.
Gedaliah - The LORD is great, or whom the LORD made great.
Gemariah - The LORD hath done it, or whom the LORD hath completed.
Gentiles - those who are not Israelites; nations, peoples, families, or persons who are uncircumcised (pagans); Fig. not converted, uncircumcised of heart.

Gammadims - guards, vigilant; pygmies.
Gibea - mountain or hill.
Gibeon - belongeth to a hill.
Gilead - rocky, hard, abrupt; hill of testimony.
Gilgal - circle of stone; to roll; reproach.
Goath - bellow.

Gog - high, mountain; Fig. lofty, arrogant.

Gomer - to complete; heat; elder son of Japheth, father of the Celts, the Gaels, and other groups that lived to the north of the Black Sea and extended into Europe.

Gomorrah - to project, to jut out; immersion.

Gozan - a cutting off.

Habakkuk - embrace of love.

Habazinia - the lamp of the LORD.

Hadadrimmon - from Hadad (powerful) and Rimmon (pomegranate), it probably translates: Hadad, he who thunders; or the powerful thunder.

Hadrach - I return for seasons.

Haggai - of the feast; or born on a feast day.

Hamath - fortress.

Hammelec - the king.

Hamonah - multitudes.

Hamongog - multitude for Gog.

Hamutal - God is new life, as the dew.

Hananiah - The LORD is full of grace; or The LORD has favored.

Hanameel - a form of Hananeel (God has been merciful).

Hanan - full of grace.

Hananeel - God is full of grace; or gift by the favor of God.

Hanes - Mercury; probably another name for Taphnes.

Haran - mountainous; strong; illuminated.

Hauran - district of caves.

Hazael - God sees; or whom God protects.

Hazarenan - court of the fountains.

Hazarhatticon - middle court.

Hazor - enclosed castle.

Hebrew - from Eber (shoot); he who comes from the other side, crossing over.

Helbon - fruitful, fertile.

Heldai - he who endures, or endurance.

Helem - strength.

Hen - grace.

Hena - troubling.

Hephzibah - my joy is in her.

Heshbon - intelligence; to calculate, or account.

Hethlon - sinister place, stronghold.

Hezekiah - The LORD is my strength.

Hiddekel - rapid; the Tigris (an arrow).

Hilkiah - the LORD is my portion.

Hinnom - lamentation.

Hittite - descendant of Heth (terror).

Holon - strong place.

Horeb - Sinai, desert.

Horonaim - two holes; double cave.

Hosea - same as Oshea or Hoshea; the LORD is help, liberation, salvation.

Hoshaiah - whom the LORD hath set free.

Iddo - honorable.

Idumea - Edom (red).

Igdaliah - The LORD is great.

Irijah - The LORD sees; or whom the LORD sees.

Isaac - laughter.

Issachar - he bringeth recompense or gain.

Isaiah - salvation from the LORD.

Ishmael - God is listening.

Israel - God prevails; or he who prevails with God: Fig. Prince with God; or he who reigns with God.

Ivah - probable.

Jaazaniah - the LORD shall hear; or whom the LORD shall hear.

Jacob - supplanter.

JAH - I; Heb. YAH; abbreviated form of the Name of God, YHWH, (I AM) which is transcribed LORD or GOD in the old English Bibles according to Jewish tradition upheld by the Lord Jesus in close to seventy direct quotes of OT Scripture in the Gospels.

Jahaz - same as Jahaza (trodden down).

Jareb - avenger, contender.

Javan - Greece.

Jazer - same as Jaazer (he helps, or whom *God* helps).

Jeberechiah - whom the LORD blesses.

Jebusite - descendants of Jebus (tread upon); descendants of Cainaan who dwelled in Jebus (Jerusalem) until they were defeated by David.

Jeconiah - The LORD establisheth; or the LORD raiseth up.

Jedaiah - The LORD hath known; or the LORD knoweth.

Jehoiachin - The LORD establisheth.

Jehoiada - The LORD knoweth.

Jehoiakim - The LORD shall raise up.

Jehoshaphat - The LORD is judge, or whom the LORD judgeth.

Jehu - The LORD is he.

Jehudi - a Jew.

Jerahmeel - God hath mercy; or whom God loveth.

Jeremiah - placed by the LORD.

Jericho - fragrant, a fragrant place.

Jeroboam - augmentor; his people are many.

Jerusalem - dwelling of peace; or founded upon peace; or possession of peace.

Jesse - gift.

Jezaniah - The LORD determines.

Jezreel - God plants; or God scatters.

Joa - The LORD is *my* brother.

Joash - The LORD sustains.

Job - hated, persecuted.

Joel - The LORD is God.

Johanan - The LORD is full of grace; or gift of the LORD.

Jonadab - The LORD is generous.

Jonah - dove.

Jonathan - God hath given.

Joppa - height, beautiful.

Jordan - flowing down; or he who descends; Fig. death.

Josedech - The LORD is righteous.

Joseph - he who adds; or let God add.

Josiah - The LORD heals.

Joshua - The LORD saves, (Jesus in Greek).

Jotham - The LORD is upright; or the LORD is eternal.

Jucal - able; or the LORD is powerful.

Judah - praise; or let God be praised.

Judea - the land of Judah.

Kadesh - holy.

Kedar - of black skin; son of Ishmael.

Kerioth - towns, cities.

Kidron - dark, obscure.

Kir - wall, town or city in Moab.

Kirheres - same as Kirhereseth.

Kirhereseth - town of bricks.

Kiriathaim - double city.

Kirjathjearim - city of the forest.

Kolaiah - the voice of the LORD.

Laish - lion.

Lachish - impregnable.

Lebanon - the white *mountain*.

Levi - joined to, united.

Leviathan - that which entangles; or that which goes round and round.

Libnah - whiteness.

Libya - Phut; those that bend the bow.

Loammi - not my people.

Loruhamah - not having obtained mercy.

Lucifer - light bearer.

Lud - contention.

Luhith - abundance of boards; made out of boards.

Lydia - Lud (strife), a people of north Africa; birth pangs.

Maachathi - depression, oppression.

Maaseiah - work of the LORD.

Maktesh - morter, hollow, depression.

Madian - contention, dispute.

Madmenah - same as Madmen (dunghill).

Magog - land of Gog; the descendants of Magog (second son of Japheth) and their land (also called Scythia) in the north of Asia and Europe.

Malachi - angel; the messenger of the LORD; or my messenger.

Malchiah - king of the LORD.

Manasseh - he who causeth to forget.

Mareshah - possession; to the head.

Maroth - bitterness.

Mattan - a gift.

Medeba - water that flows (?).

Megiddon - Meggido, place of God.

Melzar - administrator *of the wine*.

Memphis - place to adore Ptah, or Noph.

Mephaath - height.

Merathaim - double bitterness or rebellion, Fig. Babylon.

Merodach-baladan -Merodac (Marduk) hath given a son.

Meshach - who is as Acu (god of the moon) (?).

Meshec - possession; descendants of a son of Japheth who probably live in the mountains near the ancient Iberia, Armenia, and Colchis.

Michaiah - same as Micah (who is like the LORD).

Michmash - or Michmas; treasured, something hidden.

Migdol - tower.

Migron - precipice.

Micah - who *is* as the LORD.

Michael - who is like god?

Minni - division; province of Armenia.

Minnith - distribution, ration; place from which the wheat cometh.

Miriam - Mary; fat, robust, strong; bitterness, sadness.

Misgab - the high ground.

Mishael - who is what God is?

Mizpah - watchtower.

Moab - of his *own* father.

Molech - king.

Moloch - king.

Morasthite - of Moraseth (possession).

Moreshethgath - possession of Gath.

Moses - he who brings out.

Mozel - wanderer (?).

Naphtali - wrestler; or my fight.

Nebuchadnezzar - same as Nebuchadrezzar; Nebo, protect my boundary; Nebo, protect the crown.

Nebuzaradan - Nebu hath given the seed; or Nebu giveth prosperity (?).

Nahum - comforter, compassive.

Nathan - giver, gift; he (God) hath given.

Nazarite - separated, consecrated.

Nebaioth - or Nebajoth, high places.

Nebo - he who speaketh; the planet Mercury as adored by the pagans.

Nehelamite - strengthened; or he of the dream.

Nergalsharezer - nergal (lion) protect the king; refers to a pagan deity.

Neriah - my light is the LORD; or the lamp of the LORD.

Nethaniah - The LORD gave; or who the LORD gave.

Netophathite - inhabitant of Netophathi (resin or waste).

Nile - blue.

Nimrim - clear waters.

Nineveh - abode of Ninus (Nimrod).

Nimrod - rebel; founder of Babel, of Paganism.

Nisrock - the great eagle (pagan deity).

No - disrupting; Thebes, or Thebas; the site of modern Alexandria.

Noah - rest.

Nob - height.

Obadiah - servant of the LORD, worshipper of the LORD.

Omri - my portion is the LORD.

Ophir - reduce to ashes, reducing to ashes.

Orion - strong, constellation of the south.

Palestine - Philistia.

Palestinians - Philistines.

Panag - sweet, exquisite.

Paran - full of caverns.

Pashur - prosperity all around.
Pathros - a part of Egypt.
Pekah - of open eyes.
Pekod - vigilance, open eyes.
Pelatiah - The LORD delivers.
Perazim - breaches, mountain of breaches.
Persian - of Persia.
Persia - pure or splendid.
Pethuel - God delivereth.
Pharaoh - the sun, king of Egypt.
Pharaohhophra - the priest of the sun.
Philistea - Palestine, land of the sojourners.
Philistines - errant ones.
Phut - bow, Africa.
Pibeseth - the (cat) goddess Basht.
Pul - savage beast.

Raamah - earthquake.
Rabbah - or Rabbath; great, capital.
Rabmag - head or chief of the maggi.
Rabshakeh - maximum commander, head of the cupbearers.
Rabsaris - chief eunuch.
Ramah - high place.
Rachel - ewe.
Rechab - rider.
Rechabites - decsendants of Rechab.
Regemmelec - friend of the king.
Remaliah - whom the LORD hath adorned.
Rephaim - giants.
Reuben - behold a son.
Rezeph - hot stone.
Rezin - firm.

Riblah - bare place.
Rimmon - pomegranate.
Ruhamah - having obtained mercy.

Sabeans - descendants of Seba (who live in Ethiopia).
Samaria - guard.
Samgarnebo - be generous, Nebo.
Samuel - name of God; heard by God.
Saphir - beautiful, thorny.
Sarah - princess.
Sargon - he (god) established the king.
Sarsechim - head of the eunuchs
Satan - accuser, adversary, hater.
Saul - desired.
Seba - travelers.
Seir - hairy, rough.
Senir - or Shenir; snow covered mountain.
Sennacherib - Sin (the god of the moon) hath increased the brothers.
Sepharad - ancient Iberia; place of captivity of Israel near the Black Sea.
Sepharvaim - the two Sipparas; a town on the Eufrates.
Seraiah - The LORD contends; or soldier of the LORD.
Shadrach - command of Acu (god of the moon).
Shallum - recompense.
Shalman - fire-worshipper; Assyrian king who destroyed Betharbel.
Shaphan - rock badger.
Sharezer - or Sherezer; Ashur protect the king.

Sharon - or Lasharon, field or plain.
Shealtiel - or Salatiel; I have asked of God.
Shearjashub - a remnant shall escape; the remnant shall return.
Sheba - oath, covenant, seven.
Shebna - the scribe.
Shechem - shoulder.
Shelemiah - whom the LORD will repay.
Shemaiah - The LORD heareth; the LORD hath heard.
Sheshach - Babylon.
Shiloh - rest, place of rest.
Shimei - The LORD is fame; or my fame; or has heard.
Shinar - two rivers; the land of Chaldea, or Babylon.
Shittim - cedar, acasias; valley in Moab where Joshua sent the spies.
Shushan - or Susa; lily.
Sibmah - freshness, fragrance.
Sibraim - double hill.
Sihon - great, bold.
Siloah - or Shiloah; sent, spring.
Simeon - to hear and obey.
Sodom - burning.
Solomon - peace.
Syene - openness or opening; the modern Aswan.
Syria - Aram; high, exalted.
Syriack - the language of Aram or Syria; Aramaic.

Tabeal - of Tabeel; God is good.
Tabor - height.

Tahpanhes - or Tahapanes, or Tehaphnehes; head of the earth.
Tamar - palm tree.
Tammuz - son of life; pagan god equivalent to Adonis, Baal, Nimrod.
Tanhumeth - consolation.
Tarshish - or Tharshish; strength.
Tartan - general or commander.
Tekoa - or Tekoah; trumpet blast, or the sound of the trumpet.
Telabib - hill of grass, or hill of heads of grain.
Telassar - or Thelasar, hill of Ashur.
Tema - desert, scorched by the sun.
Teman - to the right hand.
Tirhakah - distance (?).
Tobijah - or Tobiah; The LORD is good.
Togarmah - robust; descendants of Gomer who live north of Armenia.
Tophet - burning.
Tubal - production, blow of a hammer; land of the descendants of Japheth.
Tyre - rock.

Uphaz - high land, fine gold.
Ulai - river in Shushan, Persia.
Urijah - or Uriah; The LORD is my light.
Uz - conciliated, fertile.
Uzziah - The LORD is my strength.

Zaanan - rich in sheepfolds, or place of sheepfolds.
Zadok - righteous, upright.
Zarephath - place to refine.

Zeboim - or Zeboiim; wild place, hyenas; one of five neighboring cities destroyed with Sodom and Gomorrah.

Zebulun - relationship, intimacy; dwelling.

Zechariah - The LORD remembereth.

Zedad - mountain side,

Zedekiah - The LORD is righteousness.

Zephaniah - The LORD hideth or treasureth.

Zerubbabel - sprout from Babylon; or scattered in Babylon.

Zidon - or Sidon; fishing.

Zimri - famous; of an antelope.

Zion - sustained or raised up.

Zoan - migration.

Zoar - smallness.

Please direct all inquiries for materials to:

Ransom Press
10160 Main Drive
Bonita Springs, Fla. 34135
U.S.A.
Telefax 941-992-2881
e-mail: gstendal@aol.com

Most titles are also available in Spanish.

All printed materials are available on a free will donation basis to anyone involved in non-commercial, not for profit distribution of Scripture or Christian literature.